WOMEN AGAINST SLAVERY

WOMEN AGAINST SLAVERY

The British Campaigns, 1780–1870

Clare Midgley

London and New York

First published 1992
by Routledge
11 New Fetter Lane, London EC4P 4EE

Simultaneously published in the USA and Canada
by Routledge
a division of Routledge, Chapman and Hall, Inc.
29 West 35th Street, New York, NY 10001

Typeset in 10 on 12 point Palatino by
Witwell Ltd, Southport
Printed in Great Britain by
Butler & Tanner Ltd, Frome and London

British Library Cataloguing in Publication Data

A CIP catalogue record for this book is available from the British Library

Library of Congress Cataloging in Publication Data

applied for

ISBN 0-415-06669-7

In memory of my grandmother,
Caroline Mary Freeman

CONTENTS

CONTENTS

Part III Women and 'universal abolition', 1834–1868

ILLUSTRATIONS

ACKNOWLEDGEMENTS

This study began as a Ph.D. thesis, and my first debts are to Professor Christine Bolt at the University of Kent for her dedicated supervision of my work and to the Economic and Social Research Council for its financial support.

In transforming the thesis into book form I have been encouraged and supported by numerous friends and academic contacts, and it is hard to single out individuals. However, I would particularly like to thank Leonore Davidoff for her guidance, Catherine Hall for her very valuable comments on the manuscript, and my editor at Routledge, Claire L'Enfant.

For their help, useful suggestions and exchange of ideas, my warm thanks to Alison Archer, Meg Arnot, Kelly Boyd, Moira Ferguson, Joan Grant, Karen Halbersleben, Susan Juster, Henk van Kerkwijk, Jane Rendall, Norris Saakwa-Mante, Cynthia, John, Nick and Tom Midgley, Kathryn Kish Sklar, Nick Spence, Clare Taylor, Susan Thorne, David Turley, Alex Tyrrell and Julie Wheelwright, among many others.

Finally, I would like to thank the staff at the following libraries and archives for their great assistance: Birmingham Central Library Archives Dept.; Bodleian Library, Oxford; Boston Public Library Manuscript Dept., Boston, Mass.; British Library; Cumbria Record Office; Darlington Branch Library; Essex Record Office; Friends House Library, London; Goldsmiths Library, Senate House, University of London; Houghton Library, Harvard University; John Rylands University Library, Manchester; Leicester Public Library and Leicestershire Records Office; Manchester City Archives Dept.; Merseyside Record Office, Liverpool; Mitchell Library, Glasgow; National Library of Scotland, Edinburgh; National Library of Ireland; Public Record Office, Chancery Lane, London; Public Record Office of Northern Ireland, Belfast; Rhodes House Library, Oxford; Sheffield Central Library; University College, London; University of Durham Dept. of Palaeography and Diplomatic; Wilberforce House, Hull.; William Clements Library, University of Michigan; Dr Williams's Library, London.

Clare Midgley, 1 November 1991

xi

ABBREVIATIONS

BCLASS   Bristol and Clifton Ladies' Anti-Slavery Society
BFASS   British and Foreign Anti-Slavery Society
BPL   Anti-Slavery Collection, Dept. of Manuscripts, Boston
           Public Library, Boston, Massachusetts
RHL   Anti-Slavery Papers, Rhodes House Library, Oxford

1

ANTI-SLAVERY AND WOMEN: CHALLENGING THE OLD PICTURE

On 20 September 1840 anti-slavery campaigner Anne Knight wrote to her friend Lucy Townsend, who fifteen years before had founded the first women's anti-slavery society in Britain. Anne called on Lucy to put herself forward for inclusion in the commemorative group portrait of the World Anti-Slavery Convention which had been held in London that June:

> My dear long silent friend my slave benefactress
> Not now would I trouble thy retirement but I am very anxious that the historical picture now in hand of Haydon should not be performed without the chief lady of the history being there . . . in justice to history and posterity the person who established woman agency . . . has as much right to be there as Thomas Clarkson himself, nay perhaps more, his achievement was in the slave trade; thine was slavery itself the pervading movement the heart-stirring the still small voice. . . .[1]

In the event Lucy Townsend was not included in the oil painting which Benjamin Robert Haydon produced, and I have been unable to locate any surviving image of the woman who initiated women's anti-slavery organisations in Britain. Nevertheless Haydon's group portrait (Figure 1) did include a number of women campaigners.[2] The bonneted figure of Mary Clarkson, accorded a place on the platform by virtue of her relationship to Convention president Thomas Clarkson, is visible in the left foreground of the picture. Other women, confined to the visitor's gallery, are mostly represented by Haydon as tiny unidentifiable figures in the background. However, because of his desire to make individual portraits of some of the women present, Haydon brought forward a group along the right-hand side of the picture, separated from the men by an almost invisible red barrier. In the key to the painting they are identified as follows: Mrs Tredgold and Mrs John Beaumont, the wives of two leading male activists; leading local women campaigners Mary Anne Rawson of Sheffield, Elizabeth Pease of

1

Figure 1 The Great Meeting of Delegates, held at the Freemasons Tavern, June 1840, for the abolition of slavery and the slave trade throughout the world.
Painting by Benjamin Robert Haydon, c. 1840.

Darlington and Anne Knight of Chelmsford; anti-slavery writer Amelia Opie of Norwich and aristocratic supporter Lady Noel Byron. A group of American women who had unsuccessfully attempted to gain admission to the Convention as delegates were not individually portrayed, with the exception of Lucretia Mott, whom Haydon accorded a tiny individual portrait in the background.[3]

Haydon's group portrait is exceptional in that it does record the existence of women campaigners. Most other memorials did not. There are no public monuments to women activists to complement those to William Wilberforce, Thomas Clarkson and other male leaders of the movement. Commemorative medallions bear the images and names of the male leadership; even a medallion bearing the symbol of a kneeling enslaved woman (see Figure 10) adopted by ladies' anti-slavery associations has on the reverse a list of male leaders and makes no mention of women activists. In the written memoirs of these men, women tend to appear as helpful and inspirational wives, mothers and daughters rather than as activists in their own right.

The nature of these memorials and memoirs provides one expla-

2

nation as to why historians have not hitherto considered it necessary to explore female contributions in order to understand the British anti-slavery movement. Another factor has been the tendency to rely on the records and publications of the exclusively male national anti-slavery committees rather than on local provincial sources. Until recently it has been, quite simply, easy to ignore women anti-slavery activists.

More recently, as historians have increasingly acknowledged the essential part played by extra-Parliamentary activities and the pressure of public opinion in achieving abolition and emancipation, more atten-tion has begun to be paid to women's activities. Paradoxically, however, while the importance of local organisations to the success of the movement has been recognised, women's contributions have continued to be devalued precisely because they were primarily community-based. The ladies' anti-slavery associations set up from 1825 onwards have, quite wrongly, been dismissed as small in scale and as auxiliary to local men's societies.[4] In fact, as valuable preliminary studies by Louis and Rosamund Billington and by Karen Halbersleben have suggested, ladies' anti-slavery associations were frequently large and autonomous organisations.[5] This study will more clearly establish their vital import-ance to the anti-slavery network by exploring their national and local initiatives, their connections with each other, their development of distinctive female approaches to campaigning and their formulation of feminine perspectives on matters of anti-slavery policy and ideology.[6]

This book takes the women campaigners placed in the background and at the margins of other anti-slavery studies and places them in the foreground, at centre stage. In so doing it creates a counter-image to Haydon's group portrait. The new picture presented here has emerged through two processes of research. The first process involved combing standard sources for anti-slavery history – memoirs of the national and Parliamentary leadership, and national society records, reports and periodicals – for information on women. The second process involved a comprehensive study of those neglected sources which specifically relate to women campaigners, many of them located in local rather than national libraries and archives: the large quantity of surviving records and published reports and pamphlets of local ladies' anti-slavery associations; the anti-slavery pamphlets and imaginative works written by women, some published anonymously as befitted feminine modesty, but nevertheless attributable to particular women or at least to a female author; and memoirs and other sources of biographical infor-mation on women activists, in some cases privately printed by relatives.

Through piecing together information from such sources, it becomes clear that women, despite their exclusion from positions of formal power in the national anti-slavery movement in Britain, were an integral part of that movement and played distinctive and at times leading roles in the successive stages of the anti-slavery campaign. Furthermore, in putting women back into the picture many aspects of British anti-slavery history are clarified. For when historians ignore the activities of ladies' anti-slavery associations, half the story of provincial anti-slavery organisation and of the generation of popular support for the movement on a nationwide basis is lost. And when historians dismiss women's contributions as merely supportive of men's, the fundamental ways in which gender divisions and roles structured the organisation, activities, ideology and policies of the movement as a whole go unnoticed. This study points out ways of rectifying these shortcomings through exploring both the sexual division of anti-slavery labour and the 'gendered' nature of anti-slavery politics.

A central preoccupation of anti-slavery historians since the work of Eric Williams in the 1940s has been to define the relationship between the rise of industrial capitalism and the growth of the anti-slavery movement.[7] This study demonstrates that any satisfactory resolution of this question must take gender into account. David Brion Davis has delineated the role of anti-slavery in the establishment of middle-class ideological hegemony, while not losing sight of the sincere religious and intellectual beliefs which motivated campaigners.[8] Here, it is demonstrated that anti-slavery ideas and motivations were as much related to issues of gender as to those of class, and that these issues interlocked. Anti-slavery ideology simultaneously raised and sought to suppress uncomfortable questions concerning the exploitation of women as well as the exploitation of labourers. Thus its relationship to feminism as well as to Chartism needs to be explored. Anti-slavery also drew on a spectrum of religious, intellectual and political perspectives and movements; the differing ways in which these influenced and affected men and women campaigners will be investigated.

The aim of this study is thus not to incorporate women into pre-existing accounts of the anti-slavery movement. It is not to add to traditional anti-slavery hagiography a clutch of minor female 'Saints' – the name given to William Wilberforce and other members of the evangelical Anglican 'Clapham Sect' of anti-slavery leaders. Rather, my aim is a disruptive as well as an informative one: to expose the need to rewrite existing general histories of anti-slavery, and to reconstruct the frameworks upon which they rest. The study of women campaigners of course forms only one part of this ongoing project: it is essential to a fuller understanding of the popular anti-slavery mobilisation which has been the subject of studies by James Walvin and Seymour Drescher.[9] Following Robin Blackburn, I see this mobilisation as bringing about slave-trade abolition and slave emancipation through its complex interaction not only with Parliamentary politics, but also with social and economic changes in Britain and with slave resistance and revolt in the Caribbean.[10] Indeed it should be stressed that the story told here, set in Britain, is only half the story of women and anti-slavery – the other half being the story, set in the West Indies, of the resistance of enslaved women themselves.[11]

As a whole, my study is inspired by the desire to realise the radical potential of women's history through what Joan Scott has described as 'the writing of narratives that focus on women's experiences *and* analyse the ways in which politics construct gender and gender constructs politics'.[12] The narrative presented here is intended both as an anti-slavery history and as a women's history. It is as a *political* movement that anti-slavery has an especial importance to the history of women: it is not simply an example of female participation in public life, but more specifically of women's involvement in one of the key mass movements for political reform of the late eighteenth and early nineteenth centuries. As such women's anti-slavery campaigning cannot be neatly slotted into the framework of female philanthropy and charitable activity which has been delineated by historians as characterising women's public work at this period.[13] On the other hand, as will be shown, it is problematic to see their campaigning as a prelude to the women's suffrage movement, that paradigm of early female political activity. Indeed one of the aims of this study is to illuminate the ambivalent and complex attitudes of women anti-slavery campaigners to their own social position: to their appropriate roles in the movement, and more widely to questions of women's duties and their rights. This is an issue which has received far more attention in relation to campaigners for abolition and feminism in the United States than in Britain.[14]

Examining women's participation in anti-slavery campaigns provides new insights not only into the history of feminism but more generally into gender roles in nineteenth-century British society, the focus of a recent major study of the English middle class by Leonore Davidoff and Catherine Hall.[15] What emerges here is a complex picture in which women abolitionists were involved in constructing, reinforcing, utilising, negotiating, subverting or more rarely challenging the distinction between the private-domestic sphere and the public-political sphere which was so central to middle-class prescriptions concerning men's and women's proper roles in society. Indeed it becomes clear that women were not negotiating their role in the anti-slavery movement in relation to an established and fixed 'public sphere'; rather, extra-Parliamentary political activities in support of anti-slavery were a key means by which both women and men developed the arena of civil society through the late eighteenth and early nineteenth centuries.[16]

'Separate spheres' ideology had most impact on the lives of those activists who were the wives, mothers, daughters and sisters of middle-class men, middle-class themselves in terms of their lifestyles though rarely in terms of their independent economic position. It was these women who formed the bulk of activists in ladies' anti-slavery associations. As will be shown, however, it would be a mistake to define anti-slavery as an exclusively middle-class movement. It also involved upper-class women and working-class women, and their differing political perspectives on and contributions to the movement, together with their relationships to the middle-class campaigners from whose organisations they were largely excluded, will also be explored. These white women together formed the bulk of female anti-slavery campaigners in Britain. However, there were also black women active against slavery in Britain. As will be shown, their actions challenged white women's representation of enslaved women as silent and passive victims.

The overall picture of women campaigners which emerges in this book is structured around the key campaigning stages of the British anti-slavery movement. The first part of the book deals with women's involvement in the campaign against slavery within Britain and against the British slave trade; the second examines their campaigning against British colonial slavery; and the third and final part discusses 'universal abolition' and especially women's aid to North American abolitionists.

Part I

WOMEN AGAINST THE SLAVE TRADE, 1783–1815

2

PARTICIPANTS FROM
THE FIRST

Women participated in the anti-slavery campaign in Britain from its earliest stages. Enslaved women brought to Britain from the sixteenth century onwards joined in black resistance to slavery through running away from their owners; white women became involved in campaigning against the slave trade from the 1780s onwards through supporting local and national abolition societies, abstaining from slave-grown produce, and writing anti-slavery verse.

ORIGINATORS

In 1766 Granville Sharp, a London clerk, was approached by John Hylas for help in recovering his wife Mary. The Hylases were Afro-Caribbeans, Barbadian slaves who had been brought to England in 1754 by their owners. The couple had married but only John had been formally freed, and after eight years Mary was kidnapped on the orders of her former owners and transported back for sale as a slave in the West Indies. Sharp successfully brought a court case against Mary's owners, the Newtons, for the return of Mary to her husband in England.[1]

The Hylases' arrival in Britain was a by-product of British involvement in slavery and the slave trade. The British slave trade dated back to the sixteenth century and at its peak between 1751 and 1807 involved the forcible transportation of more than 1.6 million Africans across the Atlantic. The majority of these African men, women and children were set to work on plantations in the British and other European colonies in the West Indies and in North America, a British colony until independence in 1776.[2]

John and Mary Hylas were two of a small number of these slaves who entered Britain itself, brought in as personal servants by slave traders, plantation owners and West Indian officials. By the eighteenth century, as society portraits of the period testify, black girls and boys had become fashionable as unwaged household servants among the aris-

9

Figure 2 The Dutchess of Portsmouth.
Painting by P. Mignard.

tocracy, by whom they were viewed as decorative status symbols (Figure 2).[3] Colonial plantations and mercantile enterprises based on the slave trade were major sources of aristocratic wealth and of raw materials and finance for the Industrial Revolution. Slaves in paintings of the aristocracy testify to the power of the British West India interest, the influence of which had to be overcome before abolition could be achieved.

The first attempts to bring about the end of slavery were made by slaves themselves. Indeed the history of slave resistance is almost as long as the history of transatlantic slavery. Barbados, the island on which the Hylases were born, was the scene in 1675 of the first substantial slave revolt in the British West Indies. The established tradition of writing separate histories of black resistance and of British anti-slavery is now rightly being challenged by scholars offering a new understanding of abolition as the product of the interaction between developments within Britain and events in the colonies. Most dramatic of these colonial events was the successful slave insurrection in 1791 in the French colony of Saint Domingue (now Haiti).[4]

Similarly, the origins of British anti-slavery in black resistance within Britain are also beginning to be acknowledged by historians.[5] It was this resistance which sparked the first white action in the form of a series of attempts by Granville Sharpe in the 1760s and 1770s to make slavery illegal within Britain and to use habeas corpus to secure the freedom of individual slaves such as Mary Hylas.[6] It is now becoming clear that slavery was effectively ended in England by the 1790s through the interaction between black self-emancipation and the legal judgments resulting from the court cases brought by Sharpe.[7]

Discussions of the history of black people in Britain have focused on men, partly because evidence from baptismal records and elsewhere suggests that they considerably outnumbered black women, and partly because of the general lack of concern for women's history among scholars.[8] Painstaking research at a local level is needed before a fuller understanding of the lives of black women such as Mary Hylas is possible. There is, however, already sufficient published evidence to demonstrate that women as well as men were involved in early resistance to slavery in Britain.

Both the existence of women slaves and their resistance to slavery are evidenced by advertisements in eighteenth-century newspapers for the sale of black girls and women for use as domestic servants and for the return of those who had run away from their owners.[9] An early example of a runaway comes from a newspaper in the reign of Queen Anne (1702–14), which offered a guinea reward for the return of 'a Negro Maid, aged about 16 years, much pitted with the Small Pox, speaks English well, having a piece of her left Ear bit off by a Dog; She hath on a strip'd Stuff waistcoat and Petticoat.'[10] One factor precipitating such women to take the courageous step of running away in a strange country was ill-treatment. In 1760, for example, a 'negro' girl 'eloped from her mistress on account of ill usage'.[11] Another circumstance which led women to flee from their owners was the threat of forced deportation to the West Indies. Though black resistance, in combination with Granville Sharpe's efforts, led to Lord Mansfield's famous 1772 judgment in the James Somerset case making forced deportations illegal, there were instances of such deportations until at least 1792. In Bristol in 1790, for example, the town's public crier offered a guinea to anyone who hunted down a black girl who had run away because she did not want to be sent back to the West Indies; when found she was forced on board ship.[12]

Other runaways were more fortunate, finding refuge in the sizeable black communities which had grown up in the slave trading ports of London, Bristol and Liverpool.[13] Indeed the presence of such

11

communities probably encouraged slaves in these cities to run away, whereas slaves isolated in country houses would have had little opportunity or chance of evading detection. Black communities were composed not only of sailors who had worked on ships involved in the 'triangular trade' and other free blacks, but also of runaways and what the London magistrate Sir John Fielding described in 1768 as 'a great number of black Men *and Women* who have made themselves so troublesome and dangerous to the Families who brought them over as to get themselves discharged'.[14] This last group, alleged Fielding, 'enter into Societies and make it their Business to corrupt and dissatisfy the Mind of every fresh black Servant that comes to England: first, by getting them christened or married, which they inform them makes them free', and which led them to demand wages for their services.[15]

There is some evidence to back Fielding's claims of black organisation. A newspaper reported that after Lord Mansfield's judgment of 1772 two hundred 'Blacks with their ladies' gathered at a public house in Westminster to celebrate. They may well have been members of the 'Black Society' whose secretary, 'Mungo', wrote a letter printed in a London newspaper, the *Public Ledger*, on 23 October 1772. This letter expressed concern for the welfare of a black maid-servant who had been declared a chattel, indicating that the Society took up individual cases which came to their attention and attempted aid. Black people also met to discuss the 1787 scheme to resettle the London black poor in Sierra Leone. There were about forty black women among more than four hundred people who were eventually transported to the African colony.[16]

Among the transportees were also some seventy white women, most of them the wives of black men. Given that London parish registers suggest that only about a fifth of blacks in London at this period were women, such intermarriage is not surprising.[17] Such evidence demonstrates the artificiality of separating black history from the history of English society as a whole: as David Dabydeen has pointed out, William Hogarth's portrayals of London life show black men and women as a part of the labouring poor, and include images of a black beggar-woman, an imprisoned black prostitute and a black man dallying with a white servant girl.[18] African abolitionist Olaudah Equiano, who played a leading role in negotiations on the Sierra Leone scheme, himself married a white woman, Susan Cullen of Ely in Cambridge.[19] An early abolitionist poem, *The Dying Negro* (1773), was based on a report in a London newspaper of a black runaway man who had been christened in order to marry a white servant woman, but had been seized and taken aboard a slave trading vessel in the Thames.[20] Hugh Honour has suggested that Henry Fuseli's powerful painting *The Negro Revenged* was inspired by the poem (Figure 3).[21]

The Negro revenged.

Vol.I.P.375.

H.Fuseli R.A. pinx.^t   Raimbach sculp.^t

Hark! he answers____Wild tornadoes,
  Strewing yonder sea with wrecks;
Wasting towns, plantations, meadows,
  Are the voice, with which he speaks.

Pub. by J.Johnson London March 1.1807.

Figure 3 The Negro Revenged. Engraving by Raimbach after
painting by Henry Fuseli (London: J. Johnson, 1807).

Interracial relationships provoked expressions of horror among the pro-slavery lobby in Britain at both black men's and working-class women's uncontrolled sexuality and at 'miscegenation'. Edward Long stated that 'the lower class of women in England, are remarkably fond of the blacks, for reasons too brutal to mention', and a caricaturist attempted to undermine the reputation of William Wilberforce by depicting him with a voluptuous, pipe-smoking, black prostitute.[22]

There is no evidence, however, that such racial antipathy was shared by English working people, who indeed are known on occasion to have given help to runaway slaves. Fielding commented in 1768 that black runaways got 'the Mob on their side', and evidence from newspapers suggests some basis for this allegation: in 1760, for example, a black girl runaway was brought to church in Westminster by two housekeepers to be baptised, an action which was believed to confer freedom, and a notice in the *Daily Advertiser* in 1772 warned people against harbouring a 'black woman belonging to Mrs Grant'.[23] There are also a few instances of black men joining organisations of radical artisans in the 1790s. Organisations like the London Corresponding Society to which Olaudah Equiano belonged were, however, male dominated, and no cases of black women's involvement have yet been uncovered.

SUPPORTERS

The origins of anti-slavery in Britain lie not only in the relationship between enslaved Africans and the British society of whom a small number became a part, but also in the transatlantic connection between white Britons and North Americans, in particular the Quaker link. British and American Quakers' considerable economic involvement in the slave trade and slavery was already being questioned by some members of the Society of Friends in the early eighteenth century.[24] Quaker opposition to slavery was linked to their belief that every individual could inwardly experience God directly. It was a belief which when applied to women or to black people implied that neither were naturally inferior. In addition, by denying the Calvinist doctrine of original sin, Friends simultaneously freed women from responsibility for the sins of Eve and blacks from responsibility for the sins of Cain.[25]

Quakers

The Society of Friends was unusual in having no formal ministry and in permitting anyone, male or female, to become a lay minister, provided they were convinced they had a calling from God.[26] Leading abolitionist Thomas Clarkson later singled out transatlantic visits by such Quaker ministers as being of vital importance in spreading knowledge of, and opposition to, slavery among British Quakers.[27] It is known that these ministers included a number of influential women, notably Rebecca Jones of Philadelphia, Catherine Phillips (née Payton) of Dudley in Worcestershire and Mary Peisley of Ballymore in County Kildare. Peisley (1717–57) and Phillips (1727–94) travelled thousands of miles together through the northern and southern states of America between 1753 and 1756 and in their memoirs both expressed their disapproval of American Quakers who bought and kept slaves. Peisley considered the activity to be irreconcilable 'with the golden rule of doing unto all men as we would they should do unto us', and Phillips expressed her pleasure that there was a growing move among Quakers to free their slaves.[28] Philadelphia minister Rebecca Jones (1739–1817), who first came to England in 1756 with Phillips and Peisley, travelled extensively as a minister in Britain and Ireland between 1784 and 1788 and took a great interest in the beginnings of the organised anti-slavery campaign at that period, advising the Quaker leadership on the wording of their abolition petitions.[29]

Despite the high value placed on their views and advice, however, women occupied a subordinate place in the hierarchy of Quaker organisation in Britain, being organised into a parallel but subordinate structure of women's meetings. The Women's Yearly Meeting in London, established in 1759, was a powerless and informal body. Even after 1784, when it was empowered to correspond with and advise local women's meetings, it lacked the power to set rules of conduct for the Society. Thus while exchanging letters with the Yearly Meeting of Women Friends in Philadelphia on the progress of the anti-slavery cause, the Women's Yearly Meeting in London could not as a body take an official position on slavery.[30] In contrast, the Yearly Meeting in London, at which decisions were taken by men only, had the power, in 1761, to effectively ban involvement by British Quakers in the slave trade by making involvement a matter for 'discipline'.[31]

Given the nature of Quaker organisation it is hardly surprising that the Quaker abolition committees formed in 1783 comprised men alone. When the committee of the non-sectarian Society for the Abolition of the Slave Trade (henceforth, the Abolition Society) was set up in 1787, with strong Quaker backing, it too had an exclusively male membership, in common with the other voluntary organisations which were being formed at this period. In Parliament, too, the campaign was of course under male direction. The same exclusion of women persisted in the African Institution, founded following the passage of the Abolition Act in 1807 with three main aims: to see that the new laws were properly enforced, to encourage 'legitimate' commerce with Africa, and to persuade other countries to follow Britain's example in ending involvement in the slave trade.

While women were thus excluded from decision-making positions within the movement at this period, it would be wrong to conclude that they made no contributions to the abolition campaign. In fact, as will be shown, these contributions were more diverse and more important than has hitherto been recognised.

Social and family network

Previous writers have singled out individual women of high social status as exerting an important 'behind-the-scenes' influence on male politicians in favour of abolition. In particular, the home of Lady Margaret Middleton at Teston in Kent is identified as having acted as a centre for evangelical Anglican supporters of abolition. Her close friend, the well-known author and moral reformer Hannah More, wrote a series of letters about the launching of the Parliamentary campaign at Teston, describing how she and Lady Middleton initiated discussions of the slave trade at dinner parties attended by leading politicians, and how the women canvassed members of Parliament by letter and personal contact.[32] Lady Middleton herself, whose husband Captain Charles Middleton (later Lord Barham and First Lord of the Admiralty) was a member of Parliament, exerted an early influence on William Wilberforce to promote the abolition cause in Parliament.[33] Indeed family friend Ignatius C. Latrobe went so far as to claim on this basis 'that the abolition of the slave trade was . . . the work of a *woman*, even Lady Middleton'.[34]

How is such a high assessment of the power of feminine influence to be interpreted? It is tempting to simply dismiss it as an example of male chivalry. However, the praise accords with the importance which evangelicals attached to women's role as guardians of religion and morality, an attitude which encouraged men to take heed of women's views on a topic such as slavery.[35] In addition, it should not be forgotten that female domestic support was essential to the public work of the male leadership of the movement, and that women, through marriage, entertaining and friendships, played an essential part in cementing the close evangelical Anglican social and family network from which this leadership drew strength and cohesion.[36] The contrast between male members of the Clapham Sect and their wives and daughters is nevertheless striking. In the historical record the women are shadowy private figures hidden behind the public men, those men who alone possessed the power to legislate to bring about the end of the slave trade.

16

Subscribers

Women's support for the campaign was not, however, confined to the assertion of informal influence and the fostering of social networks sympathetic to the cause. One aspect of their support which has hitherto been largely overlooked was financial. The subscription list which the Abolition Society published in 1788 included the names of 206 women, comprising around ten per cent of total subscribers and donating £363.3s.6d of the Society's total income of £2,760.2s.7d in 1787-8.[37] Similarly, while only one of the African Institution's initial 130 subscribers was female, by 1823 the sixty female subscribers also represented around ten per cent of total subscribers.[38]

The proportion of female subscribers is typical of philanthropic societies of the 1790-1810 period.[39] The predominance of male subscribers to the Abolition Society, as in these other groups, was the product of married women's lack of independent legal and financial status.[40] It is likely that many male subscriptions were made as 'heads of household', representing their wives and children as well as themselves. Nevertheless some married women did subscribe to the Abolition Society in their own right. In fact, most female subscribers were married: only forty-four were definitely single.[41] Thus Frank Prochaska's observation that single women contributed more generously to philanthropy than married women does not seem applicable to the Abolition Society.[42] Another interesting characteristic of the female subscribers is that only about a quarter appear to have been related to male subscribers, suggesting that women frequently made the decision to support abolition independently of their male relatives.[43] In so doing, they were implicitly recognising themselves as individuals able and willing to represent themselves.

Identification of individual women from the subscription list is difficult. It should be borne in mind that it has been easiest to identify those who were related to prominent male subscribers and those who were Quakers, given the full records kept by this denomination. A number of the women were members of leading Quaker families. Sarah Dillwyn of Walthamstow (1751-1815) had come to England around 1774 with her husband William, who became a member of both Quaker and non-sectarian abolition committees and wrote an influential pamphlet against the slave trade. Hannah Gurney of Norwich was married to wealthy abolitionist and leading Quaker minister John Joseph Gurney. Catherine Fox of Falmouth (1751-1829) was an elder in the Society of Friends and the wife of George Croke Fox, a Falmouth merchant who toured Cornwall in 1788 to stimulate abolition petitions. Susanna Boone of Birmingham (1731-89) was a Quaker minister who was married to ironmonger George Boone (1730-85). Other Quaker women who can be identified are Mary Arthington and Catherine Elam (1755–1831), both of Leeds, Ann Hirst of Farfield near Sheffield, Mrs Joseph Atkinson of Manchester, and Mary Hanbury of Stoke Newington near London.[44] The African Institution also received subscriptions from women of leading Quaker merchant and banking families: the Allens, Barclays and Hanburys, the Rathbones of Liverpool and the Foxes of Falmouth.

Other women subscribers to both societies came from the leading evangelical Anglican families of the 'Clapham Sect'. Lady Middleton and Lydia Babbington, wife of Thomas Babbington, MP for Leicester, subscribed to the Abolition Society, and Hannah More subscribed to the African Institution. Subscribers to the Abolition Society also included a group of women from wealthy Manchester Unitarian families.

The standard annual subscription rate of one to five guineas for the Abolition Society suggests that subscribers were well-to-do men and women. While E.M. Hunt has found evidence of artisan involvement in local abolition committees in the northeast of England, the national subscription rate was too high for large-scale working-class support.[45] At the other end of the social scale, few aristocrats subscribed: Lady Hatton of Lanstanton and Dowager Countess Stanhope are the only two titled women in the list. This probably reflects a combination of High Church unwillingness to support a society dominated by nonconformists combined with the vested interest of family involvements in slavery and the slave trade.[46] Lady Scarsdale, who aided leading abolitionist Thomas Clarkson, did so only after deciding that religious duties outweighed the risk of offending friends and relatives with West India interests.[47]

Patterns of subscription in specific towns suggest that local abolition societies, which like the national society had exclusively male committees, differed widely in the extent to which they sought and secured female support. The number of female subscribers varied from none at Leicester (where there were thirty-six male subscribers) to sixty-eight in Manchester, where women made up nearly a quarter of the total of 302 subscribers. Only here did the percentage of female subscriptions significantly surpass the national average of around ten per cent.[48]

An explanation for the high level of female subscribers in Manchester may be sought in those distinctive features of the local abolition society and of the town itself which E.M. Hunt and Seymour Drescher have identified as key factors leading Manchester to initiate the mass national petitioning campaign against the slave trade. These features were the prominence of Unitarians, political radicals and merchants on the Society's committee and the nature of Manchester as a fast-growing town at the hub of the Industrial Revolution.[49]

To begin with, denominational factors played a role. Many of the wives and daughters of the Unitarians who dominated the Manchester abolition committee subscribed to the Society. The Bayley, Rigby, Grimshaw, Hardman and Mather families were all members of the influential Unitarian congregation of Cross Street Chapel.[50] The Coopers were also nominal Unitarians, although the Walkers were Anglicans and the Atkinsons were Quakers. It may be suggested that Unitarian women, raised in a denomination which stressed freedom of thought, independence and individual autonomy, and which pioneered education for women, were encouraged, and felt motivated, to subscribe to the Manchester society in their own right rather than letting their husbands or fathers act as their representatives.[51] While Quakerism also gave women a considerable measure of equality, it placed less emphasis on self-assertion and more on family ties than did Unitarianism.

Another factor was the political radicalism of the Manchester committee, which was chaired by Thomas Walker, the president of the Manchester Constitutional Society, and had as secretary another leading member of the Constitutional Society, Samuel Jackson. These activists brought a radical approach to their anti-slavery work, and the Manchester abolition society led the transformation of abolition into a popular campaign mobilising public opinion to put pressure on Parliament.[52] While radicalism was male dominated in Manchester as elsewhere, Thomas Paine's call for the Rights of Man was an advocacy of individual human rights which could be extended to encompass not only slaves but also women, as Mary Wollstonecraft demonstrated in 1792.[53]

Socio-economic factors also need to be considered. Among identifiable female subscribers Mrs Rigby, Mrs Grimshaw and Mrs Hardman were all married to cotton merchants, Mrs Atkinson's husband was a hat manufacturer, and Mrs Cooper was the wife of a lawyer and natural philosopher. Hunt's research into support for abolition in northern English towns suggests that other abolition committees tended to be dominated by clergymen and professionals rather than the merchants who dominated the Manchester committee. Such businessmen, in the forefront of creating a new society based on industrialised forms of work organisation, rapid urbanisation, and the development of voluntary philanthropic organisations as a substitute for the traditional forms of individual paternalistic aid offered by rich to poor, may have been more open than most to accepting new forms of voluntary activity by their wives and daughters.

These hypothetical explanations for the high level of female subscribers in Manchester can be tested through an examination of the nature of abolitionist appeals to women in the town. The first striking fact is that Manchester abolitionists decided to *publicly* appeal for female aid as soon as they launched their campaign against the slave trade. A long letter from 'C' printed in the *Manchester Mercury* of 6 November 1787 is apparently the earliest instance of an appeal to British women to aid the abolition cause. Written at a time when radicals were increasingly using the press as a stimulant for and vehicle of public opinion, its appearance is significant in itself in suggesting a recognition of women as a constituent of the public.[54] The writer of the appeal 'publickly requested' the ladies of Manchester to take up a 'publick Opportunity' for charitable work by adding their names to a published subscription list to help cover the cost of petitioning 'for some Parliamentary interference in favour of the oppressed Africans'.[55]

While women's financial support was thus being publicly solicited it was nevertheless for an activity, petitioning, from which they themselves were excluded: only adult males signed Manchester's petitions. Female charity was thus to aid male politics. The Manchester petition, however, based its demands for action on the offensiveness of the slave traffic to humanity, justice and national honour rather than on policy considerations.[56] This was to be the general approach of abolitionists, and it was one which gave scope for female involvement in at least some aspects of the campaign:

> If any public Interference will at any TIME become the Fair Sex; if Their Names are ever to be mentioned with Honour beyond the Boundaries of their Family, and the Circle of their Connections, it can only be, when a public Opportunity is given for the Exertion of those Qualities which are peculiarly expected in, and particularly possessed by that most amiable Part of the Creation – the Qualities of Humanity, Benevolence, and Compassion.[57]

Those moral qualities on which abolitionist commitment was based were thus from the outset identified as especially 'feminine' in nature.

The writer of the appeal went on to delineate the sufferings of the female slave and the violation of family life under slavery. This was the first articulation of a theme which was to dominate women's writings throughout the history of the anti-slavery movement. Public horror at the physical and sexual abuse of enslaved women was aroused by cases such as that of Captain Kimber, who flogged a young black woman to death for refusing to dance naked for him on deck (Figure 4). Such male brutality was seen as both necessitating and justifying female opposition to slavery:

> If it be just and right; if it be what Nature requires, and what Mankind expects, that Women should sympathize with Women; that if the Brutality of the Male should at any Time reverse in his Practice the Obligation of his Species, a Female may meet, from

20

Figure 4 The Abolition of the Slave Trade. Cartoon, London, 1792.

the Pity of her own Sex, that assistance which the Inhumanity of the other may deny.[58]

Women who were privileged themselves owed this to other less fortunate women:

> Which of them, whom the kindness of Providence has blessed with even moderate Affluence, with the Attention of a Husband, and with the Smiles of a Family, can justify to her own Feelings, and her own Sense of the Duty she is under, the Omission of joining in support.

Abolition had the potential to 'Relieve the Miseries of more Females, and Miseries more Extent, than any other charitable Institution which the Exertions of Benevolence have yet brought forward.' Female suffering under slavery was blamed not only on slave holders but also on 'the Supineness and Indifference of Englishmen in this Country'. In Manchester in particular:

> If the Young Men, if the Husbands of Manchester are so much involved in the Cares of the World, in the Bustle of Trade, that the still small voice of pity cannot be listened to, it is the Duty, and I trust it will be the earnest Inclination of the Fair Sex, in this town at least, to remind them, that some Attention is due to the Humanity of our Commerce as well as to the Gains of it.

This letter is at first sight surprising in view of the evidence for the familial nature of support for abolition in Manchester. The writer's statements can be explained as a tactic for enlisting female support through evoking a role for them as guardians of morality and ameliorators of the suffering caused by the uncaring pursuit of profit. A process may be discerned whereby the commercial elite of Manchester, able to use their wealth to accord their wives and daughters the status of leisured ladies, then encouraged them to devote themselves to charitable works, and idealised them as untainted by the corrupting influence of the marketplace. As the wording of a special prologue to the tragedy of Oroonoko, spoken at the Manchester Theatre on 28 November 1787, put it:

> Our better Hopes within this Circle Rest:
> Here Pity lives in ev'ry gentle Breast.
> Folly may scoff, or Avarice may hate,
> Since Beauty comes the Negroe's Advocate.
> Let others boast in Fashion's Pride to glow,
> To lure the Lover, or attract the Beau;
> You check Oppression's Lash, protect the Slave,
> And, First to charm, are still the First to save.[59]

It may be concluded that an environment conducive to female involvement in abolition in Manchester was created by the dominance of the committee by radical Unitarian merchants whose perspectives on public campaigning and gender relations provided scope for female participation in abolition. The possible part played by women's own initiatives in this process unfortunately cannot be determined. It is unknown, for example, whether the separate 'lady's subscription' in Manchester was organised by men to encourage female support or was initiated by women themselves.[60] What is clear is that women did give valuable financial support to the Manchester abolition society, providing almost a quarter of its income in 1787-88, and thus contributing significantly to its ability to initiate the extra-Parliamentary campaign against the slave trade.

Signatories and speakers

For women themselves, their inclusion as subscribers was important both to their recognition by others and to their perception of themselves as members of the 'public' whose voluntary activities could advance a philanthropic cause. On the other hand, their exclusion from the committee and from the signing of the massive abolition petitions organised in the town marked the setting, no less firm for being assumed rather than explicitly stated, of clearly defined limits to their participation.

While Samuel Bradburn, a Methodist minister and radical who joined the Manchester abolition committee in 1792, felt that women should be allowed to sign petitions, male abolitionists were generally agreed that the petitioning of Parliament was the province of adult males.[61] Women were excluded from signing along with paupers and children.[62] This was not because of their political exclusion or limited education – working-class men were encouraged to sign – but presumably because of their dependent status. Incidents where a few 'improper' signatories slipped through caused great concern, probably because of fears that they might be used by the pro-slavery lobby to undermine the credibility of abolitionist petitions as a whole. Thus during his anti-slavery tour of Scotland on behalf of the Abolition Society, Quaker activist William Dickson was troubled that in Dundee 'by a mistaken zeal some boys and 3 women have been allowed to sign' a popular petition which had attracted two thousand signatures and that his local contact had asserted that 'there is scarce any preventing boys or at least improper people from signing'.[63]

Provincial abolitionists and the local press seem to have been less hostile than the London committee to female signatories, a reflection perhaps of their greater radicalism. The *Newcastle Courant* reported that

23

at Belford in Northumberland in 1792 it was reported of the abolition petition: 'Some of the 433 [signers] are Ladies, who were anxiously desirous to shew their abhorrence of this abominable trade.'[64] There was also talk of the possibility of sending a separate female petition to Parliament. This suggestion, published in the *Derby Mercury* of 16 February 1792 and repeated in the *York Courant* of 21 February 1792, echoed the 1787 Manchester appeal in suggesting that women should take action on behalf of other women, but extended this in calling not for subscribers but for petitioners:

> It has been said that a *Petition from the Ladies* to Parliament, for an Abolition of the Slave-Trade, would have a good effect. The idea is certainly a proper one – for, as *Female Misery* is included in the wretched Allotment of the Africans, an Appeal in their Behalf from the same Sex must carry great Weight with it.

While this suggestion was never put into practice it is significant as a subversive challenge to dominant views of proper gender roles in raising the possibility that women might be more effectively represented by other women than by men.

Reactions to the French Revolution and the effect of war with France meant that there were no public petitioning campaigns for abolition between 1792 and the passage of the Abolition Act in 1807. Instead abolitionists focused on the Parliamentary campaign and the selection and election of abolitionist candidates. Women, as non-voters excluded from Parliament, were marginal to this process. Nevertheless wealthy ladies did individually play some part in election politics. Reporting on the election in Yorkshire at which Wilberforce was elected, the *York Herald* commented that 'The FAIR SEX, as the best canvassers, were distinguishable in a high degree.'[65] Another Yorkshire paper commented that Lady Johnson of Hackness near Scarborough had subscribed £1000 in support of Wilberforce's election and sent a number of freeholders to York at her own expense, and that a 'young lady' in the Hull area had 'greatly distinguished herself by her successful exertion, in obtaining votes for that gentleman'.[66] Such activities, however, marked a continuance of earlier eighteenth-century forms of political patronage by women rather than a development of their involvement in the popular abolition campaign of 1787–92.

When abolitionist petitioning was revived in the 1810s women were again rarely given the opportunity to sign. Petitions from Inverkeithing and Harwick in Scotland represent the only two female petitions out of nearly eight hundred presented to the Government in 1814 urging it to insert clauses in peace treaties which committed other European nations to end their involvement in the slave trade.[67]

Women also rarely spoke out in public against the slave trade. In his extensive survey of newspaper reports of anti-slavery activity, Seymour Drescher has, however, identified two instances of women giving public lectures against the slave trade, both in London in 1788. The first was a speech in favour of abolition at a weekly debate at the School of Eloquence in Panton Street, Haymarket. Her speech was well received and 'The Question was carried against the Slave Trade'.[68] Admission was only 6d, and Donna Andrew's research suggests that such commercial debating societies attracted audiences of mixed sex and class, providing an alternative venue to the private male radical clubs which met in London public houses of the period, and offering discussions of such issues as love, marriage and women's roles as well as politics and morals.[69]

On the second occasion a 'Lady of distinguished ability' opened a ladies-only discussion at La Belle Assemblee, Rice's Rooms in Brewer Street, Golden Square, which was one of six or seven such women's debating societies in London at this period. The 2s.6d admission charge suggests the debate was for a slightly better off audience than was the School of Eloquence lecture; the issue was whether ladies whose husbands were peers or Members of Parliament should try to influence them to support abolition.[70] Such debating societies were an important public forum for debate on slavery by both men and women. The two public addresses by women, while exceptional, are interesting as among the earliest examples of public speaking by women in Britain outside the context of religion. Significantly, a conservative attack on debating clubs written in 1810 commented that discussions on the slave trade were 'one of the earliest tricks to attract females to their indecent discussions'.[71] Abolition, it seems, had unusual power in impelling women to take public action.

RADICALS AND REACTIONARIES

Abolition, as a non-sectarian movement which sought to elevate itself above party politics, initially attracted support from men and women of widely differing political perspectives and religious persuasions, from Tory evangelical Anglicans to radical dissenters. This unity began to collapse from 1792 onwards, however, when horror at the perceived excesses of the French Revolution and fears about the spread of revolutionary sentiment within Britain led to a crackdown on extra-Parliamentary campaigning.

Women played key roles in this pattern of radicalism then reaction, and a brief comparison of their perspectives on politics, on anti-slavery and on the position of women throws light both on the changing course of the abolition movement and on the changing relationship of women to political activism in the two decades between 1787 and 1807.

The most notorious radical woman of the 1790s, Mary Wollstonecraft (1759–97), included Thomas Cowper's abolitionist poem 'On Slavery' and a quote from Anna Laetitia Barbauld on the sufferings of slave women in her 1789 educational anthology *The Female Reader*.[72] She also included an anti-slavery message in *A Vindication of the Rights of Men*, written in 1790 as a reply to Edmund Burke's conservative *Reflections on the Revolution in France*. In her book, published before Thomas Paines' more famous response to Burke, Wollstonecraft expounded the doctrine of natural rights, to which the institution of slavery was posed as a complete antithesis. Slave traffic, she asserted, 'outrages every suggestion of reason and religion' and is a 'stigma on our nature'. The security of property should no longer be the highest principle of society. Rather, all men should be 'allowed to enjoy their birthright – liberty'. She asked: 'is it not consonant with justice, with the common principles of humanity, not to mention Christianity, to abolish this abominable traffic.'[73]

Wollstonecraft's friend Helen Maria Williams (1762?–1827), another leading radical writer of both imaginative and polemical works, included a long digressionary passage in support of abolition in her *Letters on the French Revolution*. In this she praised Mirabeau for proposing to the National Assembly that they abolish the slave trade. She hoped, however, that England would not wait for France to take a lead, for:

> I trust an English House of Commons will never persist in thinking, that what is morally wrong, can ever be politically right; that the virtue and the prosperity of a people are things at variance with each other; and that a country which abounds with so many sources of wealth, cannot afford to close one polluted channel, which is stained with the blood of our fellow-creatures.[74]

Williams' view of anti-slavery as an attempt to moralise both commerce and politics resembles the 1787 appeal to women in Manchester to get involved in the abolition campaign.

The influence of Enlightenment thinking and the optimism in human progress felt by British radicals at the beginning of the French Revolution is evident in Williams' expression of her belief that 'this system of inhumanity' would soon be abolished:

> Europe seems hastening towards a period too enlightened for the perpetuation of such monstrous abuses. The mists of ignorance and error are falling away, and the benign beams of philosophy are spreading their lustre over the nations.[75]

A similarly optimistic note was sounded by Unitarian writer and educationalist Anna Laetitia Barbauld (1743–1825) in *An Address to the Opposers of the Repeal of the Corporation and Test Acts* (1790), an argument for full religious freedom for dissenters.[76] With the triumph of freedom in France she felt that liberty now 'even extends a smile of hope and promise to the poor African, the victim of hard, inpenetrable avarice'.[77]

Such expressions of opposition to slavery as an integral element of support for the 'rights of man' were on similar lines to the writings of male supporters of the French Revolution. In *A Vindication of the Rights of Women* (1792) Mary Wollstonecraft expressed her opposition to slavery in a rather different context, comparing the position of British women to that of slave. She described women, few of whom had ever 'emancipated themselves from the galling yoke of sovereign man', as 'the most oppressed half of the species'. Her analogy, however, was as frequently with the enslavement of women in the 'oriental' harem – saying, for example, that women denied freedom 'must ever languish as exotics' – as with the enslavement of Africans in the West Indies.[78] In addition, she was not the first British to make analogies between the position of women and that of slaves of both types.[79] Nevertheless, the fact that she was writing at the height of the popular abolition campaign surely helped to encourage the reception of her book not as the reiteration of a familiar complaint but as a positive call for action to bring about change.

Wollstonecraft's analysis of the nature of women's oppression affected her views on how women should exert a good influence on society as a whole. In the absence of understanding, she believed, female influence was harmful rather than beneficial to society: 'When I call women slaves, I mean in a political and civil sense; for, indirectly, they obtain too much power, and are debased by their exertions to obtain illicit sway.'[80] Wollstonecraft argued that women should develop a rational humanity founded on knowledge, rather than be 'slaves' to their senses.[81] She considered the currently fashionable feminine sensibility to be unstable and unreliable because it was based on emotion rather than reason.[82]

The period from 1787 to 1792 was remarkable as a time when radical dissenters such as Wollstonecraft, Barbauld and Williams briefly united with conservative evangelical Anglicans such as Hannah More in the popular abolition campaign. Thereafter came a general decline in extra-Parliamentary anti-slavery activity as a direct result of the Government clamp-down on public meetings and extra-Parliamentary campaigning in reaction to the French Revolution and the war with France. The Abolition Society became inactive and the largest local society in Manchester collapsed following disagreements between radicals and Whigs on the committee and the arrest of the Society's leader, Thomas Walker, on charges of treason.[83]

The most outspoken female opponent of the French Revolution was Hannah More. A study of the *Cheap Repository Tracts* which More

27

compiled and edited in 1795 suggests that her fear of revolution spreading to Britain undermined her commitment to the anti-slavery cause. While More's biographer M.G. Jones contends that More can be credited with keeping anti-slavery sentiment alive through the 1790s, the tracts in fact include pieces which range from opposition to implicit acceptance of slavery.[84] In *The Sorrows of Yamba; or, a Negro Woman's Lament* the enslaved woman looks back in sorrow at her idyllic family life in Africa, her capture, the death of her child at sea, and her ill-treatment as a slave, and called on British slave traders to 'Mock your Saviour's name no further,/Cease your savage lust of gain'.[85] This is a poem of standard abolitionist type, and the favourable contrast it makes between 'noble savage' and hypocritical Christian slave trader resembles a poem written at this period by a pro-revolutionary woman author, Fanny Holcroft (d. 1844), daughter of leading radical Thomas Holcroft. In this poem, *The Negro* (1797), a dying slave curses his Christian masters.[86]

Three other tracts in More's compilation, however, have a more ambivalent message. In *Babay. A True Story of a Good Negro Woman* the slave is charitable because she is a Christian, and the chief purpose of the story is not anti-slavery but the pointing of a moral to the working class reader: charity is based not on advantages of birth and education but on religious conviction.[87] In the poem *The Comforts of Religion* the aim of freedom in life is replaced by a vision of slavery and other human sufferings made bearable by a religion which holds out the hope of life after death.[88] Finally, in *A True Account of a Pious Negro*, an English gentleman tells of his encounter with a slave on a North American plantation. He asks the slave whether he would not prefer liberty to slavery and the man replies:

> I have wife and children, and my massa takes care of them, and I have no care to produce any thing: I have a good massah who teach me to read; and I read good book, that keep me happy.[89]

One of the messages at the end of the tale is that 'religion, and that only will make a man content and comfortable in the lowest situations'.[90]

These poems and tales compiled by More need to be interpreted in the context of the purpose of the *Cheap Repository Tracts* of which they formed a part. These tracts, which reached thousands of readers, fulfilled More's aim of providing 'safe' books for use in Sunday schools to teach the poor to read. They were intended to combat the effect of Paineite pamphlets advocating the 'Rights of Man' which were circulating among the working class in the wake of the French Revolution. They stressed morality, loyalty and religion, encouraging people to accommodate themselves to their station in life rather than to try to change the established order.

More's reactions to the French Revolution encompassed not only calls for working-class and black passivity but also a reply to Wollstonecraft's call for liberty and equality for women. Her *Strictures on the Modern System of Female Education* (1799) stressed differences in male and female natural qualities and social roles, praised the special sensitivity of women, and called for the moral regeneration of society on a Christian basis through the moral influence of women educated not in the art of reasoning but in religion. While accepting that the supposed inferiority of both women and blacks was in part, and possibly wholly, the result of inadequate education rather than innate inability, More argued the goal of equality in this life to be unimportant in the face of the pre-existing equality of all before God: 'Christianity had exalted women to true and undisputed dignity; in Christ Jesus, as there is neither "rich nor poor", "bond nor free", so there is neither "male nor female".'[91]

Two successive images of women and freedom symbolise the move in anti-slavery and gender ideology from Wollstonecraft's radical vision of freedom as equality to More's conservative vision of freedom as the establishment of proper hierarchies. These are the radical romantic artist William Blake's egalitarian image of Europe, Africa and America as the three Graces, equal and interlinked, which was produced in 1796 as part of the abolition campaign; and Robert Smirke's contrasting hierarchical image of Britain, represented by white female figures symbolising Britannia and Justice bestowing freedom on grateful kneeling slaves, which he produced in 1809 to commemorate the abolition of the slave trade (Figures 5 and 6).

IMAGINATIVE WRITERS

Prior to 1795 Hannah More had been responsible for producing a number of major anti-slavery poems. Indeed the stress by Hannah More and other evangelicals on the especial sensitivity of women encouraged female contributions to anti-slavery literature to take the form not of tracts directed at the intellect but of poetic appeals to the heart. It was in the field of imaginative literature that women made one of their most significant contributions to the early abolition campaign.[92]

At a crude estimate female authors were responsible for around a quarter of poems and tales with an anti-slavery theme which appeared in the late eighteenth century.[93] Such literature had its origins a century earlier with the work of the woman who was possibly the first professional woman writer in England. The Restoration writer Aphra Behn (1640–89) wrote *Oroonoko; or, the Royal Slave* in 1688. It purports to be the 'True History' of an enslaved African prince whom Behn had encountered on her travels in Surinam.[94] *Oroonoko* established many of

Figure 5 *Europe Supported by Africa and America.*
Engraving by William Blake in John G. Stedman,
*Narrative of a Five Years' Expedition, against the Revolted
Negroes of Surinam in Guiana* (London, 1796).

the elements which in the late eighteenth century became the cliches of
abolitionist poetry and tales by both women and men: the noble savage,
the princely or Europeanised hero, the heart-rending tale of young
lovers torn apart by slavery, the tragic end of suicide as the only escape.
Despite Behn's claim for it as a 'true story', however, its initial publication well before the onset of an organised anti-slavery campaign
meant that it could be read simply as tragic fiction rather than as a call
for action. As such, transformed into dramatic form by Thomas
Southerne in 1696, it became an extremely popular play during the
eighteenth century. It was only in 1789 that it gained significance as
propaganda, when it was performed in Manchester and London with
the addition of anti-slavery prologues.[95]

The heyday of imaginative literature about slavery was in the 1787–

Figure 6 Steel engraving by William Henry Worthington
after painting by R. Smirke, illustrating James
Montgomery, 'The West Indies, a Poem in Four Parts', in
James Montgomery, James Grahame and E. Benger, *Poems on
the Abolition of the Slave Trade* (London: R. Bowyer, 1809).

92 period, at the height of the popular campaign against the slave trade,
and it functioned as an important part of the appeal made to public
opinion at this time.[96] Poems about slavery, often incorporating
elements of the *Oroonoko* story, were circulated by abolition societies
and were widely published in the newspapers which reported abolitionist campaigns, as well as in the burgeoning literary, denominational
and women's periodicals of the period.[97]

Poetry was an obvious choice as anti-slavery medium by women in
the late eighteenth century because, as recent studies have pointed out,
at this period a 'discernible tradition of feminine poetry' was emerging
as 'women virtually took over, as writers and readers, the territories
most readily conceded to them, of popular fiction and fashionable
poetry'.[98] Women poets such as Hannah More and Anna Laetitia

Barbauld created a corpus of highly popular work, the significance of which has until recently been obscured by critical focus on male Romantic poets such as Wordsworth.

Imaginative literature was recognised as a particularly good way of appealing to a wide public encompassing both women and men. The Abolition Society had William Cowper's poem *Pity the Poor Africans* reprinted on fine quality paper and distributed in thousands with the superscription, 'A Subject for Conversation at the Tea-Table', suggesting its suitability for polite discussion among women in the home. Lady Harriet Hesketh (1753–1807), Cowper's cousin, suggested that he write some songs on the slave trade 'as the surest way of reaching the public ear'.[99] Hannah More wrote to Lady Middleton suggesting that they persuade the manager of the Drury Lane Theatre in London, with whom More had close contacts, to put on *Oroonoko* as a way of reaching three thousand people a night with an anti-slavery message.[100] In Manchester *Oroonoko* was performed in 1787 with an anti-slavery prologue specifically addressed to women.[101]

Women writers were aware of the power they possessed to write poetry which had the potential of arousing public feeling to the extent of influencing events in the Parliamentary sphere from which they were excluded by their sex. Hannah More wrote her most famous anti-slavery poem, *Slavery*, explicitly as propaganda to aid Wilberforce at his opening of the Parliamentary campaign against the slave trade in 1788.[102] She commented to her sister: 'I grieve that I did not set about it sooner; as it must now be done in such a hurry . . . . but good or bad, if it does not come out at the particular moment when the discussion comes on in Parliament, it will not be worth a straw.'[103] Mary Leadbeater (1758–1826), an Irish Quaker teacher and writer of moral tales from Balymore in County Kildare, addressed family friend Edmund Burke in a poem entitled *The Negro. Addressed to Edmund Burke* (1789), which made an appeal to this leading politician as 'freedom's firm friend' to campaign to make slavery illegal.[104] Helen Maria Williams' *Poem on the Bill Lately Passed for Regulating the Slave Trade* (1788) praised the Act but urged the Government to go further to give full freedom.[105] Anna Laetitia Barbauld's *Epistle to William Wilberforce Esq.* (1788) praised Wilberforce's efforts but attacked the nation as a whole for failing to abolish the trade.[106]

The writing of anti-slavery poetry was not restricted to such professional authors. Amateur female poets were encouraged to take up their pens in a period which saw both the 'feminisation' of poetry and its democratisation and which was marked by the evolution of new styles which, in comparison to poetry of the Augustan Age, placed less stress on classical learning and set forms than on the expression of heartfelt sentiment and of natural talent. A collection of *Poems on Slavery* by 'Maria Falconar, aged 17, and Harriet Falconar, aged 14' appeared in 1788, and a poem 'On the Slave Trade by a Young Lady at School' was printed in the *Manchester Mercury* that same year.[107] Ann Yearsley (1752–1806), the working-class 'milkwoman of Bristol' whose poetic talent was discovered by Hannah More, published a *Poem on the Inhumanity of the Slave Trade* (1788) which pleaded with the leading inhabitants of the city to end its heavy involvement in the slave trade.[108]

Together with poems of obvious campaigning intent were others in the *Oroonoko* tradition portraying the sufferings of black people under slavery and contrasting this with a romantic and idealised view of the life of the 'noble savage' in an African Eden. A typical example in this genre is Eliza Knipe's narrative poem *Atombaka and Omaza: An African Story* (1787), the tale of a young African warrior chief and his lover, their bravery in battle, capture by the enemy and sale to slave traders. On board ship, rather than face a life enslaved, they throw themselves, 'clasp'd in a fond embrace', into the sea and drown.[109] Such tragic tales of romantic love fostered sympathy for black suffering and awareness of black resistance and helped combat pro-slavery stereotypes of black men and women's animal sexuality and licentiousness.[110]

Women poets played an important part in harnessing developing evangelical ideas about feminine sensitivity to the fashionable literary cult of sentimentalism in order to further the cause of abolition.[111] More's poem *Slavery* (1788), which includes the lines 'From head to hearts lies Nature's plain appeal,/Though few can reason, all mankind can feel'[112] was praised in the *Monthly Review* in these terms: 'The chief excellence of this poem consists in its pathetic appeal to our feelings, in behalf of our sable fellow-creatures.'[113]

The few specific poetic appeals to women to support abolition stressed feminine sensitivity and influence. In *An Appeal to England, on Behalf of the Abused Africans* (1789) the Irish Quaker Thomas Wilkinson, a friend of Romantic poets Thomas Coleridge and William Wordsworth, successively addressed himself to clergy, colleges, 'free and favour'd Britons', 'House august', 'Senators' and King, and then appealed to the tenderness of women:

> Ye British Dames! whose tender bosoms know
> To melt with pity o'er the couch of woe:
> How must your hearts commiserate his woes,
> Whose lot nor home, nor couch, nor country knows!
> These sacred rights he never must regain,
> Oh plead for such! – you seldom plead in vain.[114]

Irish Catholic actor and author James Field Stanfield (d. 1824), an abolitionist friend of Thomas Clarkson's, in his poem *The Guinea Voyage* (1789) called on women in similar terms:

A nation's councils oft your pow'r obey;
The wars of nations own your sov'reign sway
. . . .

When beauty lifts her eye in Mis'ry's cause,
Compassion wakes, and follows with applause.[115]

The anonymous *The Negro Mother's Petition to the Ladies of Bristol*, a campaign poster in the form of a poem, was produced by Edward Protheroe, who stood as Parliamentary candidate for Bristol on an anti-slave-trade platform in 1788. It was in the form of an appeal from a black woman to the women of Bristol, imploring them to 'tink on' suffering slaves, to tell their husbands, fathers and brothers about their plight, and to urge them to vote for 'massa PRODEROE', the abolitionist candidate, in the election to 'de house call Parliament'.[116]

Only one poem has been identified which was written by a woman and directed specifically at her own sex. Irish Quaker Mary Birkett's *Poem on the African Slave Trade* appealed to 'Hibernian fair, who own compassions sway' to join in the abolition campaign:

For Mercy's softest beams to you belong;
To you the sympathetic is known,
And Charity's sweet lustre – all your own;
To you gall'd Mis'ry seldom pleads in vain,
Oh, let us rise and burst the Negro's chain![117]

The poem continued with a call for women to exert their influence:

Say not – no power of your's so far extends,
These are your brothers, husbands, sons, or friends,
. . . .

Will these reject your small, your just request,
When urg'd with meekness – yet with warmth exprest?[118]

Katherine Rogers has written that in the late eighteenth century women writers were expected to write in a 'feminine' way, demonstrating delicacy of feeling, dealing with emotional distress rather than political problems, and abstaining from radical social criticism and political discussion.[119] Abolitionist verse and tales, however, demonstrate that women found a way to voice social and political criticism through the acceptably 'feminine' means of poetic sentiment and appeals to the emotions. While some poems by women were purely sentimental appeals which may have led to a selfish obsession with the reader's sensibility rather than attempts to relieve black suffering, others were clear calls for action.[120] As a complement to the tracts and pamphlets written almost exclusively by men, poetry by both sexes could, as D.B. Davis has pointed out, give 'a directness and emotional

34

intensity to rational arguments that had long been ignored'.[121] In this way 'masculine' reason and 'feminine' sensibility were enlisted as complementary qualities in the fight against the slave trade.

BOYCOTTERS

Mary Birkett's poetic appeal called on women not only to exert their influence on men but also to take action themselves by abstaining from slave-grown sugar. Abstention was seen from the first as a particularly female concern, and it provided women with another important opportunity to actively participate in the abolition campaign.[122]

It is clear from *An Address to the People of Great Britain* by leading Baptist campaigner William Fox (1736–1826), a pamphlet which launched the public abstention campaign in 1791, that the public campaign to encourage abstention got underway in response to frustration at the failure of petitioning to persuade Parliament to put a stop to the slave trade. If the government would not take action, Fox argued, then people must bring about the end of the slave trade themselves by putting economic pressure on planters and slave traders to change over to a system of free labour and to trade in free-grown produce.[123] As David Brion Davis has pointed out, such an approach had 'subversive implications', threatening to 'undercut the government's control over abolitionism'.[124]

Thus disillusionment with petitioning, a male campaign based on negotiation with Parliamentary authority, led to an increasing focus on abstention, a campaign which bypassed that authority and for which the support of women, political outsiders by virtue of their sex, was actively solicited.

Methodist Samuel Bradburn's *Address to the People Called Methodists* explicitly included the female half of the denomination in his appeal for a boycott of sugar and rum as one element of a popular campaign against the slave trade.[125] Similarly, an advertisement for a meeting in Coachmaker's Hall in London on 12 January 1792 acknowledged that abstention was a campaigning tactic which 'had been resolved upon by women as well as men'. The speaker, William Allen, a Quaker member of the Abolition Committee, couched his appeal 'to the justice and humanity of both sexes', emphasising that all could participate in the boycott and concluding by making an especial appeal to women.[126]

The inclusion of women in appeals by Quakers like Allen was related to Quaker emphasis on the individual guilt of supporting slavery through consumption of slave-grown goods, and individual responsibility to abstain was tied to the Quakers' belief in the importance of following the dictates of one's conscience.[127] The word 'abstention' laid emphasis on the self-denial involved in the refusal to *eat* slave-grown sugar, and may be contrasted with the use of the modern word 'boycott' to describe the refusal to *buy* South African produce in opposition to apartheid. In the context of the 1790s, abstention may be related to current middle-class and evangelical critiques of excessive aristocratic consumption, which placed a high value on the renunciation of worldly pleasures. Abstention was a word later used by temperance campaigners to describe the refusal to drink alcohol, and in both cases the word carried connotations of the moral righteousness of renouncing a sin.

Responsibility to abstain was seen as falling equally on women and men. In Sheffield, where Quakers led the abstention campaign, a public appeal to women to replace West Indian produce by 'food unstain'd with unoffending blood' appeared in the *Sheffield Register* in 1791.[128] The anonymous male author's 'Lines, Humbly Addressed to the Fair Sex', were printed above a letter defending the sugar and rum boycott. Slaves could be restored to liberty, the writer argued:

> If you, ye Fair (who long, too long, have been
> With us, sad partners, in the sinful act,
> And caus'd the tyrants to prolong the scene)
> Will join to end the tragic, mournful fact.[129]

Similarly, Quaker Mary Birkett's 1792 poetic appeal to Irish women urged them to follow the example of their English sisters in abstaining from slave produce, both as a way of freeing them from guilt and as a way of advancing abolition:

> Yes, sisters, to us the task belongs,
> 'Tis we increase or mitigate their wrongs.
> If we the produce of their toils refuse,
> If we no more the blood-stain'd lux'ry choose;
> . . . .
> And in our brethrens sufferings hold no share,
> In no small part their long-borne pangs will cease,
> And we to souls unborn may whisper peace.[130]

Women's actions, Birkett claimed, could and did have some effect:

> Say not that small's the sphere in which we move,
> And our attempts would vain and fruitless prove;
> Not so – we hold *a most important share*,
> In all the evils – all the wrongs they bear;
> And tho' their woes *entire* we can't remove,
> We may th' *increasing* mis'ries which they prove,
> Push far the plant for which they die.[131]

To these general assertions of women's similar responsibilities to men and their ability to participate in the boycott was added the recognition that women held the responsibility for household purchases and made the decisions about family consumption. They were thus in the position to actually take the *lead* in the abstention campaign. In a letter which appeared in the *Newcastle Courant* in 1792 its writer, 'Humanus', described women as making decisions on household consumption:

> Happening lately to be sometime from home, the females in my family had in my absence perused a pamphlet, entitled 'An Address to the People of Great Britain on the Utility of Refraining from the Use of West India Sugar and Rum'. On my return, I was surprised to find that they had entirely left off the use of Sugar, and banished it from the tea table.[132]

This decision-making role was also acknowledged in *An Address to Her Royal Highness the Dutchess of York* (1792), which urged her to proscribe sugar from her own household.[133] Similarly, in Gillray's cartoon 'ANTI-SACCHARITES,-or- JOHN BULL and his Family leaving off the use of SUGAR' (1792) Queen Charlotte is shown as the instigator of abstention from sugar in the Royal Family, for reasons both of economy and to save the 'poor Blackeemoors' from work.[134]

It was recognised that women's participation was essential to the success of the abstention campaign. As a newspaper report of sugar abstention in Biggleswade and Lincoln concluded, 'City meetings might make resolutions upon resolutions in such a business to little purpose indeed, unless we first gain over our wives and daughters.'[135] In Lincoln 'a party of oeconomical and *public-spirited* ladies' had undertaken to forward a house-to-house canvass to gain signatures to an agreement not to use sugar. While this was on account of its high price rather than for humanitarian reasons, the report is of interest in indicating that women sometimes organised abstention from sugar on a community as well as on an individual household basis.

Aristocratic women were appealed to not only as individual consumers but also as the leaders of fashions in consumer items.[136] The writer of *An Address to Her Royal Highness the Dutchess of York* (1792) requested the Duchess to place herself at the head of the body of people who had stopped using sugar. The writer hoped that the King and Queen would follow suit, and that the scheme would spread through the nobility and gentry to the middling orders and then through Europe, fired by her example.

The role of women as leaders of fashion was also exploited by Josiah Wedgwood, manufacturer of the famous jasper cameo depicting a kneeling black slave with the motto 'Am I not a man and a brother?' Wedgwood produced these cameos from 1787 onwards and they became widely adopted for decorating men's snuff boxes and ladies' bracelets and hairpins.[137] In his diary of his 1792 tour of Scotland on behalf of the Abolition Society William Dickson noted that he presented the gentlemen with whom he stayed with abolition pamphlets, their wives and daughters with cameos.[138] The abolitionist Thomas Clarkson later recalled: 'At length the taste for wearing them became general; and thus fashion, which usually confines itself to worthless things, was seen for once in the honourable office of promoting the cause of justice, humanity, and freedom.'[139] Clarkson's point about the harnessing of consumerism to political ends could equally be applied to the abstention movement.

Campaigners for abstention also appealed to women's supposed sensitivity and their influence over men. William Allen, for example, in his 1792 speech to a public debating society in London, addressed women thus:

> In THEM 'tis graceful to DISSOLVE AT WOE, And from the SMALLEST VIOLENCE to shrink! They are universally considered as the MODELS of every just and virtuous sentiment – and we naturally look up to them as PATERNS [sic] in all the softer virtues. Their EXAMPLE, therefore, in ABSTAINING FROM THE USE OF WEST INDIA PRODUCE – must silence every murmur – must refute every objection – and render the performance of the Duty as UNIVERSAL as their INFLUENCE![140]

Women's concern for the suffering of other women was also evoked. Andrew Burn, in his Second Address to the People of Great Britain, described how mothers with infants were forced to toil and subjected to whippings, stating 'Think on this, Mothers who use sugar!'[141] Cruikshank's cartoon of the Royal Family entitled 'The Gradual Abolition of the Slave Trade. Or leaving of Sugar by Degrees' has the Queen, who is trying to persuade her household to cut down on sugar consumption, saying in an imitation of black dialect: 'Now my Dear's only an ickle Bit, do but tink on de Negro girl dat Captain Kimber treated so Cruelly.' This referred to the case just described by Wilberforce to Parliament of a girl whipped to death on a slave ship for refusing to dance naked on deck. (See Figure 4.)

The extent of female support for the abstention campaign is difficult to gauge. The most reliable contemporary estimate of total abstainers, made by Thomas Clarkson on the basis of his extensive anti-slavery tour of England and Wales in late 1791 and early 1792, is not broken down on sex lines. Clarkson estimated that 300,000 'persons' of 'all ranks and parties. Rich and poor, Churchmen and dissenters' had abandoned the use of slave-produced sugar.[142] Newspaper reports of abstainers in particular towns generally gave numbers of abstaining families rather than individuals, suggestive of the domestic basis of the campaign and, by implication, of the involvement of women.[143] The fact that some grocers began to stock East India in preference to West India sugar suggests that women, who were responsible for household purchases, put consumer pressure on retailers. Further evidence for female involvement is provided by Mary Birkett's praise of English women's support for abstention, and James Mullala's praise of Irish women's participation in the campaign.[144]

There is evidence that some of the women who participated in the abstention campaign were working class. Clarkson stated that some domestic servants had voluntarily followed their masters' example and left off the use of slave-grown sugar.[145] This is interesting information in view of the important role of domestic servants, the majority of whom were women, in transmitting middle- and upper-class fashions to the rest of society.[146]

An indication that there was also support for abstention among women from artisan households is contained in the letter Lydia Hardy wrote in 1792 to her husband Thomas, a shoemaker and the leader of the radical London Corresponding Society. In the letter, written from her home village of Chesham in Buckinghamshire, where her father worked as a carpenter and builder, she stated:

> Pray let me no how you go on in your society and likewise we . . .
> [illegible word] as been donn in the parlement house concurning
> the slave trade for the people here are as much against it as enny
> ware and there is more people I think hear that drinks tea without
> sugar than there is drinks with. . . .[147]

The letter also mentions the Hardys' close friend Olaudah Equiano's anti-slavery autobiography, which he had revised while staying in their home.[148] Artisan women's support of abstention was the product of radical enthusiasm for abolition rather than the aping of middle- or upper-class fashion. However, Lydia Hardy's lack of status in the radical movement compared to her husband, and her letter, with its complaints of debt and ill-health, are suggestive of the obstacles impeding all impoverished women from participation in abolitionist activities.

The support which the abstention campaign attracted among women provoked considerable concern among the West India interest in Britain. An article in the *Gentleman's Magazine* of December 1791, by an advocate of reform rather than abolition, argued that women were taking action in vain.[149] The February 1792 issue of the magazine contained an attack on the *Address to Her Royal Highness the Dutchess of York* alongside a 'Vindication' of the use of West India sugar.[150] In March 1792 *The Times* carried a long letter purportedly written by a little boy to a young lady who had persuaded him to give up sugar. The writer suggests that the lady had been gulled by hypocritical men who actually made their fortunes from trading in other slave produce such as cotton. The lady and her mother are also accused of inconsistency for using other slave-grown produce.[151]

While such attacks suggest that the West India interest were nervous at the possible success of the abstention campaign, any adverse effect that declining consumption in Britain might have had on planters and traders was in practice cancelled out by a huge increase in imports of British colonial sugar to continental Europe in the 1790s. In Britain itself the effects of the boycott on consumer demand were obscured by its occurrence at a time of sugar shortage and rising prices.[152]

The main importance of the campaign to the abolition movement was probably the role it played in creating in large numbers of men and women a sense of individual responsibility for slavery, and a belief in the possibility of achieving its downfall through extra-Parliamentary action. For women, the campaign allowed them an active part in the abolition campaign which they had been denied in the field of petitioning. It also exposed their power as domestic consumers to have a direct effect on commerce and an indirect influence on politics. The potential effectiveness of abstention was, however, seriously undermined when it ceased to be publicly promoted by the Abolition Society after 1792 as part of the Society's general wariness of any extra-Parliamentary campaigning which might be viewed as subversive in the reactionary climate of the period.[153]

Overall, looking at the evidence for women's involvement in abolition it might be concluded that, as a consequence of the collapse of the popular abolition campaign in 1792, women, in common with men excluded from the franchise and from Parliament, made little contribution to the passage of the Abolition Act in March 1807. However, as James Walvin points out, though the Act was the 'function overwhelmingly of Parliamentary tactics and ploys' it was 'the tactics and arguments of popular abolition' which 'had served to lodge the issue securely with Parliament itself'.[154] It was in this popular campaign that women had played significant roles as runaways, as subscribers, as writers and as abstainers.

Women had also been instrumental in linking rival formulations of anti-slavery as a matter of rights or a matter of charity to contesting views of women's social role as equals with the same rights as men or as possessors of innately feminine qualities with distinctive duties.

Part II

WOMEN AGAINST BRITISH COLONIAL SLAVERY, 1823–1838

3

'CEMENT OF THE WHOLE ANTISLAVERY BUILDING'

In 1823 the attention of British campaigners switched from the slave trade to slavery itself. The campaign against British colonial slavery was launched in response to the realisation that, contrary to activists' hopes, the abolition of the British slave trade had not led to improvements in the treatment of slaves or to progress towards their emancipation in the British West Indies. A new national society was formed: the Society for the Mitigation and Gradual Abolition of Slavery Throughout the British Dominions, known popularly as the Anti-Slavery Society. It campaigned initially for the amelioration and eventual abolition of slavery, and then from 1830–31, in conjunction with the Agency Committee, for immediate and entire emancipation. Campaigners witnessed the partial achievement of their aims with the passage of the Emancipation Act in 1833.[1] The Society was revived in 1837 when, together with the more radical Birmingham-based Central Negro Emancipation Committee, it launched a campaign for the immediate abolition of the apprenticeship system which had been introduced by the Government as a transitional stage between slavery and full emancipation. This campaign ended successfully when colonial legislatures abolished all forms of apprenticeship in the five months leading up to 1 August 1838, the date set by the British Parliament for the complete freeing of non-agricultural labourers.

Despite their continuing exclusion from national committees, women played a vital part in all stages of this campaign, most notably through the anti-slavery associations which they set up to co-ordinate their activities.

ORGANISING

On 8 April 1825, two years after the national Anti-Slavery Society had been formed, the first women's anti-slavery society in Britain was established at a meeting in the home of Lucy Townsend, wife of the

Anglican clergyman of West Bromwich near Birmingham. Initially entitled the Ladies Society for the Relief of Negro Slaves, later the Female Society for Birmingham, the organisation pledged itself to the 'Amelioration of the Condition of the Unhappy Children of Africa, and especially of Female Negro Slaves'. In its founding resolutions the society stated that it intended to achieve its aims through diffusing information to arouse public abhorrence of slavery, through dispatching an 'Appeal from British Ladies to the West India Planters', and through using surplus funds to aid charitable and educational work by missionaries among the free black population of the West Indies. Annual subscriptions were set at five to twelve shillings, two secretaries and a committee of ten district treasurers were appointed, quarterly meetings were arranged, and an initial list of forty-four female suscribers was published.[2]

The foundation of the Female Society for Birmingham was followed by the formation of a network of other ladies' anti-slavery associations. Together these groups marked the change from abolition as an individual woman's commitment, to anti-slavery as a collective female endeavour. It was to be a change with major repercussions not only on the role of women in the movement but also on the nature of the anti-slavery campaign as a whole and on the role of women in British society.

The network of ladies' anti-slavery associations which was formed in the 1820s and 1830s has hitherto received little attention from historians. Early studies of the campaign against British colonial slavery focused on the activities of the male national leadership both within and without Parliament.[3] Recent studies stressing the vital importance of widespread popular support to the strength and success of the campaign have entailed some consideration of the activities of women.[4] Ladies' associations have, however, generally been misleadingly characterised as small local groups working hard within their local communities but playing a largely supportive role.[5] This recent assessment contrasts markedly with the one made in 1834 by national anti-slavery activist George Thompson. Thompson, in a letter to Chelmsford Quaker campaigner Anne Knight, stated: 'Where they existed, they did everything. . . . In a word they formed the cement of the whole Antislavery building – without their aid we never should have been united.'[6]

Thompson's assessment, as will be shown, cannot be dismissed as the case of a chivalrous male exaggerating the truth. Ladies' associations were 'not simply passive auxiliaries', as Louis and Rosamund Billington have recently made clear in their short but pioneering study.[7] Indeed, as will be demonstrated here, they were the *major* innovation in national anti-slavery organisation in the 1820s and they had a highly significant

44

impact on the course of the anti-slavery campaign as a whole.

The anti-slavery campaign of 1823–33 was a nationwide campaign involving the exertion of public pressure on Parliament to bring about legislative change. The formation of an active network of local societies was thus viewed by the Anti-Slavery Society as vital to achieving its aims. However, while local men's auxiliaries were promoted from the first, initially no thought was given to forming similar local groups for women.[8] Just as the name 'Anti-Slavery Society' appeared sex-neutral but in practice denoted a society run by an all-male committee, so the term 'auxiliary' in practice denoted a local society for men only: women were excluded but in a way which rendered their exclusion invisible and taken for granted, rather than a matter for debate. In contrast, when the first women's groups were set up in 1825 their titles made clear their sex-specific nature, thus indirectly drawing attention to the sexual division of labour in the anti-slavery movement. It was a division which, while in some ways limiting women's participation, in others expanded its significance through fostering the development of distinctive female perspectives and specialised forms of activities.

The Anti-Slavery Society's network of affiliated local societies expanded rapidly through the 1820s. The Society's records show the receipt of money from four ladies' associations and thirty-four auxiliaries in 1826, increasing to a peak of thirty-nine ladies' associations and seventy-eight auxiliaries in 1831.[9] At least seventy-three ladies' associations were active at some time between 1825 and 1833, and at least twenty-four in the 1834–8 period, (see Appendix for a full list). While men's anti-slavery groups were always more numerous than women's, the gap narrowed from a ratio of under eight to one in 1826 to two to one in 1831.

Men's auxiliaries and ladies' associations had a similar geographical spread, covering most English counties, and with a few groups in Wales, Scotland and Ireland. They were located in a wide variety of communities: county and market towns in rural areas, large urban industrial centres and ports. At a local level, however, men's and women's societies were not always in the same towns. Of the seventy-three ladies' associations active between 1825 and 1833, forty-two were in towns with active men's groups, and the remaining thirty-one in towns with no identified men's auxiliary. Thus the existence of ladies' associations considerably increased the number of towns involved in anti-slavery activism.

The establishment of this network of ladies' associations was largely the result of women's own initiatives. The Female Society for Birmingham was the first, the largest, the most influential and the longest lasting of the associations, and it played a key role in this process.[10]

The steps leading to the formation of the Birmingham society can be reconstructed in some detail and illuminate the origins of women's anti-slavery organisations. Lucy Townsend, having had the idea of forming a women's society, wrote to veteran abolitionist Thomas Clarkson for advice. Clarkson, who in 1823–24 had toured England and Wales promoting men's auxiliaries, was encouraging. He made suggestions about the title of the group and obtained pamphlets for Townsend from the Anti-Slavery Society.[11] He also suggested that she enlist the support of Samuel Lloyd, a Quaker campaigner who the previous year had been involved in setting up the local men's auxiliary, the Birmingham Anti-Slavery Society.[12]

While Lucy Townsend did inform Samuel Lloyd of her plans, the Birmingham Anti-Slavery Society did not play a formal role in setting up the women's group and it was rather to Lloyd's wife Mary that Lucy primarily turned for help in implementing her plan. Townsend, an evangelical Anglican, had met Lloyd, a Quaker, through their mutual involvement in the local ladies' branch association of the interdenominational evangelical British and Foreign Bible Society.[13] This association, which from 1812 onwards had established an extensive network of women's branches, and which had published blueprints for their organisation, provided the two women with a possible model for organising a women's anti-slavery society.[14] Indeed the formation of the group can be seen as part of the burgeoning of women's philanthropic societies at this period.

Neither the men's auxiliaries of the Anti-Slavery Society nor the ladies' branches of the Bible Society provided a model for a group on quite the lines of the Birmingham society, however. For the Birmingham society was set up as an *independent* society rather than a local auxiliary.[15] Indeed, as Louis and Rosamund Billington have pointed out, it acted more like a *national* than a local society, actively promoting the foundation of local women's societies throughout England, and in Wales and Ireland, and supplying them with information and advice.[16] Its independent status and national ambitions made it more comparable to the small number of early nineteenth-century charitable societies managed by women.[17]

The Birmingham society defined one of its chief objectives as being 'to strive to promote the formation of Ladies' Associations . . . in every part of His Majesty's Dominions to which their influence may extend'.[18] Lloyd and Townsend set about achieving this through developing a network of district treasurers, which expanded from ten women in 1825 to forty-nine by 1830, spread throughout England, with contacts also in Tenby and Monmouth in Wales, in Dublin, and even as far afield as France, the Cape of Good Hope, Sierra Leone and Calcutta.[19] These contacts were probably established through denominational networks such as Quaker women's meetings, through the Bible Society network, and through information from Thomas Clarkson, who had informed Lucy Townsend in 1825 that 'there are many ladies in different parts of the Kingdom who would embark in committees of this sort . . .'.[20]

The district treasurers, aided by advice and a supply of tracts and pamphlets from Birmingham, were encouraged to found local associations in their towns.[21] This scheme was very successful, with separate ladies' associations with links to Birmingham being formed by 1829 at Calne in Wiltshire, Bristol, Southampton, Plymouth, Manchester, Newcastle, York and Reading, at Battersea Rise, Islington and Tottenham in the London area, and at Monmouth in Wales and Dublin in Ireland.[22] The Birmingham group also had four auxiliary societies which sent it the money they raised by subscriptions; they were at Leicester, Oakham and Deddington in the English Midlands and at Moyallan in Ireland.[23]

A number of other ladies' associations also show evidence of close links with, and influence from, Birmingham. The Sheffield group (formed on 12 July 1825 and thus one of the earliest ladies' associations) was entitled the Society for the Relief of Negro Slaves, a similar name to that of the Birmingham group. In addition, a complexly worded founding resolution of the Birmingham society was replicated identically in the founding resolutions of the Society for the Relief of Negro Slaves founded in Sheffield on 12 July 1825, of the Colchester Ladies' Anti-Slavery Association (founded on 1 July 1825) and of the Liverpool Ladies' Anti-Slavery Society (founded on 17 January 1827), suggesting that the three later groups copied the Birmingham resolution word for word.[24] All three groups were supplied with tracts by Birmingham from the time of their foundation onwards.[25]

Overall, of the seventy-three ladies' associations founded between 1825 and 1833, around twenty were formed under the influence of the Female Society for Birmingham. Some, including those at Calne and Dublin, were independent; some were auxiliaries of the Birmingham society; others, including those at Sheffield and Liverpool, were auxiliary to the national Anti-Slavery Society. In contrast to this evidence of female initiative and influence only one case of a local men's society setting up a ladies' association has been identified: the ladies' association formed by the Rochester and Chatham Anti-Slavery Society in Kent in 1826.[26]

It was the initiative of women in Birmingham in setting up the first ladies' anti-slavery society which prompted the Anti-Slavery Society to decide to encourage the formation of ladies' associations. At a national committee meeting on 11 May 1825, a letter from Samuel Lloyd was read giving details of the formation of the Birmingham-centred group, and it was immediately resolved that a sub-committee be set up to 'prepare a plan suitable for the promotion of similar societies'.[27]

The decision to encourage the formation of ladies' associations did not take place without opposition from some prominent male abolitionists. The issue divided members of the influential evangelical Anglican Clapham Sect, with William Wilberforce and Thomas Babington opposing ladies' associations, while Zachary Macaulay enthusiastically encouraged them. It was women's move from the individually supportive, behind-the-scenes roles which they had played during the campaign against the slave trade to a more public role in organised groups that caused unease, particularly among the older generation of abolitionists. While women's public and organisational role in philanthropic and religious societies had become established over the past thirty-five years, the anti-slavery campaign had political dimensions which meant it could not be comfortably accommodated within this framework. Wilberforce evoked the authority of the Bible in expressing his disapproval, writing in January 1826:

> I own I cannot relish the plan. All private exertions for such an object become their character, but for ladies to meet, to publish, to go from house to house stirring up petitions – these appear to me proceedings unsuited to the female character as delineated in Scripture. I fear its tendency would be to mix them in all the multiform warfare of political life.[28]

Wilberforce continued his campaign against ladies' associations until at least July 1826, criticising Macaulay for publicising their activities in the Anti-Slavery Society's periodical, the *Anti-Slavery Monthly Reporter*.[29] Macaulay, however, ignored his advice. Wilberforce himself was losing influence over the movement at this period, having handed over leadership of the Parliamentary campaign to Thomas Fowell Buxton. He reluctantly agreed to his wife's name being included as a subscriber to one of the new associations.[30] Wilberforce's close associate, Hannah More, signalled her approval of such groups by joining the committee of the Female Anti-Slavery Society for Clifton, though she was too old to play an active part in its activities.[31]

Faced with the fact that women were organising independently, the anti-slavery leadership decided to encourage this to take a form which would be most helpful to themselves. By June 1825 a set of sample rules for ladies' associations had been prepared, and it was resolved to print three thousand copies each of rules for gentlemen's societies and rules for ladies' associations, suggesting that equal priority was given to the formation of both types of groups.[32] The issuing of rules indicates an attempt to encourage some unity of aims, structure and activities among local groups. The rules were quite basic and flexible, however, being concerned mainly with organisational structure, and including the statement that they 'can be altered and modified . . . according to circumstances'.[33] The recommended organisational structure for women's and men's groups was almost identical, and the 'special object' of both was defined as the collection and diffusion of information, with a secondary function of collecting subscriptions. Recommended campaigning methods differed, however: women were to diffuse information and collect funds through the medium of district collectors, men through the press and public meetings. In addition, men were urged to promote petitions to the legislature whereas the women's rules made no mention of petitioning.[34]

The appropriate relationship between ladies' associations and men's auxiliaries was never to be formally defined by the Anti-Slavery Society. Evidence from local society records, however, suggests that despite informal family connections, the two types of groups operated largely independently of each other.[35] This contrasts with the situation in other philanthropic societies, in which, as Prochaska has pointed out, 'committee-men often grafted female associations on to men's auxiliaries' in order to keep them under their control.[36]

The Anti-Slavery Society's enthusiasm for ladies' associations steadily increased. In 1826 two thousand copies of a circular 'Address to the Ladies' were issued.[37] This was probably the tract *Negro Slavery. To the Ladies of the United Kingdom*, which gave a wider definition of the objectives of ladies' associations than did the earlier rules, suggesting that the associations not only diffuse information and collect subscriptions but also promote petitions to the legislature, encourage the use of 'free' grown sugar, redeem female infants from slavery and fund the education of the 'rising race of females'.[38] By 1828 ladies' associations were being described as important 'means of awakening and extending public interest'.[39] Anti-Slavery Society activist Zachary Macaulay wrote to the Liverpool abolitionist James Cropper that ladies' associations 'seem to form now one main stay of our hopes', and agreed with him that they 'ought to be strenuously pushed in every direction'.[40]

When the Leicester Quaker abolitionist Elizabeth Heyrick wrote her *Apology for Ladies' Anti-Slavery Associations* in 1828 she mentioned such letters as evidence of the value attached by leading male abolitionists to ladies' associations and stated that men were now 'in the bitterness of successive disappointment, looking to *us* for co-operation their final resort'.[41] This sense of disappointment is certainly evident in the appeals to women composed by Cropper and Macaulay and issued by the Anti-Slavery Society in 1828. These began by lamenting the lack of progress in Parliament towards the implementation of resolutions passed in 1823 for the amelioration of the condition of the slaves. The main channels now left for activism were, they stated, the diffusion of information in order to arouse public opinion against slavery, and the substitution of 'free' produce for slave-grown produce. In both areas, much important work could be done by women, especially through the medium of ladies' anti-slavery associations, of which a sample plan was appended.[42]

The lack of progress by male abolitionists in Parliament, combined with recognition of female initiatives, had thus led the Anti-Slavery Society by 1828 to emphasise an extra-Parliamentary campaign in which ladies' associations were seen as having the potential to make contributions equal to, or even greater than, men's auxiliaries.

Lack of progress carried with it the danger of declining public interest and organisational inertia. Recognising this danger, the Female Society for Birmingham was again the one to take the initiative, starting a scheme of paid travelling agents, on the lines of those employed by the Bible and missionary societies. The first agent it appointed was the Rev. Dr John Philip, a leading Congregational missionary.[43] Philip, who superintended the work of the London Missionary Society in the Cape of Good Hope, was in England on an extended visit to promote African welfare, and had been travelling around the country diffusing information on the anti-slavery cause and promoting the formation of ladies' associations. In April 1829 he accepted an offer by the Female Society for Birmingham to pay his travel expenses, having been unable to obtain funding from the Anti-Slavery Society for this purpose.[44]

The following year the Female Society for Birmingham decided to put its support for agents onto a regular basis in order to promote the formation of new female anti-slavery associations and to arouse support for immediate emancipation and for the boycott of slave-grown produce.[45] Catherine Croker, the society's Killarney district treasurer, became the first female anti-slavery agent.[46] However, while female agents had already been used by philanthropic societies such as the Bible Society, the Birmingham women concentrated on funding men, probably because it was considered unacceptable for women to address public meetings and they would thus have been unable to give the cause a high public profile.[47] The women paid the travel expenses of two lecturers employed by the Hibernian Negro's Friend Society, a men's group with which it had very close links. One of these lecturers was Anglo-American abolitionist Captain Charles Stuart, who conducted a successful Irish tour which led to a flood of anti-slavery petitions to the British Parliament. The other was Edward Baldwin, Assistant Secretary of the Irish Society, who undertook a lecture tour in England.[48]

Stuart and Baldwin became the first two paid agents appointed by the Agency Sub-Committee set up within the Anti-Slavery Society, suggesting that the committee's formation on 1 June 1831 was influenced by the actions of the Birmingham women.[49] The new committee gained the financial support of thirteen ladies' associations including Birmingham, but only one men's auxiliary, indicating that support for agency was higher among women's than men's societies. According to committee promoter George Stephen, agents increased the number of societies affiliated to London from 200 to nearly 1,300 within the space of a single year.[50] How accurate this figure is, and how many of the groups were ladies' associations, unfortunately is unknown, however.[51]

Ladies' associations also played an important part in the anti-apprenticeship campaign of 1837-38. The formation of a new anti-slavery organisation, the Central Negro Emancipation Committee, by Joseph Sturge of Birmingham on 14 November 1837 was facilitated by the support of Elizabeth Pease of the Darlington Ladies' Anti-Slavery Society and Jane Smeal of the Ladies' Auxiliary of the Glasgow Emancipation Society, who encouraged other provincial abolitionists to back the radical new group.[52] The new committee established a network of auxiliaries and received contributions from eight women's groups and seventeen men's auxiliaries in 1837-38.[53] Women's groups once again took national as well as local initiatives in promoting organised female activism. The Dublin Ladies' Association's 'Second Appeal' of 26 October 1837 and 'Letter' of April 1838 urged women all over Ireland to take action against apprenticeship.[54] The Darlington Ladies' Society's *Address to the Women of Great Britain*, drawn up in March 1838 by Elizabeth Pease, urged women to organise female anti-slavery associations to campaign against apprenticeship.[55]

Probably influenced by the increasingly public role he had seen women playing in the anti-slavery movement in the United States at this period, anti-slavery lecturer Charles Stuart had tried to persuade the Darlington society to send a female delegate to the Central Negro Committee's founding conference in London.[56] Its leader Elizabeth Pease, however, was content to concentrate on doing an enormous amount of behind-the-scenes work on behalf of the committee without receiving formal recognition. Women's lack of attempts to gain admission to national committees in 1823-38, together with Pease's reluctance to take up Stuart's invitation, suggest that throughout this period women found ample scope for their anti-slavery activities within the framework of their own organisations.[57] These activities, and their significance to the movement as a whole, will now be explored.

FUNDING

Both men's auxiliaries and ladies' associations had an organisational core of officers and committee members, supported by a membership ranging from around forty to as many as four or five hundred

51

subscribers.[58] These subscribers provided the societies with their main source of income.

Frank Prochaska, in his study of nineteenth-century female philanthropy, has characterised fund-raising as the major contribution made by local women's societies to national organisations in that century.[59] Examination of Anti-Slavery Society records confirms the increasing importance of women's contributions to national funds. In 1826 of the £2,558 income of the Anti-Slavery Society from donations and subscriptions, £438, or seventeen per cent, came from men's auxiliaries, and only £104, or four per cent, from ladies' associations. By 1829, however, when national income had dropped to £1,415, donations from men's groups had decreased to £195, or fourteen per cent, whereas those from women's societies had increased to £293, or twenty-one per cent. This was because a higher proportion of ladies' associations than men's groups sent donations (rather than just payments for publications) to London: in 1829 only seventeen of the fifty-eight men's groups compared with nineteen of the thirty-three ladies' associations.[60] This evidence suggests that ladies' associations gave a higher priority to fund-raising for the Anti-Slavery Society than did men's auxiliaries.

On the other hand, neither ladies' associations nor the Anti-Slavery Society defined fund-raising as the association's main function, and women frequently used much of their funds locally rather than donating them to the Society in London. The Female Society for Birmingham, one of the largest group donors to Anti-Slavery Society funds, used most of the money it raised to produce its own propaganda. In 1826, its year of peak income, the group raised £908, a staggering amount when compared to the total income of £2,933 for the national Anti-Slavery Society for that year, and compared to the £50 to £150 annual turnover of other ladies' associations and men's auxiliaries at this period. Of this total nearly £700 was spent on its own activities, and only £80 was sent to the Anti-Slavery Society.[61]

An examination of other women's groups shows a spectrum of donation patterns of similar variability to that of men's auxiliaries, from the Sheffield Female Anti-Slavery Society's donation of no funds whatsoever to London, to the Liverpool Ladies' Anti-Slavery Society's allocation of almost all its income to the national society.[62] Prochaska's characterisation of local ladies' associations as *primarily* fund-raisers for their national societies is thus inapplicable to anti-slavery groups.

Women also made selective use of their funds to support specific campaigning initiatives, rather than simply passively handing over money to male control. The Female Society for Birmingham's use of funds to initiate a system of paid travelling anti-slavery agents has already been mentioned, as has the strong support from ladies' associations received by the Agency Sub-Committee. It is interesting also to note that the total of £320 donated by ladies' associations to the Agency Sub-Committee was roughly equal to their total donation to the funds of the Anti-Slavery Society itself in that year, whereas the total men's auxiliaries' donation of £9 to the committee was only a minute proportion of their Anti-Slavery Society contribution.[63] Clearly men's and women's societies were giving differing priorities to supporting different campaigning approaches.

As the last example suggests, for ladies' anti-slavery associations the 'power of the purse' lay not simply in the importance of women's donations to sustaining a national movement, but also in the power women had to decide precisely how to allocate the funds they raised.

Another area in which ladies' associations' allocation of funds differed markedly from that of men's societies was in their donations to various groups involved in relief and educational work among the black population of the British West Indies. Such support for black relief, education and conversion to Christianity was an extension of women's support for educational, missionary and charitable societies at this period. It reflects the philanthropic perspective from which women approached anti-slavery and their desire to combine campaigning on a matter of principle with practical aid to the suffering. As members of the Female Society for Birmingham expressed it,

> Should any persons hesitate to give their support to this Society, on the ground that the benefit to be derived by the slaves, from the expenditure of large sums in the diffusion of information in this country, may be remote and uncertain, we should beg them to consider, that *one* of our objects is to extend *present* relief to the suffering Negro.[64]

As early as 1792 Irish abolitionist Mary Birkett had put forward a vision of the colonisation, legitimate commerce and Christianisation of Africa as a positive alternative to the slave trade:

> Thy vessels crown'd with olive branches send,
> And make each injure'd African thy friend:
> So tides of wealth by peace and justice got,
> Oh, philanthropic heart! will be thy lot.
> Plant there our colonies, and to their soul,
> Declare the God who form'd this boundless whole:
> Improve their manners – teach them how to live,
> To them the useful lore of science give.[65]

The African Institution had promoted the commercial side of this vision, leaving the educational aspect to the missionary societies which had been founded by all the main Protestant denominations in Britain between 1792 and 1804. These societies attracted considerable support from women, with ten to fifteen per cent female subscribers, and also developed networks of female auxiliary societies.[66]

Missionary societies' relationship to the anti-slavery movement in the 1790–1823 period was ambivalent. In the British West Indies, as Mary Turner has pointed out, missionaries condoned rather than condemned slavery, trying to work in co-operation with planters rather than enter into political conflict with them and concentrating on the spiritual rather than the material welfare of the slaves. Nevertheless, while stressing the inferiority of 'heathen' African culture, missionaries based their work on a belief in black humanity and potential for Christianisation and civilisation which was at odds with planter stereotypes. In addition, missionary work was significant to the development of anti-slavery in that it gave missionaries first-hand knowledge of slavery and its damaging effects, encouraged links between white and black members of growing nonconformist denominations, fostered British hostility to planters who persecuted missionaries, and developed black churches which combined African and Christian beliefs and rituals and became a potent source of resistance to slavery.[67]

The link between anti-slavery and missionary work was initially strongest in the British colony of Sierra Leone in West Africa. After 1807 evangelical Anglican, Methodist, Baptist and Quaker missionaries and educators co-operated in organising schools for a flood of African children rescued from captured slave ships.[68] Among the workers who went out to the colony in the 1820s were two Quaker women, Hannah Kilham and her assistant Ann Thompson of Cooladine in Ireland. For Kilham (1774–1832), a Quaker convert, the work was seen as a way of combining her anti-slavery, missionary and charitable commitments: she had earlier supported the campaign against the slave trade as well as the Bible Society and the Society for Bettering the Condition of the Poor in her home town of Sheffield, and by 1819 had become interested in the idea of instructing Africans in their own languages.[69] In her proposal to Quakers concerning the scheme she wrote:

> The protection of the natives of Africa from the rapacious hands of slave-merchants belongs now to the government; and here, so far as regards the *persons* of the Africans, the case at present rests; but viewing it in a far higher relation, considering that these are *men*, who have *minds* to be instructed, and *souls* . . . have we, the Society of Friends, yet done for them all that is in our power to do?[70]

Kilham's representations led to the setting up of the African Instruction Fund Committee (1819–25), an unofficial Quaker group which is significant as the first Quaker committee to have both male and female members.[71]

Kilham's interlinking of anti-slavery and missionary and educational commitments became a characteristic feature of ladies' anti-slavery associations, although their initial focus was on the West Indies rather than Africa. Interest in so-called 'negroes' aid' was reflected in the original titles of women's societies at Birmingham and Sheffield: the Ladies' Society for the Relief of Negro Slaves and the Auxiliary Society for the Relief of Negro Slaves. The only men's group with a similar title, the Hibernian Negroes' Friend Society, was strongly influenced by the Birmingham women, which it praised for giving priority to 'negroes' aid' work, in contrast to the disinterest of other societies.[72]

Ladies' societies at Birmingham, Calne, Clifton, Dublin, Liverpool, St Ives and Edinburgh early resolved that surplus funds should be given to Christians involved in charitable and educational work among blacks in the West Indies.[73] Over the following years the societies gave donations to a large number of groups: the Society for the Relief of Distressed and Discarded Negroes in the Island of Antigua; the Female Refuge Society of Antigua; Moravian Sunday Schools in the West Indies; the Benevolent Society for St Kitt's; the Society for the Visitation of the Sick in Barbados; Mission House, Hatton Garden, for the purchase of adult books for plantations where missionaries were not admitted; and the London-based Ladies' Society for Promoting the Early Education and Improvement of Children of Negroes, and People of Colour (also known as the London Ladies' Negro Education Society).[74]

Anti-slavery women were, however, anxious that support for black education not detract from their prime aim of slave emancipation. After the Ladies' Negro Education Society was formed by evangelical Anglicans in 1825 a letter, probably written by Lucy Townsend, appeared in the *Christian Observer* stating that it was the colonial system which caused the debasement of slaves and thus the priority should be to 'assist in delivering them from their cruel bondage, which reduces them to the brutish and demoralized state in which we find them'. Giving priority to education rather than emancipation 'neutralizes the efforts of many otherwise noble-minded advocates . . ., and it prevents British Ladies joining hand in hand to break their bonds'.[75]

This issue of responsibility was also emphasised by Elizabeth Heyrick, who argued in 1824 that slaves would not accept Christian instruction so long as they saw their instructors violating their own lessons by their support for the 'sin' of slavery.[76] A few years later *A Vindication of Female Anti-Slavery Associations*, published by the London Female Anti-Slavery Society, stressed the distinction between educational and anti-slavery work. Female associations, it asserted, supported efforts for educating slaves while deprecating exertions which were *limited* to amelioration, and were intended as a substitute for eventual full emancipation.[77]

Increasing doubts about the value of educating slaves led some women's groups to favour concentrating aid on freed slaves in Africa. The London Female Anti-Slavery Society considered such aid to freed slaves as 'legitimate and desirable as a collateral one' to anti-slavery, which could be met without weakening support for the primary object of emancipation.[78] In 1831 a total of twenty-eight ladies' anti-slavery associations sent donations in response to a circular appeal from the London women urging them to give financial support to the school founded some ten years before by Hannah Kilham to educate girls rescued from slave ships. The Peckham Ladies' African and Anti-Slavery Society made clear its African focus in its title, stating that aid to freed blacks rather than relief to slaves accorded better with its objective of the total abolition rather than the mitigation of slavery.[79]

Women also allocated funds to the cases of individual slaves and free blacks which came to their attention. This included the 'ransoming' of individual slaves by purchasing them and then setting them free. The Female Society for Birmingham resolved in November 1826 to appropriate part of its funds to the ransom of infant slaves, but had to drop the scheme on being informed that a large-scale ransoming scheme would not be allowed by Government. A fund of £150 that had been accumulated for the purpose was then redirected into a modest plan for the ransom of a male or female slave who would be useful as a teacher of slaves.[80]

The Anti-Slavery Society's secretary, Thomas Pringle, gave personal help to a number of black slaves who had been brought to Britain by their owners. On several occasions he obtained funds from the Female Society for Birmingham, possibly because it was a society for the relief of slaves rather than an exclusively anti-slavery group and could thus use its funds in this way without causing controversy. The Birmingham women passed on information to other women's groups, including those at Salisbury, Manchester, Clifton and Dublin, and these societies often channelled their donations for individual cases through Birmingham. Individual men, women and in some cases whole families were ransomed, though the total numbers involved were small and the process often took several years.[81]

INFORMING

One of the major uses of funds at a local level was in the production and distribution of information. Ladies' associations and men's auxiliaries shared a belief that their primary role was the diffusion of information in order to arouse public opinion against slavery, and this was also a priority which was encouraged by the Anti-Slavery Society. The content of some of the pamphlets distributed by ladies' associations will be explored in Chapter 5; here, the focus will be rather on the role of associations in diffusing such information.

Both auxiliaries and ladies' associations were involved in the local distribution of the tracts, pamphlets and periodicals of the Anti-Slavery Society.[82] They occasionally also reprinted tracts or made compilations of extracts for local distribution.[83] Both groups also produced their own propaganda material. These included printed annual reports which gave information on developments in the West Indies, on progress in the anti-slavery cause, and on their own anti-slavery perspective and activities, including accounts and lists of officers and subscribers.

Many of the founding resolutions and reports of local ladies' associations were sent to the Female Society for Birmingham, which played a unique role among local anti-slavery societies, its role as the hub of a network of contacts between local ladies' associations having no male equivalent.[84] The group supplied its own propaganda to other ladies' associations on a national basis, acting as an alternative source of supply to the Anti-Slavery Society. Of the £908 it raised in 1826, it spent £498 on the production of workbags containing sets of anti-slavery documents and £195 on printing, in contrast to only £10 remitted to the Anti-Slavery Society in payment for its papers and documents. The group's total expenditure on publications amounted to almost half the amount spent by the national Anti-Slavery Society itself on publications in 1826 (£703 as compared to £1,485).[85] Clearly it played an extremely important part in diffusing information about slavery throughout Britain and Ireland.

The Birmingham women produced propaganda which made use of middle-class women's accomplishments and was designed to appeal particularly to women. Their workbags containing tracts were sewn from East India cotton, silk or satin, thus avoiding the use of slave produce.[86] This use of an acceptable feminine activity for a practical and philanthropic end is an example of the way in which women linked the 'private' sphere of domestic work with the 'public' sphere of campaigning.

The workbags were aimed at 'the affluent and influential classes of the community' and were presented to the King, to Princess Victoria, to aristocrats, to the wives of prominent male abolitionists such as Mrs Clarkson and Mrs Wilberforce, to the author Maria Edgeworth and to the prison reformer Elizabeth Fry. Workbags were also supplied to the ladies' associations with whom the Birmingham group was in contact, and in 1826 alone two thousand of the workbags were distributed through England, Wales and Ireland.[87]

Much of the propaganda produced by ladies' associations was aimed specifically at women and was intended to gain their support. Examples include 'What Does Your Sugar Cost?', published by the Female Society for Birmingham to promote female support of the slave-grown sugar boycott; A Vindication of Female Anti-Slavery Associations, published by the London Anti-Slavery Society; and George Thompson's Address to the Ladies of Glasgow, published by the Glasgow Female Anti-Slavery Society which he had founded.[88]

In towns where there was no active men's group, ladies' associations also on occasion produced tracts aimed at men as well as women. Examples are Sheffield Female Anti-Slavery Society's A Word for the Slave, and its Appeal of the Friends of the Negro to the British People, 1,500 copies of which were produced in an attempt to enlist the support of working-class men.[89]

Ladies' associations also diffused the works of individual women writers, many of whom were themselves members of local anti-slavery societies. A compilation of anti-slavery propaganda distributed in album form by the Female Society for Birmingham included poems on 'British Slavery' by Hannah More and 'On the Flogging of Women' by the popular author Charlotte Elizabeth Phelan, a district treasurer for Birmingham, as well as the pamphlet Scripture Evidence of the Sinfulness and Injustice of Oppression by the Quaker abolitionist Mary Dudley.[90] A similar album in the possession of the women's society at Liverpool included Verses on Slavery by a working-class woman called Jane Yeoman, and Leicester Quaker activist Elizabeth Heyrick's No British Slavery and Appeal to the Hearts and Consciences of British Women.[91] The Liverpool group also circulated Mary Dudley's pamphlet and Inquiries Relating to Negro Emancipation, by an unidentified female author.[92] Clifton and Bristol Ladies' Anti-Slavery Association included in its anti-slavery library Mary Dudley's pamphlet, Charlotte Elizabeth Phelan's narrative poem 'The System', local Quaker abolitionist Mary Anne Schimmelpenninck's Is the System of Slavery Sanctioned, and British Slavery Described, a pamphlet by Miss [probably Sarah] Wedgwood of the famous Wedgwood porcelain manufacturing family, published by the North Staffordshire Ladies' Anti-Slavery Society.[93] The Dublin Ladies' Anti-Slavery Society circulated poems by Charlotte Elizabeth Phelan and Hannah More.[94] A poem by Leicester activist and author Susanna Watts entitled 'The Slave's Address to British Ladies' was printed at the head of the 1828 reports of the Birmingham and Calne societies.[95] Watts was also the editor of The Humming Bird, a periodical which interspersed anti-slavery items with miscellaneous articles and included an 'Address to the Ladies of Great-Britain, in Behalf of the Negro-Slaves'.[96] Her co-worker Elizabeth Heyrick sent copies of this periodical to Anne Knight of the Chelmsford Ladies' Anti-Slavery Society, with whom she exchanged other tracts.[97] Lucy Townsend of Birmingham compiled biblical quotations opposed to slavery in a tract entitled 'To the Law, and to the Testimony', which was supplied at cost price to anti-slavery associations.[98]

Ladies' anti-slavery associations thus both stimulated the production of pamphlets by women and provided a source of distribution for them. The value of such tracts written by women for a female audience was recognised by the Anti-Slavery Society. A pamphlet written by a woman to encourage other women to join ladies' associations was republished by the Society in cheaper form in 1828, and 1,500 copies of Elizabeth Heyrick's Appeal to the Hearts and Consciences of British Women were purchased by the Anti-Slavery Society in 1828 and 1829 for distribution.[99]

Ladies' anti-slavery associations and men's auxiliaries diffused their propaganda and aroused public opinion in rather different ways. There is evidence that both set up libraries for the loan of tracts and pamphlets.[100] The main method of tract distribution used by women, however, was house-to-house canvassing, when publications were sold to the better-off or lent to the poor. This laborious but effective method of distribution was not used by men's auxiliaries and was probably inspired by the system of female district visitors to the poor used by the evangelical philanthropic societies of the period.[101]

Ladies' associations also made some use of the press as a means of diffusing information and gaining support.[102] The Sheffield Female Anti-Slavery Society occasionally made public appeals for financial support and sent reports of its activities to local newspapers, as did the Chelmsford Ladies' Anti-Slavery Society.[103] The Dublin-based Hibernian Ladies' Negro's Friend Society paid for inserting in the Dublin Evening Post in 1833 a speech by Thomas Fowell Buxton and an address from the Anti-Slavery Society in London.[104] When the minutes of the Female Society for Birmingham are compared with those of the local men's auxiliary, however, men's regular and consistent use of the press contrasts with its sporadic use by women. Possibly the press was felt to be too political a medium: women's groups seem to have preferred to use religious periodicals such as the Missionary Register, an evangelical Anglican magazine linked to the Church Missionary Society, and the Christian Advocate, organ of Wesleyan Methodism, to publicise their work.[105] This gave them a higher public profile at a national level but a lower one at a local level.

Locally, men's auxiliaries dominated the more public anti-slavery activities. Ladies' associations generally left the organisation of public meetings to men's auxiliaries. While women were encouraged to attend public meetings, and did so in large numbers, they never chaired or spoke at such meetings themselves.[106] In Birmingham the Female Society asked the men to arrange public lectures, and were hampered by not always receiving their co-operation.[107] Nevertheless, women did occasionally organise public meetings at which men were invited to speak. In 1830, in the absence of an active men's society to conduct the event, the Sheffield Female Anti-Slavery Society arranged for a vicar to give a public lecture on slavery, though only after obtaining 'the approbation of many gentlemen of influence'.[108] Prominent male abolitionists also gave lectures at the annual meetings of ladies' associations.[109]

Women's silence at public meetings did not mean that female anti-slavery debate was confined to the domestic sphere, however. While the Female Society for Birmingham held its committee meetings in members' homes, other societies made use of public meeting halls. Liverpool women held their committee meetings in the Bible Depository, women at Chelmsford and St Ives (Hunts) held their annual general meetings in the local Friends' Meeting House, and women in Sheffield held committee meetings in the Fire Office.[110]

In addition, the significance of groups of women debating political issues within the home should not be underestimated. It involved a breakdown of the division between male and female roles within the family, a division symbolised by the physical segregation of the 'public' areas of the middle-class home into the parlour, where women took tea and discussed domestic issues, and the smoking room, where men discussed politics. Politics were being brought into the feminine domain and in the process the division between public and private activities was being blurred.

ABSTAINING

One important aspect of anti-slavery work which involved this merging of the domestic and the political was the campaign for abstention from slave-grown sugar. Women now not only participated in this campaign on an individual basis as in the 1790s, but also promoted it in their local communities through ladies' associations.

The national campaign was two-pronged: individual abstention from slave-grown sugar and its substitution by 'free'-grown sugar, and pressure on Parliament to equalise the duties on East and West India sugar, thus removing the artificial price advantage enjoyed by sugar from the slave plantations. At a local level activities were broadly divided on sex lines, with men's auxiliaries concentrating on petitioning Parliament on the sugar duties, and ladies' associations focusing on the abstention issue. In other words, women concentrated on the more domestic, consumer-based aspect of the campaign, centring on issues of individual responsibility and morality; men concentrated on the question of economic policy.

Ladies' associations were encouraged to promote abstention by the Anti-Slavery Society, which saw this as one of their main functions.[111] Abstention was also prompted by Elizabeth Heyrick, the foremost female anti-slavery pamphleteer of the period. Heyrick had argued in 1824 that abstention was not simply a matter of conscience. Rather, in the absence of any progress towards emancipation by Parliament, destroying the market for the products of slave labour was the safest and speediest way of forcing planters to change from slave to free labour.[112] (The central place which abstention held in her plan for the immediate abolition of slavery will be discussed in more detail in Chapter 5.) In *An Appeal to the Hearts and Consciences of British Women*, published in 1828 and widely distributed by the Anti-Slavery Society, Heyrick specifically addressed women. She urged her sex to take a lead in the anti-slavery campaign by implementing 'a general system of decisive *practical* discouragement'. Women were appealed to because 'in the domestic department they are the chief controllers; they, for the most part, provide the articles of family consumption'.[113] In her *Apology for Ladies' Anti-Slavery Associations*, published the same year, she urged ladies' associations to concentrate their efforts on promoting the West India sugar boycott.[114]

Ladies' associations which actively promoted abstention in the 1825–33 period included those at Sheffield, Calne, Birmingham, Liverpool, Peckham, Clifton (near Bristol), Worcester, Leicester, St Ives (Hunts), Dublin and Edinburgh.[115] Comprehensive house-to-house canvasses were carried out in Sheffield and Birmingham, involving an enormous expenditure of women's time and energy.[116] During these canvasses pamphlets obtained from the Anti-Slavery Society and propaganda produced by the associations themselves were distributed. The Sheffield Female Anti-Slavery Society handed out cards bearing the information that 'by six families using East India sugar one slave less is required'.[117] The Birmingham society in 1828 issued five thousand copies of 'a little directory for the use of those ladies who visit the poor to recommend the consumption of the produce of Free Labour', entitled *'What Does Your Sugar Cost?' A Cottage Conversation on the Subject of British Negro Slavery*. A circular was sent to district treasurers suggesting that such small tracts aimed at children and the poor should be lent from door to door, while a different pamphlet entitled *Reasons for Substituting East India Sugar for West*, four thousand copies of which were printed, should be spread among the 'higher classes'.[118] Lucy Townsend's daughter Charlotte produced a little booklet on abstention, aimed at children and their mothers, entitled *Pity the Negro; or an Address to Children on the Subject of Slavery*, of which at least seven editions of two thousand copies each were published.[119]

Another tactic, used by the Worcester Ladies' Anti-Slavery

Association, was to put pressure on local shopkeepers by withdrawing custom from grocers who sold, and confectioners who used, West India sugar.[120] In Dublin lists of importers and retailers of 'free-grown' East India sugar were published.[121]

Attempts were also made by women to compile systematic registers of abstainers. The Dublin Ladies' Anti-Slavery Society decided in 1828 to keep a central register of all families who gave up using slave-grown sugar, collated from monthly lists produced by district treasurers.[122] In 1829 the Birmingham society instituted a similar scheme, and also contributed to setting up a national registry of abstainers. The aims were to show that numbers of abstainers were large and growing, to encourage competition among ladies' associations in recruiting new abstainers, and to draw public attention to the campaign by the regular publication in newspapers of numbers of abstainers. The scheme was taken up by the Anti-Slavery Society, and a National Registry was opened at 10 Gracechurch Street, London, on 20 December 1829.[123] Unfortunately, however, no lists of numbers of abstainers published by the Registry have been located, and it is thus difficult to estimate the extent of support for abstention. Elizabeth Heyrick claimed in 1826 that nine out of ten families visited agreed to abstain, and with the systematic canvass conducted by ladies' associations it seems probable that the total number of abstainers exceeded that during the abstention campaign of 1787-92.[124]

Despite women's persistent efforts there is, as Kenneth Corfield has pointed out, no evidence that the abstention campaign had any noticeable affect on the import of slave-grown sugar.[125] Certainly, it did not bring about the immediate abolition of slavery, as Elizabeth Heyrick had hoped it would in 1824. As during the earlier campaign against the slave trade, its main importance was in informing a wide range of people about British involvement in slavery and in enlisting them in some form of practical action which kept the unacceptability of this involvement at the forefront of their minds. In contrast to the earlier period when abstention was a matter of individual conscience, it was now promoted by women systematically on a local level, which must have helped foster the sense of an anti-slavery community, and in particular of a female anti-slavery community.

PETITIONING

The hundreds of thousands of women who signed anti-slavery petitions in the 1830–33 period indicate that this community of female anti-slavery suppporters had by then become a very extensive one, encompassing many women who never became members of ladies' anti-slavery associations. In two waves of petitioning, in 1830-31 and then in 1833, petitions to Parliament were presented from the female inhabitants of 108 English, 4 Welsh, 13 Scottish and 4 Irish towns and villages. In addition petitions were presented from the female members of 8 Baptist, 4 Independent, 9 Wesleyan Methodist and 4 other Protestant chapels, as well as from the committee of the Exeter Ladies' Anti-Slavery Society. In 1833 women also signed many mixed town and chapel petitions. This tide of female petitioning culminated in a massive national female petition presented in the run-up to the passage of the Emancipation Act in 1833.[126]

The mass entry of women into petitioning began at the time when the Anti-Slavery Society changed to a policy of immediate abolition and when the popular anti-slavery campaign increased greatly in intensity. This renewed surge of activity was stimulated by the Agency Sub-Committee, one of whose chief purposes was to promote petitions to Parliament calling for immediate emancipation of the slaves.

Prior to 1830 petitioning of Parliament had been presumed to be a male preserve. In the early years of the anti-slavery campaign, as during the early anti-slave-trade campaign, women did not sign the stream of petitions calling for the amelioration and gradual abolition of slavery. A single exception is a petition for gradual emancipation presented to the House of Commons on 5 July 1825, signed by two thousand women from the Birmingham area.[127] This petition was an isolated case, however, and its organisation by a few members of the Female Society for Birmingham independently of that society suggests that there may have been disagreements about its propriety.

The only other female anti-slavery petition presented during the period before 1830 was the private petition for freedom of the West Indian slave Mary Prince, presented to the House of Commons in 1829. For Prince, whose life and contributions to the anti-slavery movement will be discussed in the following chapter, it was part of her unsuccessful attempt to gain the right to return to Antigua as a free woman; for the Anti-Slavery Society it represented an aborted opportunity to introduce a bill to provide for the entire emancipation of all slaves brought to England by their owners.[128]

Male opposition and female ambivalence toward women petitioning Parliament had several sources. The dominant ideology of the period defined women's place as being in the private rather than the political sphere. Women lacked a tradition of petitioning Parliament. The segregation of anti-slavery work on sex lines had left men's societies to organise petitioning while women's groups concentrated on other aspects of campaigning. Finally, some women believed that petitioning for amelioration and gradual emancipation had no hope of achieving success, and that emancipation was more likely to be achieved through a boycott of slave-grown sugar initiated by women.[129]

In view of the factors inhibiting female petitioning, women's mass entry into petitioning in 1830 needs to be explained. The development was encouraged by several factors. First, there was the sense of urgency generated by the rising tempo of anti-slavery agitation and the process of change to the policy of immediate abolition which, as will be demonstrated in Chapter 5, many women favoured. Second, the precedent was set in February–June 1829 and again in March 1830 by small groups of petitioners from the female inhabitants of towns and members of congregations – Unitarian, Baptist, Calvinistic Baptist and Independent – urging Parliament to abolish the suttee, the Indian Hindu custom of burning widows on the funeral pyres of their husbands.[130] Third, mass anti-slavery petitioning by nonconformist denominations began in response to the increasing persecution of missionaries and slave converts in the West Indies. This entry into politics was justified in religious terms, which may have encouraged female participation as an extension of their support for missions.[131]

The issue of female petitioning was not discussed formally at meetings of the committee of the Anti-Slavery Society, though private discussions and disagreements are evident from a letter which Lord Henry Brougham, leader of the anti-slavery campaign in the House of Lords, wrote to Zachary Macaulay:

> I have letters saying that a Female Petition is disapproved of by the Society. I differ *toto coelo*, but as it requires cautious handling I shall myself undertake it, and preach from this very fruitful text.[132]

Other influential individuals agreed with Brougham. The October 1830 issue of the *Anti-Slavery Monthly Reporter* carried an address by the prominent Baptist minister Edmund Clarke calling for petitions for immediate emancipation and suggesting 'a separate petition, either to Her Majesty, or to the legislature from British *females* of every town, village and congregation'.[133] Two years later, at the annual meeting of the Anti-Slavery Society in London, leading Irish activist Daniel O'Connell issued a call for female petitions, and the following year he defended women's right to petition during an anti-slavery debate in the House of Commons.[134] Despite this, however, neither the Anti-Slavery Society's *Anti-Slavery Monthly Reporter* nor the Agency Sub-Committee's *Tourist* made any mention of the women's petitioning efforts throughout this period.

Denominational journals exhibited less reluctance to publicise female anti-slavery petitions. Clarke's 1830 address appeared in the *Baptist Magazine*, and was doubtless influential within this denomination given that Clarke was president of the South Devon and Cornwall Baptist

Association, the group which initiated Baptist anti-slavery petition-ing.[135] In addition, the evangelical Anglican magazine the *Record* gave information of female petitions in November 1830 and again in April and May 1833, and the evangelical nonconformist periodical the *Patriot* followed suit in May 1833.[136]

Changing Wesleyan Methodist attitudes may be traced in the *Christian Advocate*. The magazine reported that at meetings held in local chapels in Yorkshire in October 1830, ministers expressed regret that 'the custom of the country' did not allow women to sign petitions when 'they are admirably qualified to do it by enlightened understanding and affectionate feeling'. Women's own grief that they were not allowed to sign petitions was also noted.[137] In November the periodical published a letter from a Methodist expressing his wish that female chapel members sign petitions.[138] Methodists, however, continued to favour women petitioning the Queen rather than Parliament, presumably because this was considered a less political act.[139] On 6 May 1833, however, the *Christian Advocate* printed the full text of the national female petition to Parliament and earnestly entreated all women to sign it.[140] Females must have comprised around half of the estimated 95.2 per cent of Wesleyan Methodists – 229,426 individuals out of a denominational membership of around 241,000 – who signed anti-slavery petitions in 1833.[141]

These Methodist petitions were not the only anti-slavery petitions signed by both sexes: a circular issued by the organisers of the national female petition of 1833 recorded that in some places 'both sexes have signed mutual petitions'.[142] Later, during the 1837–38 campaign against the apprenticeship system, many petitions were 'signed promiscuously by Males and Females'.[143]

The national female petition was the most impressive example of national anti-slavery initiative by women. The petition was instigated and organised by women, and was never formally discussed at Anti-Slavery Society committee meetings or mentioned in the *Anti-Slavery Reporter*. According to Agency Sub-Committee activist George Stephen, the petition was organised by two Quaker women: Anne Knight of the Chelmsford Ladies' Anti-Slavery Society and Marie Tothill of Staines.[144] In fact, although the idea for the petition may have been suggested by these two individuals, the collection of signatures was organised by the London Female Anti-Slavery Society. This Society rivalled the Female Society for Birmingham in size and influence, having established by 1829 a network of ten district committees in the London area and enrolled a total of 415 subscribers.[145]

The group felt that at this crucial stage in the campaign women's 'efforts would have more weight if they were collected and concen-trated into one vast and universal expression of feeling from *all the females* of the United Kingdom'.[146] Signatures totalling 187,157 were collected in only ten days, following the dispatch of circular appeals and sample petitions to contacts throughout the country.[147] This national petition was described by Agency Sub-Committee activist George Stephen as a 'huge featherbed of a petition, hauled into the House by four members amidst shouts of applause and laughter'.[148] It was presented in the Commons by Thomas Fowell Buxton, whose daughter Priscilla was co-secretary of the London Female Anti-Slavery Society, on 14 May, the day the Government introduced its Emancipation Bill.

This national female petition to Parliament was followed in 1838 by another national petition by women: a female address to the Queen on behalf of the apprentices. The popular campaign against apprenticeship was launched in July 1837, when the accession of Queen Victoria and the Parliamentary election campaign presented a double opportunity for public agitation on the issue. A public meeting organised by the Anti-Slavery Society at Exeter Hall on 11 July 1837 adopted two major proposals – one directed at men, the other at women. The first was the issuing of an 'Address to the Electors of Great Britain' calling on them to elect candidates pledged to oppose apprenticeship; the second was the launching of an address to the new monarch, Queen Victoria, from the women of Great Britain and Ireland, calling for full freedom for the apprentices.[149]

The decision to recommend this address had been taken by the national committee of the Anti-Slavery Society on 3 July 1837, and it then conferred with the committee of the London Ladies' Central Negro's Friend Society.[150] As in 1833, however, the original idea may have come from women themselves: according to her biographer, Darlington abolitionist Elizabeth Pease made the suggestion in a letter of June 1837 to her friend Jane Smeal, secretary of the Glasgow Ladies' Auxiliary Emancipation Society.[151]

In England and Wales the canvassing for signatures was organised by the London Ladies' Negro Friend Society under the leadership of its Quaker co-secretaries Rachel Stacey and Mary Dudley. A circular was sent to ministers, the address was publicised in religious periodicals, and tracts and engravings showing the punishment of men and women on the treadmill were widely circulated. Locally, copies of the address were deposited in chapels for signature, public meetings were held, and committees of women organised door-to-door canvassing.[152] The separate national addresses from Scotland and Ireland were launched at large public meetings by George Thompson, a former lecturer for the Agency Sub-Committee, a public appeal to Irish women was issued by the newly formed Dublin Ladies' Association, and signatures were collected through the two countries both by ladies' associations and by informal groups of women.[153] The three national addresses against apprenticeship were signed by a huge number of women: 449,540 signed the English and Welsh address, 135,083 the Scottish address and 77,000 the Irish address.[154] In addition, a number of local addresses also collected large numbers of signatories: an address from the women of Manchester and Salford was signed by 29,386 women.[155]

It was the large number of signatories which each female petition and address attracted, rather than the number of petitions themselves, which made female petitioning a major contribution to the anti-slavery campaign. Female petitions constituted less than one per cent of a total of 5,484 anti-slavery petitions presented to the House of Commons in 1830–31 and only around two per cent of the 5,020 petitions presented in 1833. However, if total numbers of signatories are considered women's contribution assumes far greater importance. Out of the 1,309,913 signatories to anti-slavery petitions in 1833 a total of 298,785, or nearly a quarter, were women's signatures to female petitions, this total including the 187,157 signatories to the national women's petition. When female signatories to mixed petitions are taken into account – a minimum of around 100,000 if only Methodist women's signatures are counted – the total of female signatories reaches over 400,000. This represents nearly a *third* of all the signatories to anti-slavery petitions in 1833. Even more impressively, total signatories to female anti-apprenticeship addresses to the Queen in 1838 came to more than 700,000, a number around two-thirds of the total of 1,113,091 signatures to the 4,175 anti-apprenticeship petitions presented to the House of Commons in the 1837–38 period.[156] In addition, the national female petition of 1833 was the largest single anti-slavery petition ever to be presented to Parliament, and the female address against slavery was the largest single anti-apprenticeship petition, holding 'an amount of signatures wholly unprecedented . . . in the annals of petitioning'.[157] It represented for British women an impressive and dramatic public finale to their years of behind-the-scenes anti-slavery activity.

Women's petitions, though relatively few in number, were also significant because they did not simply add to the total mass of calls for the abolition of slavery. Many were distinguished by their articulation of concern for the suffering of slave women. In 1830 three identically worded petitions presented from women in the neighbouring towns of Christchurch, Poole and Southampton urged 'that all Female slaves may be immediately emancipated as the first step towards the entire abolition of Human Bondage'.[158] Other petitions presented between 1830 and 1833, including the national female petition, expressed horror at the degradation and suffering of women under slavery and urged Parliament to bring a stop to it by abolishing the system and thus allowing the black woman 'to occupy her proper Station as a Daughter, a Wife and a Mother'.[159] The national addresses to Queen Victoria also pleaded especially on behalf of women, expressing their shock that

> Women of every age, in every condition, are liable, for the most trivial faults, to be committed to houses of correction, from which they are sent on the highways, chained together by the neck with iron collars. They are placed on treadmills of torturing construction, and are subject to the dreadful punishment of flogging with the whip.[160]

Petitioning by women from 1830 onwards involved their taking on a new role in the anti-slavery movement which was both more public and more political. On the one hand this to some extent broke down the division of anti-slavery work on sex lines, especially with the advent of mixed petitions in 1833; on the other hand, in particular with the national female petition and national female addresses, it involved the creation of a distinctively female public opinion.

This new public presence of women is attested to by the large numbers of women who were also attending public meetings called by women to organise petitions to Parliament. At Doncaster in Yorkshire 'very respectable and numerous' meetings of women were held on 24 and 30 April 1833 in the Mansion House, following advertisements in the local press.[161] At Chatham in Kent a meeting of ladies was held in April 1833 in the unusually masculine venue of a tavern 'for the purpose of agreeing to a petition'.[162] While women at such meetings continued to leave the public speaking to men, the holding of such meetings resulted in a wider reporting of women's anti-slavery activities in the press. Several of these reports praised the women's efforts in organising petitions and urged others to follow suit.[163]

Female petitioning was also of great significance in bringing far larger numbers of women into the anti-slavery campaign than ever before. The total of more than 400,000 individual female signatories to petitions in 1833 compares with an estimated total of fewer than 10,000 members of ladies' anti-slavery associations. In 1837-38, despite fewer ladies' associations being active, signatories to the national addresses doubled in England and increased almost tenfold in Scotland and thirteenfold in Ireland in comparison to the 1833 national petition.

In some towns more women than men signed anti-slavery petitions. In Edinburgh an October 1830 petition for immediate emancipation was signed by around 22,000, the May 1833 petition by 162,000 women, or around a quarter of the adult female population of the town.[164] In 1833 at Doncaster over twice as many women (3,810) as men (1,627) signed petitions, and at Nottingham there were nearly three times as many female (15,001) signatories as male (5,310).[165] Ann

Gilbert of Nottingham Female Anti-Slavery Society wrote proudly to fellow activist Mary Ann Rawson of Sheffield:

> On very short notice we had petitions for signing in all the Chapels last Sabbath day, and by a vigorous canvass of only 18 hours . . . we succeeded in obtaining fifteen thousand signatures – The Gentlemen, who had been doing something of the same kind, as they fancied, for the last week or two, have, in consequence put on double spurs, but at present they are ten thousand in the rear of their truly *better halves*.[166]

This level of success, as this quote suggests, was the product both of female enthusiasm and well-organised canvassing. While men tended to organise petitions by calling a public meeting and leaving the petition for signature in the town hall, women solicited individual signatures more actively. In Whitby, for example, a report on the collection of signatures for a female petition to the Queen stated: 'the town is divided into nine districts, and two or more ladies are appointed to each district.'[167]

As well as marking an expansion in the form and scale of women's involvement in the anti-slavery movement, female petitioning represented the first large-scale intervention by women in Parliamentary politics. Public petitioning had great importance in the political system of the period. Both Peter Fraser and Colin Leys have stressed the vital role played by petitioning from the late eighteenth century through the 1830s in bringing the pressure of public opinion to bear on Parliament. A large proportion of Parliamentary time was taken up by Members of Parliament who used the presentation of petitions as an opportunity to initiate debate on issues such as slavery. These debates in turn influenced the public through their widespread reporting in the press.[168] When female anti-slavery campaigners began 'stirring up' and signing petitions they were thus encroaching on the male terrain of Parliamentary politics, implying that women were among the public whose views should be represented in national decision-making.

How important was female petitioning in bringing about the passage of the Emancipation Act in August 1833 and the end of apprenticeship in 1838? Izhak Gross, in his study of abolition and Parliamentary politics in 1832–33, places less stress on petitioning than on the anti-slavery pledges which constituents – by which he presumably means male voters – extracted from local Parliamentary candidates.[169] Taking a wider and longer-term view of the campaign, however, it can be seen that petitioning by women contributed to creating a 'climate of public opinion' in favour of emancipation which enabled constituents to represent their anti-slavery demands as indisputable and which encouraged candidates to stress their anti-slavery credentials in soliciting support.[170] The national female petition of 1833, as the largest single anti-slavery petition and the only one to represent national public opinion, played a crucial part in this. In addition, female petitions, some of which were ordered to be printed by Parliament because of their distinctive wording, encouraged Parliamentary debate to focus on the particular sufferings of women under slavery, and may have influenced the insertion of a clause in the Emancipation Act prohibiting the flogging of women.

In the case of apprenticeship the canvass for signatures from July 1837 onwards, as a correspondent to the *Irish Friend* put it, was 'one of the most efficient means used for extensively spreading information on the subject'.[171] It prepared public opinion for the extra-Parliamentary campaign launched by the Central Negro Emancipation Committee in November 1837, and the industry of women in collecting signatures was used to goad men into greater efforts.[172] In addition the female addresses contributed to the pressure on Government which led it to include a clause completely prohibiting the physical punishment of women in its Abolition of Slavery Amendment Act of April 1838.[173] Most importantly, the addresses influenced the complete abolition of apprenticeship by colonial governments in the five months leading up to 1 August 1838, the date set by the British Parliament for the complete freeing of non-agricultural labourers. As historians have pointed out, colonial assemblies were influenced to take this step through fears that massive popular agitation in Britain would both stimulate unmanageable unrest among the apprentices themselves and lead to the imposition of abolition by the British Parliament, thus diminishing their local political autonomy.[174] The female addresses represented the largest manifestation of this popular opinion, and their later description as 'the final blow to slavery in the West Indies' thus has some justification.[175]

Women, responsible as petitioners for the two largest expressions of national public opposition to colonial slavery, as well as co-ordinators of a mass campaign for the boycott of slave-grown sugar, diffusers of large quantities of information aimed at arousing public opinion against slavery, and major fund-raisers for the cause, thus played a vital role in the public extra-Parliamentary campaign against slavery.

The major organisational innovation which enabled women to play such a key part in campaigning was the institution of a network of ladies' anti-slavery associations. As we have seen, these groups were generally set up through women's own initiatives, and in particular through the efforts of the Female Society for Birmingham, an independent group which operated on a national scale. Working largely independently of local men's auxiliary societies, ladies' associations went about achieving their objectives primarily through door-to-door canvassing, men's auxiliaries through public meetings and press advertisements. Thus, to return to campaigner George Thompson's words, the 'cement of the whole Antislavery building' was consolidated as men's public appeals to mass audiences in town halls were complemented by women's face-to-face appeals to thousands of individuals in their own homes. Through their combined efforts anti-slavery became a truly popular campaign, involving hundreds of thousands of women as well as men.

4

ANTI-SLAVERY IN THE FABRIC OF WOMEN'S LIVES

MIDDLE-CLASS ORGANISERS

Despite their co-ordination of key aspects of the anti-slavery campaign, the women who formed the mainstay of ladies' anti-slavery associations in the 1825–38 period are not well-known historical figures. Women campaigners did not seek or gain fame, working collectively rather than as public individuals and often publishing their writings anonymously. Their work is celebrated in the memoirs compiled by their relatives or the obituaries written by their co-religionists rather than in the public monuments and major biographies which commemorate the male leadership. Nevertheless, a picture may be built up of the women who became the committee members and officers of ladies' anti-slavery associations and the authors of anti-slavery pamphlets. This section looks at the family, religious and socio-economic backgrounds of these women, the pattern of their personal lives, the scope of their philanthropic and other public activities, their political outlooks, the nature of their anti-slavery work, and their networks of abolitionist friends and contacts. In short, it explores the place of anti-slavery in the fabric of their lives.

As stated in the last chapter, the first women's anti-slavery society, the Female Society for Birmingham, was founded and run by two friends, Lucy Townsend and Mary Lloyd. Lucy Townsend (d. 1847) is representative of the older generation of activists of the period, having first become interested in the cause when Thomas Clarkson agitated for the slave sugar boycott during the campaign against the slave trade. In common with a number of other leading women activists she was an evangelical Anglican, and both her father and her husband Charles were clergymen. In addition to her duties as a vicar's wife, Townsend became involved in a number of philanthropic organisations. She was active in the Ladies' Bible Association, in Dorcas meetings, and in providing help to the sick and afflicted; she founded the Juvenile Deaf and Dumb Association with Mary Lloyd in 1834; and she supported campaigns for the suppression of vice and the abolition of bull-baiting and other cruel sports. Anti-slavery, however, was her main preoccupation and she acted as a very active secretary of the Female Society for Birmingham from 1825 to 1836, as well as writing an anti-slavery pamphlet in the form of Scriptural quotations. For her, as for the majority of other women activists, anti-slavery was a family concern: her husband published a sermon and her daughter Charlotte wrote a pamphlet on the issue, and her married daughter Mrs Moillet became an officer of the society her mother had founded.[1]

Lucy Townsend's friend and co-worker Mary Lloyd (1795-1865) is representative of a younger generation of activists, born too late to have been affected by the campaign for the abolition of the slave trade. In common with many leading activists, male and female, she was a Quaker, born in Falmouth to Joseph Honeychurch and Jane Treffry, a minister amongst Friends. As a single woman she nursed her ailing father for many years, then lived with a succession of relatives and family friends. At the age of twenty-eight she married Samuel Lloyd, head of the firm of Lloyds Foster & Co. at Wednesbury near Birmingham, who owned a colliery and iron foundry. The couple had ten children between 1824 and 1839, and one of her daughters was later to comment on her mother's hard work housekeeping on a fluctuating budget. Despite such heavy domestic responsibilities Lloyd found time to work with Lucy Townsend for the Bible Society and later the Juvenile Society for the Deaf and Dumb, and she also set up a Benevolent Society to benefit poor mothers, started a Provident Society to encourage the poor to save, and established a Mothers' Meeting for the wives of her husband's workmen. She became a temperance advocate and total abstainer and from 1840 she acted as a travelling minister in the Society of Friends. Anti-slavery was, however, her main concern, and the frontispiece of her memoir has a portrait of her in Quaker bonnet holding a book inscribed 'The Chain is broken AFRICA is free Aug 21st 1834' (Figure 7). She was secretary of the Female Society for Birmingham from 1825 into the 1830s and then its treasurer from 1845 to 1861. Support for anti-slavery by other family members spanned the whole duration of the movement. Her mother-in-law Rachel Lloyd (1768-1854), daughter of George and Deborah Braithwaite of Kendal, had participated in the slave produce boycott during the campaign against the slave trade and was a founding member of the Female Society for Birmingham, and her husband Samuel was a leading member of the local men's auxiliary.[2]

In their combination of domestic duties with a staggering range of philanthropic activities Lucy Townsend and Mary Lloyd are not untypical of leading women anti-slavery activists. Nottingham anti-slavery activist Ann Taylor Gilbert (1782-1866), for example, combined her

Figure 7 Mary Lloyd. Frontispiece portrait in
Sara W. Sturge, *Memoir of Mary Lloyd of Wednesbury.*
1795–1865 (1921).

duties as an Independent minister's wife with a variety of philanthropic
initiatives. Founder of a refuge for 'unfortunate' women, collector for a
Provident Society, member of a Committee for the Management of a
Free Library, visitor to the Blind Asylum, superintendent of a Sunday
School for young women, conductor of a cottage service for women,
and active in the local Ladies' Anti-Corn Law Committee in the 1840s,
she continued to take an interest in public affairs into her eighties. She
was also a successful author, composing and compiling hymns for
Sunday Schools and infant schools. Both she and her husband were
active in the anti-slavery movement, and she led the women's anti-
slavery society in Nottingham, in 1833 organising the mass collection
of signatures to a national female anti-slavery petition.[3] Gilbert con-
fessed to the difficulties she experienced in balancing her diverse
commitments in a letter she wrote in 1838 to her friend and fellow anti-
slavery activist Mary Ann Rawson of Sheffield:

This generally, is my great practical difficulty – the drawing the line correctly between *in door* and *out of doors* business . . . . Tho' I have no doubt that you could readily employ yourself at home, yet you have not so great a pressure constantly weighting you down, as I have, and must enjoy comparative leisure for the great demands of public benevolence. As a minister's wife I feel this exceedingly. . . .[4]

Gilbert was right to point out that, as a widow with only one child and as a woman of independent means who lived in her parental home, Rawson found it easier than herself to devote time to anti-slavery and other public causes. Rawson (1801–87) was the eldest daughter of Joseph and Elizabeth Reid of Wincobank Hall near Sheffield, and her father was the wealthy owner of a gold and silver smelter's business. Like Gilbert, she was an Independent who described herself as an evangelical and believed that 'Prayer without action is mockery'. She supported interdenominational societies such as the Tract Society, the British and Foreign Bible Society and missionary societies, promoted education and religion among the poor in her neighbourhood and supported the campaign about chimney-sweeping boys. She also became a supporter of Italian nationalism. Anti-slavery, however, was her main interest. She led the successive local women's anti-slavery societies in Sheffield from the 1820s to the 1850s, compiled a book of anti-slavery poetry, and became friends with leading activists such as George Thompson and the American radical abolitionist William Lloyd Garrison. Both her parents and her daughter also supported the cause, her mother acting as first treasurer of the Sheffield Female Anti-Slavery Society.[5]

Elizabeth Heyrick (1769–1831), the foremost female anti-slavery pamphleteer, was, like Rawson, an eldest daughter of well-off parents and, also like her, was widowed at a young age. Born in Leicester to John and Elizabeth (née Cartwright) Coltman, her father was a worsted manufacturer, and both parents were well-educated Unitarians. An artistic, beautiful and fashionable girl, she was married at eighteen to John Heyrick, son of the town clerk. Her husband 'was, by turns, a lawyer, a Methodist, a rake, and a soldier', and the couple had a tempestuous relationship and led an unsettled life until John died of a heart attack after eight years, leaving Elizabeth a young, childless widow. She then converted to Quakerism, renouncing worldly pleasures, reading improving authors and starting a diary devoted to her religious duties. She moved back into her father's house and he gave her a generous allowance, enabling her to devote herself to philanthropic work. She set up a school, campaigned against bull-baiting and other forms of cruelty to animals, and visited prisons. Of extremely radical political beliefs for a woman of middle-class background, she wrote a total of eighteen pamphlets, mostly philanthropic but also on the question of labour and the relation of employer to employed; an 'appeal to the Electors' in 1826 urging them to vote for anti-slavery and anti-Corn Law candidates; and a pamphlet against the New Vagrant Act. Heyrick, whose brother Samuel was also involved in the anti-slavery movement, was already a supporter of slave emancipation in the 1790s, and from 1824 she devoted herself to the anti-slavery cause, corresponding with the male leadership and writing several important anti-slavery pamphlets. She conducted a door-to-door canvass to urge the sugar boycott in Leicester, acted as a District Treasurer for the Female Society for Birmingham, and set up the local women's anti-slavery society. Her most important contribution to the cause, her 1824 pamphlet *Immediate, not Gradual Abolition*, will be discussed in the following chapter.[6]

Susanna Watts (d. 1842) was Elizabeth Heyrick's closest friend and her co-worker in the anti-slavery cause. The youngest daughter of John Watts Esquire of Dannett's Hall near Leicester, her father had died when she was young, leaving the family poor after losing money in the South Sea Bubble speculation. Her mother was an uneducated country girl who suffered from insanity, and her two sisters died of consumption. After the death of her mother in 1806–7 she turned to God and, though brought up in the Church of England, she became sympathetic to the Baptists. She remained single, but adopted a child whom she educated herself. Without inherited means, she made a living as a writer of children's books, ballads, local guides, hymns and poems, and translations from Italian and French. Like Heyrick, Watts campaigned against cruelty to animals, and around 1828 she founded a Society for the Relief of Indigent Old Age. Her main preoccupation, however, was anti-slavery: she campaigned with Heyrick in the Leicester Ladies Anti-Slavery Society, she was vice-president of a similar society at the Oakham, and in 1824–25 she edited a periodical, *The Humming Bird*, which included a large amount of anti-slavery material.[7]

The campaigner Sarah Wedgwood (1776–1856), like Watts, remained single. Whereas Watts had to earn a living, however, Wedgwood, of the famous Wedgwood porcelain manufacturing family of Staffordshire, was free to devote all her attention to good causes. Her will shows the scope of her philanthropic interests, listing donations to the Society for the Protection of Young Females, British Penitent Female Refuge, British and Foreign School Society, Society for British and Foreign Sailors, and to a range of temperance societies and missionary societies in addition to the British and Foreign Anti-Slavery Society. Her father had been a leading supporter of the campaign against the slave trade, and both she and her sister Catherine (1774–1823), also unmarried, contributed lavishly to the anti-slavery movement. A district treasurer of the Female Society for Birmingham, she was an early advocate of immediate emancipation and one of the first to support the Agency Sub-Committee.[8]

Anne Knight (1786–1862) (Figure 8) was another single woman who became very involved in the cause, though as an activist rather than a financial backer. One of eight children, her father William Knight was a prosperous Chelmsford wholesale grocer; her mother Priscilla was the daughter of William Allen, a London brewer well known in radical and nonconformist circles. Like most of her siblings Anne never married and her life until about age fifty was spent mostly at the family home, but thereafter she travelled to France and from 1847 she became an expatriate. By 1830 Knight was deeply involved in the local anti-slavery movement and had also established contact with the national leadership in London. Family friends included Chelmsford abolitionists the Marriage family, and her sister Maria wed John Candler, a Quaker active in the national abolitionist movement. In 1834 Knight asked George Thompson to undertake an anti-slavery speaking tour of France and when he declined she took up the task herself, addressing several French scientific congresses and numerous smaller gatherings. By 1840 she had become a supporter of women's rights, and her important contribution to feminist debate in the British anti-slavery movement will be discussed in a later chapter. As Gail Malmgreen points out, Knight was in some ways a typical middle-class radical nonconformist, supporting immediate emancipation, free trade and universal suffrage, and sympathetic to Chartism. In other ways, an unusual extremism is evident in her interest from the early 1830s in the work of French and British Utopian socialists and feminists, and in her links with the White Quakers of Ireland, a schismatic fundamentalist and communalist sect. She was to become an outspoken supporter of the radical 'Garrisonian' wing of the American anti-slavery movement in the 1840s.[9]

Anne Knight's friend Elizabeth Pease (1807–97) was also a Quaker of extremely radical beliefs. The daughter of Elizabeth Pease and Joseph Pease, a prominent Darlington industrialist and the first Quaker MP, she remained single until 1853, when she married John Pringle Nichol, a professor of astronomy at the University of Glasgow. Following his death in 1859 she spent the remainder of her life in Edinburgh. Her active support of a wide variety of reform movements commenced in the 1830s with her anti-slavery campaigning as leader of the women's abolition society at Darlington, which gave support to George Thompson and the Central Negro Emancipation Committee. Her role as assistant to her father in the British India Society, and her leading role in the cultivation of links with, and promotion of British support

Figure 8 Anne Knight. Photograph c. 1855.

for, radical American abolitionists, will be explored in Part III of this book, as will her developing support for women's rights, which led her to become active in the whole spectrum of feminist campaigns from the 1860s onwards. Pease was also an active supporter of political movements such as the Anti-Corn Law League, Chartism, and Italian and Hungarian nationalism and republicanism, as well as of movements for moral reform such as pacifism, temperance and anti-vivisection.[10]

Drawing on the lives of the leading women anti-slavery activists of the 1823–38 period which have been sketched above, and on the less complete information available about other important women campaigners, some general points can be made about the type of women involved and about the place of anti-slavery in the fabric of their lives.

A few members of the new ladies' associations had gained their first experience of anti-slavery work by joining in the sugar boycott of the 1780s and 1790s. This is true of Lucy Townsend and Rachel Lloyd and also of Mary Anne Schimmelpenninck (1778–1856), daughter of Samuel Galton and Lucy Barclay of Birmingham, who as a young girl was influenced by relatives to abstain from slave-labour sugar and who in the 1820s became a committee member of the Female Society for Clifton and an anti-slavery pamphleteer.[11] Other women's involvement also spanned both periods: examples are Hannah Kilham, Hannah More and Irish abolitionist poet Mary Leadbeater (née Shackleton) (1758–1826), who organised anti-slavery activities in her village of Ballitore in the 1820s.[12]

The majority of women who made up the officers and committee members of ladies' anti-slavery associations were, however, from a new generation of activists, many born during the years of the campaign against the slave trade. Some of the new activists were the daughters or wives of wealthy industrialists, manufacturers, merchants and bankers. Mary Lloyd, Sarah Wedgwood, Elizabeth Heyrick and Elizabeth Pease have already been mentioned. Mary Roberts (1798–1882), secretary of the Sheffield Female Anti-Slavery Society, was the daughter of Samuel Roberts of Park Grange, a manufacturer of silver and plated goods[13]; Mary Anne Schimmelpenninck was from the gun manufacturing and banking Galton family of Birmingham; Eliza Cropper Sturge (1801–35) was the daughter of Liverpool East India merchant James Cropper, to whose anti-slavery activities she gave vital support; and Jane Smeal secretary of the Glasgow Ladies' Emancipation Society, was the daughter of tea merchant William Smeal.

Other women were from the families of prosperous tradesmen or farmers. Anne Knight falls into this category, as does Hannah Messer (1787–1845), co-treasurer of the London Female Anti-Slavery Society who was the daughter of Joseph Messer, a druggist.[14] Mrs Ulph, treasurer of the Female Association for St Ives (Huntingdon), was the wife of J.B. Ulph, who ran a large ironmongery business.[15] Sophia Sturge (1795-1845), a leading member of the Female Society for Birmingham, a tireless canvasser for the slave-sugar boycott and the closest confidant of her brother Joseph Sturge, who played a leading role in the national anti-slavery movement, was the daughter of a well-off yeoman and grazier from Olveston near Bristol.[16]

Other women campaigners were related to clergymen or school-masters. To the names of Ann Gilbert and Lucy Townsend may be added those of Mrs Margaret Crouch, secretary of the St Ives Female Association, who was a schoolmaster's wife; and Maria Marsh (b. 1779), treasurer of the Colchester Ladies' Anti-Slavery Association, who was the wife of prominent evangelical Church of England clergyman Rev. William Marsh.[17]

Some women were themselves professional writers. Susanna Watts and Ann Gilbert fall into this category. Mrs Phelan, district treasurer at Sandhurst for the Female Society for Birmingham and writer of some anti-slavery poetry, was a popular author under the pen-name Charlotte Elizabeth. Amelia Alderson Opie (1769-1853), the Norwich novelist and poet, was also author of a number of anti-slavery poems. Her name headed the 1833 national female anti-slavery petition; she attended the World Anti-Slavery Conventions in London in 1840 and 1843; and she was a friend of the leading Quaker abolitionist John Joseph Gurney and of Lewis Tappan and J.G. Birney, leaders of the more conservative wing of the American anti-slavery movement.[18]

Such activists ranged in age from their twenties to their fifties, and up to three generations of female family members could be involved. Married, single and widowed women all participated in ladies' anti-slavery associations, with single women tending to fill the most time-consuming post of secretary whereas married women tended to act as treasurer, a post in which they could draw on their experience in managing household accounts. Single women who were leading activists were Susanna Watts, Anne Knight, Sarah Wedgwood, Elizabeth Pease, Mary Roberts, Sophia Sturge, Hannah Messer and Rachel Stacey, as well as sisters Mary Dudley (1782-1847) and Elizabeth Dudley (1799-1849) of Peckham near London, the former the author of an anti-slavery tract of biblical quotations, the latter co-secretary of the London Female Anti-Slavery Society around 1831.[19] Prominent widowed activists were Mary Ann Rawson, Hannah Kilham, Elizabeth Heyrick and Amelia Alderson Opie. Married women who were leading activists were Lucy Townsend, Mary Lloyd, Ann Taylor Gilbert and Mary Anne Schimmelpenninck. Mary Foster (1801?-1871), who was co-treasurer of the London Female Anti-Slavery Society in 1832 and secretary of the Stoke Newington Ladies

Anti-Slavery Association in 1840–45, was married but childless.[20] For most married women, as the description of the lives of Mary Lloyd and Ann Gilbert has shown, anti-slavery work had to be fitted in with a host of other duties for which middle-class women had particular responsibility: involvement in family businesses, housekeeping and the direction of domestic servants, the rearing of large families, and care for the sick and elderly.

Overall, women came from backgrounds similar to those of male activists, and abolition was frequently a family concern. Examples of families in which both male and female members were involved in anti-slavery were the Coltmans of Leicester (Elizabeth Heyrick's relatives), the Lloyds and Sturges of Birmingham, the Marshes of Colchester and Birmingham, the Knights of Chelmsford, the Robertses and Reids of Sheffield, the Wedgwoods of Staffordshire, the Gurneys of Norwich, the Buxtons of Northrepps Hall, the Staceys of Tottenham near London, the Croppers of Liverpool, the Peases of Darlington and the Smeals of Glasgow.

Within the family, however, the differing opportunities open to its male and female members affected the nature of their contribution to the cause. Samuel Gurney, George Stacey, James Cropper and Thomas Fowell Buxton were all on the national committee of the Anti-Slavery Society, whereas their wives and daughters were involved in local ladies' associations and in providing 'behind-the-scenes' support to their male relatives. Priscilla Buxton, daughter of Parliamentary anti-slavery leader Thomas Fowell Buxton, was co-secretary of the London Female Anti-Slavery Society and also her father's main adviser and confidante: abolitionist George Stephen later described her as Buxton's 'guardian angel', who acted as 'his secretary, his librarian, his comforter, and often as his adviser and guide'.[21]

In denominational terms anti-slavery drew support from a wide range of religious groups, and this is reflected in the presence of Quakers, evangelical Anglicans, Baptists, Independents and Unitarians among the officers and committee members of ladies' associations. Ann Gilbert and Mrs Ulph were Independents; the Wedgwoods were Unitarians; Susanna Watts of Leicester moved from Anglicanism to Baptism; Hannah More of Bristol, the Townsends of Birmingham, the Marshes of Colchester and the Robertses of Sheffield were evangelical Anglicans.

Most of the remaining activists who have been identified were Quakers, and some held influential positions in the Society of Friends, positions which would have given them self-confidence, experience of organising, and access to the close-knit national Quaker network. Elizabeth Dudley travelled extensively as a recorded minister and served as clerk to the Women's Yearly Meeting in London. Mary Foster was an elder in the Stoke Newington Meeting. Mrs Sarah Gundry (1775–1860), treasurer of Calne Ladies Association, was also an elder in the Society of Friends.[22] Mrs Elizabeth Robson (1771–1843), a Liverpool Quaker minister, paid an extended religious visit with her husband to the United States in the 1820s, during which she obtained an audience with President John Quincy Adams and exhorted him to use his power on behalf of the oppressed slaves.[23] Other leading Quaker women activists were Elizabeth Pease (though she was expelled from the Society on her marriage to a Presbyterian in 1853), Jane Smeal, Eliza Cropper Sturge and Sophia Sturge, Hannah Messer and Rachel Stacey. To these women born into the Society of Friends must be added Quakers 'by convincement', converts to Quakerism Elizabeth Heyrick, Hannah Kilham and Amelia Alderson Opie.

Women of different denominations were united in their evangelical religious perspective, which led to a willingness to combine with others across denominational lines in the cause of active benevolence. As the cases of Lucy Townsend and Mary Lloyd of the Female Society for Birmingham suggest, in forming a national female anti-slavery network women could thus draw not only on family and denomi-national networks but also on interdenominational links established through such groups as the Bible Society.

The Bible Society was one of a wide range of philanthropic and charitable organisations in which women activists were involved in addition to the anti-slavery movement, though in the 1825–33 period many gave priority to their anti-slavery work. In addition to the women whose lives have already been discussed in detail, Mary Dudley was involved in the education of the poor, Anna Gurney promoted safety measures for fishermen and sailors in her neighbourhood of Norwich, and Maria Marsh performed charitable duties as a vicar's wife and, like her husband, supported missionary work.[24] Overall, women anti-slavery activists tended to be involved in a wide variety of societies designed for the education and relief of the poor, for the promotion of missionary work, and for the relief of the suffering of animals. Anti-slavery and 'negroes' aid' efforts can be seen as appealing to a combination of these women's major philanthropic interests in relief and in education of the poor and helpless, especially women and children.

It would, however, be a mistake to stereotype all leading female anti-slavery activists as well-meaning lady bountifuls. Some women became involved in the main middle-class political pressure group of the 1840s, the Anti-Corn Law League, which campaigned for free trade. In addition, as we have seen, a few of the most prominent women anti-slavery activists held extremely radical political beliefs. Elizabeth Heyrick campaigned against the Vagrancy Act and supported workers' right to organise trade unions and to strike; Anne Knight supported Utopian socialism, Chartism and women's rights; Elizabeth Pease also supported Chartism. In fact a tension between the pursuit of anti-slavery as a branch of ameliorative philanthropy and the advocacy of the right of slaves to their freedom is evident in the writings of women campaigners as a whole. Women's doubts over the value and justifiability of supporting the Christian education of those still held as slaves has been mentioned in the previous chapter, and in the following chapter the nature of women's ideological approach to anti-slavery campaigning as a matter of philanthropy and as a question of principle will be explored more fully.

WORKING-CLASS PARTICIPANTS

Women campaigners' radicalism was limited by their preoccupation with establishing the respectability of their activities. Anne Knight, despite her radical views, remained within the bounds of middle-class respectability by adhering to a conventional lifestyle while in Britain. In contrast another Owenite supporter, Frances Wright (1795–1852), put herself beyond the pale of respectable society by her public advocacy of free love and birth control. Wright, an outspoken advocate of women's rights from a middle-class Scottish background, was not involved in the British anti-slavery movement, but she deserves a mention here for putting a scheme of gradual emancipation into action in America. This was the short-lived, racially mixed Owenite co-operative community she set up at Nashoba in Tennessee in 1826 with the plan that slaves, having earned their purchase price through manual labour, would be set free and settled in some suitable country.[25]

The degree of radicalism of the leaders of ladies' anti-slavery associations influenced the extent to which they attempted to gain working-class members. The total membership of ladies' anti-slavery associations probably never exceeded ten thousand and, like that of the organised anti-slavery movement as a whole, appears to have been predominantly middle class.[26] The social exclusivity of most ladies' anti-slavery associations suggests that they in part functioned as social clubs, a means of consolidating status as members of the philanthropic middle class. Like philanthropic groups, they offered women an opening for useful work combined with the opportunity to develop contacts and friendships outside the family circle in a respectable women-only milieu.

The limited membership of ladies' associations was in part the result of their lack of interest, at least in the 1825–33 period, in recruiting working-class members. Although middle-class women activists carried out door-to-door canvasses on the lines of missionary and Bible

83

societies, they made no attempt to follow these groups in collecting weekly penny subscriptions from the poor. Instead, like men's auxiliaries, they set subscription rates at five to twelve shillings a year, a large amount for a working-class woman to contribute as a lump sum. Scattered references in subscription lists to donations from 'a poor woman' and 'spontaneous offering from a servant' suggest that such contributions were exceptional, and they were anonymous donations rather than membership subscriptions.[27] The leadership of ladies' anti-slavery associations were probably inhibited from viewing poor women as potentially equal members of their societies because their existing relationship to them was one of either philanthropic benefactor or employer.

Ladies' associations did, however, enlist the support of working-class women for particular aspects of their campaign: as participants in the sugar boycott and as signatories to addresses and petitions, since both of these depended on mass participation for their impact.

As we have seen, during the abstention campaign the Female Society for Birmingham produced different pamphlets aimed at the poor and the well off. In Sheffield, where organisations of radical artisans supported the anti-slavery cause, the rich were urged to follow the example of the local poor, the majority of whom had promptly agreed to abstain.[28] In Wiltshire, however, most support was given by the more wealthy and influential members of the community and great difficulty was met in exciting the interest of the rural poor.[29] Not surprisingly, hints of class tensions between the well-to-do 'lady' campaigners and the poor women on whom they urged abstention can be discerned. The Birmingham women advised their co-workers in Wiltshire that 'the poor should be admonished of the indispensable obligation we are all under to excercise self-denial rather than continue to partake of other men's sins'. However, they also recognised the importance of making 'free'-grown sugar available at prices equivalent to slave-grown produce so that the poor could afford to participate in the boycott, and they approved of a plan to set up depositories for this purpose.[30]

Women's signing of anti-slavery petitions in 1830–33 also demonstrates the massive popular female support for anti-slavery outside the confines of the organised movement, and in particular the large-scale participation of working-class women. The estimated 100,000 women who signed the Wesleyan Methodist anti-slavery petitions in 1833 belonged to a denomination of which it has been calculated that around 62.7 per cent of members came from artisan families.[31] In the manufacturing town of Derby the local newspaper reported that nearly every adult female in the town signed the petition in 1833.[32] In 1837 the London committee for the female address to the Queen stated that they wished to 'give all classes of our countrywomen' a chance to sign.[33] In Birmingham, where the largest number of signatures was collected, the public meeting to launch the address was attended mostly by the 'working classes'.[34] A canvasser at Ruthin in Wales, forwarding sheets of signatories to London, apologised for the imperfect signatures of her semi-literate countrywomen.[35]

The widespread support for anti-slavery among working-class women is, as we have seen, evidenced in the huge numbers who expressed support for the boycott and who signed petitions. At present, however, evidence for independent anti-slavery initiatives by working women at this period is lacking, though it is possible that a thorough trawling of working-class periodicals might reveal some instances.

There are some indications of a greater readiness to attract working-class women subscribers in the late 1830s among radical activists involved with the Central Negro Emancipation Committee. The campaign against apprenticeship in 1837–38 took place in the context of a massive growth in political activism and organisation by working-class men and women involved in campaigning against the New Poor Law of 1834 and in the Chartist movement.[36] It was this atmosphere of popular unrest which led the Anti-Slavery Society's leadership to view with disquiet the extra-Parliamentary initiatives of the provincial radicals connected to the newly formed Central Negro Emancipation Committee.[37] Joseph Sturge, the Birmingham Quaker who founded the new committee, was the leading middle-class Chartist sympathiser, and his views were supported by his sister Sophia, secretary of the Birmingham Ladies' Negro's Friend Society.[38] Birmingham, a major centre of organised female Chartist activity by late 1837, was the town where the largest number of signatures to the female address to the Queen was collected, following a public meeting attended mainly by the 'working classes'.[39]

Elizabeth Pease and her Quaker friend Jane Smeal, both activists of radical views who supported Chartism, set the subscription rates of their respective societies in Darlington and Glasgow at only 2s.6d, suggesting an attempt to attract poorer subscribers, and Smeal reported to Pease in 1836 that

> The females in this city who have much leisure for philanthropic objects are I believe very numerous – but unhappily that is not the class who take an active part in this cause here – neither the noble, the rich, nor the learned are to be found advocating or countenancing our object . . . our subscribers and most efficient members are all in the middling and working classes but they evince great zeal and labour very harmoniously together.[40]

Fired perhaps by the example of Chartist women, one female supporter

of the Central Negro Emancipation Committee made a novel suggestion for a dramatic public protest against slavery by women.[41] *The British
Emancipator* of May 1838 printed a letter from the 'secretary of a ladies'
anti-slavery association in the north' to one of the male anti-slavery
delegates assembled in London in March 1838 to put pressure on
Parliament to abolish apprenticeship. This expressed women's disappointment at the failure of their address to gain a positive response
from the Queen. The writer then suggested that women hold a
demonstration in London on coronation day. Should Government
measures fall short of full emancipation, she proposed:

> That in sympathy with our afflicted brethren, the blacks in the
> West Indies, whose miseries we cannot alleviate, we should
> assume mourning garb, and that on the 28th June, the day of our
> queen's coronation, as many thousands of us as can meet in
> London, should assemble there, with black people from every
> quarter; that on that day we should appear as representatives of
> our sable friends, in mournful procession, with black flags and
> emblems of their depressed condition. . . .[42]

The writer's suggestion was never taken up, presumably because it was
considered too radical even for the leadership of the Central Negro
Emancipation Committee. Certainly such a demonstration was far
outside the sphere of activities considered appropriate for middle-class
women, or even men of their class, at this period.

BLACK RESISTERS

The letter writer's suggestion was unique also in expressing the desire
that black people should themselves be involved in the demonstration,
rather than simply being represented by others. Such demonstrators
might have protested not only against the continuance of slavery in the
West Indies but also at their own insecure status within Britain. For
there were a small number of black unwaged servants in England right
up to the enforcement of the Emancipation Act in 1834. While legally
free to leave their owners whilst in Britain, they faced relegation to
slave status if they returned to the West Indies without having been
formally manumitted. Such was the plight of Grace Jones, the domestic
slave of Mrs Allen of Antigua, who was brought to England by her
owner in 1822 then returned to slavery in Antigua the following year.
While Customs officers considered this re-enslavement to be illegal,
Lord Stowell ruled in the High Court of Admiralty in 1827 that Grace
Jones had possessed freedom only whilst resident in England and had
automatically lost this right on return to Antigua where she came
under the jurisdiction of colonial law.[43]

Fear of a similar fate lay behind the actions of another black woman brought to Britain by her owners the year after Lord Stowell's ruling. That woman was Mary Prince, whose *History*, published in London in 1831 and running into three editions, is the only known autobiography of an enslaved woman from the British West Indies.[44]

A slave who had worked for a succession of owners in the British West Indies, in 1826 she had married Daniel James, a free black man and carpenter and cooper by trade, whom she had met at Moravian Church meetings. Overworked and constantly flogged, she asked her owners, the Woods, to let her buy her freedom, but they refused. When the Woods travelled to London around 1828 she came willingly, hoping that the trip would help her recover from her rheumatic illness and encouraged by a rumour that her master now intended to free her. Once in London, however, she was still subjected to heavy laundry work, and still denied the chance to purchase her freedom. Prince recounted in her autobiography how she finally decided to leave her owners, despite this rendering remote her chances of ever returning to her husband in Antigua:

> I told her [Mrs Wood] I was too ill to wash such heavy things that day. She said, she suppposed I thought myself a free woman, but I was not; and if I did not do it directly I should be instantly turned out of doors. I stood a long time before I could answer, for I did not know well what to do. I knew that I was free in England, but I did not know where to go, or how to get my living; and therefore, I did not like to leave the house. But Mr Wood said he would send for a constable to thrust me out; and at last I took courage and resolved that I would not be longer thus treated, but would go and trust to Providence.[45]

In a bid to absolve themselves of any responsibility for her future, the Woods presented her with a paper saying she had come to England voluntarily and left them of her own free will, and vindictively diminished her chances of obtaining work by stating that she was idle.[46]

The first people Prince turned to were a shoe-blacker and a laundress, a poor working-class couple who were the only people she knew in England outside the Wood household. She was taken in for several months by the Mashes, paying for her keep with some money which she had brought with her from the West Indies. A woman called Hill then told Prince about the Anti-Slavery Society and in November 1828 went with her to its office 'to inquire if they could do any thing to get me my freedom, and send me back to the West Indies'.[47] Society secretary Thomas Pringle took up her case as one of several he dealt with at this period. In some instances he was successful, as for example with Nancy Morgan, a slave from Saint Vincent who had been brought to England by her owners, whose freedom Pringle procured through negotiating a price of £60 with her master for her and her son, £20 of which he obtained from the Female Society for Birmingham.[48]

In Prince's case, however, Pringle was unsuccessful. After his failure her position seemed hopeless, since legal investigations revealed that the British courts had no power to compel Wood to manumit her formally, and thus to prevent her return to slave status if she voluntarily returned to Antigua. The Anti-Slavery Committee thus decided to bring her case to the notice of Parliament and at the same time to introduce a bill providing for the entire emancipation of all slaves brought to England. Mary Prince's private petition, the first anti-slavery petition by a woman to the British Parliament, was thus framed as an integral part of the British anti-slavery campaign.[49] Unfortunately Wood, by providing testimonies that threw Prince's credibility into question, managed to delay the presentation of the petition until the close of the session of the House of Commons at the end of November 1829, and then left for the West Indies.[50]

Meanwhile Prince, trapped in England, had joined the ranks of the working poor, desperately trying to eke out a living in London. She survived first through work as a charwoman, then as a ladies' servant. Then, out of work, she used up all her savings in cheap lodgings and was forced to apply to the Anti-Slavery Society for assistance. Finally, in December 1829, she was taken into service by Thomas Pringle and his wife.

Despite her gratitude to the Pringles, Prince's loneliness and frustration at being trapped in England is apparent in her autobiography. She stated that she was 'as comfortable as I can be while separated from my dear husband, and away from my own country and all old friends and connections', and that 'I still live in the hope that God will find a way to give me my liberty, and give me back to my husband'. She tried to 'keep down my fretting' but admitted 'I find it a hard and heavy task to do so'.[51] Pringle, 'seeing the poor woman's spirits daily sinking under the sickening influence of hope deferred', decided to make a final effort on her behalf by gaining the help of Moravian missionaries and of the Governor of Antigua to intervene with Wood on her behalf.[52]

When this approach also failed, Mary Prince decided to make public her life history. The idea for the autobiography was her own, her purpose being to let the people of England hear from a slave what a slave had felt and suffered.[53] Published at the height of the anti-slavery campaign, it was intended to 'let English people know the truth' about slavery. As she so powerfully put it:

Oh the horrors of slavery! – How the thought of it pains my heart!

But the truth ought to be told of it; and what my eyes have seen I think it is my duty to relate; for few people in England know what slavery is. I have been a slave – I have felt what a slave feels, and I know what a slave knows; and I would have all the good people in England to know it too, that they may break our chains and set us free.[54]

In her narrative Prince recounted her personal history of her suffering under slavery, her various forms of resistance to her oppression and her final break for freedom. The *History* was more than a personal story, however: it was also a contribution to the anti-slavery campaign written by a black woman in her role as a representative of that vast mass of enslaved people in the British West Indies who had no opportunity to tell their stories to the British public. Prince should thus be seen not only as one of many individuals who resisted slavery, but also as an anti-slavery campaigner. Her narrative, as an integral part of the British anti-slavery campaign, also provided Thomas Pringle with an effective forum in which to draw attention to the fact that the system of slavery extended 'its baneful influence to this country', to point out that Prince's case was just one of many similar, and to call for 'the interference of the legislature' in passing an act which would finally make true the long-trumpeted claim that slavery could not exist within Britain.[55]

In some ways, then, Prince was integrated into the British anti-slavery movement. In other ways, however, she remained very much an outsider. This outsider status is suggested by the fact that the Anti-Slavery Society felt it necessary to check the authenticity of her account. While the word of a British gentleman was customarily taken on trust as a matter of honour, the word of a black woman slave and servant was assumed to need the backing of people of authority. Thus in his preface to her *History*, Pringle stated that he had cross-questioned her and obtained independent verification of all the story's details, and in his supplement to the *History* he reproduced the text of testimonies on her behalf.[56]

The Anti-Slavery Society's need to authenticate Prince's story was partly a reaction to Wood's attacks on her moral character. That it was more than this, however, is suggested by the Appendix to the third edition of the *History*. This is in the form of a letter from Mrs Pringle to Lucy Townsend, secretary of the Female Society for Birmingham. Written in response to a request from Townsend 'to be furnished with some description of marks of former ill-usage on Mary Prince's person', Mrs Pringle supplied her with a 'testimony' of 'full and authentic evidence' of her punishments as a slave which was 'certified and corroborated' by three other women.[57] It is clear that members of the

Female Society for Birmingham felt in need of such reassurances from women of their own race and class before making the decision to allocate £5 to start a fund for support of Prince and to recommend her *History* to their members.[58]

Mrs Pringle saw herself as Mary Prince's benefactor, educator and mistress.[59] She and her husband, who had lived in both Britain and the Cape of Good Hope, evaluated her as a good servant in these terms: 'we consider her on the whole as respectable and well-behaved a person in her station, as any domestic, white or black (and we have had ample of both colours), that we have ever had in our service.'[60] They noted her honesty, her industriousness, her anxiety to please and her gratitude to her benefactors, her 'natural sense', and her sincere Christian beliefs, and especially emphasised her *'decency* and *propriety* of conduct – and her *delicacy'*. Her 'faults' were listed as being 'a somewhat violent and hasty temper, and a considerable share of natural pride and self-importance'.[61]

Thus those very qualities which as a slave gave Prince the strength of character to stand up to her owners and eventually to make a bid for freedom, the very qualities which are evident throughout her auto-biography, are those condemned by the secretary of the Anti-Slavery Society in its supplement. For the Pringles as employers a rebellious household slave should transform into an obedient domestic servant; for the Pringles as upholders of proper gender relations a woman forcibly separated from her husband is granted the protection of the family who employs her; for the Pringles as philanthropists Prince's history of active resistance to slavery must be underplayed by present-ing her as a victim dependent on their benevolence. Thus black agency in undermining slavery is devalued and, under the auspices of the Anti-Slavery Society, freedom is granted as the gift of white philanthropists who leave class relations undisturbed.

Prince, a servant in a strange land, was indeed left dependent on the benevolence of her employers, dependent also for publication of her story on a middle-class white woman whose position as household guest contrasted with her own as household servant. With ample access to the education which Prince as a slave had been denied, Susannah Strickland was an author with access to publishers. It was she to whom Prince told her life story, she who wrote it out fully, 'with all the narrator's repetitions and prolixities', but afterwards 'pruned' it into its present shape, excluding 'redundancies and gross grammatical errors'.[62] The result, with its standard English, ordered arrangement and selec-tive exclusions, was well suited to appeal to the British public, but had doubtless lost some of the immediacy of Prince's original account. Prince's own testimony at the libel action brought by Wood against Pringle shows that Strickland omitted the information Prince had given her about living for seven years with a Captain Abbott prior to her marriage, about whipping another woman she found in bed with the captain, and about living with another man out of wedlock.[63] Stressing instances of Prince's sexual victimisation, Strickland thus suppressed instances of her attempts to exercise control over her intimate life for fear they would undermine her support from the 'respectable'.

Despite the campaigning intention of her autobiography, white middle-class women activists thus treated Prince not as a fellow-activist but rather as a victim of slavery, as a possibly unreliable individual whose account needed authentication, and as a working-class servant. Given this, it is hardly surprising that they did not think to recruit her as a member of one of their ladies' anti-slavery associations. The presence of a few black women in Britain might bridge the geographical boundary between slave and free, but it was not to blur the social boundary between the white female anti-slavery activist and the enslaved black woman on whose behalf she was campaigning. The voice of a black woman could not be allowed to displace the voices of white women speaking on behalf of their enslaved sisters.

A parallel case to that of Mary Prince is provided by a woman known only as Polly, who had been brought to England from Trinidad by her owner and in 1827 applied to a Methodist minister in Ramsgate for baptism. He informed a Quaker relation of his, Mrs Mary Capper of Clapton near London, and she obtained an interview with Polly. Polly told the English woman that 'she knew she was thought free in England, but *she* thought she was more a slave than in the West Indies, as she had none of her acquaintance to speak to'. She said she would like to live in an English family, and Mrs Capper decided to engage her as a servant, this being the most effective way of procuring her freedom. She worked for Mrs Capper for eighteen months but, like Mary Prince, became dejected at her isolation from other black people. Hannah Kilham discovered that she had originally come from Sierra Leone and it was decided to send her back there to work as a servant for Kilham's friend Maria MacFoy.[64]

For black women who gained their freedom in Britain at this period, one life course was thus the passage from unwaged slave to paid servant. For others, it was from uneducated slave to educator of fellow Africans, a transmitter of European cultural values and Christian beliefs to their race. Such was the fate of a young black woman of unknown name from Buenos Aires brought to Britain by her cruel mistress, an admiral's wife, who heard from sailors that she was free on reaching English shores. Her case was taken up by Quaker abolitionist Elizabeth Dudley, who applied for money from the Society of Friends anti-slavery fund for her clothing and board. Other Quakers in Southwark procured her freedom and obtained a place for her at the

Borough Road school of the British and Foreign School Society, in the hope that she could become a teacher to her fellow Africans.[65]

In their aid to such black women in England, white women abolitionists could satisfyingly combine practical aid to black people, the promotion of anti-slavery objectives, and support for black education. Without black women's own quest for freedom, however, no opportunity would have existed for such white philanthropy.

5

PERSPECTIVES, PRINCIPLES AND POLICIES

From its earliest stages the British anti-slavery movement contained conflicting tendencies: on the one hand, it was a philanthropic middle-class campaign promoting an imperial Christian mission; on the other, it was a popular movement for human rights regardless of race. For women these tensions manifested themselves in distinctive ways. As will be seen in the first part of this chapter, women promoted anti-slavery as a philanthropic mission to women degraded and families destroyed by slavery; on the other hand, as the second part of this chapter illuminates, women took the lead in transforming anti-slavery into a mass movement based on the slave's right to immediate emancipation. These differing approaches had differing implications for women campaigners themselves: the former was linked to an idealisation of, and the latter constituted an implicit challenge to, patriarchal relations and female subordination in British society.

PLEADING FOR HER OWN SEX

Distancing themselves from both black resistance to slavery and working-class agitation for social, economic and political rights, the white middle-class campaigners who led the British anti-slavery movement in the 1820s and 1830s predominantly attempted to develop an anti-slavery ideology within the secure bounds of white philanthropy.

For middle-class women campaigners, the assertion of a philanthropic perspective was seen as particularly necessary. It provided a way of distancing anti-slavery from politics at a time when political activism by women was considered improper. In particular it provided a means of justifying the formation of ladies' anti-slavery associations in the face of opposition from conservative evangelical male leaders, such as Wilberforce, and doubts among women themselves about the propriety of anti-slavery activism.

Campaigners' representation of slavery as a religious and moral rather than political issue made it possible for women to assert that anti-slavery lay within the sphere of religiously inspired philanthropy, an arena of public activity which they had by the 1820s established as an acceptable extension of their domestic duties.[1] As with their earlier assertion of their right to form philanthropic organisations, women represented anti-slavery as compatible with adherence to what historians have labelled 'separate spheres' ideology. This was a set of prescriptions about the proper social roles of men and especially women, which became dominant in the late eighteenth and early nineteenth centuries and which was closely linked to the evangelical religious revival of the period. The 'separate spheres' were the 'male' public sphere of business and political life, and the 'female' private sphere of domestic and family life. As will be seen, women anti-slavery campaigners drew on this ideology rather than challenging it.

Presenting anti-slavery as philanthropy, an 1825 appeal to women in *The Humming Bird* described anti-slavery as a religious activity which was simply an extension of women's work in the Bible Society and Missionary and Sunday School movements.[2] Similarly the first report of the Female Society for Birmingham questioned: 'should not British Ladies do for British slaves, who are most of them still Heathen, what so many Ladies are doing for Jews and Pagans.'[3] Several years later, when women had already established a place in the movement, the female author of *The Negro Slave* in 1830 called thus on women:

> Let not then the circle of your charities be too circumscribed, nor your zeal too much confined within the limits of home duties, for there is this blessed quality in Christian benevolence, that it is not weakened by extension, nor exhausted by constant overflow.[4]

'Feminine' characteristics were portrayed as positive encouragements to anti-slavery activism. The author of *A Vindication of Female Anti-Slavery Associations* argued that the activities of ladies' anti-slavery associations were an expression of 'pity for suffering, and a desire to relieve misery', which 'are the natural and allowed feelings of women'.[5] Similarly Leicester pamphleteer Elizabeth Heyrick, in her *Appeal to the Hearts and Consciences of British Women*, published in 1828, stated of woman: 'the peculiar texture of her mind, her strong feelings and quick sensibilities, especially qualify her, not only to sympathize with suffering, but also to plead for the oppressed.'[6] Sir James Mackintosh, in a speech at the annual meeting of the Anti-Slavery Society in 1831, praised women's anti-slavery zeal in terms which reconciled public activism with feminine propriety: 'In proportion as they possessed the retiring virtues of delicacy and modesty, those chief ornaments of women, in that proportion had they come forward to defend the still higher objects of humanity and justice.'[7] These qualities, he asserted, 'flow from the same source, and flow towards the same object', which was 'to humanize the world, to soften the hearts of men'.[8]

Ideas about women's social role and feminine character were closely related to the particular concern which women activists showed for the sufferings of women and disruption of family life under slavery. Expressions of this concern appear again and again in anti-slavery pamphlets, reports, appeals, poems, petitions and addresses written by women or addressed to them.

Concern for women and the family under slavery was also expressed by male campaigners. The resolutions for the amelioration of slavery passed by Parliament in 1823 included clauses opposing the flogging of women and the separation of families, and the Anti-Slavery Society's 1825 'Plan for the Emancipation of the Slaves' began with a statement of opposition to field work by women on the ground that it interfered with their domestic duties.[9] What *women* did was to make this concern the *raison d'être* of their organisations and in so doing to bring these aspects of slavery to the forefront of public attention.

One reason that women adopted this particular focus was their need to justify stepping outside the domestic sphere, which led them to seek to clearly define the specific contributions that women could make to the anti-slavery campaign. In contrast men, having no need to justify public and political activism, were less self-conscious about defining their role in the movement.

Women campaigners' focus on enslaved women was encouraged by a belief that women had a natural empathy with their own sex. Lord Brougham, leader of the anti-slavery campaign in the House of Lords, wrote to Zachary Macaulay suggesting that a public appeal to Lady Jersey, calling on her to reflect on the degraded condition of female slaves, would be a good way to arouse influential women to support the cause.[10] The Anti-Slavery Society's *Picture of Colonial Slavery* (1828) described anti-slavery as 'particularly worthy of the attention of the female sex' because 'the cruelly degrading and demoralizing effects of slavery on the female character are so strongly marked'.[11] Similarly, an appeal to women in 1825 suggested that the cause of the slave should lay particular claim to women's sympathies since 'it unites the claim of strangers with the claim of brethren and the claim of a fellow-sex'.[12]

Middle-class women in the late eighteenth and nineteenth centuries showed the greatest willingness to support philanthropic groups which were concerned with the relief of women and with domestic issues. As Prochaska has concluded: 'women preferred to contribute to those charities which dealt with pregnancies, children, servants, and the problems of ageing and distressed females.'[13] Such activism on behalf of other women was seen as consistent with woman's role in society and her character. In *A Dialogue*, one woman persuades another that action on behalf of female slaves is simply an extension of her domestic duties, since it is slavery which prevents women from taking proper care of their children, and slave holders who mistreat pregnant women and force the sick and infirm to work.[14] The Ladies' Association for Calne, stressing that the women had made 'such exertions as a proper attention to our domestic duties would allow us to make' for the relief especially of their own sex, continued:

> We would also record our conviction, that they who are the most desirous of preserving the delicacy of the female character will ever feel the most anxious for the deliverance of the weakest and most succourless of the human race (the female colonial slaves,) from that revolting system of degradation and debasement. . . .[15]

Similar points were made by the author of *A Vindication of Female Anti-Slavery Associations*. Tackling the question of whether it was unbecoming for women to join anti-slavery associations, the writer stated that it was not 'unbecoming' or 'unfeminine' to feel particularly acutely

> [t]he deep degradation of *our own sex* under this dreadful system, for the exposure of their persons to the lacerating whip, and the exposure of their untaught minds to the most awful licentiousness in its most debasing form, which even leads its captives to glory in their shame. Surely these things must stir up our spirits within us, when we behold so large a number of our own sex helpless victims alternately of cruelty and lust. . . .[16]

Articulation of concern for female slaves gave ladies' anti-slavery associations a distinctive focus for their work and led them to present a specific vision of freedom. Women's societies at Birmingham, Liverpool, Sheffield and Colchester expressed in their founding resolutions their determination to continue campaigning not only until Africans were no longer bought and sold but also until enslaved women were no longer flogged and 'every Negro Mother, living under British laws, shall press a free born infant to her bosom'.[17] The founders of the Birmingham society stated that they were motivated by the determination '[t]o awaken (at least in the bosom of English *women*) a deep and lasting compassion, not only for the *bodily sufferings* of Female Slaves, but for their *moral degradation*. . . .'[18] Pamphlets written to encourage women to join ladies' associations similarly focused on female suffering.[19]

The suffering of women under slavery was also used to justify female petitioning from 1830 onwards. The framers of the national female petition of 1833 stated that 'a painful and indignant sense of the injuries offered to their own sex, has peculiarly impelled them thus to step out of their usual sphere'.[20] Similarly, the Reading women petitioners of 1830 stated that they:

[h]oped that considering the injurious influence of slavery on the female character, they should not be regarded as exercising an unbecoming interference in a political question, or departing from the propriety of their sex.[21]

The fullest expression of this line of reasoning is to be found in the petition of the female members of the congregation of Carr's Lane Chapel in Birmingham. The petitioners stated:

They can no longer forbear to address your Honourable House in a cause which so deeply involves the honour and the comfort of so many of their own sex; and if in this act it should be thought that the zeal of your Petitioners has led them to overstep the line within which female influence is usually confined and unobtrusively employed, they hope it will not be attributed to any deficient sense of what is due either to themselves or to your Honourable House, but to that still deeper sense of what is due to so large a portion of their fellow-subjects.[22]

The minister of Carr's Lane Chapel was the Rev. John Angell James, a leading evangelical and the author of a number of influential works that stressed that women's philanthropic activities must be compatible with domestic duties, and that attacked women who went out canvassing and collecting from door to door.[23] The fact that he did not prevent the women of his congregation from petitioning is indicative of women's success in establishing widespread acceptance of such public and political action in the exceptional case of the anti-slavery cause.

Women focused on three main aspects of female suffering: flogging, 'moral degradation' and separation of mothers from children. Imaginative combinations of verse and engravings were used to give a vivid picture of the suffering of women under slavery. The Female Society for Birmingham's albums, which were distributed throughout the country, contained a series of specially commissioned engravings of the sufferings of slave women, accompanied by lines of verse. One of the pictures (Figure 9), depicting a woman with her sick child, was also imprinted on the society's workbags.[24] Such images helped combat planter stereotypes of the black woman as a licentious, lustful troublemaker by substituting the alternative stereotype of the weak and helpless woman which was predominant in British society.

This image of female victimisation was also purveyed by a modified version of the image on the Wedgwood cameo of 1787 which was adopted by women abolitionists in 1828. This showed a kneeling female rather than a male slave and bore the legend 'Am I not a Woman and a Sister' as an alternative to 'Am I not a Man and a Brother', used during the campaign against the slave trade (Figure 10).[25] The new slogan

The driver's whip unfolds its torturing coil.
"She only Sulks___go, lash her to her toil."

Figure 9 Engraving by Samuel Lines included in the Album of
the Female Society for Birmingham etc., for the Relief of
British Negro Slaves, c. 1825.

drew attention to the woman slave, a figure concealed by the male slave
figure used to represent the supposedly gender-neutral concept of the
brotherhood of man. This assertion of sisterhood paralleled that of
brotherhood in its evocation of family relationships and of religious
fraternities and sororities, thus acknowledging black humanity and
spiritual equality. In addition it conveyed women's particular identification with the sufferings of their own sex.

The assertion of black humanity and spiritual equality, however, went
hand-in-hand with a belief in white cultural superiority and support for
the imperial Christian mission. Women campaigners suggested that the
degradation of women under slavery was worse than that of women in
heathen societies because it was carried out by supposedly civilised
Christians. It thus undermined the missionary project of promoting
Christianity in order to 'civilise' men's attitudes to women. Mary
Dudley's pamphlet opposing slavery on Scriptural grounds included an
engraving of a kneeling woman slave, her chains broken, praying that
her master would read the Bible and learn not to be cruel (Figure 11).
Birmingham women in 1825 appealed directly to planters as professed
Christians, stating:

Figure 10 Abolitionist roundel 'Am I Not a
Woman and a Sister'.

It has wounded us to read of woman's suffering and woman's
humiliation in Countries which acknowledge British Laws, which
are governed, not by some half-wild, benighted native Race, but by
those who are connected with us by the closest ties.[26]

In this appeal slave holders are represented as anomalies who must be
reformed because they stand in the way of the missionary project, and
principles of anti-slavery and of white racial superiority are combined.

Slave holders were regarded by women anti-slavery activists as
anomalous whites because they abused rather than protected women
and thus failed to act as proper Christian gentlemen. Charlotte Elizabeth
Phelan made a similar appeal in her verses 'On the Flogging of Women':

> Bear'st thou a man's, a Christian's name?
> If not for pity, yet for shame,
> Oh fling the scourge wide;
> The tender form may writhe and bleed,
> But deeper cuts thy barbarous deed
> The female's modest pride.[27]

In the face of planters' failings white superiority was reasserted through
an idealised picture of women's position in British society. Susanna
Watts' 'The Slave's Address to British Ladies' highlighted the lot of
mothers:

This Book tell Man not to be cruel;
Oh that Massa would read this Book.

Figure 11 Engraving facing title page [Mary
Dudley], *Scripture Evidence of the Sinfulness of
Injustice and Oppression*
(London: Harvey & Darton, 1828).

> Think, how naught but death can sever
> Your lov'd children from your hold;
> Still alive – but lost forever –
> Ours are parted, bought and sold![28]

Similarly, 'The Negro Mother's Appeal', included in the *Anti-Slavery Scrap
Book*, addressed the 'white lady, happy, proud, and free' and urged her:

> Dispel the Negro Mother's fears –
> By thy pure, maternal joy,
> Bid him spare my helpless boy.[29]

This poem was illustrated with an engraving contrasting the lot of free
white and enslaved black mothers (Figure 12).

Women's petitions, like their anti-slavery pamphlets, frequently

Figure 12 Engraving accompanying poem 'The Negro Mother's Appeal' in *Anti-Slavery Scrap Book* (London: Bagster & Thoms, 1829).

contrasted the 'hapless and forlorn' condition of slave women with their own 'high privileges as British females' and represented their social position as an ideal which should be extended to other women.[30] As with their petitions against suttee, women petitioned not on their *own* behalf but on behalf of women whose lives were remote from theirs.

Women's petitions associated their own privileges with an 'enlightened' imperialism which could spread the benefits of Christianity and of British social conventions and government to the colonies. The female members of New Road Chapel in Oxford stated that they

> felt truly grateful for the just and honourable level in society which they maintain, and for the distinguished privileges which in the several characters of daughter, wife, mother, Christian, they enjoy under the benign influence of the principles of Christianity, and by the administration of the enlightened and paternal Government of this happy land.[31]

The language of female petitions thus reinforced evangelical ideology concerning gender relations and religious mission. The favourable contrast women made between their own social position and that of women slaves involved both accepting their own subordinate status and passing over the sufferings of overworked and impoverished working-class women within Britain. Their approach was in sharp contrast to those Owenite Socialists who were at this period making analogies between the position of both British workers and British wives and that of West Indian slaves.[32]

At a men's reception to celebrate the emancipation of slaves held after anti-slavery activist Priscilla Buxton's wedding on Emancipation Day (1 August 1834), Priscilla was toasted with the wish 'that she might long rejoice in the fetters put on that day as well as over those which she had assisted to break'.[33] That her female relatives and co-workers could comment without irony on this scene is further suggestive that anti-slavery involvement can be seen as in some ways blocking the development of a feminist consciousness in women.

Idealising their own social position, white middle-class British women sought to affirm their power and influence not by challenging male domination of the anti-slavery movement but by representing enslaved women both verbally and visually as the ultimate passive victims. They were described as 'the weakest and most succourless of the human race', as 'helpless victims'.[34] White middle-class British women felt it was their duty to speak on behalf of these black women because as slaves they lacked the ability to speak for themselves and were deprived of male protection. Their assertions of sisterhood were thus in part paternalistic – or perhaps the term 'maternalistic' is more appropriate – offers of help by the benevolent to the powerless. The Birmingham group's 'Appeal from British Ladies to the West India Planters' began:

> This Appeal utters a cry from the hearts of British women, to plead for those of their own sex, who have less power to plead than ourselves, who cannot speak their Misery and their shame . . . who have none with the authority and rights of husbands to protect them from insult.[35]

Lacking male protection, slave women must thus rely on British women, who have more power than either enslaved women themselves or their brother slaves.

Information on the sufferings of women under slavery was drawn directly from accounts of slave punishments in the *Jamaica Gazette* and missionary accounts as well as publications of the Anti-Slavery Society.[36] The views of enslaved women themselves are absent from these sources, with the exception of the *History of Mary Prince*; as we have seen, even this was mediated through its white female scribe and editor Susannah Strickland, and through the supplementary comments of Anti-Slavery Society secretary Thomas Pringle.

Only recently have researchers begun the process of documenting and analysing the lives of enslaved women in the British West Indies.

Their work has confirmed the special sufferings of women under slavery described by the women abolitionists. However, it has also undermined their stereotype of black women's passivity by exposing the multiplicity of ways in which women resisted and survived slavery. It has revealed the important economic and cultural roles of women in the black community under slavery, as cultivators of small provision grounds, as marketers, and as preservers of African cultural traditions. These economic and cultural roles, sources of black women's power and status within their communities and of their strength to survive slavery, were threatened rather than enhanced by white women abolitionists' promotion of British forms of marriage, family life and gender roles, British moral codes, and Christian religious beliefs and practices.[37]

It is thus important to realise that middle-class anti-slavery ideology did not only pivot on the contrast between slave and 'free' labour which David Brion Davis has highlighted. Equally significant was the contrast emphasised by women campaigners between a society run by degraded white slave holders who abused black women and undermined family life and a Christian society modelled on British lines which elevated family life and women's domestic duties. For anti-slavery campaigners freedom was equated not only with a capitalist system operating in a colonial context but also with a Christian society moulded on British lines. Women abolitionists played a vital part in developing this sense of Britain's imperial Christian mission.

IMMEDIATE, NOT GRADUAL ABOLITION

Anti-slavery never fit comfortably into the framework of the philanthropic imperial mission, however; it always carried a more radical potential as a mass movement for human rights. During the campaign against British colonial slavery it was a woman campaigner who pushed this alternative vision earliest and furthest, and in whose writings the evangelical inspiration of female activism was transformed into a vision of freedom achieved through adherence to religious principle.

In 1824 a pamphlet was published anonymously under the title *Immediate, not Gradual Abolition; or, an Inquiry into the Shortest, Safest, and Most Effectual Means of Getting Rid of West-Indian Slavery*.[38] While initially mistaken by some as the work of a man on account of its 'vigorous' style, its author was in fact the Leicester Quaker abolitionist Elizabeth Heyrick.[39] In her pamphlet Heyrick argued passionately for the immediate emancipation of slaves in the British colonies, launching a frontal attack on the policy of amelioration and gradual abolition which the Anti-Slavery Society had espoused at its inception in 1823.

As David Brion Davis has pointed out, belief in the slave's right to immediate freedom underpinned anti-slavery commitment in Britain from the eighteenth century, but in policy terms gradual abolition had always been espoused by campaigners as the best and safest approach.[40] Thus, while black slaves themselves had been attempting to, and on occasion succeeding in, achieving immediate emancipation through flight and through uprisings from the earliest days of slavery, Heyrick was the first white British campaigner to give eloquent support to their desire for undelayed freedom. There was not to be such a powerful argument for immediate abolition until a speech by the Rev. Andrew Thomson of Edinburgh in 1830.[41] It was only then that the Anti-Slavery Society finally made moves to change the cornerstone of its policy, moves which signalled the opening of the final intense phase of public campaigning and petitioning leading up to the Emancipation Act of 1833.[42]

Convinced that slavery was a sin against God, Heyrick argued that the slave 'has a *right* to his liberty, a right which it is a crime to withhold'.[43] The planter's pretended right to property in the slave is 'ill-founded, because it is opposed to nature, to reason, and to religion. It is also illegal, as far as legality has any foundation of justice, divine or human, to rest upon.[44] Liberty is a 'sacred unalienable right' the withholding of which the degradation caused by slavery should not be used to justify.[45]

In opposing slavery from the perspective of natural rights philosophy and from the religious perspective of its moral sinfulness, Heyrick drew on the eighteenth-century foundations of anti-slavery thought. Where she made a startling leap forward was in her fervent conviction that such principles should dictate anti-slavery policy. The policy of gradual abolition, she argued, had been 'the grand marplot of human virtue and happiness; – the very masterpiece of satanic policy'.[46] It was a 'wily artifice of the slave holder' who rightly perceived that delay would eventually produce public indifference and who had persuaded abolitionists to accommodate the planter's interest rather than prioritise the right of the slave.[47]

In calling for immediate emancipation Heyrick was, as she recognised, opposing 'not only the general, but almost the universal sentiment of the abolitionists'.[48] But, drawing strength from her conviction that 'truth and justice are stubborn and inflexible; – they yield neither to numbers or authority',[49] she boldly criticised the worldly politicians' who comprised the gradualist leadership in the Anti-Slavery Society and in Parliament:

they have converted the great business of emancipation into an object of political calculation; – they have withdrawn it from

Divine, and placed it under human patronage; – and disappointment and defeat, have been the inevitable consequence.[50]

Recognising that 'every idea of *immediate* emancipation is still
represented, not only as impolitic, enthusiastic and visionary, but as
highly injurious to the slave himself',[51] Heyrick set out to demonstrate
that on the contrary it was 'more wise and rational, – more politic and
safe, as well as more just and humane, – than gradual emancipation'.[52]
She argued that rather than sparking off massacres of the white
population, it would prevent the black insurrections of which planters
at present lived in constant fear.

Whereas other abolitionists tended to idealise western civilisation,
Heyrick drew attention to its violent history:

> To *polished* and *Christianized* Europeans, such abuses of liberty may
> appear natural and inevitable, since their own history abounds
> with them. But the history of negro emancipation abundantly
> proves that no such consequences are to be apprehended from the
> poor *uncultivated* and *despised* African.[53]

Where other abolitionists tended to be discomforted by evidence of
black agency, Heyrick represented slave insurrection as 'self-defence
from the most degrading, intolerable oppression', the result of enslaved
men being provoked by their inability to protect their families.[54]

Heyrick, an obscure provincial woman with no opportunity to vote
on national anti-slavery policy, to sit on the national anti-slavery
committee or to elect a Parliamentary representative, thus used the
medium of a pamphlet to publicly take issue with the policy of the male
leadership of the national anti-slavery movement. The purpose of her
pamphlet was not simply to criticise or influence the anti-slavery
leadership, however. It was also to arouse the mass of the population to
bring down slavery by their own actions. Believing that emancipation
would be achieved only through public pressure, she presented the case
for immediate abolition partly because she felt that such a plain appeal
to reason, justice and conscience would be 'better calculated to keep
alive the public sympathy' than the present cautious approach. She
opened and concluded her pamphlet with exhortations to the people –
to every individual living in Britain – to take the task of achieving
immediate abolition into their own hands: 'Too much time has been lost
in declamation and argument, – in petitions and remonstrances against
British slavery. The cause of emancipation calls for something more
decisive, more efficient than words.'[55] Endless petitioning of Parliament
for gradual abolition would achieve nothing: it was by mass abstention
from slave-grown produce that slavery would be '*most safely and speedily
abolished*'.[56] Deprived of a market for their produce, slave holders would

be forced to change to a free-labour system. Abstention was thus not simply a matter of conscience, but the most effective way of achieving abolition.

Heyrick thus believed that the perpetuation of slavery 'is not an abstract question, to be settled between the Government and the Planters, – it is a question in which we are *all* implicated' through the purchase of slave-grown produce. There was no neutral ground: 'the whole nation must now divide itself into the *active supporters*, and the *active opposers* of slavery.'[57]

Heyrick developed her arguments for immediate emancipation in two succeeding pamphlets. In *An Enquiry Which of the Two Parties is Best Entitled to Freedom? The Slave or the Slave-holder?*, also published anonymously in 1824, she tackled the general belief among abolitionists that slaves were at present unfit to be entrusted with liberty. The periodic slave revolts which occurred in the West Indies acted as flashpoints for debate and contending interpretations throughout the anti-slavery campaign. They challenged the image of the slave as passive victim propagated by abolitionists, and they were interpreted by slave holders as evidence of black people's innate violence. Heyrick recognised that to gain support for immediate emancipation it was vital to provide an alternative analysis of these insurrections, and in her *Enquiry* she took as her example the course of the recent slave insurrection in Demerara. She explained that here the slaves – distressed by new restrictions on their freedom of religious worship and hearing rumours of their impending freedom but experiencing instead increased corporal punishment as planters openly defied instructions from the British Government to limit flogging – decided to go on strike until plans for their future were explained to them. But despite the slaves' peaceful attempts to negotiate with the Governor, the troops opened fire on them, killing more than 150 and then rounding up and executing hundreds more. In presenting this account of events, Heyrick pointed to the contrast between the repressive and violent actions of whites and the peaceable resistance of blacks. While other abolitionists focused on the martyrdom of the white missionary Rev. John Smith, who was charged with having incited the slaves to rebellion, Heyrick likened the rebel slaves themselves to Christian martyrs.

The *Enquiry* aimed to bring the question of immediate emancipation 'into the open court of public opinion' in the confidence that here the slave would obtain a more favourable verdict than that passed by the anti-slavery leadership.[58] As in *Immediate, not Gradual Abolition*, Heyrick appealed to the common people of England to take the God-given task of immediate emancipation into their own hands: 'Away then with the puerile cant about *gradual* emancipation. Let the galling ignominious chains of slavery be struck off, at once, from these abused and

suffering, these patient, magnanimous creatures.'[59] And again she
argued that this could be accomplished through complete abstinence
from West India sugar, a campaign which would persuade planters to
'substitute equitable wages for the stimulant of the cart whip'.[60]

Two years later Heyrick wrote a third appeal for immediate
emancipation, this time aimed primarily at 'the more influential classes',
and especially the 'Great Leaders of the Anti-Slavery Society'.[61] She
pointed out that despite the dedicated efforts of these leaders, there
had been a total lack of progress towards either amelioration or
abolition since 1823. As in 1824, she blamed this on their adoption of
the 'hollow and treacherous' policy of gradual abolition, which was
sapping support for the cause.[62] She set out and countered various
objections to immediate emancipation and argued:

> The restoration of the poor Negroes' liberty must be the begin-
> ning of our colonial reform, the first act of justice, the pledge of
> our sincerity. It is the only solid foundation on which the
> reformation of the slave, and the still nore needful reformation of
> his usurping master, can be built.[63]

Heyrick wrote not as an isolated individual but as an active member of
the anti-slavery movement. Through her position as leader of the
Leicester Ladies' Anti-Slavery Society and district treasurer of the
Female Society for Birmingham, she was integrated into the circle of
women who belonged to the ladies' associations of which Birmingham
formed the hub. She saw these associations as providing the organisational basis for the mass movement for immediate emancipation: As
she put it in her 1828 'Apology for Ladies' Anti-Slavery Associations',
'the cause of emancipation has been pleaded in the Senate by the wise,
the eloquent, the noble. Now, it is pleaded in the workshop and the
cottage, by women and children.'[64]

As Kenneth Corfield has pointed out, ladies' associations did indeed
provide Heyrick with her earliest support.[65] Heyrick's Letters include a
quote from a letter written in 1825 by one of the founders of the
Ladies' Association for Calne of 1825 in which she expressed her
personal abhorrence of gradual abolition and expressed the hope that
'no Ladies' Association will ever be found with such words attached to it'.[66] Her wish
was fulfilled: no ladies' association appeared with the words 'gradual
abolition' in its title, though many, including societies at Calne and
Birmingham, did initially campaign for amelioration.

The first anti-slavery society in Britain to call publicly for immediate
emancipation was the Sheffield Female Society in 1827. It was clearly
influenced by Heyrick, distributing copies of her pamphlet Immediate, not
Gradual Abolition though, unlike her, it was willing to entertain the

possibility of a 'temporary feudal' system as a transitional stage between slave and waged labour.[67]

By 1828 the stereotyping of ladies' associations as in favour of immediate emancipation led the Female Society for Clifton and the London Female Anti-Slavery Society to publish *A Vindication of Female Anti-Slavery Associations* aimed at correcting the 'misrepresentation' that they were 'adverse to all plans for meliorating [sic] the condition' of slaves. While professing themselves not 'urgent for *immediate* emancipation', the women nevertheless deprecated 'those exertions which are LIMITED to amelioration merely' and argued that '*amelioration* and *emancipation* are points far distant, which must not be confounded with each other'.[68] In so doing these two groups questioned the causal link between amelioration and emancipation on which gradualist policy was based.

In contrast to ladies' associations, many local men's auxiliaries followed the lead of the Anti-Slavery Society in including the words 'mitigation and gradual abolition' in their titles and explaining this policy in their statements of objectives and reports. Furthermore, a number of auxiliaries claimed that abolitionists were uniformly opposed to immediatism. At the first annual meeting of the Newcastle Anti-Slavery Society on 16 June 1824, a speaker stated:

> It has been very unjustly imputed to us, that we desired the immediate abolition of slavery; but I can say in the name of all the friends of emancipation that we never did call upon government or the planters to adopt any such measure.[69]

In 1828, four years after the appearance of Heyrick's pamphlets, the Rochester and Chatham Anti-Slavery Society reiterated that 'the abolitionists have not the remotest idea of an immediate liberation'.[70]

In the change to support for immediate abolition by local societies between 1827 and 1830, men's auxiliaries followed rather than preceded ladies' associations. In Sheffield, where the female society had become the first group to adopt the policy in 1827, the treasurer of the local men's auxiliary, Samuel Roberts, failed to convert his society to a similar viewpoint and the group became inactive by 1830.[71] In Wiltshire the Ladies' Association for Salisbury and Calne supported immediate abolition by 1829, whereas the local men's society did not petition Parliament for immediate abolition until September 1830.[72] In Birmingham the female society decided in the spring of 1829 to fund a travelling lecturer who spoke out to other women's groups about his opposition to amelioration, and in April 1830 it stipulated that their agents should speak out against amelioration and promote the 'utter extirpation' of colonial slavery.[73] In contrast, the Birmingham men's society did not advocate immediate emancipation until August 1830.[74]

Acknowledging in 1830 that women's groups had taken the lead in this change of policy, the leader of the Dublin Negro's Friend Society stated: 'the usual policy, we think, of the Gentlemen's Anti-Slavery Societies had been at least until lately, gradual, limited and temporising.'[75]

Key members of local men's and women's societies came from the same families, and thus in espousing immediate emancipation women were not only going against the authority of the national leadership of the movement but also taking a stance in opposition to that of their fathers, husbands and brothers.

The national Anti-Slavery Society itself followed rather than led the provinces in this change of policy. It decided to drop the words 'mitigation and gradual abolition' from its title in May 1830, but initially promoted petitions to Parliament calling for the freeing of newborn children of slaves rather than immediate and total emancipation and only changed to an immediatist policy in April 1831.[76] The pattern which thus emerges is of a strong call for immediate abolition made by a woman gaining backing from some ladies' associations, followed by increasing support for immediatism among provincial men's societies, and finally a change in national policy.

Explanations for the earlier support for immediate abolition among women are suggested by the terms in which male gradualist arguments and female immediatist arguments were couched. Male and female abolitionists were agreed that slavery was an evil and a sin, an affront to religion and morality. For men and women this had different implications in terms of policy, however. Men supported gradualism on the basis of their economic and political perspective as employers of waged labourers or as middle-class professionals who identified with this group, whereas women supported immediatism on the basis of their assigned evangelical role as guardians of moral principle. Elizabeth Heyrick argued that as abolitionists believed slavery was a sin, their only consistent position was to campaign for it to be immediately abolished. In sharp contrast, the Leicester Auxiliary Anti-Slavery Society, which numbered Heyrick's brother John Coltman and a large number of clergymen among its committee members, argued against immediatism on the grounds that 'universal experience shews, that in the body politic, no less than in the natural, inveterate diseases admit only a slow and gradual cure'.[77] This organic vision of society was intrinsically conservative, since it implied that an alteration in existing social relations was fraught with danger. Behind it lay a fear of revolutionary change disrupting society and an identification with the economic interests of the planters. As members of the Beverley Anti-Slavery Association stated at a public meeting on 26 February 1824, calling for gradual rather than immediate emancipation and suggesting the possibility of financial compensation to former slave holders: 'it is far from our wish and intention to deprive the Planters of the services of the Black Population. . . . We wish to convert a set of dangerous slaves into useful, industrious labourers.'[78] This process of conversion from slave to waged labour, represented as being equally in the interests of slave and planter, was to be accomplished by the preparation of slaves for their freedom through Christian education and moral elevation.[79]

This difference in outlook was recognised by women, who attacked the anti-slavery leadership for placing political expediency before religious principle. Heyrick's attack on 'worldly politicians' who paid too much attention to planters' interests was echoed by the Sheffield Female Anti-Slavery Society, which criticised members of Parliament who proposed anything short of immediate emancipation for their 'vain attempts to make humanity and interest meet'.[80] Parliamentary politics was seen as a corrupting activity, and working-class men, excluded from Parliament like all women, were similarly appealed to as potential upholders of anti-slavery principle. Thus Sheffield women campaigners represented slavery as:

> not exclusively a political, but pre-eminently a *moral* question; one, therefore, on which the humble-minded reader of the Bible, which enriches his cottage shelf, is immeasurably a better politician than the statesman versed in the intrigues of Cabinets. . . .[81]

Women related their support for immediatism not only to their position as political outsiders but also to their special qualities as women. They attributed the gender difference on the issue of immediate abolition to women's moral superiority, their stronger adherence to Christian principle and their greater sensitivity. The founder of the Calne society, expressing her hope that ladies' associations would never advocate gradual abolition, stated in 1825 that

> men may propose only *gradually* to abolish the worst of crimes, and only to mitigate the most cruel bondage, but why should *we* countenance such enormities by speaking them in such acquiescing, unscriptural, heartless terms?[82]

The Sheffield Female Anti-Slavery Society, arguing in 1827 for immediate emancipation, stated:

> We ought to obey God rather than man. Confidence here is not at variance with humility. On principles like these, the simple need not fear to confront the sage; nor a *female* society to take their stand against the united wisdom of this world.[83]

David Brion Davis has pointed to the 'obvious links between immediate emancipation and a religious sense of immediate justification and presence of the divine spirit' characteristic of both Quakerism and the evangelical revival.[84] The particular support which women gave to immediate emancipation can be related to this religious conviction, which in turn provided an acceptable legitimation of feminine defiance of male authority. Heyrick's conversion to immediate emancipation followed her conversion to Quakerism, and her post-conversion obsession with sinfulness and self-denial can be linked to her call to people to renounce the sin of slavery and deny themselves slave-grown products. In addition, Quaker acknowledgement that women could communicate the inner voice of God as ministers, a factor which her friend Catherine Hutton suggested partly motivated Heyrick's choice of the sect, would have strengthened Heyrick's resolve to give public voice to her anti-slavery views.[85]

Nevertheless for some of her supporters consciousness of women's lack of political experience did lead to a wavering of public commitment to immediate abolition. Between outspoken statements of support for immediate emancipation in 1827 and 1830, members of the Sheffield Female Society in 1829 expressed the fear that they were 'incompetent to judge' its danger because of their limited knowledge of 'the political relations in which the question is grounded'.[86]

Women's support for immediate emancipation was strongest when it was the product of political as well as religious conviction. Elizabeth Heyrick had an extremely radical political outlook, and in the series of tracts she wrote between 1817 and 1828 she tackled a series of 'sins' which she felt should be immediately set right. Whereas the leadership of the Female Society for Birmingham distinguished between aid to the poor at home, seen as a matter of charity, from aid to the slave, viewed as a matter of justice, Heyrick was equally concerned to advocate the rights of slave and poor labourer, blaming the sufferings of both on the 'lust for wealth' among slave holder and British employer alike and making analogies between the position of waged workers and that of slaves, which middle-class abolitionists tended either to avoid or deny. Heyrick, rejecting a purely philanthropic approach, argued that charitable relief was inadequate and that justice demanded the immediate setting of adequate wages for labourers and the right of workers to strike.[87] In the case of both Britain and the West Indies, however, she stopped short of attacking the principles of the capitalist system of masters and men, profits and wages. She did not espouse the vision of communal and co-operative social organisation being developed by the Owenite socialists at this period.[88]

Heyrick's radicalism can be partly attributed to family influence and to the legacy of the 1790s: her father was a Unitarian and a supporter of religious and civil liberty whose family collection included an autograph of Thomas Paine, author of *The Rights of Man*.[89] A letter from her brother John suggests that both he and Elizabeth were fervent anti-slavery supporters in 1796, but that he like many others had by then reacted against political radicalism, whereas she had retained her Jacobin sympathies.[90] Her political distance from her brother widened in the 1810s when she espoused workers' economic rights in direct conflict with her male relatives' vested economic interests in the hosiery trade, and this family division was further exacerbated by disagreement on the issue of immediate abolition in the 1820s.

Heyrick's willingness to rebel against male authority both inside and outside the family seems to have been fostered by tensions between her own character and abilities and the limitations imposed on her activities by her womanhood. The picture which emerges from reminiscences of friends and relatives is of a passionate, romantic, talented and strong-willed young woman. She was denied the opportunity to develop her talents as a painter, and as a woman did not have the opportunity to enter the family business open to her brothers. Encouraged to become an industrious and orderly wife, she channelled her energies at eighteen into a stormy marriage with a jealous and unstable husband. Then, left a childless widow in the 1790s, she converted to Quakerism and threw herself into philanthropic work, giving most of the sizeable allowance she received from her father to charity.[91] Excluded from active participation in the economic realm herself, she acted as the moral conscience of men of her family and her class, whether it was on matters concerning British workers or West Indian slaves.

It would be wrong, however, to characterise Heyrick and other female advocates of immediate abolition as idealists unconcerned with the practicality of their policies. Rather, they saw a principled stance as the only one which would maintain public support for the anti-slavery cause and avoid 'disappointment and defeat'.[92] Staffordshire campaigner Sarah Wedgwood, stating her opposition to the infant-freeing plan adopted as a scheme for gradual abolition by the Anti-Slavery Society in 1830, wrote to Anne Knight of the Chelmsford Ladies' Anti-Slavery Society that she considered the plan 'more fatal' than amelioration because 'it will satisfy more people than the other would'. She explained:

> If the battle might be between emancipation and slavery only there would be some hope; but this 3rd thing that looks like emancipation and is not, is I fear beguiling so many that it will very much weaken the true cause.[93]

The problem for women was that they lacked the formal power to change the gradualist policy of the Anti-Slavery Society. They were excluded from its committee and, unlike delegates from local men's auxiliaries, they could not speak or vote at the Society's annual meetings. This has led both David Brion Davis and Kenneth Corfield to suggest that women, despite their pioneering advocacy of immediate emancipation, had little influence on changing national anti-slavery policy.[94] I believe, however, that this interpretation underestimates women's influence within the anti-slavery movement, as will be suggested by a detailed study of the various means by which women could and did try to bring about policy change and of the impact of their efforts.

First, women could attempt to bypass Parliament altogether and bring about abolition through methods in which they could play a leading role. Heyrick argued that through abstention from slave-grown sugar 'We, the people, the common people of England, – *we ourselves will emancipate him*'.[95] As we have seen in Chapter 3, ladies' anti-slavery associations promoted the slave-grown sugar boycott systematically from 1825 and by 1828 the Anti-Slavery Society, lamenting the lack of progress achieved by its own approach of petitioning for amelioration and gradual abolition, issued appeals to women which acknowledged that abstention was now one of the main channels left for achieving progress towards emancipation.

Second, women could attempt to influence national policy by arousing public opinion. A noteworthy aspect of the immediatist campaign by women was that it was conducted largely through public rather than private pressure. It is striking that the first anti-slavery pamphlet by a British woman was Heyrick's highly controversial *Immediate, not Gradual Abolition*. Heyrick's first pamphlet went into three editions in Britain in 1824, and her biographer stated that it 'was read by thousands both in England and America and . . . was a means of converting some who had great influence in high places, to the truth and justice of her views'.[96] In Britain it was favourably reviewed in two major religious periodicals. *The Baptist Magazine* described it as 'a well-written, argumentative, cheap pamphlet. It deserves to be generally read', though the reviewer focused on Heyrick's recommendation of abstention from slave-grown sugar rather than discussing the policy of immediate abolition which this boycott was intended to promote.[97] In its review, the evangelical Anglican *Christian Observer* explained the meaning of the term 'immediate emancipation', and described it as 'a pamphlet of extraordinary vigour' which 'cannot fail to produce considerable effect', while expressing reservations about 'the intemperance of some expressions' and 'the perfect accuracy of others'.[98]

These two reviews would have helped bring the pamphlet to the attention of the middle-class nonconformist and evangelical Anglican community who formed the backbone of organised anti-slavery support and who would have been sympathetic to its view of slavery as a religious question. This publicity was important given that the *Anti-Slavery Reporter* made no mention of the pamphlet, presumably because the views it expressed were contrary to current Society policy.

Despite attempts by the Anti-Slavery Society to ignore its existence, Heyrick's pamphlet excited the interest of provincial abolitionists, and the Society's national committee decided to procure a dozen copies for distribution to 'any member who may apply for them'.[99] A Cambridge abolitionist asked for the committee's advice on dispensing the pamphlet. A Mr Mathews of Histon in Cambridgeshire wrote a pamphlet the title of which, *The Rights of Man. (Not Paines,) but the Rights of Man, in the West Indies*, suggested a similarly radical political perspective to Heyrick's; in it he praised Heyrick's 'eloquent and powerfully written pamphlet' and reiterated many of its arguments.[100] In March 1825 Zachary Macaulay, secretary of the Society, reported that 'there has been much discussion and much correspondence among Anti-Slavery folks in London and in various parts of the country' on the issue of immediate abolition.[101]

Interest in Heyrick's ideas was also shown by men in Scotland. The Edinburgh and Aberdeen anti-slavery societies included the pamphlet on their lists of works available for loan to members in 1825 and 1826 respectively.[102] It thus seems probable that it influenced the Rev. Andrew Thomson of the Edinburgh Anti-Slavery Society, who made use of similar arguments in his influential October 1830 speech in favour of immediate abolition. Slavery, Thomson argued in words echoing Heyrick's of 1824, was 'unlawful, iniquitous, and unchristian', a sin which could not be mitigated but must be immediately abolished.[103] There is also evidence that Thomson corresponded on the immediatism issue with Lucy Townsend, secretary of the Female Society for Birmingham. She sent him her society's resolutions of April 1830 concerning putting pressure on the Anti-Slavery Society to adopt immediatism, and encouraged him to disseminate his immediatist views in pamphlet form.[104]

Heyrick's later pamphlet, *Letters on the Necessity of a Prompt Extinction of British Colonial Slavery*, the first section of which was addressed specifically to the anti-slavery leadership, received considerably more attention from the committee of the Anti-Slavery Society than her earlier pamphlet. Heyrick wrote to the Society in September 1825 enclosing a prospectus for her projected new pamphlet; this was considered by the committee, and a response was written by the Society's secretary, Zachary Macaulay, who made suggestions on its contents. He reported that she had agreed to his suggestions, and in December she forwarded the completed manuscript to him.[105] Heyrick acknowledged Macaulay's help at the beginning of the tract, stating:

Since the prospectus of the following work was issued, its title and contents have undergone considerable alteration, consequent upon the change produced in some of the writer's views of the subject, by a correspondence with one of the most able and devoted leaders of the Anti-Slavery Society.[106]

The changes seem to have been minor, however, and while more praise is accorded to the efforts of the anti-slavery leadership than in her first pamphlet, there is no weakening in her critique of this leadership for its support of gradualism. Heyrick's pamphlets, while officially ignored by the leadership of the Anti-Slavery Society, were thus privately given serious attention.

Women could also exert financial pressure on the Anti-Slavery Society for a change of policy. The Female Society for Birmingham passed the following resolution at their annual meeting in April 1830, an interesting aspect of which is its identification of the national society as the 'Gentleman's' society, indicative that they were distancing themselves as women from its policies and identifying men as the gradualists:

> This Society being anxious not to compromise their own princi-
> ples, nor to give a sanction to anything which falls short of the
> standard of Right, will appropriate £50 to the London
> Gentleman's Anti-Slavery Society when they are willing to give
> up the word *gradual* in their title, and not to recur in any terms of
> approbation to the Resolutions of the Commons House of Parlia-
> ment in 1823 – which if passed into law would only serve to
> legalize iniquity.[107]

Some seven weeks after receiving the Birmingham women's resolution, the committee of the Anti-Slavery Society resolved that the terms 'mitigation and gradual abolition' should be dropped from the Society's title, and that their aim should now be the 'entire abolition' of slavery.[108] Though pressure from male provincial delegates at the Society's annual meeting on 15 May was clearly a major force behind this change of policy, the women's financial pressure must also have played a part. The Female Society for Birmingham was one of the largest local society donors to central funds, and also had great influence over the network of ladies' associations which together had supplied over a fifth of the Society's total income from donations and subscriptions in 1829.[109] Given this, the Anti-Slavery Society could not have afforded to ignore its threat to withdraw funding.

Women were also able to promote a policy of immediate emanci-pation by their financial support for the Agency Sub-Committee of the Anti-Slavery Society, which promoted a popular campaign to bring about immediate abolition from 1830 onwards. Staffordshire abolitionist Sarah Wedgwood, a firm supporter of immediate abolition, offered a donation of £100 to 'carry the plan into operation', and this gave 'encouragement to its projectors to proceed'.[110] Ladies' associations gave greater financial backing than men's auxiliaries to the agency system. This was both because their support for immediate abolition was stronger and because they were more convinced of the importance of continued extra-Parliamentary action. A letter from the secretary of the Female Association at St Ives in Huntingdonshire to the Anti-Slavery Society, pledging her society's support for the Agency Sub-Committee, expressed frustration at the contrasting lack of support from local men who considered action was unnecessary at present because when the Reform Bill passed the abolition of slavery was sure to follow.[111]

Women thus combined promotion of immediate abolition through the mass boycott of slave-grown sugar with the application of passionate rational argument, the arousal of public opinion and the exertion of moral and financial pressure to persuade the national leadership to change to a policy of immediate emancipation. They initiated a swing in opinion within the anti-slavery movement in favour of immediatism which spread upwards through the decision-making hierarchy from an individual woman to ladies' associations through men's auxiliaries to the national committee, and inwards from the provinces to London. Elizabeth Heyrick herself, with her eloquent pamphlet *Immediate, not Gradual Abolition*, set out a reasoned case for immediate emancipation which provided a clear alternative to the movement's official policy from the first stages of the campaign against British colonial slavery.

Women's advocacy of immediate emancipation was important not only as an intervention in anti-slavery policy but also as an assertion of feminine independence. Kenneth Corfield has argued that women's radical and independent stance on immediatism 'implied no similarly radical attitude to the social and political position of their own sex'.[112] This is true in the sense that women who supported immediatism did not simultaneously claim equal rights in the anti-slavery movement or in wider society, seeing their exclusion from Parliamentary politics as the very basis of their powerful moral influence and considering that men and women had different and complementary qualities to bring to the anti-slavery campaign.[113] Nevertheless, women's outspoken criticisms of the male leadership of the campaign, and quarrels over matters of anti-slavery principle with their brother societies, involved a public questioning of male authority, an assertion of independence, and a recognition that their views were not adequately represented by men. Such an outlook might be described as 'proto-feminist' in the sense that

116

it was a necessary precursor to any formulation of demands for women's independent legal and democratic rights. Certainly it sat uneasily with the idealisation of British women's existing social position which characterised many of the anti-slavery pamphlets and petitions by women discussed in the first section of this chapter.

The links between a radical abolitionist stance and the assertion of female independence can be further clarified by looking at events in Sheffield during the campaign against apprenticeship, the system which the 1833 Emancipation Act had introduced in lieu of immediate emancipation. In their support for the Central Negro Emancipation Committee's uncompromising public campaign for the immediate abolition of apprenticeship in 1837–38, Mary Anne Rawson and other radical women anti-slavery activists who dominated the ladies' association in Sheffield came into conflict with more cautious and conservative members of the local men's society.[114]

When the local men's society in Sheffield refused to comply with requests by the ladies' committee that they organise public events to which leaders of the Central Negro Emancipation Committee be invited, the women went ahead and organised the events themselves, despite the resignation of six Anglican members of their own society who disapproved of the radical nonconformist image of the national committee. The men's committee, headed by two Anglican vicars, expressed its angry disapproval of the women's independent action. In response the women issued a forthright declaration in which they described the 'present interference' as 'uncalled for' and stated that they represented an *entirely independent Society* which had never been auxiliary or subordinate to the men's society though it had tried to co-operate with it.[115] Considering an anti-apprenticeship petition organised by the men's society to have been too compromising in its demands, and feeling that they had 'the mass of popular . . . [support?]' on the side of *immediate emancipation*', the women's committee then organised petitions from both the male and female inhabitants of Sheffield calling for immediate, unconditional and complete freedom for the West Indian apprentices.[116] Their success in collecting signatures suggests that they were more in tune with the predominantly nonconformist radical artisan population of Sheffield than were the conservative Anglicans who dominated the men's society.

In Sheffield in 1838 female support for immediate full emancipation was thus linked to a radical nonconformist outlook and to the willingness to seek mass public support and to act independently of male guidance; while male support for gradualism was linked to conservative High Church politics, to a reluctance to seek working-class support, and to a horror at insubordinate female behaviour.

The attitude of male abolitionists in Sheffield towards independent anti-slavery action by women has much in common with the views expressed by the author of a pamphlet attacking female anti-slavery petitioning as a threat to the social order. Attributed to an anonymous 'Englishwoman' who was a High Church Tory suspicious of radical nonconformist enthusiasm, it first appeared as an article in the London newspaper *John Bull* in 1833 and was then published in the form of a pamphlet entitled *An Address to the Females of Great Britain, on the Propriety of Their Petitioning Parliament for the Abolition of Negro Slavery*. The author stated that for women to 'outstep propriety' by petitioning Parliament was an 'interference' which was 'a vote of censure upon those whom we are bound to acknowledge as our superiors – our fathers, our husbands, our brothers; for if they perform their part, our assistance cannot possibly be requisite'.[117] The home was women's 'only province' and women had been honoured in the past because 'they knew their rank in society to be a subordinate one, and they dignified it by the fulfilment of its obligations'.[118] Female petitioning was thus represented as a threat to the proper hierarchical ordering of society. In a reference back to the 1790s and to Mary Wollstonecraft, the only precedent for political action by women was stated to be in that 'most calamitous period' when 'the females of a revolutionary and fanatical age' forgot their proper position.[119]

Part III

WOMEN AND 'UNIVERSAL ABOLITION', 1834–1868

6

THE TRANSATLANTIC
SISTERHOOD

The abolition of British colonial slavery, with the implementation of the 1833 Emancipation Act in 1834 and the end of the apprenticeship system in 1838, did not herald the end of the British anti-slavery movement. Rather, campaigners now focused on the welfare of emancipated slaves and the abolition of slavery throughout the world. It is on women's participation in the universal abolition movement, and in particular their aid to abolitionists in the United States and their contacts with their sister campaigners there, that this chapter will focus.

UNIVERSAL ABOLITION

Three new national societies were set up in Britain in 1839 following the termination of the apprenticeship system: the African Civilization Society, the British India Society and the British and Foreign Anti-Slavery Society (BFASS). Of these only the BFASS was to survive beyond 1843.

The African Civilization Society, founded by Sir Thomas Fowell Buxton with the aim of eradicating the foreign slave trade by promoting legitimate commerce, education and Christianity in Africa, was the most aristocratic of the new anti-slavery bodies.[1] It was also the one with the lowest level of formal participation by women: of its 361 initial subscribers only 23 were female, several of these being titled ladies.[2] The society organised mass meetings and set up some local men's auxiliaries, but its periodical, The Friend of Africa, made no mention of the formation of any ladies' associations.

Despite the lack of public participation by women in the African Civilization Society's activities, Buxton's married daughter, Priscilla Johnston, and his wife's cousin, Anna Gurney, did vital work behind the scenes, drafting Buxton's speeches, editing his pamphlets and compiling information for his use.[3] Other women promoted the African Civilization Society at a local level, distributing prospectuses and pamphlets of the society and attempting to attract further female support.[4] In addition, Buxton co-operated with the London-based Ladies' Negro Education Society on schemes for missionary work and African education.[5]

The African Civilization Society collapsed in 1841, following the disastrous failure of the Niger Expedition, an attempt to establish an inland trading post and model farm in West Africa.

The British India Society was also short-lived, though more successful. It was formed in response to the continued existence of slavery in British India, for the 1833 Emancipation Act had not affected the status of more than a million serfs in debt bondage there.[6] The society also hoped that by encouraging land reforms in India to increase the efficiency of cultivating tropical produce they could decrease British dependence on slave-grown cotton and sugar from the United States and elsewhere and thus contribute to the downfall of the slave system.[7]

Women also lacked formal positions in the British India Society, but Darlington abolitionist Elizabeth Pease played a key unofficial role, working closely with her father, Joseph Pease, and with George Thompson in promoting the work of the society.[8] She acted as her father's secretary, collecting information, writing leaflets and articles for the provincial press, and informing American abolitionists about the issue, and she accompanied Thompson on his lecture tours, acting as his adviser.[9]

Elizabeth Pease also acted as secretary of the Darlington Ladies' Anti-Slavery and British India Society, which raised funds for the British India cause. Other women's societies which raised funds and disseminated information on the issue were the Edinburgh Ladies' Emancipation Society and the Ladies' Auxiliary of the Glasgow Emancipation Society.[10] Elsewhere, however, the contesting demands of the African Civilization Society and the BFASS caused problems in gaining support. At Sheffield, for example, women concerned with the situation in the British East Indies decided that they had insufficient money or resources to take up the issue.[11]

The British India Society ceased operations in 1843, the year that the Indian government passed an act removing the legal basis of slavery.[12] In contrast, the third society formed in 1839, the BFASS, became the only national anti-slavery society to continue its activities throughout the 1840s and 1850s. It defined its objectives as 'the universal extinction of slavery and the slave trade, and the protection of the rights and interests of the enfranchised populations in the British possessions, and of all persons captured as slaves'. In keeping with the prominence of Quakers on its committee, the society resolved to employ only 'those means which are of a moral, religious, and pacific character'.[13]

In origin the BFASS was a replacement of the Central Negro

Emancipation Committee, which had co-ordinated opposition to the apprenticeship system. Like that group, it was set up through the initiative of Joseph Sturge of Birmingham and drew support mainly from those middle-class nonconformists who had provided the core of anti-slavery activism in the 1820s and 1830s. The new society attempted to recreate the network of local societies which had existed in the earlier period.[14] It issued an 'Address to the Women of England' and gave priority to the formation of ladies' associations rather than men's auxiliaries, since these were considered 'the more valuable of the two'.[15]

In June 1840 the BFASS organised the first World Anti-Slavery Convention, which was held at Exeter Hall in London in June 1840. It was largely a transatlantic convention of British and American abolitionists, and it became the arena in which British campaigners' decision to focus primarily on slavery in the United States was clarified and in which the recent division in the American anti-slavery movement spilled over into the British movement. Events at the convention thus had lasting repercussions on the future form of the British anti-slavery movement.

The division within the American movement, which had come to a head a month prior to the convention, was between radical abolitionists led by William Lloyd Garrison, who had taken control of the American Anti-Slavery Society, and his evangelical opponents, led by Lewis Tappan, who had seceded to form a new society, the American and Foreign Anti-Slavery Society. Differences centred on the Garrisonians' combining of anti-slavery with a number of other radical causes, especially women's rights, non-resistance and 'no human government' (anarchistic forms of pacificism which were associated with hostility to any political action against slavery), and unconventional religious beliefs (especially Hicksite Quakerism, whose 'quietist' supporters were labelled infidels or heretics by members of the opposing mainstream of evangelical Quakerism).

The dispute on the 'woman question' that was caused at the convention by the refusal of the BFASS to accept the credentials of a group of women delegates sent by Garrisonian societies, and its impact on the development of feminism in Britain, will be discussed in the following chapter. In terms of the future organisation of the British anti-slavery movement, the vital point to make here is that American abolitionists, lacking widespread public support in their own country, weakened by ideological divisions, and admiring British abolitionists' successes, attached great importance to gaining financial and moral support in Britain and Ireland.[16] Following the 1840 Convention the two rival American societies thus dispatched their representatives on tours of Britain in attempts to gain support for their own factions.[17]

The BFASS had already, in refusing to accept female delegates, aligned itself with the American and Foreign Anti-Slavery Society. By 1844 its agents had succeeded in establishing a network of twenty-two ladies' associations and twenty-five men's auxiliaries supporting their line. Most of them were in England, where activists had formerly been involved with Joseph Sturge's Central Emancipation Committee and where women in particular had close links with anti-Garrisonian agent Charles Stuart.[18] American Garrisonian agents met with most success in Ireland and Scotland, where there was a tradition of anti-slavery organisation independent of London, and where George Thompson was particularly influential among women's societies, which had established links with American Garrisonians in the 1830s. By 1846 independent women's groups aligned with the Garrisonians were in existence at Glasgow, Edinburgh, Perth and Kirkcaldy in Scotland, and at Cork, Belfast and Dublin in Ireland, as well as at Bridgewater, Rochdale and Carlisle in England. Support for Garrisonians continued to be through such independent groups, following the failure of an attempt to set up a network of male and female auxiliaries linked to the Anti-Slavery League, a central co-ordinating body intended to rival the BFASS.

In England, where Stuart and others were successful in aligning most local men's and women's societies behind the BFASS, a handful of women were the leading initial supporters of Garrison. Elizabeth Pease was the leading supporter and adviser to John Collins during his fund-raising tour on behalf of the American Anti-Slavery Society in 1840–41, and she engaged in a heated debate with John Scoble, secretary of the BFASS, over his refusal to recognise Collins.[19] Pease maintained an extensive correspondence with American Garrisonians, who recognised that in cementing the radical transatlantic abolitionist network she ranked in importance alongside George Thompson and the leading Irish abolitionist Richard D. Webb of Dublin.[20]

Other English women who gave early support to the Garrisonians included author Harriet Martineau, who contributed an introductory letter to Collins' pamphlet in defence of the American Anti-Slavery Society; the educationalist Elizabeth J. Reid; and radical abolitionists Mary Anne Rawson of Sheffield and Anne Knight of Chelmsford.[21] In 1840 Pease asserted:

> If we count by *numbers*, England may be called regularly new organized; but, if we come to those who will throw their souls into the work, I am not so sure as regards the *women*, at any rate.[22]

While anti-slavery underwent a general decline in the final years of the 1840s, women's societies remained more active than men's. For example, in 1847 independent female societies at Glasgow, Edinburgh and Dublin were still thriving, though local men's societies were becoming moribund.[23] The number of men's societies donating to the BFASS decreased between 1844 and 1850 from twenty to only three, whereas the decrease in women's groups was less: from twenty-two to eleven.[24] Thus by 1850 women's societies had come to outnumber men's groups for the first time in the history of the anti-slavery movement. This numerical dominance of active women's societies became even more noticeable during the 1850s when between eight and thirteen ladies' auxiliaries contributed each year to BFASS funds, whereas the number of contributing men's auxiliaries varied from none to six. The BFASS's 1854 report, praising the work of local societies both auxiliary to and independent of it in a move which marked increasing rapprochement between the two sides of the movement, acknowledged the receipt of printed reports from five women's groups and one mixed group but made no mention of any men's groups. In 1859 the BFASS singled out two women's groups – the Birmingham Ladies' Negro's Friend Society and the Edinburgh Ladies' Emancipation Society – as the chief amongst various provincial organisations forwarding its work.[25] In addition, though a few new men's societies were formed during the 1850s, there was nothing to equal the two extensive new networks of female societies: the twenty-six Free Labour Associations promoted by Anna Richardson in 1850–51, and the fifteen new ladies' anti-slavery associations formed by Julia Griffiths in 1856–59. The American Garrisonian abolitionist J. Miller McKim reported in 1854 of his British visit:

The most active abolitionists were, with few exceptions, to be found among women. In Bristol, Leeds, Edinburgh, Belfast, the principal work was performed by ladies, and on them everywhere the cause seems to depend for its life and vigour.[26]

Part of the reason for women's increasing prominence in the British anti-slavery movement through the 1840s and 1850s lay in the serious decline in male anti-slavery activism. This stemmed from the political marginalisation of anti-slavery in Britain after 1838. Activities on which local men's groups had previously focused – petitions to Parliament, the influencing of electors and the canvassing of MPs – were of little relevance when confronting slave trading and slave holding in foreign countries over which the British government had no jurisdiction. In contrast, areas of work in which female societies had established prominence, such as fund-raising, boycotting slave-grown produce and exerting moral pressure, now became the main courses of action open to abolitionists as a whole.

Financial support was particularly valued by American campaigners, who directed their financial appeals largely at women. The American female supporters of rival anti-slavery factions instigated annual bazaars to raise funds for their societies, and British women responded to their appeals for aid by making and collecting 'useful and fancy articles' which were boxed and shipped out for sale in the United States.[27]

Support for bazaars was divided on political lines, and women had to make a choice as to which American groups to support. Female societies which were auxiliary to the BFASS contributed in the 1840s to the bazaars at New York and Boston run by the Tappanite wing of the American anti-slavery movement and to the bazaar in Philadelphia in aid of the Liberty Party, a group opposed by Garrison because it advocated political action against slavery rather than the exclusive use of moral pressure.[28] Female supporters of Garrison formed a rival network of collectors through Britain and Ireland for the Boston Bazaar, an event organised by Maria Weston Chapman of the Boston Female Anti-Slavery Society which provided a vital source of funding for the *Anti-Slavery Standard*, the official paper of the American Anti-Slavery Society.[29] Women also contributed to the *Liberty Bell*, an anti-slavery annual connected to the bazaar. Harriet Martineau wrote several pieces, and her friend Elizabeth Barrett Browning sent in her two powerful anti-slavery poems, 'The Runaway Slave at Pilgrim's Point' and 'A Curse for a Nation'.[30] From 1846 British and Irish women also began collecting for the Rochester Anti-Slavery Bazaar, organised to support the work of Frederick Douglass, who had decided to work more independently of Garrison and set up his own anti-slavery paper, the *North Star*, in Rochester, New York, to represent the black community.[31] From 1856 donations were collected through the network of new ladies' societies set up by Julia Griffiths, Douglass' principle British supporter.

In the 1850s women also gave financial support to groups in America and Canada who were aiding runaway slaves. In Scotland support for fugitives through donations to the New York Vigilance Committee was co-ordinated by the Glasgow Female New Association for the Abolition of Slavery, formed by evangelical women who had left the 'infidel' Garrisonian Female Anti-Slavery Society in 1850.[32] In Ireland the Dublin Ladies' Anti-Slavery Society and the Clogher Ladies' Association supported fugitive aid through donations to the New York and Philadelphia Vigilance Committees. In addition, the ladies' associations at Clogher, Bury St Edmunds and Edinburgh responded to appeals for donations for the relief and education of fugitives in Canada.[33]

Another female fund-raising initiative during the 1850s was the Birmingham women's collection of a national tribute to Harriet Beecher Stowe, from the readers of her best-selling anti-slavery novel,

Uncle Tom's Cabin. A total of £1,800 was eventually contributed to this so-called 'Penny Offering', mainly in the form of small donations from working- and middle-class people. The total compared favourably with the total annual income of the BFASS at this period of some £1,100. In addition, a separate testimony totalling £1,000 was organised by societies independent of the BFASS in Scotland, and other collections were made by independent societies in Dublin and Leeds. As British women wished, Stowe eventually spent the money from the testimonial on promoting both abolition and black Christian education.[34]

Overall, British and Irish women were responsible for most of the foreign financial aid which was sent to the American anti-slavery movement in the 1840s and 1850s. Their help was vital since American anti-slavery societies suffered from constant financial crises due to the lack of a wide base of popular support and splits caused by sectarian infighting.

CO-OPERATION AND SISTERHOOD

Through the 1840s and 1850s formal contacts between female societies in Britain and America and between the women organisers of American anti-slavery bazaars and their British networks of collectors were cemented by the development of personal friendships between leading individual activists who exchanged information and views not only on anti-slavery but also on a wide range of other political and philanthropic issues. A transatlantic sisterhood of abolitionists developed, particularly among supporters of William Lloyd Garrison. This formed an integral and crucial part of the transatlantic abolitionist network.

Transatlantic anti-slavery links had their origins in links established by Quaker men and women during the eighteenth century.[35] During the 1823–33 period links with American abolitionists had been formed both by the Anti-Slavery Society and by ladies' anti-slavery associations. The Liverpool Ladies' Anti-Slavery Society transmitted workbags and pamphlets obtained from the Female Society for Birmingham to abolitionists in Philadelphia, Baltimore and New York. Among those supplied was Benjamin Lundy, editor of the abolitionist magazine the *Genius of Universal Emancipation*, who devoted a large amount of space to publicising the efforts of British women and urging American women to follow their example.

The three leading male abolitionists who did most in the 1833–38 period to establish transatlantic links – William Lloyd Garrison, Charles Stuart and George Thompson – were all leading promoters of female anti-slavery activism with strong links to women's societies. Their efforts provided the foundations for the growth of the transatlantic sisterhood of women abolitionists which flourished in the 1840s and 1850s.

William Lloyd Garrison (1805-79), who was to become leader of the radical wing of the American anti-slavery movement in the 1840s, first became aware of the activities of British women through his editorial work for Benjamin Lundy's *Genius of Universal Emancipation*. When he split on policy grounds with Lundy in 1831 and founded the *Liberator* to promote immediate emancipation, he continued to publicise British women's activities and to urge his countrywomen to follow their example. On his anti-slavery mission to Britain from May to August 1833 he was particularly impressed with the national female petition, expressing the hope that it would excite 'a spirit of emulation, in the redemption of our slave population, among the numerous female anti-slavery societies' in America.[36]

After Garrison formed the American Anti-Slavery Society to promote his objectives, he issued an appeal to British abolitionists for aid; in response the Agency Sub-Committee decided to make worldwide emancipation its goal. Now known as the Universal Abolition Society, its aims were defined as aiding American abolitionists and campaigning against foreign involvement in the slave trade.[37]

Charles Stuart and George Thompson, the leading agents of the Society, attached high priority to fostering links between British and American women abolitionists. When Stuart and Thompson undertook tours of the United States beginning in 1834, they were particularly concerned to stimulate the formation of women's societies in America on similar lines to their British counterparts.[38] On his return to Britain Thompson travelled around Scotland, England and Ireland lecturing on developments in America and setting up both men's and women's universal abolition societies. Thompson emphasised in his talks to women the 'zeal, heroism, and perseverance' of female abolitionists in the United States. He also suggested ways in which British women could further aid their American co-workers.[39]

Some of the new female societies which Thompson founded channelled donations to America through the Glasgow Ladies' Auxiliary Emancipation Society.[40] This group became the hub of transatlantic links between female abolitionists, creating a network of honorary and corresponding members which included leading American and British women campaigners and which paralleled the network of male honorary and corresponding members established by their brother group, the Glasgow Emancipation Society.[41]

Another key group in fostering transatlantic contacts was the Darlington Ladies' Anti-Slavery Society, under the leadership of Elizabeth Pease. To drum up British support following Thompson's visit, the Ladies' Associations of New England issued an address 'To the

Women of Great Britain'.[42] To this the Darlington women responded with an address expressing solidarity with the American women. The American women, very encouraged by this response, hailed the Darlington women as 'coadjutors in the holy cause', and secured the address's publication in all the American anti-slavery periodicals.[43] In Britain the address was held up in the press as an example to other women on the grounds that 'there is nothing to which the Americans are more sensitive than the expression of public opinion in this country', and early in 1837 a similar address was sent by another group formed by Thompson, the Newcastle Ladies Emancipation Society.[44]

Formal addresses were followed by general letters to American female anti-slavery societies and correspondence between the secretaries of particular British and American female anti-slavery societies. This was sufficiently extensive for many American groups to appoint special foreign correspondence secretaries. Maria Weston Chapman, secretary of the Boston Female Anti-Slavery Society, corresponded with the female anti-slavery societies of Glasgow, Edinburgh, Seaport, Darlington, Sheffield, Taunton, Exeter, Liverpool and Manchester; Juliana Tappan of the New York City Female Anti-Slavery Society corresponded with Glasgow, Edinburgh and Sheffield. This correspondence involved the mutual exchange of information about the American anti-slavery campaign and the British anti-apprenticeship campaign, American requests for and British offers of advice and moral support, and mutual expressions of friendship, admiration, solidarity and sympathy.[45]

At this period women saw their struggles on either side of the Atlantic as interlinked. A letter to Thompson from Abby Ann Cox, corresponding secretary of the New York City Ladies' Anti-Slavery Society, expressed this clearly:

> We have some powerful and binding interests in common, as they have now to labour for the abolition of the cruel apprenticeship System – and here we would remind them, as an additional motive to their zeal, that the speedy success of this question in England, must and will have a most auspicious influence upon the question of Immediate Emancipation in America.[46]

To promote the cause of immediate emancipation in America the Philadelphia Ladies' Society decided in 1836 to republish Elizabeth Heyrick's *Immediate, not Gradual Emancipation*.[47] Heyrick's importance was stressed by Garrison who, urging women to attend the first Female Anti-Slavery Convention, called on them to follow the example of England where Heyrick had 'enkindled a blaze which unfolded new scenes of action, and pointed out new paths of duty'.[48]

There was also a major new British woman writer who inspired male and female abolitionists on both sides of the Atlantic at this period. Harriet Martineau (1802–76) was born into a Norwich Unitarian family of French Huguenot origin and forced by the loss of the family fortune to earn her living by writing. Martineau had written an anti-slavery article in 1830, and 'Demerara', one of the first popular tales for her *Illustrations of Political Economy*, dealt with the economic benefits of free as opposed to slave labour.[49] She had not otherwise been active in the anti-slavery movement, however, and when she travelled to the United States in August 1834 it was not on a specifically anti-slavery mission. Nevertheless slavery became her major preoccupation during her two-year stay.[50] She had discussions with slave holders, with members of the American Colonization Society and with supporters of immediate emancipation. On 19 November 1834 she attended a meeting of the Boston Female Anti-Slavery Society despite threats of attack from pro-slavery mobs. She accepted a request to offer a word of public sympathy to the abolitionists, expressing her support for their principles on the grounds that slavery was 'inconsistent with the law of God'. She based her decision to speak out on her belief that slavery 'was a question of humanity, not of country or race; a moral, not a merely political question; a general affair, and not one of city, state, party, or nation'.[51]

Martineau's action, like that of Thompson, was reviled in the press and she was soon shunned by polite society and threatened with death if she dared return to the South.[52] Her public stand, however, had won her the admiration of William Lloyd Garrison, who felt that she had 'shown true moral courage' and had made an even greater impact than had Thompson.[53] Another leading abolitionist, James G. Birney, considered that her writing would do more good than all the agitation stirred up by Thompson, because prior to her taking a public stand she was established as a popular figure in the United States.[54]

Martineau's alliance with the radical female abolitionists of Boston was cemented by her election in August 1836 as life member of the Massachusetts Anti-Slavery Society. In her note of thanks she expressed her pleasure that she was now 'one of your sisterhood in outward as well as inward relation'.[55]

As a well-known writer, the most valuable contribution Martineau could make to the American cause was literary. The two books based on her travels, *Society in America* (1837) and *Retrospect of Western Travel* (1838), gave some information on the activities of the radical abolitionists and argued that both slavery and prejudice against free blacks were completely against the principles of the United States constitution.[56] To arouse British sympathy and support for the radical American abolitionists Martineau then wrote a series of articles on 'The Martyr Age of the United States' for the *London and Westminster Review* of December 1838. As her biographer Richard Webb has pointed out, the articles were 'the first full-scale introduction for the general public to the work of the abolitionists' in America.[57] They contained much information on women's activities, culled from the annual reports of the Boston Female Anti-Slavery Society written by its secretary Maria Weston Chapman, a close friend of Martineau. The articles extravagantly praised the radical American abolitionists, especially Garrison, Chapman, and the Grimké sisters, portraying them as anti-slavery martyrs who courageously persisted despite verbal and physical abuse.

Martineau's writings had a considerable impact on abolitionist circles on both sides of the Atlantic. In America Garrison published extracts from *Society in America* and *Retrospect* in the *Liberator*, where the former was also favourably reviewed. The American Anti-Slavery Society printed two thousand copies of 'The Martyr Age', and published as a pamphlet that part of *Society in America* dealing with slavery.[58] In Britain 'The Martyr Age' was reprinted in pamphlet form in 1839 as *A Review of Right and Wrong in Boston in 1835*, and in 1840 the Newcastle-upon-Tyne Emancipation Society republished it with the addition of an appeal written by Martineau on behalf of the Oberlin Institute, a seminary in Ohio for the education of both black and white men and women.[59] Richard Davis Webb, the Dublin abolitionist who became a leading supporter of Garrison in the 1840s and 1850s, later claimed that his interest in American slavery had arisen in part from reading 'The Martyr Age'.[60]

The appreciation of American women for British women's support was expressed at the first national convention of anti-slavery women, held in New York in May 1837, at which a special committee was appointed to send an expression of 'deep gratitude for the aid and encouragement and strengthening sympathy of the women of Great Britain'.[61] That same year the Boston Female Anti-Slavery Society publicly expressed its thanks to its British friends, with whom the members felt united 'by the firmest of all ties – those which bind Christians to the accomplishment of righteous exertions'.[62] The following year the Boston society held up 'the example of our British sisters' in organising the massive female anti-apprenticeship address to the Queen as an example to American women.[63]

After the end of the British anti-apprenticeship campaign in 1838, transatlantic links moved from a pattern of mutual support to one of British support for American abolitionists. The spirit of unproblematic transatlantic co-operation, however, was disrupted in 1839–40 when the American movement split into two factions. From this period it was on the Garrisonian side that transatlantic links developed most strongly, stimulated by personal contacts made at the 1840 World Anti-

Slavery Convention in London. There were important links between both male and female campaigners, but with the decline of local men's anti-slavery societies in Britain through the 1840s and 1850s links between women became increasing vital in maintaining the transatlantic network. The extensive surviving correspondence between British and American women campaigners reveals the developing friendships and discussion of 'non-resistance', free trade and the Anti-Corn Law League, Chartism and women's rights, as well as anti-slavery. A transatlantic sisterhood of radical nonconformist reformers was developing, and some 1,500 letters written by American Garrisonians to and from 66 different British and Irish women survive.[64] In contrast, women who sided with the Tappanites had much more limited contacts with American abolitionists, who concentrated on corresponding with the male leadership of the BFASS.[65]

British women's aid to American abolitionists took the form not only of major donations to anti-slavery bazaars, but also of the exertion of moral pressure through the dispatch of anti-slavery addresses which made use of the language of sisterhood to call on American women to use their influence to bring about the end of slavery. In 1847 three independent Scottish women's societies – the Edinburgh Ladies' Emancipation Society, the Glasgow Female Anti-Slavery Society and the Kirkaldy Female Anti-Slavery Society – collected large numbers of signatures (45,000 in Glasgow and 10,337 in Edinburgh) to addresses from Scottish women to free American women calling on them to oppose slavery; these were exhibited at the Boston bazaar.[66] In 1850 the Glasgow Female New Association for the Abolition of Slavery issued an address 'to their Christian Sisterhood in the United States of America', urging women to arouse public opposition against the Fugitive Slave Law.[67] Finally, in 1853, women were responsible for the single most impressive attempt to exert moral pressure on Americans to abolish slavery: the Stafford House (or Shaftesbury) Address from British women to their American sisters. This address will be discussed in more detail in the final section of this chapter.

LEADERSHIP AND INDEPENDENCE

Harriet Martineau, Elizabeth Pease and Anne Knight, the three key original British members of the transatlantic anti-slavery sisterhood, were joined in the 1840s and 1850s by three other British women: Mary Estlin, Eliza Wigham and Anna Richardson. As will be seen, these important activists took initiatives, formed independent anti-slavery societies, and demonstrated strong leadership qualities.

Five of the six British women at the hub of the transatlantic sisterhood were single – only Anna Richardson was married. The predominance of unmarried women among the female anti-slavery leadership, already evident in the 1823–38 period, was even more striking later. Single women were able to devote a large proportion of their time and energy to the movement, and they made the transatlantic abolitionist network a major focus of their personal lives and friendships. They must be given a large portion of the credit for keeping alive the British anti-slavery movement in the period after 1838.

The transatlantic abolitionist sisterhood always involved the active exchange of information and ideas rather than the passive following by British women of instructions from their American co-workers. This is very evident from the history of the two local anti-slavery societies which were most active in Britain in the 1850s: the Bristol and Clifton Ladies' Anti-Slavery Society and the Edinburgh Ladies' Emancipation Society. The respective leaders of these two independent groups, Mary Estlin and Eliza Wigham, were both supporters of Garrison, and both conducted an extensive correspondence with radical abolitionist men and women in the United States.

The Bristol and Clifton Ladies' Anti-Slavery Society had been founded in 1840 as an auxiliary of the BFASS. Its members, however, became increasingly frustrated in this role owing to the failure of the BFASS to make practical suggestions for action, the petering out of communications with Tappanite American abolitionists, and snubs to secretary Fanny Tribe's attempts to obtain from the BFASS a clear explanation of its policy towards the American societies.[68] Things came to a head in 1851, largely as the result of the efforts of new committee member Mary Estlin to make the society take more initiative and give some support to the Garrisonians.

The women's first initiative was on the controversial issue of church fellowship, and it took the form of pressure on American churches to condemn the Fugitive Slave Act of 1850, which made it legal for Southern slave holders to recapture runaway slaves in the Northern states. Early in 1851 the Bristol and Clifton Ladies' Anti-Slavery Society published a compilation of 'Clerical Teachings on Slavery' and an address which urged ministers attending the annual conferences of their denominations in London not to offer access to their pulpits, or fellowship, to any American clergy who refused to condemn the Fugitive Slave Act. These documents were distributed to nearly 250 nonconformist ministers and religious associations in England and Scotland, as well as to 53 anti-slavery associations and 300 other individuals. The women's initiatives preceded action taken by the BFASS on the issue, and their parent society's decision to act was partly in response to the women's prompting. As a result of both efforts.a number of religious associations, as well as ladies' anti-slavery societies at Birmingham, Edinburgh, Newcastle, Manchester, Chelmsford, Liverpool and Kendal, agreed to take up the issue.[69]

Irritation among society members at the BFASS's attempt to claim all credit for this church fellowship campaign, combined with longer-standing dissatisfaction with the BFASS's leadership, made the group receptive to the influence of Frances Armstrong and Mary Estlin, two local Unitarian women whom American Unitarian minister Rev. Samuel May Jr had won over to Garrison in 1843. Frances Armstrong, an established member of the committee, was backed by her husband, the Unitarian minister Rev. George Armstrong, also a strong supporter of Garrison. Mary Anne Estlin (1820-1902), newly appointed to the committee in February 1851, was backed by her father, Dr John Bishop Estlin, a pioneering opthalmologist by profession who became a leading financial supporter and propagandist for the Garrisonians in England.[70] Mary herself conducted an extensive correspondence with leading American Garrisonians, especially with Maria Weston Chapman, the co-ordinator of the Boston Anti-Slavery Bazaar.[71]

The Estlins' and Armstrongs' efforts were helped by the good impression made by Chapman, Garrison, May and others during their visits to Bristol. Most importantly, Garrisonians offered women a channel for their energies in the form of collecting for the Boston bazaar, sources of direct information on developments in America, and the opportunity to become part of a lively transatlantic abolitionist network. Lured by these attractions, and spurred by Mary Estlin, the Bristol and Clifton Ladies' Anti-Slavery Society voted on 13 November 1851 to sever its connection with the parent body and become an independent group.[72] It was the first and only auxiliary of the BFASS to take this drastic step.

The Bristol women were not content to just quietly leave the BFASS. Instead, Mary Estlin compiled a list of eight charges against the BFASS, and the women set about drawing the attention of all other associations affiliated to the BFASS to the grounds of their separation from the parent society.[73] The BFASS committee clearly took this attempt to undermine its auxiliary network seriously: it asked John Scoble to prepare a response, and agreed to request editors to publish it in newspaper columns opposite the women's charges.[74]

The launch of the Bristol and Clifton Ladies' Anti-Slavery Society as an independent organisation marked the beginning of a period of intense national propaganda by the group under Mary Estlin's leadership.[75] Pamphlets in defence of the Garrisonian American Anti-Slavery Society written by R.D. Webb and the American abolitionist Mr Edmund Quincy were distributed to local anti-slavery associations and in towns 'infested with' BFASS supporters. Mary Estlin compiled a pamphlet contradicting attacks on American Garrisonians made by a

Dr Campbell in January to March 1852 in the *British Banner*, organ of the Independent denomination.[76] The women also produced a *Special Report* explaining their course of action; this was widely circulated to local anti-slavery associations and newspaper editors.[77]

After splitting with the BFASS, the Bristol society remained formally independent of both wings of the anti-slavery movement and made up its own mind on policy issues rather than looking to America for guidance. Mary Estlin explained to American Garrisonians that they must be content with a 'co-alition [sic] and not a union', and in 1853, when the BFASS's vehemently anti-Garrisonian secretary John Scoble was replaced, Mary Estlin successfully sought a rapprochement with the new secretary, Louis Chamerovzow.[78] That winter, after consulting Mary Estlin, Frederick Chesson, along with his father-in-law George Thompson, launched the Manchester Anti-Slavery Union in co-operation with BFASS leaders Louis Chamerovzow and Joseph Sturge. Mary Estlin then became involved in preparing an address to the American Anti-Slavery Society, to come from the new union as an auxiliary of the BFASS. The purpose of this address was to have the BFASS indirectly endorse the Garrisonian wing of the American movement.[79] When the group collapsed in disputes over control, Estlin advised on the foundation of a new Garrisonian group, the Manchester Anti-Slavery League.[80]

Estlin had little confidence in the league, fearing that it would 'crumble through poor management' by incompetent British men. In fact, exhibiting great confidence in women's powers of leadership, she expressed the view that Eliza Wigham of Edinburgh and herself were the only two in the country with 'combined knowledge of what is wanted and faculty or means of *taking steps* in accordance with the demands of the occasion'.[81]

Chesson again solicited Mary Estlin's support when he organised a conference on 1 August 1854 for Garrisonian abolitionists under the auspices of a new group, the North of England Anti-Slavery League.[82] At the same time Chamerovzow approached Estlin, seeking to repair the breach between the Garrisonians and the BFASS.[83] Estlin managed to set up a successful meeting between him and Maria Weston Chapman when both were in Paris, and soon afterwards the first advertisement for the Boston bazaar, which Chapman ran to raise funds for Garrisonians, appeared in the *Anti-Slavery Reporter*.[84]

Mary Estlin was thus a national activist whose advice was actively sought by leading male campaigners. Her independent stance can be compared to that adopted by her friend Eliza Wigham, secretary of the Edinburgh Ladies' Emancipation Society.

Eliza Wigham (1820–99), daughter of John Wigham III, a shawl manufacturer, and his first wife Jane Richardson, was a Quaker who acted as a minister in the Society of Friends. Like her father, she supported a wide variety of social, political and philanthropic movements. In addition to anti-slavery she was active in the peace movement, she acted as vice-president of the Scottish Women's Christian Temperance Union, she became a leading activist for women's rights, and she organised a penny savings bank and mothers' meeting for the poor and helped run a home for destitute young girls.[85]

Wigham corresponded with American Garrisonians from the mid-1840s into the 1870s, keeping in particularly close touch with leading Unitarian activist Rev. Samuel May Jr.[86] Her family was part of a network of leading Quaker anti-slavery families of the period: her stepmother Jane was a member of the Smeal family of Glasgow and had acted as secretary of the Glasgow Ladies' Emancipation Society before her marriage; her sister Mary married Joshuah Edmundson of Dublin; and a member of another branch of the family married into the Richardson family of Newcastle.[87]

This network, cemented by intermarriage, was threatened by differences among its members over which group of American abolitionists to support. In the 1840s John Wigham III, Eliza's father, steered the Edinburgh Emancipation Society into an alliance with the BFASS, whereas his wife Jane joined with his daughter Eliza in promoting the Garrisonians through their leadership of the Ladies' Emancipation Society.[88] Thus, in contrast to the situation in Bristol where Mary Estlin worked in close co-operation with her father, John Bishop Estlin, in promoting the Garrisonians, in Edinburgh male and female members of the leading anti-slavery family were divided in their views of Garrison. It is noteworthy that, despite their subordinate and dependent familial roles as wife and daughter, Jane and Eliza did not allow family loyalty to take priority over anti-slavery principle.

The Edinburgh women plunged headlong into anti-slavery controversy in the 1840s. They promoted the controversial Garrisonian 'Send Back the Money' campaign against the Free Church of Scotland's acceptance of funds from slave holders in the Southern states of the US, launched in 1846 by the Garrisonian Glasgow Emancipation Society.[89] The Edinburgh group appealed especially to women in its Remonstrances to the Free Church, and some of its committee members were involved in setting up a Free Church Anti-Slavery Society, which had a male managing committee and a subsidiary female committee.[90]

Religious differences remained at the centre of anti-slavery controversies in Scotland, and in 1850 the evangelical majority on the ladies' committee voted to sever all connections with American Garrisonians because of their alleged religious infidelity.[91] Jane and Eliza Wigham's decision to remain members of the Edinburgh Ladies'

Emancipation Society after it withdrew support from Garrison drew strong criticism from other Garrisonians including Andrew Paton of the Glasgow Emancipation Society, who accused them of cowardice and compromise.[92] Their tactics, however, succeeded in keeping female abolitionists in Edinburgh united and active at a time when Paton's group was severely weakened by dissension.

The Edinburgh Ladies' Emancipation Society chose an independent path in relation to anti-slavery factions rather than becoming an auxiliary of the BFASS or an openly anti-Garrisonian body.[93] In 1853 Eliza Wigham and her stepmother Jane supported Mary Estlin's attempts at fostering co-operation between Garrisonians and the BFASS.[94] The Edinburgh society subscribed to a wide range of periodicals and produced valuable annual summaries of developments in the United States drawn from a wide range of published sources and direct American contacts. These reports, quoted and highly recommended in the *Anti-Slavery Reporter*, came to act as a nationwide information source.[95]

The BFASS recommendation was a symptom of a more general move on the part of the BFASS leadership from an attempt to exert tight centralised control of the movement in the 1840s, to greater willingness to tolerate and even encourage independent female initiatives as public support for anti-slavery waned in the 1850s. This is evident also in the case of the 'free' produce movement, which was initially promoted by both men and women, with women, as in 1825–33, concentrating on the consumer side of the campaign and men on petitioning Parliament against the abolition of protective duties for 'free'-grown sugar from the British West Indies. The BFASS campaign for protective duties failed, however, partly because it was opposed by provincial abolitionists who were ardent free-traders.[96] As a result the BFASS was led from 1846 to focus on the consumer side of its campaign. The society's 1846 address 'On the Disuse of Slave Produce' was directed especially at 'the female heads of families'.[97]

The boycott campaign was concerned not only with sugar but increasingly also with the import of slave-grown cotton from America.[98] The Birmingham Ladies' Negro's Friend Society, the most active BFASS auxiliary, organised a memorial to the Queen, urging her to set an example by using only 'free'-labour produce and to give encouragement to the cultivation of 'free'-grown cotton in British India.[99] The memorial, read out at the Yearly Meeting of the Society of Friends in London and signed by 59,686 women from all parts of the country, was presented to the Queen in March 1850.[100] While the Queen did not respond to the memorial's requests, it was viewed by both the BFASS and women themselves as a success in terms of the information diffused and the resulting revival of 'almost dormant' interest in the anti-slavery cause among the public.[101]

Having initially promoted the 'free'-produce movement, by the 1850s the BFASS was content to leave it to develop independently under the supervision of the Quaker activist Anna Richardson.[102] Richardson (c. 1806-92), daughter of Esther and Samuel Atkins of Chipping Norton in Oxfordshire, had married Henry Richardson of Newcastle in 1833. Her interest in anti-slavery and in particular in the 'free'-produce movement was inherited from her mother, who abstained from slave-grown sugar, and Anna and her husband were already involved in anti-slavery campaigning in the 1830s. The couple were also active in many other reform and philanthropic causes, including peace, the Bible Society, aid to European emigrants, prison visiting and temperance.[103]

Anna Richardson, a member of the BFASS, had founded the independent Newcastle Ladies' Free Produce Association in 1846 and had issued a circular encouraging women to form similar local groups.[104] From 1847 she also issued 'Monthly Illustrations of American Slavery', in which she provided up-to-date information to nearly a hundred newspaper editors.[105] Then in 1850 she persuaded an American ex-slave, Rev. Henry Highland Garnet, to come to Britain to promote women's involvement in the movement.[106] As a result, around twenty-six free-labour associations were rapidly formed, progress that was recorded in *The Slave*, a periodical launched by Richardson and her husband Henry to promote the movement.[107] In 1853, when a woman wrote to the BFASS secretary Louis Chamerovzow for information on the movement, he forwarded her letter to Anna Richardson explaining that it was a 'ladies' question' and that she had 'this matter under her more immediate direction'.[108] Underlining that the 'free'-produce movement was under her control, Chamerovzow wrote to Richardson of his 'desire to lend a strong helping hand', and asked her to supply him with a list of free-labour associations and sources of 'free'-grown produce.[109]

The major practical problem facing the free-labour movement was obtaining sufficient quantities of guaranteed free-labour cotton goods of high quality and reasonable price. To help solve this problem, a 'free-labour depot' was eventually opened by Mrs Bessie Inglis in London in May 1853 as a non-profit-making enterprise, and women also set up free-labour warehouses in both Dublin and Glasgow.[110]

The London Depot had close links with Ladies' Olive Leaf Circles, a network of peace groups linked to the League of Universal Brotherhood and composed primarily of young middle-class Quaker women.[111] The league had been founded by an American, Elihu Burritt, who came to live in Britain around 1846 and who was a keen proponent of the free-labour movement as an important element of work 'affecting the union and brotherhood of man'. Burritt's magazine, *The Bond of Brotherhood*, carried frequent articles on the free-labour issue, and

Burritt kept in close contact with Anna Richardson who, like Bessie Inglis, was involved in her local Olive Leaf Circle.[112] In 1855, when Anna was forced to cut down on her 'free'-produce work owing to the illness of her husband, Burritt took over the editing of *The Slave*.[113] The 'free'-produce movement thus retained its independence from the BFASS and its close links with Ladies' Olive Leaf Circles.

The 'free'-produce movement continued to be promoted by Anna Richardson and by other Quaker women until 1860 but, despite their efforts, it had little effect.[114] As Louis Billington has pointed out, the export of American cotton to Britain more than tripled between 1840 and 1860, and the United States continued to provide at least eighty per cent of Britain's cotton supply.[115] The movement was nevertheless significant as an example of female organisation and initiative, as a moral protest against slavery, and as an effective means of keeping concern about American slavery alive among British women.

Another area of work in which women played the leading role was in support for fugitive slaves who had fled to Britain. Ellen Richardson, Anna Richardson's sister-in-law, successfully raised funds for the ransom of Frederick Douglass in 1846 and of another leading African-American abolitionist, William Wells Brown, in 1854, enabling them to return to America without fear of re-enslavement.[116] The Glasgow Female New Association raised funds to ransom from slavery the Weims family, whose daughter had fled to Britain.[117] It should be noted, however, that some women opposed the ransoming of individuals on the grounds that it constituted an acknowledgement of their status as slaves.[118]

Other women concentrated on giving practical aid to fugitives. Eliza Wigham of Edinburgh helped to raise funds for William and Ellen Craft. They were given board and tuition at an agricultural school at Ockham in Surrey partly owned by anti-slavery supporter Lady Byron.[119] Other aid was co-ordinated by the Ladies' Society to Aid Fugitives from Slavery, founded at a meeting on 4 November 1853 in the BFASS offices in London. The group was promoted by the BFASS as a means of avoiding criticism that it was using its own funds for purposes not strictly related to anti-slavery. Sarah Ann Alexander (1817–1918) of Stoke Newington Ladies' Anti-Slavery Association, who was the wife of George W. Alexander, a wealthy London Quaker banker who had helped found the BFASS, acted as joint secretary of the society together with Sarah Cogan, the leader of Walthamstow Free Labour Produce Association and the daughter of Unitarian minister, social reformer and anti-slavery supporter Rev. Eliezer Cogan, and Mrs J. Horman-Fisher, whose husband acted as treasurer of the new society.[120] By April 1855 subscriptions and donations of £107 had been collected from more than two hundred individuals, mainly women, and from ladies' anti-slavery associations at Chelmsford, Walthamstow, Birmingham, Halstead, Peckham and Sunderland. Before its demise in January 1856 the society spent a further £60 on aid to fugitives.[121]

The society remained a small-scale affair with limited objectives, soliciting money privately rather than courting publicity. Nevertheless it gave useful practical aid to a small group of friendless and destitute refugees. Its report of 1855 listed five fugitive slaves and three free black people, including two women, who were aided in finding work or education in Britain or helped with passage money for their resettlement in Canada or Africa.[122]

RACE, SEX AND CLASS

Black activists and racial segregation

That the presence of destitute fugitives from slavery in Britain could be dealt with by white abolitionists within the traditional framework of philanthropic patronage of the black victim was a view challenged by the presence of African-American abolitionists such as Frederick Douglass. Such activists might be fugitive slaves, but they were also articulate lecturers who played a leading role in the transatlantic anti-slavery movement.

White attitudes to black abolitionists were ambivalent, and intersecting ideas about proper relations of gender, race and class can be discerned in responses to Douglass and his white British assistant Julia Griffiths; to William and Ellen Craft, fugitive slaves who became involved in the British anti-slavery movement; and to Sarah Parker Remond, a free black woman who toured Britain as an anti-slavery lecturer.

Frederick Douglass, a man of striking looks, fiery oratory and great intelligence and education, made a particularly strong impression on women abolitionists during his anti-slavery lecture tours of Britain and Ireland in the 1840s.[123] Leading Bristol abolitionist John Bishop Estlin, however, rather than praising the important support Douglass was able to raise for the cause among women, instead expressed concern that his popularity would turn his head:

> While observing him at Liverpool, I could not but tremble for his future domestic comfort when he returns to the U.S. You can hardly imagine how he is noticed, – *petted* I may say by *ladies*. Some of them really a little exceed the bounds of propriety, or delicacy, as far as appearances are concerned; yet F.D.'s conduct is most guardedly correct, judicious and decorous. I doubt if he forms intimacies much with gentlemen. . . . My fear is that often associating so much with white women of education and refined

taste and manners, he will feel a 'craving void' when he returns to his own family.[124]

Estlin's male jealousy at the attention Douglass attracted from women took a racialised form in his concern that a black man, in associating with white women, was getting ideas above his station, and in his assumption that an uneducated black wife could not hope to rival the attractions of refined white women. Any interracial contact between the sexes, Estlin implied, holds the danger of impropriety and the potential to disrupt appropriate intraracial sexual relationships. Estlin, who also expressed concern that Mary Carpenter's attempts to involve working-class women in the movement in Bristol would undermine its respectability, clearly saw bonds between black men and white women formed through the anti-slavery movement as threatening to disrupt proper relations of gender, race and class. In a similar vein a white speaker at a British abolitionist meeting in 1853 argued that providing a proper college for black West Indians would be 'stirring up the conceit of the coloured people, who would soon be aspiring to the hands of the daughters of the whites, and seeking to place themselves entirely on a level with them, which could not be tolerated'. It was a black abolitionist who opposed this statement.[125]

This reluctance to treat blacks as social equals, manifested in antipathy to interracial unions, surfaced in the attempts of rival abolitionists in the 1850s to discredit Douglass after his decision to split with Garrison. A key way in which this was done was by hinting at improper relations between him and his unmarried white English helper, Julia Griffiths. Griffiths, a friend of Anna Richardson from Beckenham in Kent, was so impressed by Douglass during his visit to Britain in 1846–47 that she decided to take the dramatic step of travelling to the United States to aid his anti-slavery campaigning. A truly transatlantic abolitionist, Griffiths remained in Rochester, New York, for six years, giving Douglass vital help in running his newspapers and acting as secretary to the Rochester Ladies' Anti-Slavery Society, which co-ordinated collections for the Rochester bazaar, a bazaar which received more valuable goods from Britain and Ireland than from within the United States.[126] Through her untiring efforts she succeeded in rescuing Douglass from his serious debts and placing his papers on a secure financial footing.[127] Douglass himself was later to acknowledge Griffiths' contribution: 'to no one person was I more indebted for substantial assistance'.[128]

In 1855 Julia Griffiths returned to Britain to raise further funds for Douglass.[129] She was never to return to the United States, though she remained in correspondence with Douglass after her marriage in 1859 to the Rev. H.D. Crofts of Halifax. Between 1856 and 1859 she travelled through Scotland, England and Ireland, forming a network of fifteen 'Christian' female societies in rivalry to the network of 'infidel' Garrisonian groups, to collect for the Rochester rather than the Boston bazaar (see Appendix for list of societies).[130] These female societies constituted the largest group of new anti-slavery societies since the formation of local auxiliaries by BFASS agents in the early 1840s.

The *Anti-Slavery Advocate*, bitter at Griffiths' outspoken attacks on the Garrisonians for their alleged religious infidelity, did not scruple to indulge in character assassination, portraying her as an interfering woman exerting a baneful influence over Douglass and having an inappropriate involvement in his private financial affairs.[131]

William and Ellen Craft's relationship to the British movement was somewhat different to that of Frederick Douglass: rather than being visiting lecturers they were fugitive slaves who lived in England for nineteen years and became members of the British anti-slavery movement. Their lives in Britain show a successful process of extricating themselves from the patronage of upper- and middle-class abolitionists and establishing themselves as a self-sufficient working-class couple who played important roles in the anti-slavery movement.

Ellen Craft (1826–90) and William Craft (1824–1900) were Georgia slaves who had staged a celebrated dramatic escape from slavery with Ellen dressed as a man and posing as the white master of her husband.[132] They became active in the anti-slavery movement in Boston, but with the passage of the Fugitive Slave Act in 1850 they were forced to flee to Britain. In Britain the Crafts joined fellow black abolitionist William Wells Brown on anti-slavery platforms around the country. Harriet Martineau arranged for them to spend two years at Ockham school in Surrey, a vocational training school funded by Lady Byron and under the superintendence of the abolitionist Dr Lushington and his daughters.[133] They were then offered positions as superintendent and matron of the industrial department, but decided instead to open a lodging house in London, where William could also continue his trade as a cabinet maker. They continued to be active in the anti-slavery movement; both provided hospitality to visiting black abolitionists and William lectured on behalf of the 'free'-produce movement. In 1859 both became members of the London Emancipation Committee, and in the 1860s Ellen worked in the Freedmen's Aid movement while William spent several years in Dahomey working for the African Aid Society. In 1869 they returned to America and in 1875 established a farming co-operative and school in Georgia.[134] Ellen's forthright hatred of slavery was expressed in 1853 when, in response to rumours that she was tired of life in freedom, she issued a public statement that she 'had much rather starve in England, a free woman, than be a slave for the best man that ever breathed upon the American continent'.[135]

Ellen Craft was not the only African-American woman to become actively involved in the British anti-slavery movement at this period. Sarah Parker Remond (1826–94) was the daughter of a prosperous free black tradesman from Salem, Massachusetts, and the sister of prominent Garrisonian abolitionist Charles Lenox Remond, who had travelled to Britain as an anti-slavery lecturer in the 1840s. Sarah Remond herself had been appointed in 1857 as a travelling lecturer for the American Anti-Slavery Society.[136] From her own account, it is clear that she came to England for three reasons: to 'for a time enjoy freedom' from the pro-slavery atmosphere and racial segregation in America, to 'serve the anti-slavery cause', and to gain access to the education denied to her as a black woman in the United States.[137]

On arrival in England she undertook a gruelling series of anti-slavery lecture tours in Britain and Ireland between January 1859 and January 1861. These were of great importance as the first public talks by a woman to mass mixed British audiences on the anti-slavery question; their significance to the development of the women's rights movement in Britain will be discussed in the following chapter.

Deciding to remain in England for an extended period, Remond, who stated that her 'strongest desire through life has been to be educated', enrolled at Bedford College for Ladies in London.[138] She boarded with its founder Elizabeth Reid, a pioneer in women's education and a supporter of Garrison. In 1866 Remond worked in London University Hospital training as a nurse; a few years later she was to move to Italy to train as a physician and there to settle and to marry.[139]

Remond's major anti-slavery lectures in Britain were attended by thousands of people, and perhaps because she was removed from British class politics and gender conventions by virtue both of her race and her nationality, she was able to appeal to audiences ranging from male factory operatives in Yorkshire to fashionable ladies in London. Between December 1859 and February 1860 she lectured successively in Warrington, Ireland, Bristol, Manchester, Bury, and the Leeds area; from October 1860 to February 1861 she spoke in Scotland at Edinburgh, Hawick, Glasgow and Dumfries, and south of the border at Carlisle and Ulverstone.[140]

Remond was an experienced public speaker, clear and forceful.[141] Stressing that she was the agent of no society, though she identified herself with the Garrisonians, she presented herself as a representative of her race and spoke out against both slavery and racial discrimination in the United States. She pleaded especially on behalf of her own sex, who were suffering under the 'cruelty and licentiousness of their brutal masters', relating cases of women who would rather die and kill their own children than continue to live under the debasing system of slavery. Remond stressed that the plight of the enslaved woman was

143

far worse than that of the English seamstress, and urged English women to 'demand for the black woman the protection and rights enjoyed by the white'.[142]

In her speeches Remond stressed the sexual exploitation of black women under slavery:

> In the open market place women are exposed for sale – their persons not always covered. Yes, I can tell you English men and women, that women are sold into slavery with cheeks like the lily and the rose, as well as those that might compare with the wing of the raven. They are exposed for sale, and subjected to the most shameful indignities. The more Anglo-Saxon blood that mingles with the blood of the slave, the more gold is poured out when the auctioneer has a woman for sale, because they are sold to be concubines for white Americans. They are not sold for plantation slaves.[143]

The presence of 800,000 'mulatto' slaves in the Southern states was, she claimed, proof of the licentiousness of white Southern men.[144] This, then, was the truth about interracial sex: not the lust of black men for white women conjured up by pro-slavery advocates and also haunting some white abolitionists, but the sexual exploitation of black women slaves by the white men who owned them.

After one of Remond's first speeches, in Warrington, a local abolitionist, Mrs Walter Ashton, made a speech in which she 'said she felt proud to acknowledge her as a sister' and presented her with a watch inscribed 'Presented to S.P. Remond, by Englishwomen, her sisters, in Warrington. February 2nd, 1860'. Sarah Remond responded emotionally:

> I do not need this testimonial. I have been received here as a sister by white women for the first time in my life. I have been removed from the degradation which overhangs all persons of my complexion; and I have felt most deeply that since I have been in Warrington and in England that I have received a sympathy I never was offered before. I have therefore no need of this testimonial of sympathy, but I receive it as the representative of my race with pleasure. In this spirit I accept it, and I believe I shall be faithful to that race now and for ever.[145]

In this way Remond, who as a free, educated and Christian black woman visiting Britain as an abolitionist might have been granted exceptionally favourable treatment, transformed an assertion of sisterhood made to her as an individual into a claim for white Englishwomen's sisterhood with all her race.

Remond saw herself as a representative of both enslaved and free blacks, and she played an important role in drawing British abolition-ists' attention to the disabilities suffered by free black people through-out the United States. In her short autobiography, published in Britain in 1861, she stressed that 'prejudice against colour has always been the one thing, above all others, which has cast its gigantic shadow over my whole life', and she condemned the establishment of separate churches and schools for black people by supposed well-wishers as 'based completely on prejudice against colour' and leading to 'immense dis-advantage to the descendant of the African race'.[146] She continued to fight against racial discrimination whilst in Britain, drawing public attention to two incidents – one involving discrimination against her sister Caroline R. Putman on a Cunard liner during her passage to Liverpool, the second the refusal of the American legation in London to stamp a visa in her American passport for a visit to Paris on the grounds that blacks were excluded from American citizenship.[147]

The issue of racial discrimination and racial segregation in the United States, however, was never focused on by the majority of British abolitionists. Rather it occasionally surfaced as a divisive controversy. The issue was most forcefully addressed by Elizabeth Pease, whose opposition to racial segregation in American Quaker meetings was expressed in her pamphlet on 'The Society of Friends, in the United States – their views of the anti-slavery question and treatment of the people of colour'. This pamphlet presented testimonies from Quakers and black activists concerning the lack of support among the Quaker leadership for abolition and the existence of separate Negro pews in Quaker meeting houses. Pease's aim was to persuade British Quakers to send a remonstrance to their co-religionists in America, but her pamphlet was strongly condemned and she was accused of being an enemy of the Society of Friends.[148] While this response may partly be attributed to ill-feeling between Pease, a Garrisonian, and the pro-BFASS leadership of the Society of Friends, and partly to internal religious conflicts in the Society between evangelicals and Hicksites, it nevertheless exposed the unwillingness of the British Quaker leader-ship to take a firm stand on the issue of racial segregation.

The influence of *Uncle Tom's Cabin*

Transatlantic anti-slavery campaigners had never viewed black people in general as social equals, though exceptions were always made for the Western educated and Christian. Pro-slavery stereotypes of violent, licentious and lazy blacks were combated by an alternative racial stereotype of the passive, degraded victim. This image had widespread appeal to the British public, as was demonstrated by the tremendous reception accorded to Harriet Beecher Stowe's famous anti-slavery

145

novel, *Uncle Tom's Cabin*, published in Britain in 1852. The novel led to a dramatic upsurge in public interest in the cause which abolitionists eagerly exploited.

Uncle Tom's Cabin became a best-seller in Britain, and within a year more than one million copies had been sold.[149] The book had a strong appeal to women, and the secretary of the Manchester Ladies' Anti-Slavery Society reported an increase in female anti-slavery activism in the town stimulated by the novel.[150] The source of the novel's appeal to women lay partly, as Jane Tompkins has argued, in its status as the prime example of the popular domestic and sentimental novel of the nineteenth century, written 'by, for, and about women'. Tompkins describes it as 'the story of salvation through motherly love' which 'represents a monumental effort to reorganise culture from the woman's point of view'.[151] Although Tompkins' analysis certainly helps to explain the novel's strong impact on British women schooled in evangelical ideology and the cult of feminine sensitivity, it suffers from her failure to explore the racial dimensions of its appeal.

Stowe became a symbol of white women's philanthropic and mission-ary power to bring freedom and Christianity to grateful black slaves. This was a racially based power which crossed class lines, for it was one in which even the humble female chapel-goer and mission supporter could participate. The ladies of Surrey Chapel described the silver inkstand they presented to Stowe on her visit to England thus:

> The female figure is intended to represent yourself presenting the precious Book of God to a fettered slave. In a devotional attitude, he blesses his Heavenly Father for the gift, and asks that he may use the freedom which he anticipates aright. . . .[152]

The fettered slave may be taken to represent the character of Uncle Tom from Stowe's novel, a figure of Christian patience and passive suffering recalling the emblem of the fettered victim of slavery used by the British anti-slavery movement since the 1780s. The image of Stowe herself may be compared with the engraving of a white woman representing Liberty reading from the Bible to a group of black children, which appeared on the cover of an almanac produced in London to celebrate Stowe's novel (Figure 13).[153] In both these images the spiritual freedom brought by Christianity is emphasised over the physical liberty brought by abolition.

Among African-Americans, 'Uncle Tom' has become a term of abuse for a passive black who is seen to collaborate with slavery and white supremacy. As Angela Davis and others have pointed out, Stowe made use of racist stereotypes of blacks for anti-slavery purposes; illus-trations in the British edition of the novel capture this image clearly. Jacqueline Kaye's attempt to reinterpret Uncle Tom as a positive figure

THE

UNCLE TOM'S CABIN

ALMANACK

OR

ABOLITIONIST MEMENTO.

FOR

1853.

LONDON:
JOHN CASSELL, LA BELLE SAUVAGE YARD, LUDGATE HILL;
AND ALL BOOKSELLERS.

PRICE ONE SHILLING.

Figure 13 Cover sheet, *The Uncle Tom's Almanack or Abolitionist Memento, 1853*
(London: John Cassell, 1853).

of Christ-like self-sacrifice fails to address the question: positive for whom? Uncle Tom was a positive figure for white abolitionists since he left them a role in bringing about the end of slavery. For this role to be maintained, black nobility had to be represented by white abolitionists as characterised by passive suffering rather than active resistance.[154]

As Tompkins points out, it would seem that Stowe's aim was to achieve a change of heart in the reader rather than to inspire specific actions against slavery.[155] British abolitionists, however, were keen to convert the generalised anti-slavery sentiment evoked by the novel into practical action. Appealing especially to women, the book elicited the most important campaigning response from them. It was they who organised the 'Penny Offering' from readers of the book, and it was members of the Glasgow Female New Association for the Abolition of Slavery who invited Stowe to visit Britain, where she carried out a successful anti-slavery tour.[156] Women were also responsible for the major campaigning response to Stowe's novel: the 'Affectionate and Christian Address of Many Thousands of the Women of England to Their Sisters, the Women of the United States of America'.

This Stafford House Address marked a new departure in female anti-slavery campaigning since it originated not with the middle-class nonconformist women who had previously dominated female anti-slavery organisation, but with a group of aristocratic Anglican 'ladies' and the members of the fashionable London literary set who met at Stafford House, London home of Harriet Elizabeth Georgina Leveson-Gower, Duchess of Sutherland (1806–68), Mistress of the Robes to Queen Victoria and patroness of the Ladies' Negro Education Society.[157]

The address, launched on 26 November 1852, originated in a proposal by the prominent philanthropist Anthony Ashley Cooper, Seventh Earl of Shaftesbury, a Factory Act campaigner and a leader of the Ragged School Union. Shaftesbury was himself responsible for its wording, which controversially did not call for immediate emancipation, the principle long since adopted by all committed anti-slavery campaigners in both the United States and Britain. Instead it called on women to use their influence to bring about the amelioration and eventual removal of slavery, stating:

> We do not shut our eyes to the difficulties, nay, the dangers that might beset the immediate abolition of that long-established system; we see and admit the necessity of preparation for so great an event . . . .[158]

This wording may be attributed partly to Shaftesbury's ignorance of the policy of the established anti-slavery movement, partly to aristocratic fear of sudden change in the established order of things, and partly to the failure of *Uncle Tom's Cabin* to make clear Stowe's own position on immediatism. The committee of the BFASS, who had not been consulted on the wording, unsuccessfully tried to get it changed 'on behalf of many ladies of our acquaintance, deeply interested in the anti-slavery cause'.[159] Women activists associated with the BFASS thus decided to adopt an amended address which declared the supposed dangers of immediate emancipation to be morally irrelevant in the face of the 'Christian duty to terminate, without delay, a system which deprives man of his rightful freedom'.[160]

Women were very successful in obtaining signatures to one or other of the addresses, organising door-to-door canvasses, and contacting local ministers, anti-slavery societies and Olive Leaf Circles.[161] People ascribed their success to the popularity of *Uncle Tom's Cabin*, which had 'found its way into almost every family of all grades'.[162] By March 1853 the original address had amassed 562,848 signatures, the amended ones around 200,000. The addresses were presented to Mrs Stowe for transmission to American women.[163]

These totals were similar to the number of signatories to the ladies' anti-apprenticeship address to the Queen of 1837–38, and the address represents the largest single British anti-slavery effort of the period. It represented the climax of British attempts to exert moral pressure on Americans to abolish the slave system. It gained more public attention, positive and negative, in both Britain and the United States than any other British anti-slavery activity of the period.

In the United States the address provoked predictably polarised reactions. It was enthusiastically received by abolitionists but was subject to virulent attack in the Southern and pro-slavery press.[164] The Duchess of Sutherland's hope that an address from women would be seen as free from 'political motives' and as a reflection of 'domestic' rather than 'national' feeling proved ill-founded.[165] The most widely circulated condemnation, by Juliet Gardiner (1820–89), wife of ex-president and Virginia slave plantation owner John Tyler, contrasted Southern women, portrayed as ideal wives and mothers who presided benevolently over the domestic economy of slave plantations, with English women who went outside their proper sphere by interfering with the internal concerns of another country.[166] It was, as Evelyn Pugh has pointed out, 'not only a defense of slavery, but a classic justification of the role and life-style of the idealized Southern woman'.[167]

Working-class antagonism

In contrast to this defence of the plantocracy, criticisms of the address in Britain reflected and exploited working-class antagonism to the aristocracy. A pamphlet in the form of a letter from an 'Englishwoman' concerning slavery at home argued that it was hypocritical for fashion-able ladies to lecture American women while poor seamstresses toiled to supply them with fripperies. The seamstress, portrayed as the pathetic slave of fashionable ladies, was a focus of concern among socially conscious artists and poets at this period.[168] *Reynolds Newspaper*, a popular radical paper which delighted in attacking the aristocracy, carried an editorial describing 'The Titled Conclave at Stafford House' as 'the vampire-brood which preys upon the vitals of our industrial population'. It asserted that independent working-class women had for the most part 'wisely abstained' from signing the address, and argued that working women had been too much oppressed by these ladies 'for any union or coalition to take place'.[169] Another male attacker adopted a tone of masculine superiority towards the 'pretty little parliament' at Stafford House, asserting that popular clamour for emancipation was useless unless led by government and nation: only then could 'manly, practical results' be secured.[170]

Such attacks were replied to both in editorials in the *Anti-Slavery Reporter* and by female abolitionists like Sarah Cogan, co-secretary of the committee which organised the amended address, and Mrs Henry Grey, wife of an Edinburgh minister and one of the many women who had signed the address. Starting from the position that it was women's duty to exercise a moral influence against slavery, they argued that the attacks were in fact written by pro-slavery male editors rather than women, that the position of poor women in Britain was better than that of slaves, and that women abolitionists were in any case involved in philanthropic work among their own poor as well as in anti-slavery campaigning.[171]

Class tensions in the anti-slavery movement in the 1840s and 1850s can be related to the views which working-class activists and middle-class women abolitionists held of each other. The extent to which working-class women either supported or expressed hostility to the anti-slavery cause at this period is difficult to determine. Leaders of female societies of all alignments were middle-class women from similar backgrounds to those who had supported anti-slavery in the 1820s and 1830s. Patricia Hollis has emphasised class antagonism and Chartist disruption of anti-slavery meetings in the 1840s, and there is some evidence in support of this interpretation in relationship to women.[172] In 1840 Elizabeth Fry's daughter Katherine wrote with horror of an anti-slavery meeting at Norwich which she and other ladies had been forced to leave when it was disrupted by Chartists calling for the rights of English white slaves. Among them were 'some women who excited the men, and whose shrill voices out-screamed the roar of the men. I heard they were three well-known Socialist sisters, the vilest of the vile'.[173] Chartist women referred to the suffering of working-class women as 'the wrongs of sisters in slavery'.[174] Class antagonism among women was made explicit by Owenite socialist lecturer Emma Martin, whose 1844 criticism of philanthropic ladies who wept over the sufferings of people in distant countries while ignoring the exploitation of poor women in their own land referred specifically to supporters of foreign missions but could equally have been applied to abolitionists.[175]

Nevertheless, there is also evidence about women to back Betty Fladeland's contrasting stress on the involvement of Chartist leaders in anti-slavery organisations, and support for Chartism by middle-class abolitionists.[176] In the first place, there is evidence that some working-class women supported anti-slavery. In Bristol, Mary Carpenter succeeded in interesting poor women in the cause despite opposition from leading local abolitionist John Bishop Estlin, who considered that 'it is the more educated classes here that can alone benefit the A.S. movement'.[177] In Scotland the 'deep poverty' of the young women who were active in the Perth Ladies' Anti-Slavery Society was remarked upon, and it was stated that most earned their own livelihood 'by their head or their hands'.[178] The Glasgow Female Anti-Slavery Society, like the Ladies' Auxiliary Emancipation Society it replaced, opened itself to working women by setting no minimum subscription and obtaining a considerable number of members who subscribed only a shilling.[179] While there is no definite evidence for Chartist women's involvement in anti-slavery organisations in Glasgow, this seems probable given that Chartist men are known to have been involved in the men's society, and that an American Garrisonian, Abby Kimber, wrote to George Thompson in 1840 praising the public activism of the 'Lady Chartists of Glasgow'.[180]

There is also evidence that some middle-class women anti-slavery campaigners in Britain, like leading male abolitionists, were sympathetic to Chartism. This applied to Harriet Martineau, Anne Knight and Elizabeth Pease.[181] Pease, in a series of letters to her American abolitionist friends, informed them about Chartism and her own sympathy for the movement. She described herself as an *'ultra radical'* who fully sympathised with the 'moral force' Chartists, though she condemned those who appealed to physical force. Just as working-class Chartist women were considered particularly 'vile' by philanthropic ladies, so Pease's support as a middle-class woman for Chartism was considered by her friends to be *'ungenteel'* and *'vulgar'*. Her Chartist sympathies threatened her image of respectability and thus her status as a lady: 'It is thought most unaccountable for a *gentleman* to say he sees nothing wrong in these – but for a lady to do so is almost outrageous.'[182]

The particular opprobrium directed at middle-class women who held radical views was also suffered by Edinburgh anti-slavery activist

Harriet Gairdner, who wrote thus to Garrisonian fund-raiser John Collins in 1840:

> In this country a woman who holds really liberal opinions is even more out of place than a man . . . this latter is only blamed as rash, wrong headed, or at the worst infidel but still only his judgment is called in question and that is bad enough. But the former had also to encounter the obloquy of being supposed to have both heart and head depraved, she is shunned as unfeminine and that then is obliged constantly to converse on only the most indifferent topics or else hold one's peace . . . .[183]

Pease based her support of Chartism not on philanthropic sympathy for the oppressed but on 'the grand principle of the natural equality of man – a principle alas! almost buried, in this land, beneath the rubbish of an hereditary aristocracy and the farce of a state religion'.[184] Not shrinking from the analogy between the position of workers and of slaves made by Chartists themselves, she described the contention that working people were not ready for full rights to be 'nothing but a slaveholder's argument'.[185] Despite her own family's position as wealthy manufacturers and employers, Pease expressed her total sympathy for workers who went on strike and attacked factories in Lancashire and Yorkshire, arguing that they were driven 'almost to desperation' by those who 'consider they are but chattels made to minister to their luxury and add to their wealth'.[186]

Pease was in close contact with Chartists in her home town of Darlington, exchanging information with them and helping to distribute their pamphlets. She believed that the working and middle classes should form an alliance against the aristocracy, and was thus enthusiastic about Joseph Sturge's organisation of a Complete Suffrage Union. She took an even more radical line than Sturge, however, accusing him of pandering too much to middle-class prejudices in rejecting the name 'Chartist' and for taking initiatives without adequately consulting the working-class Chartist leadership.

More broadly, Pease attributed most of the evils afflicting British society to 'class legislation' such as the Corn Laws, monopoly, and union of Church and state.[187] She reported enthusiastically on the Anti-Corn Law campaign, and on women's involvement in organising a national bazaar and preparing a memorial to the Queen. She felt that aristocratic resistance to this campaign was doing immense good in

> teaching the middle classes their powerlessness to resist the Aristocracy and landocracy and shewing them that the political liberty and equality of the people, whose rights they have too long

treated with neglect or disdain, is necessary to *their own* independence.[188]

Pease nevertheless wished anti-slavery to remain a single-issue
campaign, and warned Collins that Garrisonian attempts to enlist
Chartist support in their battle with the BFASS would compromise
anti-slavery principles and independence of action:

> What had the resolution about universal suffrage to do with the
> object of the meeting if they will not permit you to be *abolitionists*
> on your own ground, without subscribing to their views as well, I
> wd have no more to do with *them*, than I wd with those among the
> clergy who require submission to *their* domination.[189]

Pease's conviction of the identity of working- and middle-class
interests, a view she shared with other middle-class supporters of
Chartism such as her anti-slavery rival Joseph Sturge, involved an
overlooking of working-class resentment at middle-class employers like
Pease's own father. This led to her failure to understand Chartists'
ambivalent attitude towards the anti-slavery movement: on the one
hand, working women and men could identify with the suffering of
slaves and saw anti-slavery and Chartist objectives as indivisible; on the
other hand, resentment at anti-slavery campaigners from a class
responsible for their exploitation led them to disrupt anti-slavery
meetings with calls for their own rights.

7

THE 'WOMAN QUESTION'

From its earliest stages, women's participation in the British anti-slavery movement raised central questions concerning women's role and position in society. These surfaced both in debates on the role of women in the movement and in comparisons between the position of enslaved women in the British colonies and 'free' women in Britain.

As we saw in the first part of this book, between 1825 and 1833 British women anti-slavery campaigners succeeded in establishing that their activities were an acceptable extension of their domestic and religious duties as defined in the dominant and mutually reinforcing ideologies of 'separate spheres' and evangelicalism. Women did not challenge their exclusion from positions of formal power and authority within the movement, and female voices remained silent at meetings of national committees or conferences or public meetings. Finding sufficient scope for their activities within women-only organisations, women campaigners' approach may be described as feminine – self-consciously female – rather than feminist. The women may be labelled maternalist activists: they were hieresses of Hannah More in the sense that they celebrated women's unique qualities and existing social roles as wives and mothers, stressed the domestic basis of female duties and represented their anti-slavery campaigning as a duty rather than a right. Preoccupied with maintaining their respectability, they distanced themselves from the egalitarian feminist legacy and unconventional private life of Mary Wollstonecraft, who had used the language of citizenship to stress women's rights and who had compared the position of British women to that of slaves.

Given the way in which women *represented* their anti-slavery activities, one might conclude that anti-slavery did not provide a fertile ground for the development of feminism in Britain. However, if we focus on what women actually *did* we see that in practice it could provide such a ground. Women campaigners were not simply philanthropists: they were involved in a political movement, the leading reform movement of the period, one that pioneered methods of extra-Parliamentary agitation in order to bring about legislative change. They played a central role in shaping public opinion and in applying pressure to Parliament. Their involvement led them to develop independent organisations, to form a national female network, to co-ordinate mass petitions, to articulate a specifically feminine campaigning perspective focused on concern for enslaved women and the disruption of family life under slavery, and to engage in systematic canvassing. In addition, on the issue of immediate abolition women showed a willingness to challenge male authority on a key matter of policy.

Thus, while women campaigners stressed that they were satisfied with their present social position and indeed wished to extend it to enslaved women, their experiences as anti-slavery organisers provided them with the skills, self-confidence, connections, sense of collective identity, and commitment to public and political activism which were essential to the development of organised feminism.

That this feminist potential was to some extent translated into reality was in part the result of developments external to the British anti-slavery movement, and in particular to the growth of abolitionist-feminism in America from 1837 onwards. This chapter will explore the varied response of British abolitionists to their American co-workers' open demand for women's rights, a demand which threatened to upset the balance which British women had achieved between reinforcing, accepting, negotiating, subverting and challenging their social roles in the course of the campaign against British colonial slavery. The evolving relationship between anti-slavery and feminism will then be traced through the 1840s and 1850s into the 1860s and 1870s.

A DAWNING AWARENESS

American women abolitionists, who in the late 1820s and early 1830s had looked to British women for guidance and formed separate ladies' anti-slavery societies on similar lines to British groups, by 1837 began to expand the range of their campaigning activities and organisations beyond those of their British sisters in several ways. In May 1837 they organised a successful national women's Anti-Slavery Convention which attracted more than a hundred female delegates, both black and white. These delegates were addressed by Angelina Grimké, a white Quaker abolitionist from the American South, who urged women to break their own bonds so that they could aid enslaved women more effectively. Grimké went on in late 1837 to address large meetings of both men and women as a travelling anti-slavery lecturer, following a precedent set by black Boston abolitionist Maria W. Stewart in 1831–33. Persisting in the anti-slavery activities despite the public condemnation of Congregational ministers, in February 1838 Grimké became the first woman to address the Massachussetts legislature. Her activities were wholeheartedly supported by her sister, Sarah Grimké, who in 1838 wrote the first serious American discussion of women's rights, *Letters on the Equality of the Sexes, and the Condition of Women*. The Grimkés also gained the support and encouragement of leading male abolitionists such as William Lloyd Garrison.[1]

News of these American developments reached leading British women abolitionists through their American contacts, through reports in periodicals and through Harriet Martineau's descriptions in 'The Martyr Age', in which she praised American women activists for both fulfilling their duties and exercising their rights.[2] Martineau's *Society in America* (1837) contained her first explicitly feminist statements – which her biographer V.K. Pichanick has rightly described as 'a too much neglected early manifesto of the women's rights campaign'.[3] Breaking with the dominant tendency among British women abolitionists to contrast their own position with that of enslaved women, Martineau likened the position of 'free' women in North American society to that of slaves. Both women and slaves, Martineau argued, were denied the rights to independence and property 'on no better plea than the right of the strongest'. The acquiescence of many women to their present powerless position, like the fear of some slaves about freedom, 'proves nothing but the degradation of the injured party'. Arguments against women engaging in politics on the grounds of its incompatibility with their other duties were as invalid as Tory arguments against the enfranchisement of artisans and planters' opposition to the freeing of slaves.[4]

The influence of American women abolitionists on Martineau's feminist ideas is evident in her defence of their public actions on the grounds that 'fidelity of conscience' must take precedence over false notions of 'retiring modesty'. Openly challenging the ideology of 'separate spheres' in words echoing those of the Grimké sisters, she argued that women's sphere should not be that appointed by men and 'bounded by their ideas of propriety' but rather 'the sphere appointed by God, and bounded by the powers which He has bestowed'.[5]

Martineau's writings formed part of the first stirrings of agitation for women's rights among women and men of all classes in Britain. Analogies between the position of women and slaves were made by Owenite socialist feminists, as in, for example, the articles by 'Kate' and public lecturer Mrs Leman Grimstone published between 1835 and 1839 in the *New Moral World*.[6] Some Chartists supported the inclusion of women in their demand for universal suffrage. Lady Caroline Norton in 1836 embarked on a campaign to secure women's right to custody of her children following divorce. In the temperance movement, in which many women anti-slavery campaigners had become involved since its beginning in 1829, Clara Lucas Balfour shocked respectable opinion in 1837 by lecturing in public to mixed audiences on the evils of drink.[7]

Such developments, in combination with news of events in the United States, affected a small number of influential British women anti-slavery campaigners. Chelmsford activist Anne Knight became a supporter of women's rights at this period, influenced both by English and French utopian socialists and feminists and by contact with American women abolitionists.[8] In 1834, unable to obtain George Thompson for an anti-slavery speaking tour through France, she herself addressed several French scientific congresses and numerous smaller gatherings.[9] From around 1838 she began corresponding with radical American abolitionists Angelina Grimké, William Lloyd Garrison and Maria Weston Chapman. Her letters reveal her admiration of American women abolitionists' courageous stand in the face of attacks from both pro-slavery and anti-feminist opponents. She described the Grimké sisters and Margaretta Forten, a leading black member of the Philadelphia Female Anti-Slavery Society, as 'brave *Amazons*', and wrote an admiring letter to Angelina Grimké in which she likened her to Joan of Arc and signed herself 'thy fellow-warrior though quite a subaltern'.[10] Knight similarly wrote to Maria Weston Chapman of Boston: 'I fear your women to be far above us in the attitude of christian action and endurance'.[11] At this stage, however, Knight did not attempt to introduce the women's rights issue into the British anti-slavery movement.

Praise of American women abolitionists was also expressed, if in rather more measured tones, by the Darlington abolitionist and Chartist sympathiser Elizabeth Pease. She corresponded with the Grimké sisters and William Lloyd Garrison in 1837–38 on developments in American abolition, including the role of women in the movement. In December 1837 Sarah Grimké wrote to Pease about her sister Angelina delivering public lectures on slavery to mixed audiences of men and women, stating that 'Wherever we went the question came up, what right have *women* to hold public meetings', to which their reply had been that 'the fact that women had been qualified to plead the cause of the dumb was the best argument in favor of their *right* to do it'.[12] In response Elizabeth Pease expressed her admiration of the Grimkés for moving 'steadily onward in your path of duty'. She believed it to be their duty just as 'any female minister in our Society is required to preach the Gospel'.[13] Pease's Quakerism thus made her sympathetic to women speaking out when they felt impelled by their conscience to do so, though she stressed that the Grimkés' action was, and would remain, exceptional:

unusual tho' it may be, and *unusual* it will doubtless continue to be, *few* indeed of our sex being qualified to stand so conspicuously forward, as advocates for the oppressed.[14]

Pease was also concerned to distinguish women's duty to the anti-slavery cause from the advocacy of women's rights for its own sake. She admitted that she was 'rather startled' to hear of the Grimkés' intention to advocate the 'rights of women', feeling that it was a *'delicate subject'* which she had much rather 'remained unassailed by *words* at least'. She questioned whether those who censured women speakers were not better silenced, and the fastidious more readily convinced 'by *actions* than by words', asking:

> is not the right of woman to act on all moral questions, and her determination to maintain that right *most* securely established, by a modest yet resolute and unflinching perseverance in *doing all she can* heedless of the scorn and the jeers, the ridicule of the opposition of those who are striving to build up the kingdom of darkness?[15]

For Pease the women's rights issue was at this period one to be discussed in terms of American abolition rather than introduced into the British anti-slavery movement. Unlike Harriet Martineau, Pease was unwilling to challenge the ideology of 'separate spheres' which had hitherto provided the framework for women's anti-slavery effort. Her position was similar to that taken by the Ladies' Auxiliary of the Glasgow Emancipation Society under the leadership of her Quaker friend Jane Smeal. The members of this group, while extravagantly praising the forthright stand of Boston women abolitionists in the face of mob violence in 1837, defined their *own* role as auxiliary and supportive and stressed that they had 'no desire to step beyond their appropriate sphere'.[16]

CONTROVERSY AND DEBATE

Up to 1840 dissension among American abolitionists over women's rights could be, and largely was, ignored by all but a minority of female and male anti-slavery campaigners in Britain. The World Anti-Slavery Convention, organised by the British Foreign Anti-Slavery Society (BFASS) and held in London in 1840, completely altered this situation. In a dramatic public way it introduced into the British arena a crucial point of dissension between supporters and opponents of William Lloyd Garrison in the United States: the right of women abolitionists to fully participate in mixed assemblies as office holders, public lecturers and delegates. For the first time the 'woman question' was openly discussed by men in a British anti-slavery forum, and for the first time many British women abolitionists began to consider the issues involved.

The point of contention was straightforward: Garrisonian American abolitionists appointed a number of female delegates to attend the conference, but the committee of the BFASS refused to accept the women's credentials. The women's male supporters challenged this decision, and as a result the first day of the convention was devoted to a heated debate on women's rights.[17] This debate was between men: British women abolitionists witnessed these events as silent spectators, since they were allowed to attend only as non-participating visitors, seated apart from the men (see Figure 1). The conference was the forum in which for the first time women's hitherto taken-for-granted exclusion from national anti-slavery committees and delegate conferences became the subject of debate; it was also the point at which the BFASS converted female exclusion into explicit policy and at which a small number of men for the first time argued for the full and equal participation of women.

Ten British men spoke out either against the acceptance of the women delegates or against raising the issue at the convention, whereas only three spoke in favour of the women. The group opposed to female delegates, which included five clergymen, was not against all female activity outside the home. Indeed these men stressed the high value they attached to women's efforts in the anti-slavery cause – provided that these remained within their appropriate sphere. George Stacey, speaking on behalf of the BFASS committee, began by praising the 'bright example and philanthropic efforts of our female friends' before continuing by arguing that 'the custom of this country' was that 'In all matters of mere business, unless females are especially associated together . . . they do not become a part of the working committee'. He explained that when the BFASS committee had framed its orginal invitation it 'had no reference to, nor did the framers of it ever contemplate that it would include, females', and when there appeared to be a misunderstanding over this the committee had issued a revised invitation addressed specifically to men.

Stacey's points were backed by the Rev. J. Burnet, Carlisle delegate Captain Wauchope and William Cairnes of Edinburgh. Charles Stuart, who was a leading promoter of female anti-slavery societies in both Britain and America, took his stand on the basis of his knowledge of the American movement, arguing that those in favour of female delegates were in a minority there as in Britain.

Several speakers argued that it was inappropriate that 'the abstract question of the rights of woman' – a matter separate from the anti-slavery cause, one that was 'almost new' in Britain and was a source of discord – was diverting the time and attention of the convention and causing an uproar which might bring the proceedings into discredit. They disagreed, however, as to whether this was because it was too important or too insignificant a issue: for the leading Birmingham evangelical Rev. John Angel James it was a question involving 'far wider considerations than even the Anti-Slavery cause itself'; for the Rev. Stovel, it was a 'paltry question' detracting from the great object of anti-slavery.

Only one speaker tackled the 'abstract question' directly, and he was a minister who evoked dominant evangelical prescriptions of women's social role. The Rev. A. Harvey of Glasgow made explicit the 'separate spheres' ideology in which the presumption of female exclusion – 'the custom of this country' – was grounded. He argued that it was a question of conscience, that God had assigned women a particular sphere and that voting in favour of admitting women delegates would be 'in opposition to the plain teaching of the word of God'.

Aligned against the group were three radicals who supported the women with varying degrees of enthusiasm: Dr John Bowring (1792–1872), a prominent Unitarian politician and Anti-Corn Law League activist; George Thompson, a leading supporter of Garrison with close links to both British and American women abolitionists; and the radical lawyer and Owenite sympathiser William Henry Ashurst Sr (1792–1855). George Thompson took his stand as a supporter of Garrison rather than an enthusiast for women's rights. He deprecated 'the introduction of the abstract question' of women's rights, but he shrewdly pointed out, 'It appears that we are prepared to sanction ladies in the employment of all means, so long as they are confessedly unequal with ourselves.' The exclusion of women delegates, he argued, affronted not them alone but also the societies which they represented. This could not be justified when American women had led the anti-slavery cause in America and ran the most vigorous societies there. Dr Bowring, focusing on the British end of the question, pointed out that to argue that women were customarily excluded from such public participation was inconsistent given that Britain was ruled by a woman and that the anti-slavery movement was closely linked to the Society of Friends, which gave women great prominence. Mr Ashurst was most forthright in his support for the women. Taking his stand on principle, he argued that at a convention meeting 'on the principles of universal human benevolence' it was inconsistent to be exclusionary by commencing by 'disenfranchising one-half of creation'. Women were as competent as men to 'judge on the principles of Christianity' and thus there was no principled ground for their exclusion.

Five main points of disagreement may be discerned between British men who opposed female delegates and those who supported them. First, opposers argued that the custom of the country did not allow such roles for women, supporters that women already participated in public life. Second, opposers claimed that women could and did play a central and honoured role in the movement without being delegates, supporters that it was unfair to welcome women's contributions but then exclude them from full and equal participation. Third, opposers argued that the subject of women's rights was irrelevant to the convention, supporters that it was inconsistent to exclude women from a convention called on the principle of universality. Finally, opposers argued that in acting as delegates women went outside their proper sphere, supporters that women had as much grasp of anti-slavery principles as men.

What then were the reactions of British women abolitionists to this debate among their male co-workers? This is a question which has received little attention from historians despite the light it might throw on the development of feminism in Britain.[18]

Elizabeth Pease and Anne Knight, already friends and supporters of the Garrisonians prior to the convention, tried to arrange a separate female conference to meet with the women on a more official basis, but they were prevented by obstruction from the leadership of the BFASS. Pease wrote of the American women that 'every obstacle was thrown in the way and no public opportunity was ever afforded them for a free interchange with their English sisters', and added: 'I regretted it deeply and several of us mourned our utter inability to help it – had we been at our homes, we might have exerted an influence, but here we felt ourselves to be powerless.'[19] Nevertheless, informal meetings between the British and American women did take place both during and after the convention.[20]

The American women found the powerlessness of their British sisters depressing. Lucretia Mott, a Quaker activist sent as a representative of the American Anti-Slavery Society, complained of the meeting eventually held with a company of twenty or thirty women anti-slavery activists at her lodgings: 'stiff – poor affair – found little confidence in women's action either separately or con-jointly with men, except as drudges'.[21] Sarah Pugh, who led the American women's delegation, commented: 'they had little to tell us – and had but little desire to hear anything we had to say – seemed very insensitive – fearing they might get "out of their sphere" should they speak aloud even in a social circle. . . .'[22]

American supporters of Garrison were nevertheless hopeful that the agitation at the convention would help change this situation. Garrison observed that it had 'done more to bring up for the consideration of Europe the rights of women, than could have been accomplished in any other manner'.[23] Some fifty years later, recalling her own visit to the convention, the American women's suffrage leader Elizabeth Cady

Stanton asserted that the convention had indeed 'stung many women into new thought and action' and given 'rise to the movement for women's political equality both in England and the United States'.[24]

There is evidence to suggest that Stanton's assertion, while exaggerated in respect to developments in Britain, did contain an element of truth. Anne Knight, herself already a convinced feminist, found that the convention opened up opportunities for her to discuss the women's rights issue with other British and Irish abolitionists. She told Boston abolitionist Maria Weston Chapman that she and other women were now explaining to male abolitionists that with anti-slavery agitation women had been 'driven into the forefront of the battle'. Men should be listening to their counsel rather than excluding them with 'the puny cry of *custom*'.[25] Her anger at the treatment of the women delegates was a factor spurring her into devoting as much energy to women's rights as to anti-slavery through the 1840s. In 1851 she was involved in the formation of the first women's suffrage society in England, the Chartist-aligned Sheffield Female Reform Association.[26]

Other women who attended the convention also wrote enthusiastically on the stimulus of the women's rights debate. Maria Waring, an Irish anti-slavery campaigner who attended the convention, found the debate over the female delegates 'extremely interesting' and described their exclusion as 'silly'.[27] Elizabeth Pease was also indignant at 'the spirit of exclusion manifested towards those noble women'. After the convention she came into conflict with Charles Stuart, who was attempting to obstruct British support for the 'woman-intruding society', as he called the American Anti-Slavery Society.[28] In her arguments with Stuart, Pease emphasised both her full knowledge of the origin and history of the 'woman question' in America, and her conviction as a Quaker that it could not be right to allow human authority to interpose between woman and her conscience.[29] In a letter to John Collins, who arrived in Britain in late 1840 on a fund-raising mission for the Garrisonians, she explained her current very crude and 'undefined' position on women's rights. While not as 'ultra' as Harriet Martineau, she believed that women should have been admitted to the convention. For 'on *moral questions*, they ought to stand in equality with their "masters" '. She concluded:

> I believe there are few persons whose *natural feelings* are so opposed to *women* appearing *prominently* before the public, as *mine* – but viewed in the light of *principle* I see, that prejudice – custom and other feelings which will not stand the test of truth, are at the bottom, and must be laid aside.[30]

By 1843 Pease was publicly expressing her agreement with Garrison that the exclusion of women from anti-slavery and other philanthropic assemblies 'proceeds from a paltry, ill-founded, unscriptural and anti-Christian prejudice', comparing it with the racial prejudice which segregated black people in the 'negro pew' in Quaker meeting houses in America, and stating that she now saw it to be her duty to protest against it, feeling 'far differently from what I once did'.[31] Pease's developing feminism, as will be shown, was to lead her to active participation in feminist campaigns in the 1860s and 1870s.

Other women who attended the convention were also impressed by the women delegates and disturbed at their exclusion, and they likewise became supporters of Garrison and correspondents of American feminist abolitionists. While they included some of the most prominent feminist activists of the 1840s and 1850s, anti-slavery was not, however, their prime concern, and they were not among the most prominent female anti-slavery campaigners. Rather, for women like Elizabeth Reid, Mary Howitt and the Ashurst sisters anti-slavery and women's rights were two of a range of radical reforms to which they gave their support. While events at the convention and links established with Garrisonians clearly stimulated or in some cases initiated their interest in women's rights, the women can more accurately be labelled radical reformers rather than given the narrower designation of abolitionist–feminists appropriate to some American Garrisonians. A brief examination of their lives will clarify this point.

The author Mary Howitt (1799–1888), daughter of Ann Wood and Samuel Botham, a land-surveyor and iron-master, attended a school in Sheffield run by anti-slavery campaigner and African education pioneer Hannah Kilham. She then worked as a governess and ladies' companion before marriage in 1821 to William Howitt, who ran a chemist's. The couple had five children between 1824 and 1839, two of whom died young. Quakers by upbringing, she and her husband became Unitarians in the 1840s. They worked together as writers and editors of weeklies aimed at the working class which gave support to both anti-slavery and labour causes. The Howitts supported a spectrum of radical causes including anti-slavery, the Anti-Corn Law League and universal suffrage. In the 1840s Mary developed friendships with both Garrison and Frederick Douglass; in 1853 she was on the women's committee which organised the Stafford House Address; and in 1856 she demonstrated her feminist commitment by becoming secretary of the committee for a petition for a married women's property act.[32]

Another woman who became a member of this committee was the Unitarian educationalist Elizabeth J. Reid (1789–1866), founder in 1849 of Bedford College, the first college run by women for women. She entertained visiting American abolitionists from both sides at her home during the convention, but she aligned herself with the Garrisonians, being a close friend of Harriet Martineau and later a friend of Sarah

Parker Remond, who studied at her college. Like Remond, she became a member of the Garrisonian London Emancipation Committee in 1859.

Two other London radical Unitarian activists who attended the convention were Matilda Ashurst Biggs and Elizabeth A. Ashurst, daughters of London lawyer and radical leader William Henry Ashurst Sr, who spoke in support of the women delegates. Matilda was the wife of radical Leicester businessman Joseph Biggs, and, according to her daughter, was aroused to support women's rights by events at the convention.[33] Anne Knight sent her a packet of paper slips with feminist statements around 1847 accompanied by a letter asking her to support her call for suffrage for all men and women.[34] When at the end of 1859 a Northern Reform Society was established in Newcastle-upon-Tyne with universal suffrage as its objective, Mrs Biggs complained that they meant only male suffrage and argued that women's suffrage should be included.[35] Her daughter, Caroline Ashurst Biggs, became editor of the feminist *Englishwoman's Review* from 1870 to 1889.

Matilda's sister Elizabeth A. Ashurst (c. 1820–50), who married French artisan Jean Bardoneau-Narcy in 1849 and died the following year in childbirth, became a friend and correspondent of radical abolitionists including Lucretia Mott, Garrison and Pease following the convention. She was a member of the 'Muswell Hill Brigade', an activist circle in northeast London with interests in women's rights, anti-slavery, the Anti-Corn Law League and Italian nationalism.[36]

A more direct link between anti-slavery and feminism is represented by Marion Reid. The eldest daughter of a Glasgow merchant, Mr Kirkland, she married Hugo Reid in 1839 and moved to Edinburgh. While her name does not appear among the subscribers to the ladies' emancipation societies in Glasgow or Edinburgh, she attended the 1840 convention in London. Three years later she produced an important early feminist tract, *A Plea for Woman*. Headed by the quote 'Can man be free, if woman be a slave?', the book compared the position of women to that of slaves, and held up the success of the British anti-slavery campaign as an inspiration to women beginning to campaign for equal rights.[37] The book went into several editions in Britain and the United States and impressed Harriet Martineau, Anne Knight and Elizabeth Pease, who recommended it to Garrison. Knight's annotated copy survives as a vivid document of this interest, covered in her feminist stickers, interleaved with her anti-slavery and feminist broadsides and interspersed with her detailed comments on Reid's line of argument.[38]

Reid's comments about the British anti-slavery campaign suggest that it was not only admiration for American women but also pride in their own achievements which encouraged British women abolitionists to support women's rights. Further evidence for this is provided by the anonymous evangelical Anglican author of *Domestic Tyranny, or Women in Chains* who, calling in 1841 for married women to be given property rights, held up the successful efforts of large numbers of British women in favour of black emancipation 'as a pledge and forerunner of their own emancipation from the state of civil bondage'.[39]

Some women, however, while supporting the American women delegates in principle, were worried that the 'woman question' would divert energy from anti-slavery activism, which they felt should be kept a single-issue campaign. The outspoken anti-slavery activist Mary Ann Rawson of Sheffield considered 'that both parties have made the question respecting women's rights of too great importance'. She viewed slavery as the greatest social evil and in attempting to eradicate it was willing to unite with either the upholders or opposers of women's rights. Esther Sturge of London, though soon persuaded of the women's case by Maria Weston Chapman, initially took a similar line, urging Garrisonians to keep to anti-slavery alone, for:

> Ever since I have heard of the questions mooted as to the equality of women etc. I have thought it would prove only as a strategem to divert the minds of valuable labourers from the point.[40]

Aligned against those British women who supported Garrison where those who aligned themselves with the BFASS and the Tappanite wing of the American movement and who expressed hostility to calls for women's rights as disruptive of proper relations between the sexes. Eliza Conder, wife of Independent publisher Josiah Conder of London and thus a member of the denomination which in the United States had exhibited the most hostility to the mingling of anti-slavery and women's rights, was most scathing of the American women. For her such public assertiveness by women was not respectable: she described the 'vulgar clamour' at the convention and ridiculed the women as 'most untidily arrayed'. She was afraid that women's rights would contaminate English women and disrupt the proper ordering of society:

> If we are thus to start out of our spheres, who is to take our place? who, as 'keepers at home' are to 'guide the house', and train up children? Are the gentlemen kindly to officiate for us?[41]

Similar hostility was expressed by Mary Caroline Braithwaite, Quaker secretary of the Kendal Ladies' Anti-Slavery Society, who wrote to Joseph Birney of the American and Foreign Anti-Slavery Society asking him to recommend American women abolitionists with whom members of her society could establish contact, because they were not 'disposed to extend our sympathy to the Women's Rights Party'. Clearly influenced by Charles Stuart, who had revived her society, Braithwaite described the American Anti-Slavery Society as a 'Women's Rights Party' which had appointed 'inconsistent representatives', and stressed that her own anti-slavery activities were 'consistent with needful attention to other duties'.[42]

This renewed need to emphasise the compatability of anti-slavery activism with domestic duties is also evident in a letter by Sarah Dymond, Quaker secretary of the Taunton Ladies' Anti-Slavery Society and also an associate of Stuart, who wrote to the secretary of the BFASS:

> I will engage to get up a public meeting, which I think I can do without stepping out of my *proper* sphere; I am decidedly opposed to the woman question, but when *men will* not work in the cause *women must*.[43]

In some cases, then, the controversy at the convention, rather than opening up new opportunities for women activists, forced them onto the defensive as they felt impelled to once again justify their more public forms of campaigning while distancing themselves from support for women's rights.

The clearest statement of the distinction between public anti-slavery activism and support for women's rights was made by Anne Taylor Gilbert (1782–1866), an evangelical hymn-writer who, like Eliza Conder, was married to an Independent minister. Gilbert had organised a mass women's petition against slavery in Nottingham in 1833 and had stated then that she had 'no scruple, as to female petitions, in the cause of humanity'. However, when asked by Anne Knight to lend her support to a campaign for women's rights, she replied that she was not in favour of women having the vote. She explained that she considered women were adequately represented by their menfolk and that the 'division of labour' and of 'spheres' was both the natural and the scientific way to organise society. It was a scheme, she believed, which avoided creating conflict within the family and burdening women with extra responsibilities on top of their already heavy load of domestic and philanthropic duties.[44]

What is evident in the stance of these anti-feminist women anti-slavery campaigners is the intertwining of principled opposition to women's rights with practical concern over the difficulties for women of combining political activism with domestic responsibilities.

There is also evidence that the controversy over women's rights was intertwined with religious controversy. Many leading anti-slavery campaigners, including the Quaker leadership of the BFASS, were evangelicals. Evangelical beliefs about women's moral duties were central to the dominant 'separate spheres' ideology and provided the foundation on which women had traditionally based their support for anti-slavery. Evangelicals combined advocacy of 'separate spheres' with a stress on biblical authority and on church unity and interdenominational alliances.[45] In contrast, Garrisonians stressed women's *right* to campaign against slavery, rather than their *duty* to do so. They tended to be unorthodox 'Hicksite' Quakers or Unitarians who gave priority to the following of the individual conscience, questioned all forms of established civil and religious authority, subscribed to an anarchistic form of pacifism known as 'non-resistance', and undermined the 'separate spheres' ideology by their demand for a perfectionist moral standard for all. Evangelicals accused Garrisonians not only of religious 'infidelity' but also of defying divine ordinances about the role of women.[46]

The strength of evangelical tradition in British anti-slavery was such that the potential which Garrisonianism offered for a break with traditional women's roles in anti-slavery was never fully exploited. In Glasgow, where local men's and women's societies split in the aftermath of the controversies at the convention, even those women who supported Garrison and were angered at the exclusion of the American women delegates made it clear that they had no desire to follow the American women's example. Fears among local Congregational ministers that local women might now attempt to insert themselves into public and leadership roles in the Glasgow anti-slavery movement thus proved unfounded.[47]

The same pattern is evident nationally. The short-lived Anti-Slavery League, set up in 1846 as a central co-ordinating body for British and Irish Garrisonians, had an all-male organising committee, and the independent local societies which supported the Garrisonian wing of the American anti-slavery movement were segregated on sex lines as were the auxiliaries of the BFASS.

STEPS TOWARDS EQUALITY

It was not until the 1850s that tentative moves towards more equal participation by women in the British anti-slavery movement were initiated. These moves occurred simultaneously with the beginnings of the organised feminist movement.

Elizabeth Pease was able to report to Garrison in 1852 that the cause of women's rights was progressing slowly, with increasing support for women's education and decreasing horror at women's public speaking on philanthropic issues.[48] Some of the women who led these developments were anti-slavery supporters. Elizabeth Reid, who founded Bedford College in 1849, has already been mentioned. Another Unitarian supporter of Garrison was Mary Carpenter (1807–77), a single woman from Bristol who is famed as the founder of the first reformatory for girls in England, and who in 1852 became the first woman to give evidence before a Parliamentary commission.

Within the anti-slavery movement itself the first move towards female equality was marked by the formation in February 1853 of the Leeds Antislavery Association. With its mixture of male and female officers, committee members and subscribers, it followed an organisational form common in American anti-slavery circles since 1840 but marked a break with the pattern of single-sex organisation established in the anti-slavery movement in the 1820s and hitherto standard in all forms of voluntary societies in Britain.[49] The initial impetus for the new society came from two women: Sarah Pugh, a Quaker supporter of Garrison who had led the American women's delegation to the 1840 World Anti-Slavery Convention and who had acted as treasurer of the mixed-sex Pennsylvania Anti-Slavery Society since 1843; and her friend Harriet Lupton, a local Unitarian supporter of Garrison with an interest in women's rights.[50] Pugh and Lupton initially formed a ladies' committee to collect signatures for the Stafford House Address, and their hopes of then founding an independent ladies' society developed into a plan for a mixed group.[51]

The Leeds Antislavery Association was remarkable in that it gained support both from Garrisonians and from evangelicals traditionally hostile to Garrisonian 'infidelity' and women's rights. With a total of 110 female and 77 male subscribers, it had an interdenominational committee of both sexes, including Quakers Mr and Mrs Wilson Armistead, Unitarians Mr and Mrs Joseph Lupton and their daughter Harriet, Independents the Rev. and Mrs William Guest and Mrs E. Baines, wife of the editor of the *Leeds Mercury*, and Baptists the Rev. and Mrs John Walcott.

The new association adopted an emblem, a variant of the traditional Wedgwood plaque, which showed the figures of two slaves, one male and one female, with the slogans 'Am I not a woman and a sister' and 'Am I not a man and a brother'.[52] In practice, however, women and men did not have completely equal roles in the group. While women slightly outnumbered men on the committee, and Harriet Lupton and Mrs Guest held important posts as its secretaries, men took on the more public roles of president and vice-president, which involved chairing public meetings. At the group's founding meeting, men proposed the motions, women seconded them. This pattern was probably encouraged by the familial basis of support for the society, leading to a tendency for patriarchal authority and the sexual division of labour within the family to be replicated in the society.[53]

This local development was followed in November 1854 by a move towards the involvement by women in national decision making. The BFASS called a conference to which British abolitionists of all persuasions were invited, with the aim of reaching agreements on united action. On receiving information of the planned meeting, Harriet

Lupton sent a circular to independent women's societies offering to pay the expenses of any ladies who would consent to attend as delegates 'for the purpose of testing the woman question'.[54] The circular stimulated considerable debate among independent women's societies over the issue of female delegates. The Bristol and Clifton Ladies' Anti-Slavery Society, whose leader Mary Estlin was a friend of Harriet Lupton and was apparently involved in the scheme, received communications from Leeds, Manchester, Bridgewater, Edinburgh and Glasgow, all expressing the desire that the right of women to attend such conferences should be established.[55] The responses testify to the growth in feminist sentiment among Garrisonian women abolitionists in Britain in the 1850s.

The two women who eventually agreed to attend the conference as delegates were Rebecca Moore and Rebecca Whitelegge of the Manchester Ladies' Anti-Slavery Society. Mrs Rebecca Moore (née Fisher) was an Irish Quaker who with her sisters Susanna and Charlotte had been active supporters of Garrison in Limerick since 1841. She had eloped to Manchester with barrister and Anti-Corn Law League lecturer Robert R.R. Moore. After he left her she stayed in the town, founding the Manchester Ladies' Anti-Slavery Society in 1847 to collect for the Boston bazaar and later becoming active in the women's suffrage movement.[56] Her namesake Rebecca Whitelegge is known to have collected subscriptions to the British Garrisonian paper the *Anti-Slavery Advocate*. Mary Estlin thought highly of her contribution to the cause, describing her and Eliza Wigham in 1855 as 'the two main props of the enterprise in Great Britain'.[57]

While the Manchester women were the only female delegates to the conference, the Edinburgh Ladies' Emancipation Society sent a male delegate, Duncan McLaren, bearing a long letter containing suggestions about matters they felt should be prioritised at the conference and also calling for women's full participation in the movement.[58] The letter recommended holding a World Anti-Slavery Convention in 1855, providing it was 'on a broad and comprehensive platform'. It argued for the inclusion of women as representatives of enslaved women:

> When it is considered that of those whose interests the Convention will meet to advocate, one half at least are *women* . . . and that during the interval since West India Emancipation, a great share of anti-slavery work and duty had devolved on the *women* of Britain, we would respectfully suggest that *ladies* should be specially invited to attend the conference, and thus have the opportunity of representing the wrongs of their sisters who are in bonds.[59]

Before the London conference women's groups made enquiries of the

BFASS committee as to whether it would accept female delegates. Surprisingly, assurances were obtained that female delegates would be received 'as a matter of course'.[60] This demonstrated a complete change in attitude from the World Convention in 1840. It is also surprising in the light of worries over female delegates being expressed by BFASS committee members as late as November 1853.[61]

The BFASS's apparent change of attitude between 1853 and 1854 was less the product of a sudden conversion to women's rights than the product of increased co-operation and conciliation between anti-slavery factions. The new mood was, however, short lived. The conference ended in disarray when the BFASS refused to succumb to pressure from Garrisonians to grant full recognition to the American Anti-Slavery Society. The BFASS then further alienated Garrisonians by publishing a report of the conference which both omitted pro-Garrisonian speeches and failed to mention the female delegates.[62] In this context the snubbing of the women seems primarily to have been a method of attacking the Garrisonians.

Rebecca Moore wrote after the convention that the acceptance of women delegates was 'of little consequence if the American [Anti-Slavery] Society is to be passed by'.[63] Her reluctance to prioritise women's rights seems to have been shared by other British women abolitionists, for there were no new developments on the issue for several years. Meanwhile, however, the organised feminist movement in Britain was getting underway. In 1855 a married women's property committee was set up by Barbara Leigh Smith, an old friend of Harriet Martineau, and she initiated a petitioning campaign for legal change on the issue. In 1857 the first British feminist periodical, the *Englishwoman's Journal*, was set up by a group of London women, and in 1858 women set up an Association for the Promotion of the Employment of Women. At the same time women began to play a full part in the Association for the Promotion of Social Science.

This was the state of affairs when African-American abolitionist Sarah Parker Remond arrived in England to undertake a series of lecture tours of Britain and Ireland between January 1859 to January 1861. Her lectures were the first public talks by a woman to mass mixed audiences on the anti-slavery issue.

Remond was a supporter of women's rights, who had appeared on the platform at the National Women's Rights Convention in New York in 1858 and whose brother Charles Remond had refused to participate in the 1840 World Anti-slavery Convention as a gesture of solidarity with the excluded women delegates. Sarah Remond nevertheless made no attempt to advocate women's rights or other controversial Garrisonian views from the anti-slavery platform. As a result she was welcomed by Garrisonians and non-Garrisonians alike, and her tour helped foster co-operation between the two sides. At her main lecture in London, leading Garrisonian George Thompson was joined on the platform by Louis Chamerovzow of the BFASS, who for the first time publicly praised the work of the American Anti-Slavery Society. Chamerovzow's endorsement of Remond, while motivated by his desire for rapprochement with the Garrisonians, also reflected his acceptance of new roles for women in the British abolition movement. Acknowledging that it was unusual for women to speak in public, he asserted that whenever they did so 'the cause they advocated benefited by their support of it'.[64] His statement was symptomatic of the increasing acceptance in middle-class circles of a public role for women in organised philanthropy in this period.[65]

British Garrisonians were also encouraged by their American colleagues at this time to set up a national committee with both male and female members. American Unitarian abolitionist the Rev. Samuel May wrote to the leading Irish Garrisonian Richard D. Webb of his desire to see a 'living association' to replace the BFASS with a committee of both men and women. He put forward a list of possible committee members which included Eliza Paton and Elizabeth Pease (now Mrs Nichol following her marriage in 1853 to John Pringle Nichol, a professor of astronomy at the University of Glasgow), Eliza and Jane Wigham of Edinburgh, Mary Estlin and Mrs Stephens of Bristol, and Mrs Turner and Miss Whitelegge of Manchester as well as nine men.[66] Webb was sceptical that such a league could be formed, considering the people listed by May to be an 'incongruous medley' who lacked the money to promote a new society. The women he described variously as 'great stayers at home', 'good as gold', 'a good deal swallowed up in [her husband]', 'does not much like personal publicity', 'a good woman – but is also a [warm?] wife', 'w[oul]d be hardly like to help much in council'. While his comments suggest his own reluctance to support equal participation by women they also highlight the problems which women did face in attending meetings away from home, and their own continuing reservations about independent public action.[67]

Garrisonians under the leadership of F.W. Chesson and George Thompson nevertheless did succeed in setting up a mixed central co-ordinating committee in London in June 1859. The London Emancipation Committee was made up of both men and women, blacks and whites. Women were thus admitted to the central decision-making body of an anti-slavery organisation for the first time in Britain. They included two African-American abolitionists, Sarah Remond and Ellen Craft. The other women members of the new committee were, like Ellen Craft herself, mostly the wives of male committee members (Mrs Chesson, Mrs Thompson, Mrs Dennis McDonnell,

Mrs T.E. Thoresby), but they also included women's rights campaigner Elizabeth Reid.[68]

The formation of the new committee was welcomed by local
Garrisonian groups. Dissension soon arose, however, when Chesson
and Thompson failed to invite Sarah Parker Remond to address the
public meeting held in London on 1 August 1859 to celebrate the
twenty-fifth anniversary of the abolition of British colonial slavery.
Maria Weston Chapman tried to placate Remond, but the *Anti-Slavery
Advocate* publicly condemned the omission, which it blamed on 'the
prejudices of some influential persons present' against public speaking
by women.[69] The Bristol and Clifton Ladies' Society and the Edinburgh
Ladies' Emancipation Society wrote letters of complaint to the committee about the incident, and Harriet Martineau publicly criticised the
committee in the *Anti-Slavery Standard*.[70] The controversy was still alive
in January 1860, and the resulting erosion of female support probably
contributed to the collapse of the London Emancipation Committee:
Sarah Remond did not attend its meetings again and it only met
erratically after August 1859, finally terminating operations in February 1860 at a meeting attended by men only.[71] The attempt to unite
abolitionists on equal terms across racial and sexual lines in a national
committee was thus short lived.

ANTI-SLAVERY AND ORGANISED FEMINISM

In 1887 an article on 'the emancipation of women' appeared in the
Westminster Review in which it was claimed that 'the public work of
women began appropriately with the Anti-Slavery agitation', and in
which a path was traced from this through the temperance and anti-
Corn Law movements to the campaign against the Contagious Diseases Acts and the women's suffrage movement.[72] In fact, however,
these movements cannot be placed in such simple chronological succession. In particular, the anti-slavery movement, while it began earlier
than the others, continued through the 1860s, as will be shown in the
next chapter.

Many of the women most active in the anti-slavery and Freedmen's
Aid movements in the 1860s became leaders of feminist campaigns in
the late 1860s. This link has already been recognised in the case of the
feminist campaign against the Contagious Diseases Acts in 1869-86.
Judith Walkowitz, in a study of the Ladies' National Association (LNA)
which co-ordinated this campaign, has identified ten of its thirty-three
leaders as having been involved in anti-slavery. Seven of the ten were
also involved in the women's suffrage movement, four in promoting
higher education for women, and two in the campaign for a married
women's property act. They included leading anti-slavery activists of

172

the 1840s and 1850s – Harriet Martineau, Mary Estlin, Eliza Wigham and Elizabeth Pease Nichol – along with younger women anti-slavery campaigners such as two of the sisters of leading Quaker anti-Corn Law activist John Bright: Margaret Bright Lucas (1818–90), a member of the committee of the London Ladies' Emancipation Society; and Priscilla Bright McLaren (1815–1906), wife of the radical lord provost of Edinburgh, Duncan McLaren, and a member of the committee of the Edinburgh Ladies' Emancipation Society.[73] The other anti-slavery supporters listed by Walkowitz are LNA leader Josephine Butler; Emilie Ashurst Hawkes Venturi, one of the daughters of radical lawyer William Henry Ashurst Sr; Margaret Tanner (1817–1905), a Bristol Quaker; and Mrs H. Kenway, a Birmingham Quaker. To these can be added several women abolitionists mentioned by Paul McHugh as important local activists in the campaign against the acts: the Clarks of Street in Somerset and the Priestmans and Mrs Charles Thomas of Bristol.

Josephine Butler, leader of the LNA, and Elizabeth Pease Nichol, one of its committee members, were involved in both anti-slavery and all the major feminist campaigns of the period. A comparison of the two women sheds some light on the varied nature of links between anti-slavery and feminism at this period.

Elizabeth Pease Nichol had been a leading anti-slavery activist since the late 1830s. In 1859, on the death of her husband, she moved to Edinburgh, where she joined her friend Eliza Wigham as one of the leaders of the Edinburgh Ladies' Emancipation Society. Nichol's interest in women's rights was as long standing as her commitment to anti-slavery, and had been fostered by her meetings and correspondence with leading American abolitionist–feminists. While she had supported her American friends' stand, however, she had never pushed women's rights in the British anti-slavery movement. Only in her sixties did she become active in the women's movement, and she can be seen as representative of that generation of female abolitionists for whom the winding down of the British anti-slavery movement released reforming energies which were channelled into the newly organised women's rights movement. Indeed, it may be tentatively suggested that one reason why feminist organisations burgeoned in the late 1860s was because of this release of women reformers from anti-slavery work. Josephine Butler (1828–1906), some twenty years Pease's junior, is representative of the generation of feminists who were too young to have been involved in the height of the British anti-slavery movement in 1823–38, but who came from families which had supported the cause. Her own anti-slavery convictions led her to early support for the North during the American Civil War, and to donating to the Freedmen's Aid movement. Butler later credited her unpopular stand during the war with providing useful training for her work in the controversial campaign against the Contagious Diseases Acts: 'The feeling of isolation was often painful . . . but the discipline was useful.'[74]

Butler admired Garrison for his uncompromising anti-slavery stance, his stress on moral suasion and his fervent desire to combat suffering.[75] She and her co-workers in the LNA referred to themselves as 'abolitionists' campaigning in the 'New Abolition' movement, and her rhetoric was imbued with references to slavery. She described the Contagious Diseases Acts as a 'legislative movement for the creation of a slave class of women for the supposed benefit of licentious men'.[76] Like women abolitionists before her, she saw her new campaign as a religious mission, drawing inspiration from a conviction that equality and liberty were the basis of Christ's teachings. Drawing on the woman–slave analogy, she argued that just as slaves had found arguments against slavery in the Scriptures despite the sanction they might appear superficially to give, so women had found arguments for their liberation from 'legal thraldom' and from 'chains which had been riveted by the traditions of centuries'.[77] In Walkowitz's account of how women like Butler viewed the prostitutes on whose behalf they were campaigning as their 'less fortunate sisters' who were the innocent and passive victims of male lust, may be discerned many echoes of women anti-slavery campaigners' expressions of concern for female slaves.[78] Both sets of propaganda show the desire of middle-class women to counter the stereotype of voracious working-class/black female sexuality by emphasising an alternative stereotype of the passive and inarticulate female victim.

As well as drawing on anti-slavery for its ideological approach, the developing feminist movement made use of the network of female abolitionists in creating its own network and leadership. This network overlapped with the networks of Quaker and Unitarian families, denominations which provided the leadership of both anti-slavery and feminist movements. The honorary secretary of the Ladies' London Emancipation Society which was formed in 1863 was Mentia Taylor (née Doughty), the wife of Leicester MP Peter Taylor, whose home at Aubrey House in Notting Hill, London, was a centre for radical movements. Caroline Ashurst Biggs asserted of Mentia Taylor, known as the 'mother' of the women's suffrage movement, that 'when she began her efforts for women's suffrage, the English abolitionists were among the first correspondents to whom she applied, and they nearly all responded cordially'.[79] This statement is backed by evidence of the large number of London Ladies' Emancipation Society officers, committee members and pamphleteers who became leading figures in the women's movement. Mentia Taylor herself acted as secretary and treasurer of the London Women's Suffrage Society, and other leading feminists involved in the Emancipation Society included veteran abolitionists Mary Estlin, Harriet Martineau and Sarah Parker Remond as well as new recruits like Frances Power Cobbe (1822–1904), a journalist who became a leading anti-vivisection campaigner and whose public support for women's rights dated back to 1862; Isa Craig (1831–1903), assistant secretary to the Association for the Promotion of Social Science; Emilie Shirreff (1814–97), a leading campaigner for women's higher education from 1870; Elizabeth Malleson (1828–1914), a supporter of women's suffrage from the 1850s and a campaigner against the Contagious Diseases Acts; Harriet Taylor (1807–58), wife of John Stuart Mill, who wrote in favour of women's rights in the 1850s; Emily Davies (1830–1921), a pioneer of higher education for women; Margaret Bright Lucas, Mary Priestman of Bristol and M. Merryweather, all on the committee of the LNA; and Mrs Hensleigh Wedgwood, a women's suffrage campaigner.[80]

The link with abolition was also evident in the case of leading male supporters of the women's movement: the London Negro Aid Society, the mixed-sex successor of the Ladies' London Emancipation Society, included on its committee the leading Parliamentary supporters of women's suffrage: Professor Henry Fawcett, John Stuart Mill and Mr Peter A. Taylor.

Outside London the links between anti-slavery and feminism are equally striking. The strongest women's suffrage societies in the 1860s were in London, Manchester, Bristol and Edinburgh, and in all cases women who had led the local ladies' anti-slavery societies became leaders of the local women's suffrage committees. Rebecca Moore, founder of the Manchester Ladies' Anti-Slavery Society and the first woman to attend a British anti-slavery conference as a delegate, became a member of the executive committee of the Manchester Society for Women's Suffrage. Mary Estlin, leader of the Bristol and Clifton Ladies' Anti-Slavery Society, acted as treasurer of the Bristol and West of England branch of the Women's Suffrage Society, as well as being a member of the executive committee of the LNA. Eliza Wigham, secretary of the Edinburgh Ladies' Emancipation Society, acted as secretary of the Edinburgh Women's Suffrage Society, while her stepmother and fellow anti-slavery activist Jane Wigham also joined the suffrage committee. In addition, Elizabeth Pease Nichol acted as its treasurer and Priscilla Bright McLaren, who had joined the committee of the Edinburgh Ladies' Emancipation Society in the 1860s, became its president. Eliza Wigham, Elizabeth Pease Nichol and Priscilla Bright McLaren also served on the executive committee of the LNA.[81]

Such women brought to the women's movement a tradition of public activism, experience in organising women, in canvassing, in fund-raising, in propagandising, and in petitioning Parliament, as well as their valuable contacts and friendships with an extensive network of activists. Many had long-established links with American abolitionist-feminists. Leading female supporters of Garrison, in Britain as in America, became leading women's rights activists, and London, Manchester, Bristol and Edinburgh, which had the most active radical female anti-slavery societies, gained the strongest women's suffrage societies.

Links between women allied to the BFASS and the feminist movement were less common, as would be expected given the BFASS's history of opposition to women's rights. Nevertheless the treasurer of the Birmingham Ladies' Freedmen's Aid Association, Mrs W. Middlemore, became a member of the local women's suffrage committee, as did Miss Sturge and Miss Albright, members of the two leading Quaker anti-slavery families of the town.[82]

Radical British and American abolitionists discussed and exchanged information on the developing women's rights movements in their correspondence. Mentia Taylor, Elizabeth Pease Nichol, Mary Estlin, Eliza Wigham and Harriet Lupton conducted a transatlantic correspondence on women's suffrage with Samuel J. May Jr, Sarah Pugh, William Lloyd Garrison and Oliver Johnson.[83] Mary Estlin sent information on the campaign against the Contagious Diseases Acts to Maria Weston Chapman.[84] Rebecca Moore of Manchester wrote occasional articles for *Revolution*, journal of the Stanton–Anthony wing of the American women's suffrage movement. Garrison, while he approved of her articles, wrote to Elizabeth Pease Nichol criticising this wing of the movement for its opposition to giving black men the vote before white women and its dubious alliance with the racist George Francis Train.[85] Garrison's visit to Britain in 1877 was welcomed by feminists who felt that he would lend a 'high moral and religious tone' to the movement and that his association with the successful anti-slavery cause would encourage people to believe in the women's suffrage movement.[86]

Looking at the connections between anti-slavery and feminism in 1860s Britain as a whole, a number of conclusions can be drawn. The end of the Freedmen's Aid movement released the energies of women's rights supporters for the new feminist campaigns. Experience of supporting an unpopular cause during the American Civil War helped give women strength to launch a controversial campaign against the Contagious Diseases Acts, in which women abolitionists' traditional concern for the 'degraded' woman was transferred from slave to prostitute. Anti-slavery also provided local and national networks of reformers, predominantly Quakers and Unitarians, from which feminism drew much of its leadership. Finally, close contacts between radical women abolitionists in Britain and Garrisonian abolitionist–feminists in America provided a stimulating exchange of information and source of support.

Taking a wider and longer-term view, the relationship between anti-slavery and feminism in Britain between the 1820s and the 1860s can be clarified by comparison with the United States. Sklar has pointed to the importance of comparing not only the internal history of the anti-slavery movement and women's political culture but also the ways in which 'the larger political environment encouraged or discouraged women's participation'.[87] She has argued convincingly that American women abolitionists were more inclined to feminism than their British counterparts because they were 'more profoundly challenged to alter the social-political status quo, and less deeply rooted in class and other social distinctions'.[88] While it is not possible to explore this argument in any depth here, it is clear that in Britain slavery was a colonial and later a foreign issue, that there was a widespread public consensus in favour of abolition, and that anti-slavery activism aimed to expand existing British political culture and gender ideology on a global scale; in contrast in the United States slavery was an established domestic institution, abolition was the cause of an unpopular minority who risked social ostracism and racist mob violence, and anti-slavery posed a challenge to American political culture. More conscious of a gender than a class identity, less constrained by religious orthodoxy, their contributions viewed as more vital by male abolitionists who saw themselves as an embattled minority, and already challenging convention by supporting abolition, American women were more willing than their British sisters to advocate women's rights as a matter of principle.

It remains the case, however, that there was an important connection between anti-slavery and feminism in Britain. Anti-slavery was more than one of a number of philanthropic causes which encouraged women to become public activists and led them to develop a consciousness of the limitations imposed by dominant ideas about their proper social roles. It was a political movement central to the development of an extra-Parliamentary but public female political culture.

8

A LINGERING CONCERN

The 1860s, which saw the growth of an organised women's movement in Britain, was also the period when anti-slavery activism wound down as reformers increasingly focused on other causes, as new forms of virulent racism gained hold, and as popular support for abolition waned. The period was marked by two dramatic events abroad to which anti-slavery campaigners and the British public as a whole responded: the American Civil War of 1861–65, and the Jamaica Insurrection and Governor Eyre controversy of 1865–68. It was also the period of the Freedmen's Aid movement, the final large-scale effort by anti-slavery campaigners.[1]

WAR AND POLARISATION

As scholars have pointed out, British reactions to the attempted secession of the Southern states from the Union and to the outbreak and course of the American Civil War were complex and did not follow simple pro- and anti-slavery lines. British abolitionists were confused by the initial failure of the North to come out in favour of slave emancipation. The leaders of the British and Foreign Anti-Slavery Society (BFASS) and other Quakers and pacifists found it impossible to support war for however worthy a cause. Those allied to the Garrisonians were bewildered at the sudden about-turn of their American co-workers from a non-resistant, non-political and disunionist stance to support for the Union and the North and acceptance of the use of violent means to overthrow slavery.[2]

With both the BFASS's *Anti-Slavery Reporter* and the Garrisonian *Anti-Slavery Advocate* failing to take a clear line on the war prior to President Lincoln's Emancipation Proclamation of 22 September 1862, Harriet Martineau's firmly pro-Northern leaders for the *Daily News* on the war initially provided almost the only public opposition to the pro-Confederate stance of the bulk of the British press. The leading Irish abolitionist Richard D. Webb, whom Harriet Martineau replaced as

178

correspondent for the American Garrisonian *Anti-Slavery Standard* in the 1860s, considered that 'there is nobody in Europe who has done so much to promote anti-slavery views and uphold the northern cause in England'.[3]

Martineau's view of the American Civil War was influential because of her well-established reputation as a journalist, her personal familiarity with America, and her close contacts with leading American abolitionists. In contrast to many other British radical abolitionists, she joined George Thompson in immediately accepting American Garrisonians' abrupt change from an anti-war and disunionist position to a pro-Union stance. From the outset of the war she stressed that slavery was 'the great question which underlies the whole quarrel', and 'the one irresistible cause of the existing civil war'.[4] While critical of Lincoln's initial failure to adopt an emancipationist policy, she presented cumulative evidence of the North's progress towards such a policy and interpreted developments as indicating that the war would inevitably result in abolition.[5]

Martineau's was the main voice countering the predominantly pro-Confederate stance of the British press at this period. This dominant viewpoint was in part based on fears about the disruption of British trade with the South and a belief that the war was about the South's right to self-determination rather than the issue of slavery. It led to pressure on the British government to abandon its policy of neutrality and take the Confederate side, break the Northern blockade of Southern ports and even enter the war.

The pro-Confederate viewpoint also marked a reversal of the dominant anti-slavery sentiment of the press. It was characterised both by references to the economic decline in the British West Indies suggesting that black people were unsuited for free labour and that emancipation would herald economic ruin, and by the evocation of the India Mutiny of 1857 and the St Domingue revolt of 1791 fuelling expectations that emancipation would lead to a terrible servile war.[6] Martineau combated such assertions by arguing that, on the contrary, emancipation was the only security against insurrection, and that it would actually increase planters' profits because free labour costs less than the upkeep of slaves.[7] She argued, in words echoing Elizabeth Heyrick's in the 1820s, that 'immediate emancipation' didn't mean 'letting loose a race of barbarians to run amuck in society', but simply that there was no possible intermediate stage between the status of chattel and that of human being. Drawing on the history of the British West Indies, Martineau contrasted the success of immediate full emancipation in Antigua with the failure of the apprenticeship system, and pointed out that black insurrection had occurred when there was no prospect of emancipation, rather than as the result of freedom.[8]

President Lincoln's Emancipation Proclamation of 22 September 1862, granting freedom to slaves in the rebel states from 1 January 1863, brought anti-slavery closer to being an official war aim. It convinced the majority of abolitionists that the North was now worthy of support, and in November 1862 a group of influential radical politicians joined with veteran Garrisonian abolitionists, including George Thompson and Frederick W. Chesson, to form the London Emancipation Society to propagandise about the war and its roots in Southern aggression.[9]

A particular impetus to female activism was given at this time by Harriet Beecher Stowe's open letter to British women 'in behalf of many thousands of American women'. This took the form of a belated reply to the 1853 Stafford House Address. Stowe turned the wording of that address on British women, urging them to forward the emancipation of American slaves by giving support to the Unionist cause.[10]

Stowe's fame ensured her open letter widespread publicity. It was published in pamphlet form and printed in full in the *Anti-Slavery Reporter* and in the pro-Northern London papers the *Daily News* and the *Morning Star*, and it met with a very positive response from women.[11] The Edinburgh Ladies' Emancipation Society issued a Scottish response and a *Rejoinder* was rapidly produced 'in behalf of Englishwomen' by the journalist Frances Power Cobbe.[12] While Cobbe had not previously been involved in the anti-slavery movement, she articulated the traditional feminine approach to slavery, stressing the sufferings of women and portraying slavery as a matter of moral and religious principle which transcended politics. English women, she asserted, abhorred slavery as human beings, as women and for itself. They had witnessed with 'solemn joy' the picture of 'your country purging herself, even through seas of blood, from the guilty participation in the crimes of the past', and they were convinced that the conflict would end in abolition. Such were 'the beliefs and hopes of the Women of England, whose hearts the complicated difficulties of politics, or the miserable jealousies of national rivalry, do not distract from the great principles underlying the contest'.[13]

In London women responded to the interest stirred up by Stowe's *Reply* by setting up a new society, the Ladies' London Emancipation Society. Formed in March 1863 on the basis that slavery was 'a question especially and deeply interesting to women', it worked in co-operation with the London Emancipation Society while retaining its independence from the men.[14]

The new group was founded by Mentia Taylor, wife of Unitarian radical MP Peter Taylor, who was treasurer of the men's society. It was the first national female anti-slavery society, in the sense that it recruited more than two hundred members from all over England, though Londoners predominated and it had no local auxiliaries.[15] Frances Power Cobbe was a member of its executive committee, as were veteran abolitionists Mary Estlin of Bristol, Sarah Parker Remond and Harriet Martineau. Among its subscribers were other established activists including George Thompson's daughter Amelia Chesson, fugitive slave Ellen Craft, Mrs Cropper of Liverpool and Harriet Lupton of Leeds, and female members of the leading radical families the Ashursts and Biggs. It is notable, however, that the majority of the committee had not previously been prominent in the anti-slavery cause. Their presence marks the input of new energies into the movement. Some committee members, like Mrs T.B. Potter, Mrs Lucas, Mrs W. Malleson, Miss Bright and Mentia Taylor herself, were the relatives of men who were also newly prominent in the movement as leaders of the London Emancipation Society and the Manchester Union and Emancipation Society. Some, like Mrs Stansfield, Mrs Wedgwood, Mrs Courtauld, Mrs T.B. Potter and Mrs Harriet Taylor, were Unitarians like Mentia Taylor; others, such as Mrs Lucas and Miss Bright, were Quakers. Most, with the notable exception of the Tory Miss Cobbe, were Liberals, and the European political connections of the new group are reflected in the presence of Italian nationalists Signor Mazzini as the sole male subscriber and General Garibaldi as honorary member.[16] Many were also involved in the developing women's rights movement. They were the kind of pro-Northerners whom the Tory *Standard* decried as 'Atheists, Socialists, advocates of "free love", or universal licentiousness, of woman's rights, and every other abomination or absurdity . . .'.[17]

Like its brother society, the Ladies' London Emancipation Society saw one of its prime aims to be the circulation of tracts 'explanatory of slavery as it now exists in the United States, and of its bearing on the present struggle between North and South'. Between 1863 and 1864 it produced twelve tracts, of which more than twelve thousand copies were circulated, supplementing the propaganda produced by the London Emancipation Society and the Manchester Union and Emancipation Society. Half of the tracts were written or compiled by women connected with the society. Taken together these tracts combated pro-Confederate sympathies in Britain through revelations about the true nature of slave-holding Southern society. Emily Shirreff's *The Chivalry of the South*, for example, contrasted the healthy morals and high respect for women in the Northern states with the licentiousness and degradation of women in the South, where the supposedly chivalrous landed proprietors lauded in the British Tory press even sold their own children who had some black blood. Frances Power Cobbe's *The Red Flag in John Bull's Eyes* attempted to counteract slave holders' propaganda that the Emancipation Proclamation would lead to servile insurrection by presenting evidence that newly emancipated slaves were non-violent, industrious, disciplined, courageous and unvindictive.[18]

Other tracts stressing the sufferings of women under slavery were promoted by or addressed to British women at this period, and together their focus on the present suffering and sexual exploitation of black women at the hands of white men provided an alternative vision to combat the pro-Confederate focus on the future danger to white women from lustful and violent emancipated black men. Tract no. 2 of the London Ladies' Emancipation Society was a compilation of extracts from the most famous of these, Frances Ann Kemble's *Journal of a Residence on a Georgian Plantation in 1838–1839*. Kemble, a well-known English actress, had kept a journal of her horrific experiences as wife of Pierce Meace Butler, owner of a Georgia rice plantation worked by approximately seven hundred slaves. She was finally driven to publish her journal in 1863 by her dismay at widespread British sympathy for the Southern Confederacy.[19] A chapter of the journal detailed the sufferings of women under slavery, and it was this section that was particularly remarked upon by reviewers.[20] In it Kemble contrasted the lot of slave mothers, who had entreated her to not let them be forced to resume hoeing the field immediately after childbirth, with her own privileges as a mother. She also contrasted the lot of the wife of a slave mechanic, worn down by hard labour in the field without time off after childbirth, with an idealised picture of the lot of a British artisan's wife, whose husband could earn enough for them both, enabling her to concentrate on housework and childcare.

A similar emphasis on female suffering is evident in Edward Yates' *A Letter to the Women of England* (1863). Yates was an English barrister who had travelled extensively in the South. He addressed women as especially sensitive beings, calling on them in rather high-flown language to use their feminine influence to support emancipation and the free North and to end the degradation of their own sex under slavery.[21]

A year earlier a narrative of slavery related by a former slave woman herself had been published in London. *A Deeper Wrong; or, Incidents in the Life of a Slave Girl* was the autobiography of Harriet Brent Jacobs, an African-American fugitive slave.[22] Like the earlier *History of Mary Prince*, it was edited by a white woman abolitionist and author, and it was similarly produced for a campaigning purpose. Brent Jacobs related her story 'in behalf of my persecuted people' in order 'to arouse the women of the North to a realizing sense of the condition of two millions of women at the South, still in bondage'. She painted a horrific picture of the breaking up of families under slavery, the anguish of mothers who gave birth to children destined to be sold away from them as slaves, the sexual exploitation of black women by their masters, the hatred and jealousy of planters' wives towards their husbands' black mistresses and illegitimate children, the degradation caused by slavery and the spirit of resistance of slaves like herself. She told the story of how she ran away from her master in order to escape becoming his mistress, and hid in a cramped attic space for seven years before eventually escaping to freedom in the North. The book helped rekindle the anti-slavery zeal of British women, and Amelia Chesson, George Thompson's daughter, wrote a long review of the book for the *Morning Star*, which, under the editorship of her husband F.W. Chesson was one of the few newspapers to take a pro-Northern line during the Civil War.[23]

Another important tract was Eliza Wigham's *The Anti-Slavery Cause in America, and its Martyrs* (1863), which was circulated by both the Edinburgh and London ladies' emancipation societies.[24] This was a succinct summary of the history of the American anti-slavery movement, set in the context of political developments in the United States. It concentrated on the Garrisonian wing which Wigham herself had supported, and emphasised women's contributions to the movement. Wigham stated that the aim of her pamphlet was to arouse British people's determination to guard their country from any tendency to ally itself with the Confederacy, which she described as 'having for its corner-stone American Slavery'.

Abolitionists were also concerned about the effect of the American Civil War on the British economy, in particular the cotton famine in Lancashire brought about by the North's naval blockade of the Southern ports which were the outlet for the American cotton on which the Lancashire factories depended. This led to widespread unemployment among cotton operatives.

Women abolitionists supported the giving of practical aid to these distressed cotton workers as a part of the anti-slavery cause. Harriet Martineau, seeing the workers as innocent victims of the cotton famine, acknowledged that this was a case where it was right to abandon the dogma of political economy and her belief that charity stunted self-help. She urged that steps be taken to sustain the 'lives, character and self-respect' of the operatives, suggesting that possible measures were emigration, public works, recruitment to the armed forces, and the training of young women for household employment.[25]

It was the philanthropic alleviation of female distress that particularly preoccupied female abolitionists. At a meeting of the Birmingham society in September 1862 an outline was given of a plan for employing young Lancashire women who had been deprived of their livings. Ladies in several large towns had gathered them together to make up clothing for the poor, to be disposed of at the cost of the material. It was hoped that 'at a time of forced idleness and pressing need' this would both give the women a means of subsistence and enable the ladies to exert a useful moral influence on the women, who as young, unmarried and financially independent workers were considered by middle-class reformers to be of dubious moral reputation.[26] Quaker women were prominent among those who organised sewing, cooking and reading classes for young unemployed women in Lancashire which by March 1863 had been attended by more than 41,000 women.[27]

Little information is available on the attitudes to the Civil War of the tens of thousands of women who composed slightly more than half the work-force of the cotton factories.[28] Lancashire working women lack visibility in the contemporary record because they were not prominent as leaders of textile unions, they did not make public speeches or edit working-class newspapers, and their opinions were generally not recorded by the leadership of the anti-slavery movement. It is known, however, that abolitionists' general expressions of admiration for the patient suffering of cotton operatives were extended to women workers by George Thompson, who had always taken a particular interest in women's anti-slavery efforts. At Christmas 1862 he wrote to Garrison, saying he was sure he could collect twice the number of signatories as those to the Stafford House Address to an address calling on Lincoln and Congress to give immediate and unconditional freedom to all slaves. He could not promise that as many aristocratic names would appear as before, but:

> I think I might guarantee that there should be the names of at least two hundred thousand women, who are at this moment heroically and uncomplainingly suffering from the suspension of our supply of slave-grown cotton, and who are willing to continue to suffer, rather than see the triumph of the slave holder, or a compromise of the principles of liberty on the part of the Northern States.[29]

Thompson's statement was made immediately prior to the famous meeting of the working classes in Manchester Free Trade Hall on 31 December 1862, which resolved to send an address to Lincoln on the abolition of slavery. As Mary Ellison has pointed out, Lancashire working-class newspapers of the period show widespread pro-Southern sympathies, and this meeting was not the spontaneous expression of working-class feeling which it was claimed to be by abolitionists but in fact a carefully arranged event chaired by the mayor and attended by many members of the Manchester Union and Emancipation Society.[30] In this context Thompson's unsupported claims of the anti-slavery zeal of women textile workers cannot be fully relied on. This is not, however, to deny the effectiveness of his image of self-sacrificing womanhood as anti-slavery propaganda.

A contemporary account of the cotton famine by a member of the Central Relief Committee suggests that women did not in practice always passively and gratefully join the sewing and reading classes formed by well-off ladies to await the victory of anti-slavery forces abroad. At Stalybridge in March 1863 women were involved in a riot against the low level of relief, and at the trial of the rioters a crowd of women and girls gathered illegally outside the court and 'continually insulted the soldiers and police, and chaffed the male bystanders for their cowardice'. Women also took part in raids on provision stores.[31] More research needs to be done on local sources, however, before a clearer picture of women workers' attitudes to slavery and the Civil War in America can be reconstructed.

FREEDOM AND AID

As more and more slaves were freed between the implementation of Lincoln's Emancipation Proclamation in January 1863 and the end of the American Civil War in 1865, British abolitionists became increasingly preoccupied with providing them with practical aid. As Christine Bolt has pointed out, the Freedmen's Aid movement which resulted was a continuance of the fight against slavery and involved many families with a history of anti-slavery campaigning.[32]

Ladies' anti-slavery associations in particular had always combined anti-slavery work with support for educational, missionary and relief work among black people in the West Indies and Africa. After emancipation some abolitionists felt that their responsibility to the West Indian slaves had now been discharged, but many did turn their attention to the education and Christian instruction of former slaves. They felt that it was their duty to 'elevate' those debased by slavery by helping fund missionaries, sending out Bibles and school materials, and giving grants for establishing schools and places of worship. While both male and female abolitionists supported black education, they did so in different ways. Ladies' anti-slavery associations at Birmingham, Woodbridge, Peckham, Liverpool and London, which had already supported 'negroes' aid' work, were transformed into 'negroes' friend and instruction' societies.[33] In contrast, men, with no tradition of supporting black education through their anti-slavery societies, more frequently disbanded their societies and supported education through other channels.

Birmingham provides a clear illustration of these different approaches. There the men's anti-slavery society was disbanded in January 1834 and on its reformation in July 1835 concentrated on campaigning against apprenticeship.[34] Its leading activists later organised support for black education through a separate group, the Jamaica Education Society, which they set up in 1837 in co-operation with

Baptist missionaries.[35] In contrast, the Ladies' Negro's Friend Society at Birmingham had decided in 1833 that when slavery was abolished ladies' anti-slavery associations should 'merge into Societies for the education of the African race' in order to 'undo as much as possible the miserable and demoralizing effects' of slavery.[36] Following the passage of the Emancipation Act, its members stated: 'we cannot now deliver the enslaved Negroes in our colonies from their short remaining term of bondage; but we may, with the help of God, assist in training them to the principles and *practice* of our holy religion.'[37] The society was to contribute regularly to educational projects in both the West Indies and Africa, and to maintain a personal correspondence with missionaries in the field, until its final demise in 1919.[38]

British women gave particular support to the education of black girls and women, a preoccupation in tune with the particular concern they had evinced for the suffering of women under slavery. The London Central Negro's Friend Society stated that it wished 'to be made instrumental in raising the character of the sable females of our slave colonies by intellectual and moral culture'. Aided by the Birmingham women, the group funded the sending of an English woman to conduct a school for the training of school mistresses in Spanish Town, Jamaica.[39] The Peckham Ladies' Negroes' Friend and Instruction Society continued to send regular support to the schools for girls founded by Hannah Kilham in Sierra Leone, successfully soliciting support from Quaker women as far afield as Belfast.[40] The Sheffield Ladies' Association raised subscriptions for George Thompson's School for Negro Girls at Kettering in Jamaica, intended to train female teachers for the West Indies and Africa.[41]

Women saw support of African education as part of a broader project of civilisation and Christianisation intended to promote the downfall of slavery and eradicate other aspects of African societies which they found objectionable. 'We consider', the Edinburgh Ladies' Emancipation Society stated in their 1864 report, 'that the civilization and Christianization of Africa afford the best antidotes for the slave trade, native slavery, and the dreadful human sacrifices.'[42] Similarly, commenting in the 1860s on progress at the Mendi Mission schools it helped fund in West Africa, the Birmingham Ladies' Negro's Friend Society stated that 'very pleasing accounts are constantly received of the readiness among the people to listen to Christian instruction, even when it conveys reproof of war, polygamy, slavery, and intemperance.'[43]

Missionaries and abolitionists thus maintained an attitude which combined conviction of the inferiority of African culture to European with a firm belief in Africans' innate humanity. By the 1860s this was a viewpoint which was being undermined by increasingly widespread acceptance of derogatory views of black ineducability being disseminated by individuals such as the anthropologist James Hunt, founder in 1863 of the Anthropological Society of London, who led a revival in polygenist theory that blacks are an inferior species and that missionary efforts were thus doomed to failure. Such views were challenged by women such as Mrs Moseley, the widow of the late chief justice at Cape Coast Castle on the Gold Coast of West Africa, who in 1866 gained support from British women abolitionists for educational projects in the area and who was held up to other English women as an example at a time when missionary zeal appeared to be collapsing.[44] Mrs Moseley put forward what Douglas Lorimer has described as 'the amorphous child-savage stereotype of the Negro' to justify missionary efforts.[45] In an appeal to English children she stated that black children were not the monkeys many of them had been taught to believe, but had a natural intelligence, though they were 'sunk in superstition, idolatry and ignorance'. To adults she argued that the 'negro character is as capable of gratitude, affection, and fidelity, as it is of intelligence, when treated with consideration, justice, and straightforwardness.'[46]

Between 1863 and 1868 women abolitionists focused mainly on providing aid to the American freed slaves. Aid for American fugitive slaves that had been continued by ladies' societies in Birmingham and Edinburgh through the 1850s into the early 1860s, at a time when men's groups had become inactive, merged from 1862–63 into aid to freed slaves.[47] Women took some of the first initiatives in this area. In 1862 Eliza Wigham, secretary of the Edinburgh Ladies' Emancipation Society, wrote to the editor of the *British Friend* urging Quakers to follow the example of her society in sending donations in aid of the education of emancipated American slaves.[48] At the beginning of 1863 women in Bristol issued an appeal 'to the friends of abolition' urging them to contribute money towards the education and clothing of freed slaves through a network of female collectors in England, Scotland and Ireland.[49]

When the London Freedmen's Aid Society was formed in April 1863, however, its Quaker-dominated committee was exclusively male, being drawn mainly from the committee of the BFASS. Women were also excluded from the Central Committee of the Society of Friends for the Relief of the Emancipated Negroes of the United States, formed in March 1865; from the National Committee of British Freedmen's Aid Associations (1865–66); and from the committees of the National Freedmen's Aid Union and the British and Foreign Freedmen's Aid Society (1866–68). Although the national committees were exclusively male, on the local level there were both men's and women's committees, with at least sixteen women's committees out of a total of approximately fifty societies (see Appendix, list 3e).[50] Unlike men, however, women did not send delegates to national committees.[51]

Women were encouraged to engage in practical work for the freed slaves rather than take leading organisational roles. The sexual division of labour in the Freedmen's Aid movement is exemplified by the Alsops, a couple from Stoke Newington near London. Both were prominent ministers in the Society of Friends, but whereas Robert Alsop was a member of the committee of the London Freedmen's Aid Society his wife Christine (1805–79), née Majolier, a Frenchwoman who had settled in England in the 1820s, organised local ladies' sewing circles.

Such sewing circles became the main focus of female work in aid for the freed slaves. They proliferated throughout Britain, replacing the bazaar committees of the 1840s and 1850s. Quaker activist Mrs J.B. Braithwaite set up twenty-five to thirty circles in the London area in 1864–65. In Bristol by late 1865 nearly a hundred women were meeting in sewing circles, £100 a month was being raised to purchase materials, and each month five or six boxes of clothing containing up to two thousand garments each were being forwarded to America. The circles, while often set up by women who were committed anti-slavery activists, drew in many women with no history of involvement in abolition, many of whom probably viewed the work as simply another philanthropic duty and social activity in which they could made use of their feminine accomplishments. In Bristol, for example, where a sewing circle of eighty to ninety Unitarian women was set up by veteran abolitionist Frances Armstrong, her co-worker Mary Estlin noted that 'no one whom I spoke to had an idea what the cause was wh[ich] brought them together'.[52] In other cases working-class women's support was enlisted. Louisa Brown of Leighton Buzzard promoted the formation of such circles by Friends conducting mothers' meetings, and was 'much cheered by the practical sympathy, evidenced by gifts of well worn, neatly mended garments, pence, and testaments, brought by the very poorest', and their rapid sewing of 150 garments for the cause.[53]

As earlier, exclusion from national committees did not prevent women abolitionists from taking national initiatives. In February 1864 the Female Society for Birmingham set up a committee of twelve to consider how to raise funds for aid to the freed slaves. They issued a printed circular urging the collection of funds, which was forwarded to more than a hundred places around Britain and to ministers of all denominations in Birmingham itself. By June 1865 a total of £280 16s.8d had been received from approximately three hundred individuals, mainly in small sums of 2s.6d to 10s.[54]

At the Birmingham society's annual meeting in May 1864 a novel proposal for aiding the freed slaves was made by Mrs Hannah Joseph Sturge (c. 1816–96), née Dickinson, the second wife of BFASS leader Joseph Sturge and the founder of the Birmingham Ladies' Temperance

Society as well as an anti-slavery activist. She suggested that a vessel should be freighted with clothing and agricultural implements for the use of the former slaves, 'as an appropriate return for the cargoes of bread-stuffs so beneficently sent from America to relieve our Irish and cotton famines'. The women did not feel able to carry out this scheme themselves, however, and it was put to male abolitionists who formed the Birmingham and Midland Freedmen's Aid Association to carry it into effect. This group became one of the major Freedmen's Aid organisations in Britain.[55]

The Birmingham Ladies' Negro's Friend Society and the Birmingham and Midland Freedmen's Aid Association maintained close working links and publicised each other's activities. Their co-operation was facilitated by family connections: the Quaker secretary of the women's society, Lydia Sturge (1807–92), was married to Edmund Sturge, the founder of the new group, and was the sister of Arthur Albright, a leading Birmingham activist who in 1866 became leader of the National Freedmen's Aid Union. Lydia and her husband Edmund were also involved in movements for peace, abstinence and suppression of the opium trade.[56]

The Birmingham men offered £5 to any congregation or circle of ladies who would raise another £5 for the purchase of material to make up clothing for the freed slaves. This scheme proved very popular and resulted in the receipt of goods worth £684 from ladies' sewing circles both in Birmingham and elsewhere in England, Scotland and Ireland in 1864–65.[57]

Freedmen's Aid work reached a climax in the immediate aftermath of the end of the Civil War in 1865, when the problem of catering for the physical needs and education of the four million emancipated slaves was most acute. At this period large numbers of women attended public meetings on the subject in both London and the provinces.[58] Specific appeals were made to women by the male leadership of the Freedmen's Aid movement, calling on them to honour their tradition of commitment to the anti-slavery cause: '[A]s you pleaded for the liberty of your sisters in slavery, so you are now pledged for their elevation.'[59] The two rival national societies set up in 1866, the National Freedmen's Aid Union (NFAU) and the British and Foreign Freedmen's Aid Society (BAFFAS), both adopted the sewing-circle subsidy scheme started in Birmingham. The NFAU described the work of sewing circles as the most 'pressingly indispensible' form of practical aid to the former slaves, and urged manufacturers and drapers to donate materials to sewing circles.[60]

Such appeals to women helped revive flagging interest in the cause.[61] In February 1866 alone £2,000 worth of goods was forwarded to America on behalf of the BAFFAS, and during 1866 and 1867 numerous boxes of garments made up by women were also dispatched by the NFAU, the Birmingham and Midland Freedmen's Aid Association, and by women themselves. Garments were contributed by individual women, by informal groups, by local sewing circles – some associated with church congregations including Wesleyans, Congregationalists and United Presbyterians – and by more formal ladies' associations.[62] Commenting on the work of these groups in its final report in October 1867, the committee of the NFAU spoke in high terms of the strenuous efforts of the groups' members. The goods they had forwarded had 'been not merely excellent in quality, but admirably adapted to the wants of the coloured people'.[63] The majority of the large quantities of clothes contributed to the emancipated slaves were made up by women's sewing circles.

Women also contributed money to the movement through their subscriptions and donations to local and national Freedmen's Aid societies though, in the absence of complete lists detailing individual donors, it is impossible to estimate what proportion they contributed of the estimated £120,000 raised in Britain for aid to former slaves between 1863 and 1868.

REBELLION AND REACTION

In 1866 the British Freedmen's Aid movement split over the question of whether to send aid only to the American freed slaves or to aid those in Jamaica and elsewhere as well. The division was largely the result of the so-called Governor Eyre controversy. This began in October 1865 with a riot by blacks outside the courthouse in Morant Bay in Jamaica over a disputed fine for squatting on land. A number of people were killed both by the rioters and by the volunteer militia. The British governor, Edward John Eyre, fearing a general uprising of the black population against the white – a spectre which had earlier been raised by planters and pro-slavery advocates as the inevitable consequence of emancipation – immediately declared martial law and sent in the troops. More than four hundred black people were killed, six hundred men and women were flogged and over one thousand homes burnt down. In addition George William Gordon, a 'coloured' member of the Jamaican House of Assembly accused of inciting the riot, was given a summary court martial and hanged.[64]

Confused accounts reaching Britain resulted in exaggerated stories of terrible atrocities committed by the black rioters, and abolitionists split over the best way to respond to the events.[65] The events also polarised British public opinion, with the majority of the middle and upper classes, backed by most newspapers, coming out in support of Eyre, whereas a minority of middle-class radicals and working-class leaders demanded his prosecution. As demonstrated by analyses of British reactions to the events made by Bernard Semmel, Douglas Lorimer and Christine Bolt, these reactions need to be set in the contexts of the development of a virulently racist ideology, of upper- and middle-class fears of Fenian unrest in Ireland, and of working-class trades union and suffrage agitation in the lead-up to the 1867 Reform Act.[66]

The two rival committees formed in Britain in 1865 in response to the events, the Jamaica Committee and the Eyre Defence Committee, were both composed entirely of men. In the case of the Jamaica Committee, formed to campaign for Eyre's prosecution, this was not because its members were hostile to women's rights. Indeed its leader, John Stuart Mill, was a leading proponent of women's suffrage. Rather, female exclusion resulted from the desire of the committee to recruit members with the greatest public power and influence, and women had little of either. The committee was dominated by MPs and clergymen, occupations which respectively carried the greatest political and moral weight, but which were both closed to women.

British women aligned themselves on both sides of the controversy. Women abolitionists, excluded from membership of the Jamaica Committee, nevertheless backed its work. The Edinburgh Ladies' Emancipation Society stressed the importance of the men's work in 'vindicating the law, providing constitutional safeguard against the recurrence of such abuse of prerogative' and defending 'the safeguards of life throughout the breadth of our vast empire'.[67] The group circulated the committee's pamphlets and contributed to the Jamaica Investigation Fund. The fund also received donations from the Aberdeen and Preston ladies' anti-slavery societies and the Birmingham Ladies' Negro's Friend Society.[68] Women also gave practical aid to victims of destitution in Jamaica caused by Eyre's reprisals. The Birmingham society sent £100 worth of clothing and other goods to Jamaica in 1865–66, and Edinburgh women contributed a small sum to a Restitution Fund for Sufferers in Jamaica.[69]

Women abolitionists based their support for the Jamaica Committee on their own knowledge of developments in Jamaica. The Edinburgh Ladies' Emancipation Society considered that:

> Although the rising at Morant Bay was the first act of violence, it is well known that the unhappiness of the people had just grounds in the oppressive tariffs, the low rate of wages, the with holding of wages, and the impossibility of procuring legal redress.[70]

The Birmingham society's continuing support for missionary and educational support among the black population of the West Indies involved it in extensive correspondence with missionary teachers.

These teachers gave them first-hand information on events and stressed the temperate and hard-working character of the black population.[71] Birmingham women had campaigned against the importation to Jamaica of indentured labour from China and India.[72] They had also compiled a pamphlet on the state of Jamaica, which, by laying the blame on inefficient plantation management, combated claims such as those made by Thomas Carlyle in his 1849 'Occasional Discourse on the Nigger Question' that the economic ruin of the plantations was the result of black laziness.[73] They were well aware of the depressed state of the island at the time of the Morant Bay riot.[74] At a meeting attended by fifty women on 6 February 1866, several months after the riot, letters the society had recently received from Jamaica were read and a resolution was passed which, while strongly condemning the murders committed by the rioters, also expressed the belief that the Government Commission of Inquiry would prove:

> that these barbarous acts were no part of a general conspiracy to exterminate the white population of the island, and that therefore the indiscriminate slaughter of the numbers that perished under martial law, with the flogging of women and the suffering of children, calls for the strongest condemnation, and, as far as possible, for redress from the English people.[75]

This image of suffering black women and children contrasted with the spectre of savage black male lust for white women that was conjured up by British newspapers sympathetic to Eyre. In their 1866 report the Birmingham women, while repeating their condemnation of the rioters, attacked opponents of the anti-slavery cause for using the riots to stereotype blacks as savages on whom attempts at education were · wasted. It was unfair to condemn all for the misdeeds of the few, for 'we believe that these acts cannot fairly be attributed to any *peculiar* depravity of the negro race'. Rather, they asserted that black character was similar to 'the character of the labouring classes in our own land', which 'rises and falls in no inconsiderable degree with that of the classes above them'. Black people, however, were not viewed in an identical way to poor whites: counterposing the pro-slavery stereotype of the savage with the missionary stereotype of the childlike innocent, the women argued that the influence of bad example would 'operate more powerfully with a race naturally impulsive and imitative in a high degree'. In Jamaica, where blacks were dealt with 'by those who despise and hate them', it was inevitable that bad consequences would follow.[76] If proper efforts had been made for black education, the catastrophe of 1865 might have been avoided.[77]

The Edinburgh Ladies' Emancipation Society, donating £20 towards education in Jamaica in 1867, stated:

The best compensation it is in the power of their friends in this country to provide, is to send means of education, so that, under careful protection, these poor people may be able to expand to the moral dignity of free citizens, and to understand contracts, regulations of wages, and other arrangements which materially affect them, and in which they have been so grievously imposed upon by the white race.[78]

Here freedom is equated with the ability to understand the operations of the capitalist system of waged labour, and the blame for the state of affairs is laid as much on black ignorance as on white exploitation.

For abolitionists the most shocking aspect of the Eyre controversy was the spectacle of the majority of the press and middle-class public siding with the governor. Worries had earlier been expressed at the tendency of the press and the well-off to side with the Southern Confederacy during the Civil War, but it had been possible to attribute this partly to confusion about the objectives of the North. The openly racist tone of support for Eyre, however, forced abolitionists to acknowledge that the earlier tide of public opinion in favour of anti-slavery had now been reversed. The Birmingham society deplored the spectacle of the upper and middle classes urging the Government to restore and reward Eyre.[79] The Edinburgh Ladies' Emancipation Society expressed its particular disgust at finding English women applauding as a hero a man who had been accessory to the flogging and slaughter of women.[80]

One of the earliest condemnations of British reactions to the affair came from African-American abolitionist Sarah Parker Remond, who condemned the racism inherent in support for Eyre in a letter to the editor of the London *Daily News* in response to an article in the London *Times* which claimed that the uprising proved blacks were unfit for freedom. Remond, who in 1860 had expressed pleasure at the absence of racial prejudice among Britons, stated in 1865: '[T]here is a change in the public opinion in Great Britain in reference to the coloured race.' She had, she asserted, 'never read more insulting attacks upon the negro race than I have read within the last four years in some of the London journals'. Black people themselves were 'in no way to blame' for this change. Rather, Southern Confederates in alliance with West Indian planters had tried to undermine public support for blacks. Slaves freed after eight generations in slavery were judged unfit for freedom because they did not immediately attain perfection, whereas the terrible cruelty of slave holders had been forgotten. Remond argued that if blacks in Jamaica had committed crimes during the recent insurrection then they should have been entitled to legal trial just as other British subjects were. Those found guilty should then have been properly punished, but the incidents should not be made 'the occasion of the most insulting and unjust attacks upon the whole race, on account of a difference of complexion'.[81]

The termination of the national Freedmen's Aid societies in 1868 was in part the result of this growth in scientific racism and decline in public sympathy for former slaves which had crystallised during the Governor Eyre controversy. The need for support of the newly free had never been greater. In 1868, the very year that British aid was discontinued, an illustration appeared in *Harpers Weekly* which vividly highlighted the rise in racist violence in the American South (Figure 14).

Only a handful of activists maintained an interest in the plight of free blacks after the 1860s. Prominent among them was Catherine Impey (1847-1923), an English Quaker who was too young to have played much part in the anti-slavery or Freedmen's Aid movements of the 1860s. The daughter of Quakers Robert and Mary Impey of Street in Somerset, she remained single and devoted her life to public work, becoming a member of the urban district council and the local Board of Guardians. On a visit to Boston, Massachusetts, in 1878 as a delegate to the International Conference of the Temperance Order of Good Templars, she met with former leaders of the American abolition movement and leading black churchmen. She was told of the colour bars in occupations and on public transport, and of the self-satisfied indifference to black people's plight which was prevalent even among abolitionists. Her black contacts, who impressed her with their education, stressed that they did not want patronage but simply a fair and equal chance. Writing to the *Friend* of her experiences, she argued that the stereotype of African inferiority was unjust, since some black men and women were 'highly educated, refined and intelligent'. The social disabilities of blacks were 'the remains of slavery'. The few in America who were 'continuing to fight the battle of freedom under this new aspect' looked to the 'unprejudiced Christianised common sense of the British people' for moral support. 'Should we not, then', she asked, 'disregard the cry of "British interference", and endeavour, both by act and word, as opportunity may offer, to obtain the recognition of the dark-skinned man as truly a *man* and a *brother*.'[82]

Catherine Impey retained her opposition to racial prejudice, editing a periodical called *Anti-Caste* between 1888 and 1895, which was 'devoted to the interests of the coloured races', particularly African-Americans. In her opening address to readers she stated that distinctions and disabilities based on differences in social rank or on physical characteristics such as sex or race were 'contrary to the mind of Christ'. She gained the support of Hannah Joseph Sturge, president of the Birmingham Ladies' Negro's Friend Society at this period.[83]

Figure 14 Patience on a Monument. Engraving by Thomas Nast in *Harper's Weekly*, 10 October 1868, p. 648.

Catherine Impey was also involved in the mid-1880s in the formation of the Society for the Furtherance of Human Brotherhood. This society issued an address which appealed to people to 'complete the work of the Anti-Slavery Movement by securing, not mere *declarations of emancipation*, but the full enjoyment of FREEDOM, EQUAL OPPORTUNITY, AND BROTHERHOOD within the pale of the one great human family'. While chattel slavery in America had been abolished twenty years before, it had been replaced by racial prejudice, persecution and violence. The few Northerners still fighting for equality, and the leaders of the black community, needed support from outside America for their work. The new society had thus been formed 'with a view to rendering this support to the surviving Anti-Slavery sentiment of our sister nation, and also of instilling principles of *justice* and human brotherhood in our own people *at home*, in India, and in the Colonies (who are far from blameless in this matter of race-prejudice)'.[84]

A list of names of both men and women was appended to the appeal, headed by Edinburgh abolitionists and feminists Eliza Wigham and Elizabeth Pease Nichol, which suggests that it was they who initiated the group. Other female signatories included Mary Estlin, Mary Carpenter, Josephine Butler, Mary Priestman, Margaret Tanner, and Helen Bright Clark, a Quaker from Street in Somerset who was active in both the Freedmen's Aid and women's suffrage movements in the 1860s. The list thus provides evidence of the overlap between the black and women's rights movements in terms of both personnel and chronology and indicates that preoccupation with feminism did not result in a complete neglect of issues of race and slavery.

Nevertheless, the feminist movement, which provided a new focus for female reform and activism from 1866 onwards, can be identified as an important element in the ferment of political and social reform in Britain which Christine Bolt has argued was a major reason for the end of the organised anti-slavery and Freedmen's Aid movements in 1868.[85] The diversity of issues and priorities at this period is highlighted in an account by Frances Power Cobbe of a gathering of reformers, all men and women who had played leading parts in the anti-slavery movement, at Mentia Taylor's home in London. A discussion of 'what *is* the great cause of the age?' led to various responses of Parliamentary reform, industrial schools, teetotalism, theism and women's suffrage. Only Sarah Parker Remond, the sole black participant, continued to give priority to the eradication of slavery.[86]

The popular anti-slavery movement was thus not transformed into a lasting mass campaign of either practical aid or political support for the emancipated. Among women as well as men concern for black welfare dwindled both as white philanthropic mission and its more politically radical manifestation as support for black rights to freedom and legal equality. For many leading British women abolitionists, feminism became the new focus of their political energies, and concern for the suffering of enslaved and freed black women abroad was displaced by growing awareness of the subordinate position of women within British society. The long-term effects that this shift had on the relationship between feminism and imperialism in late-nineteenth-century Britain merit further attention from scholars.

9

ANTI-SLAVERY AND WOMEN: A NEW PICTURE

The Female Society for Birmingham, the first ladies' anti-slavery society to be founded in Britain, was also the longest-lasting local society. It continued to meet until 1919, and was the only local anti-slavery society to remain active beyond the 1860s. In 1875 the Birmingham group produced a *Retrospect* of its half century of activism, summing up its work for both anti-slavery and black education. The *Retrospect* was a tribute to female efforts in the cause, singling out for special praise the work of its founders Lucy Townsend and Mary Lloyd, of local activists Rachel Lloyd and Sophia Sturge, of the pamphleteer Elizabeth Heyrick and of the educationalist Hannah Kilham.[1] The little booklet is an insignificant memorial when measured against the public statues, biographies and histories of the male leadership of the campaign. It is hoped that this new study will act as a more substantial testimony to women's contributions to the cause, so that future histories of the anti-slavery movement may be informed by an under-standing of women's contributions and of the gender dimensions of the campaign, and so that future histories of women's lives in the nineteenth century may be enriched by an understanding of their roles in anti-slavery. In such ways we can break out of the restricting boundaries which have tended to confine the study of women to the field of social history while defining political history as the study of the public activities of men.

A study of women campaigners, as we have seen, can illuminate the nature of anti-slavery as a nationwide popular extra-Parliamentary campaign by exposing the differing ways in which public support could be enlisted and the variety of forms which 'pressure from without' could take. It has been established that ladies' anti-slavery associations, founded from 1825 onwards, operated largely independently of local men's auxiliary societies rather than being subsidiary groups of the type common in many philanthropic organisations of the period. In addition, far from being groups which obediently implemented the policies decided by the male leadership of the movement in London, ladies' associations provided a setting in which women were able to develop their own ways of working, produce their own propaganda, decide on their own campaigning priorities and create their own networks. Men's and women's groups tended to target members of their own sex and went about achieving their objectives in correspondingly different ways – men primarily through public meetings, women through house-to-house canvassing. Women's methods of work, while more time consuming than those adopted by men, reached a wider section of the community, beyond those already sufficiently interested in the cause to attend a public meeting. Specifically, they reached other women in their own homes, encouraging them to harness their domestic duties to anti-slavery ends.

Women's anti-slavery activities defy restrictive categorisation: they ranged from approaching friends, relatives and neighbours in the local community to taking national initiatives, from behind-the-scenes assistance to male relatives to the public and political action of petitioning Parliament and the formation of independent societies. At Birmingham the first female anti-slavery society was set up as an independent society with no formal relationship to the national society. From the late 1830s onwards increasing numbers of new independent women's societies were formed, and these established direct links with abolitionist groups in the United States. Over the course of the anti-slavery campaign women were responsible for a number of vitally important national initiatives. In the 1820s the Female Society for Birmingham successfully encouraged the formation of other women's anti-slavery groups throughout Britain. Women also organised the only three national petitions against slavery, the first to Parliament in 1833, the second to the Queen in 1838, and the third to American women in 1853. All of these were signed by enormous numbers of women, and they represent the three largest anti-slavery protests ever organised by British abolitionists.

Individual women also played important roles at a national level. Birmingham society founder and secretary Lucy Townsend, pamphleteer Elizabeth Heyrick, journalist Harriet Martineau, 'free'-produce campaigner Anna Richardson, Frederick Douglass' assistant Julia Griffiths and African-American anti-slavery lecturer Sarah Parker Remond were all campaigners of national stature. Women were also key members of the network of British and American abolitionists. From the 1840s particularly strong transatlantic links were forged between supporters of William Lloyd Garrison, and an essential element of these links was the sisterhood of radical abolitionists developed by British women such as Elizabeth Pease of Darlington, Mary Estlin of Bristol and Eliza Wigham of Edinburgh and the American women with whom they corresponded on a wide variety of political and social issues including pacifism, Chartism and feminism as well as abolition. Overall, women in the organised anti-slavery movement came from a similar range of backgrounds as male activists, and frequently from the same families. However, as we have seen, the differing positions of men and women within the family, within religious denominations and in relationship to the political sphere and to economic life influenced the nature of their involvement in the cause.

In terms of family life, the dominant ideology of 'separate spheres', which prescribed women's prime sphere as being the domestic, fostered the development in women of a distinctive outlook on slavery which focused on the disruption of family life and the suffering of black women. Slavery, women campaigners emphasised, was not only a system of unfree, unwaged labour but also a systematic attack on the private and personal lives of the enslaved. In this way women campaigners made a political issue of the personal suffering of women who were sexually exploited by their masters, brutally flogged when pregnant, and forcibly separated from husbands and children. My contention has been that anti-slavery ideology was as much concerned with 'proper' relations of gender as with those class relations stressed by David Brion Davis in his persuasive analysis of anti-slavery as a key site of the drive to establish middle-class ideological hegemony – to make middle-class values seem 'common sense' – during the Industrial Revolution.

The dominant vision of anti-slavery which has emerged in this study was a hierarchical one based on a belief in Britain's imperial Christian mission. It was a vision linked to evangelical Protestantism, and it combined a belief in black humanity with a conviction of African cultural inferiority. It was often linked to a combination of philanthropy and social conservatism at home, in which the limits of reform were set at the point at which existing hierarchies of class and gender threatened to be overturned. It is hardly surprising that many middle-class women anti-slavery campaigners adopted this perspective, given that many came to anti-slavery from support for missionary work and other forms of evangelical enterprise. The evangelical emphasis on anti-slavery as a religious and moral crusade both roused women to action and provided a justification for acting. The approach enabled women to represent their public activism on a political issue not as a challenge to the existing social order which Wilberforce had feared it would become, but rather as an extension of their support for black Christian education, as a duty incumbent upon women in their assigned role as guardians of morality, and as the product of their desire to extend to enslaved women their own 'privileges' as British women whose 'proper' place was in the home.

There remained a tension in anti-slavery thought, however, between

200

A NEW PICTURE

this hierarchical vision and an egalitarian vision rooted in late eighteenth-century radical arguments for the natural rights of men. As has been shown, these opposing visions can be clearly traced through a comparison of the writings of two prominent women who were supporters of anti-slavery in the 1790s, Mary Wollstonecraft and Hannah More. The radical and feminist Wollstonecraft advocated the rights of men and of women from an egalitarian perspective; the conservative evangelical Hannah More believed in the spiritual equality of men and women, black and white, but was convinced that social order could only be maintained by retaining hierarchical social relations. In the 1820s, when her hierarchical vision had become dominant, the alternative egalitarian vision was most strikingly articulated by a woman schooled in the radicalism of the 1790s, Elizabeth Heyrick. Heyrick was also a woman who had experienced an intense religious conversion to Quakerism and her major pamphlet, *Immediate, not Gradual Abolition*, powerfully combined the language of natural rights with a denunciation of slavery as a sin against God. The Society of Friends – a sect to which many leading women anti-slavery campaigners belonged – combined a stress on spiritual equality with opposition to worldly hierarchies. This perspective, I have argued, fostered an egalitarian approach to anti-slavery, encouraged women to view themselves as the spiritual equals of men, and gave women the strength to follow the inner voice of their consciences regardless of male opinion.

There is evidence, too, that women's principled stand on the issue of immediate emancipation was in part the product of their exclusion from the manoeuvrings and compromises of Parliamentary party politics. This exclusion led them to develop forms of campaigning such as the community-based boycott of slave-grown produce which bypassed Parliament altogether and which involved an appeal directly to the people to bring about the downfall of the slave system by direct action. Ladies' associations' development of such forms of campaigning which were independent of developments within Parliament seems also to have facilitated the associations' transformation into flourishing societies for black education and universal abolition in the period following the passage of the 1833 Emancipation Act. In contrast many of the men's societies, which had always focused on bringing about change through Parliament, became inactive once slavery had become an issue on which the British government could exert little influence.

Men's and women's differing approaches to anti-slavery can be related not only to differing political positions but also to differing economic positions. In particular, the two approaches to slave-grown produce adopted by middle-class men and women campaigners can be related to their distinct sources of power and influence in industrial capitalist society: women as controllers of household consumption,

201

men as managers of commercial and industrial enterprises. This difference led women campaigners to focus on the evil of consuming slave-grown produce, men to concentrate on lobbying Parliament to remove protective duties favouring such produce. Women's approach had the effect of assigning responsibility for slavery to the buyer – commonly female – of slave-grown sugar and cotton in Britain, as much as to the slave holder in the West Indies. In other words, women's approach 'brought home' the issue of slavery, turning it from an issue of colonial and commercial policy into a domestic matter.

Thus women, despite their lack of formal power at a national level, influenced the form and direction of campaigns both locally and nationally. They were not passive supporters of male-defined campaigns, but active and innovative. Without their contributions the movement would have been less well funded and less widely supported, it would have involved a more limited range of activities, and middle-class ideology would have been articulated through anti-slavery in a narrower way. This would have made the anti-slavery movement less effective. A study of women thus enriches our understanding of both the nature of the anti-slavery movement and the reasons for its widespread public support and its successes.

In turn, a study of anti-slavery throws new light on women's relationship to public life and politics, on the development of feminism, and on divisions and alliances between women along lines of class and race.

The anti-slavery movement, the first great British pressure group, which preceded and inspired other reform movements, was an important arena in which middle-class men defined a masculine identity centred on male extra-Parliamentary organisations which formed part of a new public sphere clearly separated from the home. As this study has demonstrated, the movement was also the first large-scale political campaign by middle-class women, and the first movement in which women aroused the opinion of the female public in order to put pressure on Parliament. These women campaigners, only exceptionally challenging their exclusion from male organisations, instead created a distinctive female approach to anti-slavery. Ladies' associations meeting to discuss anti-slavery politics in domestic settings, women canvassers going from door to door, slave-grown sugar abstainers operating a female consumer boycott, and women using their domestic skills to make goods for anti-slavery bazaars – all these efforts made interconnections between domestic and political life and between private and public activities. In so doing, women campaigners blurred the boundaries between 'masculine' public and 'feminine' private spheres which their menfolk were so concerned to establish and to maintain.

It has become clear, however, that there was no simple line of development from anti-slavery to feminism in Britain. The majority of women represented their anti-slavery activities, whether they involved forming associations or petitioning Parliament, not as their *right* but rather as their *duty* to other women. They described their actions as a response to a system which denied enslaved women the 'privileges' of patriarchal protection. Far from explicitly challenging their own subordinate roles in British society, middle-class women expressed the desire to replicate abroad British middle-class ideals concerning gender relations. There were thus powerful ideological factors inhibiting the development from anti-slavery to women's rights in Britain.

On the other hand, anti-slavery propelled women into independently organising together for political ends, into developing an approach to campaigning which was rooted in concern for other women, into emphasising on their own responsibility for the perpetuation of slavery and thus viewing themselves as responsible adults, and into challenging men on policy matters and thus acknowledging that their views were not always adequately represented by their male colleagues. All these activities sat uneasily with their legal status as *femmes couvertes*, lacking an independent legal and political identity. While some women anti-slavery campaigners expressed hostility to American women who attempted to introduce the women's rights issue into British anti-slavery at the World Anti-Slavery Convention in 1840, many leading women anti-slavery campaigners of the 1840s to 1860s became involved in feminist campaigns, and many leading feminists of the period were supporters of anti-slavery.

The concern for women which formed the basis of women's commitment to the causes of both anti-slavery and feminism carried the possibility for female alliances across the lines of class and of race. We have seen, however, that in practice the majority of the white, middle-class women who controlled ladies' anti-slavery associations articulated and acted on their concern for other women in ways which frequently reinforced existing class and racial hierarchies among women. Often supporters of missionary work to 'heathen' women and among poor women in Britain, and themselves the employers of working-class women as domestic servants, middle-class white women campaigners tended to view both working-class and black women as passive victims on whom they had the power to bestow benefits rather than as equals and co-campaigners.

One result of this was that middle-class women tended not to recruit working-class women to ladies' anti-slavery associations but rather to enlist their support for particular campaigning initiatives which depended on mass participation for their success – in particular, petitioning and the boycott of slave-grown produce. Working women, in their participation in the boycott and most strikingly in their mass signing of petitions, demonstrated, like working men, their over-whelming opposition to slavery. At the same time, however, working women shared with working men considerable suspicion of, and even hostility towards, the middle-class campaigners who dominated the organised anti-slavery movement. Poor women resented well-to-do 'ladies' urging the morality of using expensive 'free'-grown sugar rather than cheaper slave-grown produce. Women who were politically active in the Owenite, anti-Poor Law and Chartist movements attacked the hypocrisy of middle-class and upper-class campaigners who focused on distant suffering at the expense of their suffering in Britain. Like the male activists, they made analogies between the position of waged labourers and slaves, but they added a female perspective to such critiques, comparing the exploitation of working women and the destruction of family life under the new Poor Law of 1834 with the oppression of the enslaved. Some middle-class women reacted to such attacks with alarm and hostility; many others complacently dismissed them as unjustified given their commitment to philanthropic aid to the poor. A few leading women campaigners, however, both made attempts to involve working women in their organisations, and gave outspoken public support to Chartism and Owenism despite the risks they faced of being branded as unladylike by men and women of their own class.

Women's approach to anti-slavery campaigning was affected not only by class ideology but also by racial ideology. The adoption by ladies' anti-slavery associations of the slogan 'Am I not a woman and a sister' in the 1820s echoed the slogan 'Am I not a man and a brother' coined by male campaigners in the 1780s. It marked a similar acknowledgement of black humanity, while carrying the additional message of sympathy for, and perhaps even empathy with, enslaved women. The egalitarian implications of both slogans, however, were undercut by being accompanied by images of kneeling slaves appealing to the white British viewer (see Figure 10). Such images, in sharp contrast to William Blake's 1790s image of sisterhood across racial boundaries (see Figure 5), conveyed the powerlessness of black men and women to overthrow slavery and their dependence on white men and women to grant them freedom.

The visual image of black powerlessness was reinforced by images of black women as victims of physical punishment (see Figures 4 and 9). The relationship of these enslaved women to white women campaigners was visually represented not by the image of sisters but by the image of mother and child, an image which portrayed white women as the protectors of powerless black people (see Figure 6 and 13). Here maternalism becomes the female equivalent of paternalism. The imperial mother – Britain represented by the female figure of Britannia or Justice or Liberty or Queen Victoria – bestows the blessings of freedom, Christianity and western civilisation on her enslaved colonial offspring. David Dabydeen has pointed out how portraits of eighteenth-century aristocratic English women and their black child slave-servants drew on the iconography of madonna and child to portray as affectionate the exploitative relationship of mistress and slave (see Figure 2). In the vision of anti-slavery as imperial Christian mission, this image was transformed into an anti-slavery one while preserving its inherent hierarchy.

In such images all black resistance to slavery is invisible, and in particular no record is made of the multiple ways in which black women resisted their particular forms of oppression under slavery both in the colonies and in Britain itself. In Britain, as we have seen, black women joined black men in initiating anti-slavery action by running away from their owners, and black women such as Mary Prince, Ellen Craft and Sarah Parker Remond played key roles in the British anti-slavery movement. The image of Ellen Craft, an enslaved black woman, disguised as a white male slave owner during her escape from slavery, provides a striking counter-image to the dominant representation of black women in anti-slavery texts and engravings. Here, indeed, is 'the world turned upside down'.

In creating a new picture of British anti-slavery which centres on women I hope that this book, intended to complement studies focusing on the resistance to slavery by enslaved women themselves, will lead to the restoration of women to anti-slavery history and of anti-slavery to women's history, and that in future women campaigners will be remembered 'in justice to history and to posterity', as the abolitionist and feminist Anne Knight so fervently expressed more than 150 years ago.

APPENDIX:
LADIES' ANTI-SLAVERY
ASSOCIATIONS

(1) 1825-33

Alton, Battersea and Clapham, Beverley, Birmingham etc., Bradford, Bridlington, Brighton, Calne and Salisbury, Camberwell, Carlisle, Charlbury, Chelmsford, City District (London), Clifton and Bristol, Clonmel, Colchester, Colebrookdale, Cork, Deddington, Dorking, Dublin, Durham, Edinburgh, Exeter, Glasgow, Gracechurch Street (London), Grantham, Hemel Hempstead, Huddersfield, Hull and East Riding, Hythe, Ipswich, Kendal, Kingsbridge, Kingston, Leicester, Liverpool, London, Manchester, Moyallen, Newbury, Newcastle-under-Lyme, Newcastle-upon-Tyne, Northeast London, North London and Islington, North Staffordshire, Norwich, Nottingham, Oakham, Oxford, Peckham, Plaistow and West Ham, Plymouth and Stonehouse, Ramsgate, Reading, Rochester and Chatham, St Albans, St Ives (Hunts), Sheffield, Southampton, Southwark, Spalding, Stafford, Staines, Stoke Newington, Taunton, Tenby, Tottenham, Westminster, Woodbridge, Woodgreen (Staffs), Worcester, York.

(2) 1833-38

Aberdeen, Alton, Bath, Birmingham, Brighton, Cork, Darlington, Dublin, Edinburgh, Exeter, Glasgow, Hull, Liverpool, London, Newcastle-upon-Tyne, Nottingham, Peckham, Reading, Rotherham, Sheffield, Southampton, Southwark, Taunton, Woodbridge.

(3) 1839-68

(a) Donating to the British and Foreign Anti-Slavery Society

Aberdeen, Banbury, Bath, Birmingham etc., Bury St Edmunds, Bond Street Chapel (Birmingham), Brighton, Bristol and Clifton (until 1851), Carlisle, Chelmsford, Cheltenham, Dartmouth, Derby, Devizes, Evesham, Exeter, Falmouth, Helston, Hull, Kendal, Leicester, Liskeard,

Liverpool, Manchester, Newton Abbot, Newcastle-upon-Tyne, Norfolk and Norwich, North Shields, Nottingham, Penzance, Plymouth, Redruth, Saffron Walden, Sheffield, Southwark, Stratford-upon-Avon, Stoke Newington, Taunton, Torquay, Totness, Truro, Woodbridge, York.

(b) Independent Ladies' Associations

Belfast, Bridgewater, Bristol and Clifton (from 1851), Carlisle, Clogher, Cork, Dalkeith, Darlington, Dublin, Dundee, Edinburgh, Free Church (Edinburgh), Falkirk, Glasgow (three separate societies), Halstead, Handsworth, Kelso, Kirkcaldy, Ladies' London Emancipation Society, Leeds (mixed society), Ladies' Society to Aid Fugitives from Slavery (London), Liverpool, Manchester, Manchester Anti-Slavery League, Nottingham, Perth, Preston, Rochdale, Ulverston.

(c) Ladies' Free-Labour Produce Associations, 1840s–50s

Alnwick, Birmingham and West Bromwich, Braydon, Bristol, Carlisle, Coldstream, Darlington, Dunse, Gateshead, Hartlepool, Hitchin, London, Luton, Maryport, Middlesborough, Newcastle-upon-Tyne, Newport, North Shields, Peckham, South Shields, Stockton, Sunderland, Walthamstow, Worcester, Whitehaven, Winlaton, Workington.

(d) Ladies' Associations Founded by Julia Griffiths, 1856–57

Aberdeen, Barnsley, Bradford, Coventry, Derby, Doncaster, Dublin (Irish Metropolitan), Edinburgh (Ladies' New), Halifax, Huddersfield, Liverpool, Mansfield, Rotherham, Sheffield, Wakefield.

(e) Ladies' Freedman's Aid Societies, 1862–68

Birmingham, Brighton, Bristol, Camden, Camden Road (Holloway), Cardiff, Dublin, Erdington, Frome, Glasgow, Hertford, Leeds, London (Negro Aid Society), Newcastle-upon-Tyne, Stoke Newington, Tunbridge Wells.

NOTES

1 ANTI-SLAVERY AND WOMEN: CHALLENGING THE OLD PICTURE

1 Letter from Anne Knight to Lucy Townsend, Paris, 20 September 1840, in Lucy Townsend, 'Autographs', p. 102, MSS Brit. Emp. S.5, in RHL.
2 There is an interesting discussion of the painting in Alex Tyrrell, ' "Woman's mission" and pressure group politics in Britain, 1825–60', *Bulletin of the John Rylands University Library*, vol. 63 (1980), pp. 194–230.
3 *Description of Haydon's Picture of the Great Meeting of Delegates Held at the Freemasons' Tavern, June 1840, for the Abolition of Slavery and the Slave Trade Throughout the World* (London: Charles Reynell, [c. 1841]); Tom Taylor (ed.), *The Autobiography and Memoirs of Benjamin Robert Haydon (1786–1846)*, new edition (London: Peter Davies, 1926), vol. II, p. 694, diary entry for 29 June 1840.
4 James Walvin, 'The propaganda of anti-slavery', in James Walvin (ed.), *Slavery and British Society, 1776–1846* (London: Macmillan, 1986), section on women, pp. 61–63.
5 Louis and Rosamund Billington, ' "A burning zeal for righteousness": Women in the British anti-slavery movement, 1820–1860', in Jane Rendall (ed.), *Equal or Different: Women's Politics, 1800–1914* (Basingstoke: Macmillan, 1985), pp. 82–111; Karen Irene Halbersleben, ' "She hath done what she could": women's participation in the British antislavery movement, 1825–1870', unpublished Ph.D. thesis, State University of New York at Buffalo, 1987.
6 The present study is a development from Clare Midgley, 'Women anti-slavery campaigners in Britain, 1787–1868', unpublished Ph.D. thesis, University of Kent, 1989.
7 Eric Williams, *Capitalism and Slavery* (Chapel Hill: University of North Carolina Press, 1944).
8 David Brion Davis, *The Problem of Slavery in the Age of Revolution, 1770–1823* (Ithaca: Cornell University Press, 1975); David Brion Davis, 'Reflections on abolitionism and ideological hegemony', *American Historical Review*, vol. 92, no. 4 (October 1987), pp. 797–812.
9 Seymour Drescher, *Capitalism and Antislavery: British Mobilization in Comparative Perspective* (Basingstoke: Macmillan, 1986).
10 Robin Blackburn, *The Overthrow of Colonial Slavery, 1776–1848* (London: Verso, 1988); see especially p. 465.
11 Hilary McD. Beckles, *Natural Rebels: A Social History of Enslaved Black Women in*

Barbados (London: Zed Books, 1989); Barbara Bush, *Slave Women in Caribbean Society, 1650–1838* (Bloomington: Indiana University Press, 1990).

12 Joan Wallach Scott, 'Survey article: Women in History. II. The Modern Period', *Past and Present*, no. 101 (November 1983), p. 156.

13 Frank Prochaska, *Women and Philanthropy in Nineteenth Century England* (Oxford: Oxford University Press, 1980).

14 Key studies of American abolitionist–feminists include Blanche Glassman Hersch, *The Slavery of Sex: Feminist–Abolitionists in America* (Urbana: University of Illinois Press, 1978); Jean Fagan Yellin, *Women and Sisters: The Antislavery Feminists in American Culture* (New Haven: Yale University Press, 1989).

15 Leonore Davidoff and Catherine Hall, *Family Fortunes: Men and Women of the English Middle Class, 1780–1850* (London: Hutchinson, 1987).

16 Geoff Eley, 'Re-thinking the political: social history and political culture in eighteenth and nineteenth century Britain', *Archiv für Sozialgeschichte*, vol. 21 (1981), 427–57.

2 PARTICIPANTS FROM THE PAST

1 For a short account of the case see Peter Fryer, *Staying Power: The History of Black People in Britain* (London: Pluto Press, 1984), pp. 118–19.

2 C. Duncan Rice, *The Rise and Fall of Black Slavery* (London: Macmillan, 1975), chs 2, 3, 4.

3 David Dabydeen, *Hogarth's Blacks: Images of Blacks in Eighteenth Century English Art* (Manchester: Manchester University Press, 1987), pp. 17–40.

4 C. L. R. James, *The Black Jacobins: Toussaint L'Ouverture and the San Domingo Revolution* (1938); Robin Blackburn, *The Overthrow of British Colonial Slavery, 1776–1848* (London: Verso, 1988).

5 For recent attempts to integrate black actions into British anti-slavery history see Seymour Drescher, *Capitalism and Antislavery: British Mobilization in Comparative Perspective* (Basingstoke: Macmillan, 1986), ch. 2; James Walvin, *England, Slaves and Freedom, 1776–1838* (Basingstoke: Macmillan, 1986); Douglas Lorimer, 'Black slaves and English liberty: a re-examination of racial slavery in England', *Immigrants and Minorities*, vol. 3, no. 2 (July 1984), pp. 121–50.

6 For a detailed account of the court cases, especially the famous Somerset case of 1772, see F. O. Shyllon, *Black Slaves in Britain* (London: Oxford University Press, 1974).

7 Fryer, *Staying Power*, especially p. 203; Drescher, *Capitalism and Antislavery*, ch. ii. In Scotland slavery had been made illegal by the judgment in the Knight v. Weddeburn case in 1778.

8 See Walvin, *England, Slaves and Freedom*, pp. 47, 53; Drescher, *Capitalism and Antislavery*, p. 28.

9 For examples of such sale advertisements see James Walvin, *The Black Presence: A Documentary History of the Negro in England, 1555–1860* (London: Orbach & Chambers, 1971), p. 80; Shyllon, *Black Slaves in Britain*, p. 7; Drescher, *Capitalism and Antislavery*, p. 196, n. 61. Drescher identifies the last public sale of a slave in England as taking place in Liverpool in 1782.

10 Unidentified newspaper, quoted in John Ashton, *Social Life in the Reign of Queen Anne. Taken from Original Sources* (London: Chatto & Windus, 1882), p. 81.

11 *Lloyds Evening Post*, 3–5 November 1769, quoted in Drescher, *Capitalism and Antislavery*, p. 188, n. 24. Lorimer (Lorimer, 'Black slaves and English

liberty', p. 139) suggests that black men had more job opportunities than black women, and thus faced fewer obstacles in attempting to gain freedom. Clear evidence for this is lacking, however.

12 Letter from Hannah More to Horace Walpole, Cowslip Green, July 1790, quoted in William Roberts (ed.), *Memoirs of the Life and Correspondence of Hannah More* (London: R. B. Seeley, 1834), 2nd edn, vol. II, p. 235. Shyllon gives information on the sale and forced deportation of another girl in Bristol in 1792 (Shyllon, *Black Slaves in Britain*, p. 170).

13 Estimates of the black population of England in the late eighteenth century vary, but it was probably approaching 20,000. (See Walvin, *England, Slaves and Freedom*, p. 47.)

14 Sir John Fielding, *Extracts from Such of the Penal Laws, as Particularly Relate to the Peace and Good Order of This Metropolis*, new edn (London: H. Woodfall & W. Straham, 1768), p. 144. Emphasis added.

15 Fielding, *Extracts from such of the Penal Laws*, p. 144. While the Yorke–Talbot court ruling of 1729 had declared that baptism did not make slaves free, the belief that it did was widespread among black people. (See Shyllon, *Black Slaves in Britain*, p. 26.)

16 Stephen J. Braidwood, 'Initiatives and organisation of the black poor 1786–1787', *Slavery and Abolition*, vol. 3, no. 3 (December 1982), pp. 211–27.

17 Ibid.

18 Dabydeen, *Hogarth's Blacks*, pp. 18–20, 37, 50, 62–64, 121.

19 Drescher, *Capitalism and Antislavery*, p. 34.

20 [Thomas Day and John Bicknell], *The Dying Negro, a Poetical Epistle* (London: Flexney, 1773).

21 Hugh Honour, *The Image of the Black in Western Art* (Houston: Menil Foundation, 1989), vol. IV, part 1, pp. 91–93.

22 A Planter [Edward Long], *Candid Reflections Upon the Negro Cause* (1772), p. 48–49, as quoted in Shyllon, *Black Slaves in Britain*, p. 151 (see also pp. 162–63); caricature in Radio Times Hulton Picture Library reproduced in Susanne Everett, *The Slaves* (London: Bison Books, 1978), p. 141.

23 Fielding, p. 144; report in *Lloyds Evening Post*, quoted in Drescher, *Capitalism and Antislavery*, p. 188, n. 24; *Daily Advertiser*, 4–9 September 1772.

24 See A. T. Gary, 'The political and economic relations of English and American Quakers (1750–1885)', D.Phil. thesis, Oxford, 1935.

25 For Quaker views of black equality before God see J. William Frost (ed.), *The Quaker Origins of Antislavery* (Norwood, PA: Norwood Editions, 1980), p. 2.

26 See Thomas Clarkson, *A Portraiture of Quakerism*, 3 vols (London: Longman, Hurst, Rees, & Orme, 1806), vol. III, ch. 18.

27 Thomas Clarkson, *The History of the Rise, Progress and Accomplishment of the Abolition of the African Slave Trade by the British Parliament* (London: Longman, Hurst, Rees & Orme, 1808), p. 129–30.

28 *Memoirs of the Life of Catherine Phillips: to Which Are Added Some of Her Epistles* (London: James Phillips, 1797), p. 68; *Some Account of the Life and Religious Exercises of Mary Neale, Formerly Mary Peisley. Principally Compiled from Her Own Writings* (Dublin: John Gough, 1795), p. 92.

29 William J. Allinson (compiler), *Memorials of Rebecca Jones*, 2nd edn (Philadelphia: Longstrelt, 1849), especially pp. 144–45.

30 Letters no. 28 and 38, Women's Yearly Meeting (London), 'Epistles sent and received 1768–1778', MSS in Friends House Library, London.

31 See Alan M. Rees, 'English friends and the abolition of the slave trade', *The*

NOTES

Bulletin of the Friends Historical Association, vol. 44, no. 2 (Autumn 1955), pp. 74–87; J. William Frost, 'The origins of the Quaker crusade against slavery: a review of recent literature', *Quaker History*, vol. 67, no. 1 (Spring 1978), pp. 42–58; Judith Jennings, 'The American revolution and the testimony of British Quakers against the slave trade', *Quacker History*, vol. 70, no. 1 (Spring 1986), pp. 99–103. None of these accounts deals with women's contributions.

32 Roberts, *Memoirs of the Life and Correspondence of Hannah More*, 2nd edn, vol. II, especially pp. 71, 152; letter from Hannah More to Lady Middleton, Cowslip Green, 10 September [1788], quoted in Lady Georgina Chatterton (ed.), *Memorials, Personal and Historical, of Admiral Lord Gambier* (London: Hurst & Blackett, 1861), p. 173. See also M. G. Jones, *Hannah More* (Cambridge: Cambridge University Press, 1952).

33 Robert I. and Samuel W. Wilberforce (eds), *The Life of William Wilberforce*, 5 vols (London: Murray, 1838), vol. I, p. 142–46. See also discussion of Lady Middleton's influence in John Pollock, *Wilberforce* (Tring: Lion, 1978), p. 53.

34 Latrobe, a Moravian missionary, made the remark in a letter to his daughter on 5 December 1815, quoted in Wilberforce and Wilberforce, *The Life of William Wilberforce*, vol. I, p. 146.

35 For evangelical ideology concerning women see Catherine Hall, 'The early formation of Victorian domestic ideology', in Sandra Burman (ed.), *Fit Work for Women* (London: Croom Helm, 1979), pp. 15–32.

36 Ernest Marshall Howse, *Saints in Politics: the 'Clapham Sect' and the Growth of Freedom* (London: George Allen & Unwin, 1953).

37 *List of the Society, Instituted in 1787, for the Purpose of Effecting the Abolition of the Slave Trade* (London, 1788). This is the only surviving list of the Society. The proportion of female subscribers is a minimum estimate: the donations from some eighty anonymous individuals doubtless conceal further female contributions.

38 *Report of the Committee of the African Institution* (London: William Phillips, 1807); *Fifth (to Seventeenth) Report of the Directors of the African Institution* (London: Ellerton & Henderson, 1808 (to 1823)).

39 See Frank Prochaska, *Women and Philanthropy in Nineteenth Century England* (Oxford: Oxford University Press, 1980), Appendix I.

40 Ray Strachey, *The Cause: A Short History of the Women's Movement in Great Britain*, reprint of 1st edn of 1928 (London: Virago, 1978), pp. 14–17.

41 Though it should be borne in mind that many older single women adopted the courtesy title of Mrs (see F. K. Prochaska, 'Women in English philanthropy, 1790–1830', *International Review of Social History*, vol. 19 (1974), p. 433).

42 Prochaska, *Women and Philanthropy*, p. 41.

43 A woman with the same surname and town of residence as a male subscriber is taken to be related to the man.

44 Identification of Quaker women is based on the multi-volume typescript 'Dictionary of Quaker biography' in Friends House Library, London.

45 E. M. Hunt, 'The North of England agitation for the abolition of the slave trade, 1780–1800', MA dissertation, University of Manchester, 1959, ch. iv.

46 For the rarity of titled subscribers and patrons of nonconformist philanthropic societies in general see Prochaska, 'Women in English philanthropy', p. 433.

47 Clarkson, *The History of the Rise*, pp. 222, 235.

48 Other figures are 2 women among 100 subscribers in Birmingham, 12 among 264 in Sheffield, 9 among 73 in Bristol, 8 among 60 in Exeter, 3 among 53 in Leeds, 1 among 44 in Rotherham, and 9 among 63 in York (see *List of the Society*). Separate lists located for Nottingham show 16 women among 185 subscribers, and for Edinburgh 6 among 67 (see *Nottingham Journal*, 1 March 1788; *Two of the Petitions from Scotland, Which Were Presented at the Last Parliament, Praying the Abolition of the African Slave Trade* (Edinburgh: Printed by Order of the Society Established at Edinburgh, for Effecting the Abolition of the African Slave Trade, 1790), p. 12).

49 E. M. Hunt, 'The anti-slave trade agitation in Manchester', *Transactions of the Lancashire and Cheshire Antiquarian Society*, no. 79 (1977), pp. 46–72; Drescher, *Capitalism and Antislavery*, pp. 67–73.

50 Sir Thomas Barker, *Memorials of a Dissenting Chapel* (London, 1884).

51 For support of female education and women's rights by Unitarians see Raymond V. Holt, *The Unitarian Contribution to Social Progress in England*, 2nd edn (London: Lindsey Press, 1952), pp. 147–55. For Unitarian stress on the autonomous individual and on independence see John Seed, 'Gentlemen dissenters: the social and political meanings of rational dissent in the 1770's and 1780's', *Historical Journal*, vol. 28, no. 2 (1985), pp. 299–325, especially pp. 316–18.

52 For the radicalism of the Manchester abolition committee see Hunt, *Transactions of the Lancashire and Cheshire Antiquarian Society*, no. 79 (1977), pp. 46–72. For the political radicalism of Unitarians at this period see John Seed, 'The role of unitarianism in the formation of liberal culture, 1775–1851: A Social History', Ph.D. thesis, University of Hull, 1981, ch. 2; for a study of radicalism in 1790s Manchester see James Walvin, 'English Democratic Societies and Popular Radicalism, 1791–1800', Ph.D. thesis, York University, 1969, pp. 605–702.

53 See Edward Royle and James Walvin, *English Radicals and Reformers, 1760–1848* (Brighton: Harvester, 1982), pp. 185–88 for a discussion of women and radicalism.

54 For the press and public opinion see J. A. W. Gunn, *Beyond Liberty and Property: The Process of Self-Recognition in Eighteenth-Century Political Thought* (Kingston, Ontario: McGill-Queen's University Press, 1983), ch. 3. A second public appeal to women in May 1792 was similarly made in the context of a renewed appeal by radical abolitionists to public opinion (*Manchester Herald*, 19 May 1792, in an article entitled 'Slave trade' by 'B. C.'. The *Manchester Herald* was set up March 1792 as a mouthpiece for Manchester radicals).

55 *Manchester Mercury*, 6 November 1787.

56 See Drescher, *Capitalism and Antislavery*, p. 73.

57 *Manchester Mercury*, 6 November 1787.

58 Ibid. For the possibility that Manchester abolitionists, living in 'a town of the uprooted', should be particularly concerned about loss of kin, home and community see Drescher, *Capitalism and Antislavery*, p. 72–73.

59 *Manchester Mercury*, 4 December 1787.

60 For the 'Lady's subscription' see letter to *Manchester Mercury*, 11 December 1787.

61 Samuel Bradburn, *An Address to the People Called Methodists; Concerning the Evil of Encouraging the Slave Trade* (Manchester: T. Harper, 1792), p. 13.

62 Drescher, *Capitalism and Antislavery*, pp. 78, 85; *Northampton Mercury*, 24, 30 March 1792.

63 William Dickson, 'Diary of a Visit to Scotland on Behalf of the London

Abolition Committee', entry for Dundee, 25 February 1792. Temp. MSS 10/4, Friends House Library, London.

64 *Newcastle Courant*, 3 March 1792.

65 *York Herald*, 6 June 1807.

66 *Iris, or Sheffield Advertiser*, 9 June 1807.

67 Betty Fladeland, 'Abolitionist pressures on the concert of Europe, 1814–1822', *Journal of Modern History*, vol. 38 (1966), pp. 355–73; Jerome Reich, 'The slave trade at the congress of Vienna – a study in English public opinion', *Journal of Negro History*, vol. 53, no. 2 (April 1968), pp. 129–43; *Edinburgh Evening Courant*, 11, 21 July 1814.

68 *Morning Herald*, 27 February 1788.

69 Donna Andrew, 'Women and debating societies in late eighteenth-century London', seminar paper given at the Institute of Historical Research, London, 19 May 1989.

70 *Morning Chronicle*, 7 April 1788.

71 *A Warning to the Frequenters of Debating Clubs, Being a Short History of the Rise and Progress of Those Clubs* (London, 1810), p. 3, cited in Drescher, *Capitalism and Antislavery*, ch. 4, n. 44.

72 Mr Cresswick [Mary Wollstonecraft], *The Female Reader* (London: J. Johnson, 1789), pp. 171, 321. See also Claire Tomalin, *The Life and Death of Mary Wollstonecraft* (New York: Harcourt, Brace, Jovanovich, 1974).

73 Mary Wollstonecraft, *A Vindication of the Rights of Men, in a Letter to the Right Honourable Edmund Burke: Occasioned by His Reflections on the Revolution in France*, 2nd edn (London: J. Johnson, 1790), pp. 24, 128–30.

74 Helen Maria Williams, *Letters on the French Revolution, Written in France, in the Summer of 1790, to a Friend in England: Containing Various Notices Relative to That Interesting Event, and Memoirs of Mons. and Madame Du F–*, 1st American edn (Boston: J. Belknap & A. Young, 1791), p. 33.

75 Ibid.

76 For biographical information see Anna Letitia Le Breton, *Memoir of Mrs Barbauld, Including Letters and Notices of her Family and Friends* (London: Bell, 1874).

77 A Dissenter [Anna Laetitia Barbauld], *An Address to the Opposers of the Repeal of the Corporation and Test Acts*, 2nd edn (London: J. Johnson, 1790), p. 33.

78 Mary Wollstonecraft, *A Vindication of the Rights of Women* (New York: Norton, 1975 edition), pp. 35, 37.

79 For early eighteenth-century examples see Katherine M. Rogers, *Feminism in Eighteenth-Century England* (Brighton: Harvester, 1982). For a discussion of the significance of early use of the analogy see Moira Ferguson (ed.), *First Feminists* (Bloomington: Indiana University Press, 1985), p. xii.

80 Wollstonecraft, *A Vindication of the Rights of Women*, p. 167.

81 Ibid., p. 61.

82 Ibid., p. 192.

83 Fair Minute Books of the Committee for the Abolition of the Slave Trade, 1787–1819, 3 vols, British Museum Add. MSS 21254–6: entries show that meetings decreased in frequency after August 1793 and none were held between April 1797 and May 1804; Hunt, 'The anti-slave trade agitation in Manchester'.

84 M. G. Jones, *Hannah More*, p. 91.

85 Hannah More, 'The sorrows of Yamba; or, a negro woman's lamentation', [Hannah More (ed.)], *Cheap Repository Tracts, Published During the Year 1795* ([London]: J. Marshall, [1797]), vol. I. Quote from verse 15, lines 3–4.

86 Fanny Holcroft, 'The Negro', *Monthly Magazine*, vol. IV (October 1797), p. 286.

87 [More], *Cheap Repository Tracts*, vol. I, pp. 3–5.

88 Ibid., p. 6.

89 Ibid., pp. 7–12, quote from p. 8.

90 Ibid., p. 12.

91 Hannah More, *Strictures on the Modern System of Female Education, With a View to the Principles and Conduct Prevalent Among Women of Rank and Fortune*, vols VII and VIII of *The Works of Hannah More* (London: T. Cadell Jr & W. Davies, 1801), p. 33, quote from p. 34.

92 A number of detailed studies of British imaginative literature about Africans and slavery have been made by literary historians: Eva B. Dykes, *The Negro in English Romantic Thought, or a Study in Sympathy for the Oppressed* (Washington DC: Associated Publishers, 1942); Wylie Sypher, *Guinea's Captive Kings: British Anti-Slavery Literature in the Eighteenth Century*, reprint of original 1942 edn (New York: Octagon, 1969); Hoxie Neale Fairchild, *The Noble Savage: A Study in Romantic Naturalism* (New York: Columbia University Press, 1928); Victor Casco Dinani Mtubani, 'Slavery and the slave trade in English poetry to 1833', unpublished Ph.D. thesis, University of Exeter, 1980.

93 This estimate is based on the list of imaginative literature in Peter C. Hogg, *The African Slave Trade and Its Suppression: a Classified and Annotated Bibliography* (London: Frank Cass, 1973), taking into account only those works for which the sex of the writer is known.

94 Aphra Behn, *Oroonoko; or, the Royal Slave: a True History* (London: Canning, 1688).

95 *Manchester Mercury*, 4 December 1789; *The Times*, 2 November 1789.

96 Clarkson, *The History of the Rise*, ch. iii; Roger Anstey, *The Atlantic Slave Trade and British Abolition 1760–1810* (London: Macmillan, 1975), ch. 4; David Brion Davis, *The Problem of Slavery in the Age of Revolution, 1770–1823* (Ithaca: Cornell University Press, 1975), pp. 368–73; Mtubani, 'Slavery and the slave trade', pp. 344–45.

97 See poems by Gratia Williams in *New Lady's Magazine*, vol. II (September 1787), p. 473, and vol. III (May 1788), pp. 267–68; and verse by men in the *Lady's Magazine*, vols XXI (1790) and XXIII (1792).

98 Marlon B. Ross, *The Contours of Masculine Desire: Romanticism and the Rise of Women's Poetry* (Oxford: Oxford University Press, 1989), p. 202; Roger Lonsdale (ed.), *Eighteenth Century Women Poets: an Oxford Anthology* (Oxford: Oxford University Press, 1989), p. xxxv.

99 Thomas Wright, The Life of William Cowper (London: T. Fisher Unwin, 1892).

100 Letter from Hannah More to Lady Middleton, Cowslip Green, 10 September [1788?], Chatterton, *Memorials*, p. 169. Possibly as the result of More's suggestion, the play was performed at Drury Lane in 1789 (review of the play in *The Times*, 2 November 1789).

101 *Manchester Mercury*, 4 December 1787.

102 Hannah More, *Slavery, a Poem* (London: T. Cadell, 1788). The poem was reprinted under the title 'The slave trade: a poem' in *The Works of Hannah More*.

103 Roberts, *Memoirs of the Life and Correspondence of Hannah More*, vol. II, p. 97.

104 Mary Leadbeater, *Poems* (Dublin: Martin Keene, 1808), p. 88.

105 Helen Maria Williams, *A Poem on the Bill Lately Passed for Regulating the Slave Trade* (London: T. Cadell, 1788), p. 23.

106 Anna Laetitia Barbauld, *Epistle to William Wilberforce, Esq. on the Rejection of the Bill for Abolishing the Slave Trade* (London: J. Johnson, 1791).

107 Maria Falconar and Harriet Falconar, *Poems on Slavery* (London: Egostons, Murray & Johnson, 1788); *Manchester Mercury*, 4 March 1788.

108 Ann Yearsley, *A Poem on the Inhumanity of the Slave Trade. Humbly Inscribed to the Right Honorable and Right Reverend Frederick, Earl of Bristol, Bishop of Derby, etc., etc.* (London: G. G. J. & J. Robinson, [1788]).

109 Eliza Knipe, *Six Narrative Poems* (London: printed for the author, 1787), pp. 51–60.

110 For the role of the tales in combating such stereotypes see David Brion Davis, *The Problem of Slavery in Western Culture* (Ithaca: Cornell University Press, 1966), pp. 468–70.

111 For More's views of feminine sensitivity see More, *Strictures on the Modern System of Female Education* vols. VII and VIII of *The Works of Hannah More*.

112 More, *Slavery, a Poem*, verse 13, lines 3, 4 (p. 11).

113 *Monthly Review*, vol. LXXVIII (1788), p. 246.

114 Thomas Wilkinson, *An Appeal to England, in Behalf of the Abused Africans. A Poem* (Dublin: sold by R. Jackson & W. Sleaton, 1792), verse 35 (p. 20).

115 James Field Stanfield, *The Guinea Voyage. A Poem in Three Books* (London: James Phillips, 1789), book III, verse 15 (p. 33).

116 Protheroe poster, p. 179, MS Letterpress Book, I, Fuller Papers, Duke University Library, as quoted in Davis, *The Problem of Slavery in the Age of Revolution*, ch. 9.

117 M. Birkett, *A Poem on the African Slave Trade. Addressed to Her Own Sex* (Dublin: J. Jones, 1792), part I, verse 26, lines 4–8 (p. 13).

118 Ibid., part II, verse 20, lines 15–16, 21–22 (pp. 21–22).

119 Rogers, *Feminism in Eighteenth-Century England*, p. 170.

120 See Mtubani, 'Slavery and the slave trade', pp. 118–20.

121 Davis, *The Problem of Slavery in Western Culture*, p. 481.

122 This point is made both by Kenneth Allan Corfield, 'English abolitionists and the refusal of slave-grown goods 1780–1860', unpublished MA dissertation, University of London, 1983, p. iv, and by Drescher, *Capitalism and Antislavery*, pp. 78–79.

123 William Fox, *An Address to the People of Great Britain, on the Propriety of Abstaining from West Indian Sugar and Rum*, 25th edn (London: M. Gurney, n.d.).

124 Davis, *The Problem of Slavery in the Age of Revolution*, pp. 435, 436.

125 Samuel Bradburn, *An Address to the People Called Methodists; Concerning the Evil of Encouraging the Slave Trade* (Manchester: T. Harper), pp. 12–18.

126 *Woodfall's Diary*, 5 January 1792.

127 For Quakers and abstention see Ruth Ketring Nuermberger, *The Free Produce Movement. A Quaker Protest Against Slavery* (Durham, NC: Duke University Press, 1942), which focuses on the American movement.

128 *Sheffield Register*, 16 December 1791. For the Quaker campaign see *Sheffield Register*, 11 November 1791; *Sheffield Advertiser*, 27 January 1792.

129 Verse 7 of 'Lines, Humbly Addressed to the Fair Sex', *Sheffield Register*, 16 December 1791.

130 Birkett, *A Poem on the African Slave Trade*, part I, verse 26, lines 9–13, 18–20 (pp. 13–14).

131 Ibid., part I, verse 31, lines 1–7 (p. 15). Emphasis in original.

NOTES

132 *Newcastle Courant*, 7 January 1792.
133 *An Address to Her Royal Highness the Dutchess of York, Against the Use of Sugar* (n.p., 1792).
134 The cartoon, the original of which is in the British Museum, is listed as no. 8074 in Mary Dorothy George, *Catalogue of Political and Personal Satires Preserved in the Department of Prints and Drawings in the British Museum*, vol. VI (London: British Museum Publications, 1978).
135 *Chester Chronicle*, 2 December 1791.
136 For aristocratic women's role as leaders of fashion in the context of the 'consumer revolution' of the period see Neil McKendrick, John Brewer and J. H. Plumb, *The Birth of a Consumer Society: The Commercialization of Eighteenth-Century England* (London: Europa Publications, 1982), especially pp. 119, 142.
137 For Wedgwood's exploitation of public events for commercial ends and his explicit targeting of fashionable women as clients see ibid., ch. 3.
138 Dickson, 'Diary of a visit to Scotland'.
139 Clarkson, *The History of the Rise*, vol. II, p. 192.
140 [William Allen], *The Duty of Abstaining from the Use of West India Produce, A Speech, Delivered at Coach-Maker's-Hall, January 12, 1792* (London: T. W. Hawkins, [1792]), pp. 22–23.
141 Andrew Burn, *Second Address to the People of Great Britain: Containing a New, and Most Powerful Argument to Abstain from the Use of West Indian Sugar* (London: M. Gurney, 1792), p. 4.
142 Clarkson, *History of the Rise*, vol. II, p. 350.
143 *York Courant*, 20 December 1791; *Leeds Intelligencer*, 8 November and 13 December 1791; *Gloucester Journal*, 6 February 1792; *Northampton Mercury*, 7 January 1792; *Lincoln, Rutland and Stamford Mercury*, 30 March 1792; *Norfolk Chronicle*, 5 November 1791; *Sheffield Advertiser*, 2 December 1791.
144 James Mullala, *A Compilation on the Slave Trade, Respectfully Addressed to the People of Ireland* (Dublin, 1792), as cited in Douglass C. Riach, 'Ireland and the campaign against American slavery, 1830–1860', Ph.D. thesis, University of Edinburgh, 1975, ch. 1.
145 Clarkson, *History of the Rise*, vol. II, p. 349.
146 See for example Neil McKendrick, 'Home demand and economic growth: a new view of the role of women and children in the industrial revolution', in Neil McKendrick (ed.), *Historical Perspectives: Studies in English Thought and Society in Honour of J. H. Plumb* (London: Europa Publications, 1974), p. 189.
147 Letter from Lydia Hardy to Thomas Hardy, Chesham, 2 April 1792, Public Record Office, Chancery Lane (ref: TS 24/12/1).
148 Ibid.; *Memoir of Thomas Hardy* (London: James Ridgeway, 1832), p. 15.
149 'Reflections on the slave-trade; with remarks on the policy of its abolition. In a Letter to a Clergyman in the County of Suffolk. By G. C. P.', *Gentleman's Magazine*, December 1791, p. 1124. Footnotes to the article refer to Barbauld's *Epistle to William Wilberforce* and Fox's *An Address to the People of Great Britain*.
150 *Gentleman's Magazine*, February 1792, p. 158.
151 *The Times*, 30 March 1792. The letter also appeared in the *European Magazine and London Review*, vol. XXI (March 1792), pp. 185–86.
152 Drescher, *Capitalism and Antislavery*, p. 79.
153 Davis, *The Problem of Slavery in the Age of Revolution*, p. 436.
154 Walvin, *England, Slaves and Freedom*, p. 121.

3 'CEMENT OF THE WHOLE ANTI-SLAVERY BUILDING'

1 For the major terms of the Emancipation Act see W. L. Burn, *Emancipation and Apprenticeship in the British West Indies* (London, 1937), pp. 118–19.

2 *Ladies Society for the Relief of Negro Slaves. Founding Meeting Held West-Bromwich, 8th April 1825* [printed sheet]. The society changed its name several times, and will henceforth simply be referred to as the Female Society for Birmingham.

3 For the Parliamentary campaign and actions of the male leadership the standard works are still Sir Reginald Coupland, *The British Anti-Slavery Movement* (London: Frank Cass, 1964 edition) and Frank Joseph Klingberg, *The Anti-Slavery Movement in England: A Study in Humanitarianism* (New Haven: Yale Historical Publications, 1926).

4 For useful surveys of recent approaches see Christine Bolt and Seymour Drescher (eds), *Anti-Slavery, Religion and Reform: Essays in Memory of Roger Anstey* (Folkestone: Dawson, 1980); and James Walvin (ed.), *Slavery and British Society, 1776–1846* (London: Macmillan, 1982).

5 Edward Royle and James Walvin, *English Radicals and Reformers 1760–1848* (Brighton: Harvester, 1982), p. 186; James Walvin, 'The propaganda of anti-slavery' in Walvin (ed.), *Slavery and British Society*, pp. 49–68; James Walvin, *England, Slaves and Freedom, 1776–1838* (Basingstoke: Macmillan, 1986), pp. 157–59.

6 George Thompson to Anne Knight, 14 November 1834, Friends House Library, London, Box W.

7 Louis Billington and Rosamund Billington, ' "A Burning Zeal for Righteousness": Women and the British anti-slavery movement, 1820–1860', in Jane Rendall (ed.), *Equal or Different: Women's Politics, 1800–1914* (Oxford: Blackwell, 1987), p. 90.

8 Accounts for 1823 and 1825 list the printing of 1,000 and 1,500 copies of a sheet entitled 'Resolutions recommended to auxiliary associations' (see *Account of the Receipts and Disbursements of the Anti-Slavery Society, for the Years 1823, 1824, 1825, and 1826: with a List of Subscribers* (London: Bagster & Thoms, 1826) pp. 3, 6). In 1823 and 1824 the veteran abolitionist Thomas Clarkson toured England and Wales promoting men's auxiliaries (see 'Committee on Slavery Minute Book', entry for 9 June, 1823, MSS Brit. Emp. S.20 E 2/1, in RHL).

9 *Account of the Receipts and Disbursements of the Anti-Slavery Society.* These numbers represent only the more active groups. The first report of the Anti-Slavery Society stated that there were 220 auxiliaries in existence whereas the receipts of the Society list only 31 such groups. (*Report of the Committee of the Society for the Mitigation and Gradual Abolition of Slavery Throughout the British Dominions* (London: printed by Richard Taylor, 1824)).

10 The Society was active until 1919. Many of its printed reports, together with manuscript minutes and other material, are located in the Archives Dept. of Birmingham Central Library, and have also been published as *Records Relating to the Birmingham Ladies' Society for the Relief of Negro Slaves, 1825–1919*, two reels of microfilm (East Ardsley: Microform Academic Publishers, n.d.).

11 Extracts of letters from Thomas Clarkson, dated 30 March 1825, 30 May 1825, in Lucy Townsend, 'Scrap Book on Negro Slaves', pp. 115–18, MSS Brit. Emp. S.4, in RHL.

12 *Account of the Receipts and Disbursements of the Anti-Slavery Society*, p. 14. The men's society apparently became inactive for it had to be refounded in 1826

(see Birmingham Anti-Slavery Society, Minute Book, entry for 6 December 1826, Archives Dept., Birmingham Central Library).

13 See Sara W. Sturge, *Memoir of Mary Lloyd of Wednesbury, 1795–1865* (printed for private circulation, 1921), p. 30.

14 Frank Prochaska, *Women and Philanthropy in Nineteenth Century England* (Oxford: Oxford University Press, 1980), pp. 24–27; Charles S. Dudley, *An Analysis of the System of the Bible Society* (London: R. Watts, 1821) pp. 375–6, 397–8.

15 For information on typical ladies' branch associations see Prochaska, *Women and Philanthropy*, pp. 22–29.

16 Billington and Billington, ' "A Burning Zeal for Righteousness" ', pp. 85, 87.

17 Prochaska, *Women and Philanthropy*, p. 32 and Appendix IV, which lists both local and national societies; see also F. K. Prochaska, 'Women in English philanthropy, 1790–1830', *International Review of Social History*, vol. 19 (1974), p. 430, which lists seventeen national ladies' societies founded between 1795 and 1830.

18 *Ladies Society for the Relief of Negro Slaves*, [meeting, Walsall, 8 December 1825: resolutions].

19 *Fifth Report of the Female Society for Birmingham . . . for the Relief of Negro Slaves* (Birmingham: B. Hudson, 1830).

20 Townsend, 'Scrap Book on Negro Slaves', p. 115.

21 *Third Report of the Female Society for Birmingham . . . for the Relief of British Negro Slaves* (Birmingham: B. Hudson, 1828), p. 18.

22 *Second Report of the Female Society for Birmingham . . . for the Relief of British Negro Slaves* (Birmingham: B. Hudson, [1827]); Lucy Townsend, 'Autographs', p. 318, MSS Brit. Emp. S.5, in RHL; 'Minute Book of the Ladies Society for the Relief of Negro Slaves, 1825–52', entries for 29 January 1929, 7 April 1829, 26 November 1829, MSS in Birmingham Central Library; 'Ledger belonging to the Female Society for the Relief of British Negro Slaves', MSS in Birmingham Central Library; *Rules and Resolutions of the Dublin Ladies' Anti-Slavery Society* (Dublin: Napper, 1828), resolution 1, [p. 4].

23 *First Report of the Female Society for Birmingham . . . for the Relief of British Negro Slaves* (Birmingham: B. Hudson, 1826), pp. 31–32; *Third Report of the Female Society for Birmingham*, pp. 19, 21; lists of subscribers at Leicester and Oakham in *Fifth Report of the Female Society for Birmingham*; 'Minute Book of the Ladies Society for the Relief of Negro Slaves', entries for 10 July 1827, 26 November 1828.

24 The resolution was that the society should continue its exertions 'till the time may come when the lash shall no longer be permitted to fall on the persons of helpless Female Slaves, when our fellow-creatures shall no longer be advertised like beasts for sale, and sold like beasts at a West India slave Market, and when every Negro Mother, living under British Laws, shall press a free-born infant to her bosom' (compare *Ladies Society for the Relief of Negro Slaves. Founding Meeting; First Report of the Ladies Association for Liverpool* (Liverpool: George Smith, 1828); *Auxiliary Society for the Relief of Negro Slaves* [founding resolutions of the Sheffield Female Anti-Slavery Society, 12 July 1825]; *Rules of the Colchester Ladies Anti-Slavery Association* (Colchester, 1825)).

25 'Ledger belonging to the Female Society for the Relief of Negro Slaves', pp. 11, 89; accounts at back of 'Album', MSS D/CR/12, Cropper family papers, Merseyside Record Office, Liverpool.

26 *First Report of the Rochester and Chatham Anti-Slavery Society* (Strood: J. & H. Sweet, 1828).

27 'Committee on Slavery Minute Book', entry for 11 May 1825.

28 Robert Isaac and Samuel Wilberforce, *The Life of William Wilberforce*, 5 vols (London: John Murray, 1840), vol. V, p. 264, quotation from letter dated 31 January 1826.

29 R. Isaac Wilberforce and S. Wilberforce, *The Correspondence of William Wilberforce*, 5 vols (London: John Murray, 1838), vol. II, pp. 93, 94.

30. Ibid., vol. II, pp. 493–4.

31 *Second Report of the Female Society for Clifton, Bristol, and its Neighbourhood in Aid of the Cause of Negro Emancipation* (Bristol: T. D. Clark, [1828]), p. 3.

32 'Committee on Slavery Minute Book', entries for 8 and 15 June, 1825.

33 *Genius of Universal Emancipation*, vol. II, no. 27 (Baltimore, 12 May 1827), p. 213.

34 [Anti-Slavery Society], *Rules for Anti-Slavery Associations. (Ladies')* (London: Knight & Bagster, [n.d.]); [Anti-Slavery Society], *Anti-Slavery Society*, [rules for men's societies] (London: Ellerton & Henderson, [n.d.]). The women's rules were reprinted in the *Genius of Universal Emancipation*, vol. II, no. 27 (12 May 1827), p. 213.

35 Note, for example, the lack of references to each other's activities in the Minute Books of the Birmingham Antislavery Society and the Ladies Society for the Relief of Negro Slaves.

36 Prochaska, *Women and Philanthropy*, p. 27.

37 *Account of the Receipts and Disbursements of the Anti-Slavery Society*, p. 8; 'Committee on Slavery Minute Book', entry for 25 January 1826.

38 *Negro Slavery. To the Ladies of the United Kingdom* (London: Ellerton & Henderson, [n.d.]).

39 *Anti-Slavery Monthly Reporter*, vol. II, no. 12 (May 1828), p. 213.

40 Letter from Z. Macaulay to [James Cropper], London, 16 February 1828, MS 10275, Brougham Papers, University College, London.

41 The full text of this pamphlet was given in the *Genius of Universal Emancipation*, 3rd series, vol. II, no. 7 (December 1831), pp. 110–12; no. 8 (January 1832), pp. 133–35; no. 9 (February 1832), pp. 149–52.

42 [Anti-Slavery Society], *Ladies' Anti-Slavery Associations* (London: Bagster & Thoms, [1828]); [Anti-Slavery Society], *A Picture of Colonial Slavery, in the Year 1828, Addressed Especially to the Ladies of Great Britain* (London: Bagster & Thoms, [1828]). (For evidence of Cropper's authorship of the former see letter from James Cropper to Joseph Sturge, Liverpool, 14 July 1827, quoted in Anne Cropper, 'Extracts from Letters of the Late James Cropper' (Liverpool, 1850), MSS in Friends House Library London, p. 61; for evidence of Zachary Macaulay's authorship of the latter see 'Committee on Slavery Minute Book', 2 September 1828).

43 For the importance of travelling agents to early nineteenth-century philanthropic societies, including the Bible Society, see Prochaska, *Women and Philanthropy*, p. 25.

44 Letter from John Philip to Lucy Townsend, London, 29 April 1829; Townsend, 'Autographs', p. 317; and 'Committee on Slavery Minute Book', entry for 2 September 1828.

45 'Minute Book of the Ladies Society for the Relief of Negro Slaves', entry for 8 April 1830.

46 *Seventh Report of the Ladies' Negro's Friend Society, for Birmingham* (Birmingham: B.

Hudson, 1832), p. 61; 'Minute Book of the Ladies' Society for the Relief of Negro Slaves', entry for 12 April 1831.

47 See Prochaska, *Women and Philanthropy*, p. 25.

48 Charles E. H. Orpen, *The Principles, Plans, and Objects of the 'Hibernian Negro's Friend Society'* (Dublin, 1831), p. 10; 'Minute Book of the Ladies Society for the Relief of Negro Slaves', entries for 23 December 1830, 12 April 1831.

49 For contemporary reports of the committee's inception see 'Committee on Slavery Minute Book', entry for 1 June 1831; and *Report of the Agency Committee of the Anti-Slavery Society* (London: S. Bagster, Jr, 1832), pp. 1–8. George Stephen, *Antislavery Recollections* (London: Thomas Hatchard, 1854), p. 127, describes its formation as the result of a schism within the national committee. The fullest recent discussion of the committee, which stresses its internal development from an earlier committee of correspondence, is Ruth Moshingley, 'The role of the Agency Committee in the anti-slavery campaign, 1831–1833', unpublished B.Phil. thesis, University of Oxford, 1973, p. 13. The importance of provincial pressure is highlighted in Anthony J. Barker, *Captain Charles Stuart, Anglo-American Abolitionist* (Baton Rouge: Louisiana State University Press, 1986), pp. 45–63.

50 Stephen, *Antislavery Recollections*, Letter 10.

51 For new ladies' associations in England see *The Anti-Slavery Record*, vol. I, nos. 1–14 (May 1832–April 1833); for a new group in Scotland see George Thompson, *Substance of an Address to the Ladies of Glasgow* (Glasgow: Robertson, 1833).

52 Anna M. Stoddart, *Elizabeth Pease Nichol* (London: J. M. Dent, 1899), p. 60.

53 'Corrected List of Subscriptions. To the 1st September, 1838', *British Emancipator*, no. XXX (31 October 1838), p. 176; and corrections to this list in no. XXXI (14 September 1838).

54 *Irish Temperance and Literary Gazette*, vol. I, no. 51 (28 October 1837), p. 103–04; 'A letter from the Ladies' Anti-Slavery Society to their countrywomen', *The Irish Temperance and Literary Gazette*, vol. II, no. 77 (28 April 1838), p. 310.

55 Stoddart, *Elizabeth Pease Nichol*, p. 64.

56 Letter from Elizabeth Pease to William Smeal, Darlington, 14 February 1841, MS A.1.2. vol. XI, p. 68, in BPL; Barker, *Captain Charles Stuart*, p. 129.

57 Stoddart, *Elizabeth Pease Nichol*, pp. 55, 60–62, 65; letter from Elizabeth Pease to Thomas Pease, 4 February 1838, in Darlington Branch Library (Ref. D/ XD/5/263).

58 For the range in membership numbers of men's auxiliaries compare *Second Annual Report of the Edinburgh Society for Promoting the Mitigation and Ultimate Abolition of Negro Slavery* (Edinburgh: Anderson and Bryce, 1825), which lists 502 subscribers, with *First Report of the Suffolk Auxiliary for the Mitigation and Gradual Abolition of Slavery* (Ipswich: King and Garrod, 1825), which lists 38 subscribers. For ladies' associations compare *Third Report of the Female Society for Birmingham*, which lists 396 donors and subscribers, with *Report of the Sheffield Female Anti-Slavery Society* (Sheffield: Iris, 1832), which lists 38.

59 Prochaska, *Women and Philanthropy*, ch. 1, especially pp. 23–27.

60 All the figures quoted here are derived from the *Account of the Receipts and Disbursements of the Anti-Slavery Society*. Contributions from men's auxiliaries and ladies' associations were not, of course, the only source of funds for the Anti-Slavery Society: some individuals contributed directly to central funds, with the number of men (113–132 annually) and much smaller number of women (only 11–27 annually) remaining stable over the period.

The largest single source of funds was an annual block donation from the Society of Friends of £500 to £1,500, given most but not all years. It is unknown what proportion of this money came from Quaker women.

61 *First Report of the Female Society for Birmingham; Account of Receipts and Disbursements of the Anti-Slavery Society*, p. 33.
62 [Anti-Slavery Society], *Ladies' Anti-Slavery Associations*, p. 7; *First Report of the Ladies' Association for Liverpool*; *Report of the Sheffield Female Anti-Slavery Society* (Sheffield, 1827), p. 15. For intermediate positions see *Third Annual Report of the Ladies' Association for Salisbury, Calne . . .* (Calne: T. P. Bailey, 1828), [p. 36]; *Second Report of the Female Society for Clifton*, p. 22; for the variability among men's auxiliaries contrast the account in *Report of the Committee of the Manchester Society, for the Furtherance of the Gradual Abolition of Slavery* (Manchester: Smith, 1827), p. 9, which shows £200 of £438 raised was remitted to London, with the statement of accounts in *Second Annual Report of the Edinburgh Society for Promoting the Mitigation and Ultimate Abolition on Negro Slavery*, which shows no donation to London from an income of £114.
63 Compare list of subscribing societies in the *Report of the Agency Committee* with list in *Account of the Receipts and Disbursements of the Anti-Slavery Society for the Year 1831*.
64 *Second Report of the Female Society for Birmingham*, p. 10.
65 M. Birkett, *A Poem on the African Slave Trade. Addressed to Her Own Sex* (Dublin: J. Jones, 1792), part I, pp. 12, 13.
66 Prochaska, *Women and Philanthropy*, p. 29 and Appendices; Prochaska, 'Women in English Philanthropy', pp. 427–28 and Appendices.
67 Mary Turner, *Slaves and Missionaries: The Disintegration of Jamaican Slave Society, 1787–1834* (Urbana: University of Illinois Press, 1982), especially chs 1, 3.
68 Philip D. Curtin, *The Image of Africa. British Ideas and Action, 1780–1850* (London: Macmillan, 1965), ch. 11.
69 Sarah Biller (ed.), *Memoir of the Late Hannah Kilham, Chiefly Compiled from Her Journal* (London: Darton and Harvey, 1837); Mora Dickson, *The Powerful Bond – Hannah Kilham 1774–1832* (London: Dennis Dobson, 1980).
70 'Report of the "Committee of African Instruction" to the Subscribers: Read at the Yearly Meeting of Friends, 1825', *The Yorkshireman*, no. 9, 2nd edn (15 December 1832), p. 162. Emphasis in original.
71 Ibid.
72 Orpen, *The Principles, Plans, and Objects of the 'Hibernian Negro's Friend Society'*, p. 12.
73 Eighth founding resolution of the Ladies' Association for Calne, 11 August 1825, quoted in [Elizabeth Heyrick], *Letters on the Necessity of a Prompt Extinction of British Colonial Slavery* (London, 1826), p. 162; *Second Report of the Female Society for Clifton*, p. 22; *First and Third Reports of the Ladies' Association for Liverpool*; *Second Report of the Female Association for St Ives* (St Ives: S. Gardner, [1832]), [p. 31]; *Rules and Resolutions of the Dublin Ladies' Anti-Slavery Society* (Dublin: R. Napier, 1828), p. 13; *Report of the Hibernian Ladies' Negroes' Friend Society* (Dublin: M. Goodwin, 1833), p. 7; *Resolutions and Rules of the Edinburgh Female Anti-Slavery Association* (Edinburgh: Ballantyre, 1830), pp. 10–11.
74 *Ladies Society for the Relief of Negro Slaves. Founding Meeting*, resolution 7; *First to Fifth Reports of the Female Society for Birmingham*; *Seventh and Eighth Reports of the Ladies' Negro's Friend Society for Birmingham*. For the formation of mission schools in Jamaica from 1822 and their reliance on British charitable support see Turner, *Slaves and Missionaries*, p. 87.
75 *The Christian Observer*, vol. XXV, no. 11 (November 1825), pp. 715–16; no. 12

(December 1825), pp. 749–51. Townsend, 'Scrap Book on Negro Slaves', pp. 151–55, contains an amended and lengthened version of the letter in Lucy Townsend's hand, suggesting that she may also have been the author of the published version.

76 [Elizabeth Heyrick], *Immediate, not Gradual Abolition: or, an Enquiry into the Shortest, Safest and Most Effectual Means of Getting Rid of West Indian Slavery* (London: Knight and Bagster, 1824), p. 8.

77 *A Vindication of Female Anti-Slavery Associations* (London: printed for the Female Anti-Slavery Society, [n.d.]), pp. 6–8. An identically worded section is included in *Second Report of the Female Society for Clifton*, pp. 5–8.

78 *Fourth Report of the London Female Anti-Slavery Society* (London: S. Bagster Jr, 1832), pp. 9, 14–15. The text of the circular is given in *Seventh Report of the Ladies' Negro's Friend Society for Birmingham*, pp. 31–34.

79 Quote from 'The objects and proceedings of Peckham Ladies' African and Anti-Slavery Association' in the *Missionary Register* (London), February 1830, pp. 83–84.

80 *Second Report of the Female Society for Birmingham*, pp. 26–27; 'Minute Book of the Ladies Society for the Relief of Negro Slaves', entry for 8 April 1830.

81 *Fifth Report of the Female Society for Birmingham*; 'Report of the Female Society for Birmingham . . .', *The Christian Advocate*, no. 80 (2 May 1831), no. 72 (16 May 1831); *Seventh and Eighth Reports of the Ladies' Negro's Friend Society for Birmingham*; 'Minute Book of the Ladies' Society for the Relief of Negro Slaves', entries for 12 April 1831, 3 April 1832; *Report of the Hibernian Ladies' Negroes' Friend Society*, p. 7.

82 See *Accounts of Receipts and Disbursements of the Anti-Slavery Society* for payments for publications purchased by local anti-slavery societies.

83 Examples produced by ladies' associations are: *A Concise View of Colonial Slavery* (Newcastle: Hodgson, for the Newcastle Ladies' Anti-Slavery Association, 1830); and *An Address to the Public*, 5th edn (London: printed for the Female Anti-Slavery Society by Bagster & Thoms, 1828). Sheffield Female Anti-Slavery Society printed five hundred copies of a Parliamentary speech by Brougham (see *Fifth Annual Report of the Sheffield Ladies' Anti-Slavery Society* (Sheffield: J. Blackwell at the Iris Office, 1830), [p. 3]).

84 See 'Minute Book of the Ladies Society for the Relief of Negro Slaves' for information on the Female Society for Birmingham's receipt of reports from other ladies' associations; *First Report of the Ladies' Association for Liverpool* included an extract from the report of the Female Society for Clifton, and the album in the society's possession ('Album', Cropper Family Papers, Merseyside Record Office, Liverpool) contained the First Report of the Birmingham society.

85 Compare *Account of the Receipts and Disbursements of the Anti-Slavery Society*, pp. 8–9, with *First Report of the Female Society for Birmingham*, p. 23.

86 The workbags are described in Sturge, *Memoir of Mary Lloyd of Wednesbury*, p. 30; and in *The Genius of Universal Emancipation*, new series, vol. I, no. 16 (Baltimore, 20 October 1827), p. 126.

87 'Cash Book, belonging to the Female Society for the Relief of British Negro Slaves for Birmingham', Birmingham Central Library; 'Minute Book of the Ladies Society for the Relief of Negro Slaves', entries for 30 October 1827, 8 April 1828, 12 April 1831; 'Ledger belonging to the Female Society for the Relief of British Negro Slaves for Birmingham'; *First Report of the Female Society for Birmingham*, p. 6.

88 'What Does Your Sugar Cost?' A Cottage Conversation on the Subject of British Negro Slavery (Birmingham: Richard Peart, 1828); A Vindication of Female Anti-Slavery Associations; Thompson, Substance of an Address to the Ladies of Glasgow.

89 The Ladies of the Sheffield Anti-Slavery Association, A Word for the Slave (Sheffield: J. Blackwell, 1830); Appeal of the Friends of the Negro to the British People; on Behalf of the Slaves in Their Colonies (Sheffield: J. Blackwell, 1830); Fifth Annual Report of the Sheffield Ladies' Anti-Slavery Society.

90 'Female Society for Birmingham etc., for the Relief of British Negro Slaves. Album', in Birmingham Central Library, Archives Dept.; [Mary Dudley], Scripture Evidence of the Sinfulness of Injustice and Oppression (London: Harvey & Darton, 1828).

91 Jane Yeoman, Verses on Slavery (Birmingham: B. Hudson, 1826); [Elizabeth Heyrick], No British Slavery; or, an Invitation to the People to Put a Speedy End to It (London: sold by Hatchard & Son, 1824); [Elizabeth Heyrick], Appeal to the Hearts and Consciences of British Women (Leicester: A. Cockshaw, 1828).

92 [Dudley], Scripture Evidence; Inquiries Relating to Negro Emancipation (London: J. Hatchard & Son, 1829); 'Album', Cropper Family Papers (note the handwritten list of pamphlets distributed by the Liverpool society at the back of the album).

93 Second Report of the Female Society for Clifton, pp. 16–17; [Dudley], Scripture Evidence; Charlotte Elizabeth [Phelan], The System; a Tale of the West Indies (London: Frederick Westley & A. H. Davis, 1827); [Wedgwood, Miss ?Sarah], British Slavery Described (Newcastle: sold for the Benefit of the North Staffs Ladies' Anti-Slavery Society, 1828) (for its attribution to Miss Wedgwood of Camp Hill see letter from Elizabeth Heyrick to Ann Knight, Leicester, 25 August 1828, Knight Family Papers, Temp. MSS 725, D.10, Friends House Library, London). No copy of Schimmelpenninck's pamphlet could be traced.

94 Rules and Resolutions of the Dublin Ladies' Anti-Slavery Society, p. 16.

95 Third Report of the Female Society for Birmingham; Third Report of the Ladies' Association for Salisbury, Calne (1828).

96 The Humming Bird, vol. I, no. 1 (December 1824) to vol. I, no. 12 (November 1825). The 'Address to the Ladies' is in vol. I, no. 7 (June 1825), pp. 195–203. For letters to Susanna Watts concerning contributions to The Humming Bird see p. 261 of Susanna Watts, 'Scrapbook', Leicester Public Library.

97 Letters from Elizabeth Heyrick to Anne Knight, Leicester, 25 August 1828, 5 April 1830, Knight Family Papers, D.10, Friends House Library , London.

98 Lucy Townsend, 'To the Law, and to the Testimony', or Questions on Slavery Answered by the Scriptures, and Presumed to be Worthy of Particular Consideration on the National Fast Day (London: Hamilton, Adams and Co., 1832).

99 Account of the Receipts and Disbursements of the Anti-Slavery Society, for the Years 1827 and 1828, p. 5; Account . . ., for the Years 1829 and 1830, p. 3; A Lady, A Dialogue Between a Well-Wisher and a Friend to the Slaves in the British Colonies (London: S. Bagster, Jr, [n.d.]).

100 Second Report of the Female Society for Clifton; Third Report of the Female Society for Birmingham; 'Auxiliary Society for the Relief of Negro Slaves. Instituted at Sheffield . . .' [Minute Book], entries for 10 April 1831, 18 January 1833, Rawson Family Papers, MSS in John Rylands University Library, Manchester; Report of the Hibernian Ladies' Negroes' Friend Society. Some men's societies also organised libraries – see 'Birmingham Antislavery Society Minute Book', MSS in Birmingham Central Library.

101 Prochaska, *Women and Philanthropy*, pp. 105–08; Ford K. Brown, 'Fathers of the Victorians', reprint from *Virginia Quarterly Review*, July 1936, pp. 424–28.

102 For an example of the systematic use of the press by a men's society see 'Birmingham Antislavery Society Minute Book'.

103 'Auxiliary Society for the Relief of Negro Slaves. Instituted at Sheffield . . .', [Minute Book], entry for 1 October 1831; *Sheffield Iris*, 24 October 1826 (report of annual meeting), 5 October 1830 (advertisement for anti-slavery bazaar); *The Essex Standard, and Colchester and County Advertiser*, 21 April 1832.

104 *Report of the Hibernian Ladies' Negroes' Friend Society*, [p. 7].

105 *The Missionary Register*, extracts of reports of ladies anti-slavery associations in volumes for 1826 to 1830; the *Christian Advocate* printed the full text of the Sixth Report of the Female Society for Birmingham, no. LXX (2 May 1831), no. LXXII (16 May 1831).

106 For encouragement of women to attend public meetings see advertisement in *Sheffield Iris*, 17 January 1826. The *Yorkshire Gazette* of 23 October 1830 reported that ladies outnumbered gentlemen by some six or seven to one at a public meeting on anti-slavery in York.

107 'Birmingham Antislavery Society Minute Book', entry for 3 May 1831. These minutes show the frequent organisation of public meetings by a men's society.

108 'Auxiliary Society for the Relief of Negro Slaves. Instituted at Sheffield . . .', [Minute Book], entry for 24 July 1830.

109 Joseph Ivimey, *The Utter Extinction of Slavery an Object of Scripture Prophesy* (London: Messeder, 1832), title page.

110 'Minute Book of the Ladies' Society for the Relief of Negro Slaves'; [Anti-Slavery Society], *Ladies Anti-Slavery Associations*, p. 6; Ivimey, *The Utter Extinction of Slavery*, title page; *Second Report of the Female Association, for St Ives*, [p. 5]; 'Auxiliary Society for the Relief of Negro Slaves. Instituted at Sheffield . . .', [Minute Book].

111 *Negro Slavery. To the Ladies of the United Kingdom*, p. 3; [Anti-Slavery Society], *Ladies' Anti-Slavery Associations*, pp. 1, 5, 6; *Anti-Slavery Monthly Reporter*, vol. I, no. 14 (July 1826), p. 212.

112 [Heyrick], *Immediate, not Gradual Abolition*, quote from p. 4.

113 [Elizabeth Heyrick], *Appeal to the Hearts and Consciences of British Women* (Leicester: A. Cockshaw, 1828), quotes from pp. 4, 6.

114 [Elizabeth Heyrick], 'Apology for Ladies' Anti-Slavery Associations', pamphlet reprinted in full in *The Genius of Universal Emancipation*, see especially 3rd series, vol. II, no. 7 (December 1831), p. 111; no. 9 (February 1832), pp. 150–51.

115 *First and Third Reports of the Ladies' Association for Liverpool*; *Reasons for Using East India Sugar* (London: Howlett and Brimmer, printed for the Peckham Ladies' African and Anti-Slavery Association, 1828); *Second Report of the Female Society for Clifton*; *Third Report of the Female Society for Birmingham*, p. 21; *A Brief Sketch of the Life of Elizabeth Heyrick* (Leicester: Crossley and Clarke, 1862), pp. 17–18; *Second Report of the Female Association for St Ives*; *Rules and Resolutions of the Dublin Ladies' Anti-Slavery Society*; *Report of the Hibernian Ladies' Negroes' Friend Society*; *Resolutions and Rules of the Edinburgh Female Anti-Slavery Association*.

116 *Report of the Sheffield Female Anti-Slavery Society* (1827), p. 3; 'Minute Book of the Ladies' Society for the Relief of Negro Slaves', various entries, 1827–29; *Second and Third Report of the Female Society for Birmingham*. See also *Third Annual Report of the Ladies' Association for Salisbury, Calne*, pp. 7, 20.

117 *East India Sugar* (Sheffield: J. Blackwell) [card].

118 'Minute Book of the Ladies Society for the Relief of Negro Slaves', entry for 16 November 1826. The pamphlet was also circulated by the female societies at Sheffield and Dublin.

119 [Charlotte Townsend], *Pity the Negro; or An Address to Children on the Subject of Slavery*, 7th edn (London: Westley and Davis, 1829).

120 *Third Report of the Female Society for Birmingham*, p. 21.

121 *Rules and Resolutions of the Dublin Ladies' Anti-Slavery Society*, p. 17.

122 Ibid., p. 10.

123 'Minute Book of the Ladies Society for the Relief of Negro Slaves', entries for 26 November 1829; 'Committee on Slavery Minute Book', entries for 6 and 20 October 1829; *The Genius of Universal Emancipation*, 3rd series, vol. II, no. 5 (September 1831), pp. 73–74.

124 [Heyrick], *Letters on the Necessity of a Prompt Extinction of British Colonial Slavery*, Letter V.

125 Kenneth Allan Corfield, 'English Abolitionists and the Refusal of Slave-Grown Goods 1780–1860', unpublished MA dissertation, Birkbeck College, University of London, 1983, p. 33.

126 *Journals of the House of Commons*, vols 86 to 88 (1830–33); *Journals of the House of Lords*, vols 62 to 65 (1830–33); *First to Forty-First Reports of the Select Committee on Public Petitions* (February to August 1833).

127 *First Report of the Female Society for Birmingham*, p, 11; Townsend, 'Scrapbook on Negro Slaves', p. 14; *Journal of the House of Commons*, session 1825–26, vol. LXXX, p. 629; *Appendix to the Votes and Proceedings of the House of Commons, Session 1825*, p. 777.

128 *Journal of the House of Commons*, session 1829, vol. LXXXIV, p. 404; Moira Ferguson (ed.), *The History of Mary Prince, a West Indian Slave, Related by Herself*, new edn (London: Pandora, 1987), pp. 87–88, Appendix I, p. 116.

129 [Heyrick], *Immediate, not Gradual Abolition*, pp. 11–12.

130 *Journals of the House of Commons*, session 1829, vol. LXXXIV, pp. 28, 192, 370, 406; session 1830, vol. LXXXV, pp. 148, 184, 235.

131 A valuable account of Baptist involvement is K. R. M. Short, 'A study in political nonconformity: the Baptists 1827–1845; with particular reference to slavery', unpublished D.Phil., Oxford University, 1972.

132 Viscountess Knutsford, *Life and Letters of Zachary Macaulay* (London: Arnold, 1900) p. 433.

133 *Anti-Slavery Monthly Reporter*, vol. III, no. 69 (20 October 1830), p. 452.

134 *Anti-Slavery Monthly Reporter*, vol. V, no. 5 (May 1832), p. 166; T. C. Hansard, *The Parliamentary Debates*, 3rd series, vol. XVIII (London: Hansard, 1833), column 309.

135 *Baptist Magazine*, vol. XXII (1830), pp. 482–84.

136 *Patriot*, 11 May 1833; *Record*, 1 November 1830, 19 April 1833, 16 May 1833.

137 *Sheffield Iris*, 12 October 1830; *Christian Advocate*, vol. I, no. 42 (18 October 1830); vol. I, no. 43 (25 October 1830).

138 *Christian Advocate*, vol. I, no. 44 (1 November 1830).

139 *Christian Advocate*, vol. I, no. 49 (6 December 1830); vol. II, no. 80 (2 May 1831); *Court Journal*, no. 83 (27 November 1830); *To Her Majesty Queen Adelaide. The Humble and Dutiful Address of the Undersigned Female Inhabitants of the City of Bristol and its Vicinity* (Bristol: Wright & Bagnall, [1830]). The petition from Bristol was signed by six thousand women, headed by veteran abolitionist Hannah More.

140 *Christian Advocate*, vol. IV, no. 175 (6 May 1833), p. 140.

141 Seymour Drescher, 'Two variables of anti-slavery: religious organisation

and social mobilization in Britain and France, 1780–1870'; Bolt and Drescher (eds), *Anti-Slavery, Religion and Reform*, ch. 2, table 2. David Hempton, *Methodism and Politics in British Society, 1750–1850* (London: Hutchinson, 1984), pp. 208–10, gives an official membership figure of 260, 491 in 1833. Even if Hempton's higher figure is taken, however, it remains true that the vast majority of Methodists signed the petitions.

142 'Female Petition for the Abolition of Negro Slavery', [printed circular appeal].

143 *Reports of the Select Committee of the House of Commons on Public Petitions*, session 1837–38, p. 477.

144 Sir George Stephen, *Anti-Slavery Recollections: In a Series of Letters Addressed to Mrs Beecher Stowe* (London: Thomas Hatchard, 1854), pp. 196–97.

145 'Minute Book of the Ladies Society for the Relief of Negro Slaves', entry for 26 November 1829.

146 London Female Anti-Slavery Society, 'Female Petition for the Abolition of Slavery', 29 April 1833 [printed circular appeal]. See also 'The Ladies of the London Female Anti-Slavery Society . . .'(London, May 1833) [printed circular thanking those who helped with the petition].

147 The *Record*, 16 May 1833; 'Female Petition for the Abolition of Negro Slavery'.

148 Stephen, *Anti-Slavery Recollections*, pp. 196–97.

149 See the notices of the meeting in the *Christian Advocate*, vol. VIII, no. 394 (July 1837), p. 225, and *The Philanthropist*, 13 July 1837, p. 3. For the full text of the female address see *Christian Advocate*, vol. IX, no. 425 (19 February 1838), p. 63.

150 'Committee on Slavery Minute Book', entry for 3 July 1837.

151 Stoddart, *Elizabeth Pease Nichol*, pp. 55–56.

152 Letters among MSS Brit. Emp. S18, C2/5-99, C3/1-77, Anti-Slavery Collection, in RHL; *The Patriot*, vol. IV, no. 352 (17 August 1837), p. 525; no. 354 (24 August 1837), p. 541; no. 357 (4 September 1837), p. 564; *The Christian Advocate*, vol. VIII, no. 395 (24 July 1837), p. 237; no. 400 (28 August 1837), p. 276; *The Philanthropist*, 20 July 1837, pp. 1–3; 3 August 1837, p. 3; 31 August 1837, p. 2.

153 For Scotland see *Petition to her Majesty, Queen Victoria, from the Ladies of Glasgow; Anti-Slavery Meeting – Delegation to London. From the Glasgow Argus of 13th November 1837; Caledonian Mercury*, 31 July 1837, p. 1; *Christian Advocate*, vol. VIII, no. 399 (21 August 1837), p. 269; vol. IX, no. 429 (19 March 1938), p. 89; *Patriot*, vol. VI, no. 367 (9 October 1837), p. 645. For Ireland see *An Appeal from the Dublin Ladies' Association, Auxiliary to the Hibernian Negro's Friend Society, to Their Christian Countrywomen* (Dublin, 21 August 1837); *The Irish Temperance and Literary Gazette*, no. 40 (12 August 1837), p. 160; no. 42 (26 August 1837), p. 166; no. 43 (2 September 1837), p. 167; no. 44 (9 September 1837); no 63 (20 January 1838), p. 252; *The British Emancipator*, no. 3 (17 January 1838); no. 41 (16 May 1838).

154 *Christian Advocate*, vol. IX, no. 425 (19 February 1838), pp. 56, 63; no. 439 (28 May 1838), p. 171; *British Emancipator*, no. 8 (21 March 1838), p. 43; *Anti-Slavery Meeting – Delegation to London; The Irish Friend*, vol. I, no. 2 (1 December 1837), p. 14; *The Irish Temperance and Literary Gazette*, no. 53 (11 November 1837), p. 212.

155 *Manchester Times*, 24 March 1838, p. 3. For other local addresses see *Brighton Herald*, 5 May 1838, p. 2; *Christian Advocate*, vol. IX, no. 430 (26 March 1838); no. 439 (28 May 1838), p. 171; *British Emancipator*, no. 41 (16 May 1838).

156 *Reports of the Select Committee of the House of Commons on Public Petitions*, session 1837–38, p. 660.

157 *The British Emancipator*, no. 7 (14 March 1838), p. 36.

158 *Journal of the House of Lords*, session 1830–31, vol. LXIII, pp. 152, 456, 491; *The Record*, November 1830.

159 This quote is from a petition of the females of Spilsby, Lincolnshire, to the House of Lords, dated 28 March 1833 (*Journal of the House of Lords*, session 1833, vol. LXV, p. 121). For other petitions making similar points see *Journal of the House of Lords*, session 1832, vol. LXIII, p. 420; session 1833, vol. LXV, pp. 183, 208, 314, 325, 349; *Appendix of the Votes and Proceedings of the House of Commons*, session 1830–31, pp. 78, 216; *Nineteenth Report of the Select Committee on Public Petitions* (London: House of Commons, 1832), Appendices 673, 675; report of Reading women's petition in *Berkshire Chronicle*, 25 December 1830; report of Bolton women's petition in *Bolton Chronicle*, 25 December 1830.

160 *Christian Advocate*, vol. IX, no. 425 (February 19, 1838), p. 63.

161 *Doncaster, Nottingham, and Lincoln Gazette*, 26 April, 3 May 1833.

162 *Rochester Gazette*, 30 April 1833.

163 *Bolton Chronicle*, 4 May 1833; *Doncaster, Nottingham, and Lincoln Gazette*, 10 May 1833; *Nottingham Review*, 10 May 1833. For other newspaper reports of female petitions see: *Berkshire Chronicle*, 25 December 1830; *Birmingham Journal*, 11 May 1833; *Derby and Chesterfield Reporter*, 16 May 1833; *Devizes and Wiltshire Gazette*, 25 April and 9 May 1833; *Doncaster, Nottingham, and Lincoln Gazette*, 26 April, 3 May and 17 May 1833; *Edinburgh Evening Courant*, 16 May 1833; *Newcastle Chronicle*, 18 May 1833; *Nottingham Review*, 7 December 1832, 3 May 1833; *Rochester Gazette*, 30 April 1833; *Sussex Advertiser*, 13 May 1833.

164 *The Anti-Slavery Reporter*, vol. IV, no. 2 (5 January 1831), p. 32; *Twentieth Report from the Select Committee on Public Petitions* (London: House of Commons, 23 May 1833), petition no. 7719. The total population of Edinburgh at this time was around 162,000 (see Eric J. Evans, *The Forging of the Modern State: Early Industrial Britain, 1783–1870* (London: Longman, 1983), Appendix Eiii, p. 408).

165 *Doncaster, Nottingham, and Lincoln Gazette*, 17 May 1833; *Nottingham Review*, 3 May and 10 May 1833. In Birmingham, in contrast, the proportions were reversed, with 11,000 male signatories to around 7,000 female (*Birmingham Journal*, 11 May 1833).

166 Letter from Ann Gilbert to Mary Ann Rawson, Nottingham, 10 May 1833, 'Autographs – The Bow in the Cloud', p. 151, Rawson Family Papers, Raymond English Deposit, John Rylands University Library, Manchester.

167 *Christian Advocate*, vol. IV, no. 172 (15 April 1833), p. 118.

168 Peter Fraser, 'Public petitioning and Parliament before 1832', *History*, vol. 46 (1961), pp. 195–211; Colin Leys, 'Petitioning in the nineteenth and twentieth centuries', *Political Studies*, vol. III, no. 1 (February 1955), pp. 45–64.

169 Izhak Gross, 'The abolition of negro slavery and British Parliamentary politics 1832–3', *Historical Journal*, vol. 23, no. 1 (1980), pp. 63–85.

170 For the argument that 'frequently renewed petitions' created a 'climate of opinion' against slavery, see Seymour Drescher, *Capitalism and Antislavery: British Mobilization in Comparative Perspective* (Basingstoke: Macmillan, 1986), p. 94.

171 *Irish Friend*, vol. I, no. 5 (1 March 1838), p. 38.

172 *The British Emancipator*, no. 3 (17 January 1838); no. 9 (2 April 1838), p. 45; *The Christian Advocate*, vol. IX, no. 430 (26 March 1838), p. 97.

173 See Edith F. Hurwitz, *Politics and the Public Conscience: Slave Emancipation and the Abolitionist Movement in Britain* (London: George Allen & Unwin, 1973), p. 76.

174 Izhak Gross, 'Parliament and the abolition of negro apprenticeship, 1835–1838', *English Historical Review*, vol. 96 (1981), pp. 575–76; Alex Tyrrell, 'The "Moral Radical Party" and the Anglo-Jamaican campaign for the abolition of the negro apprenticeship system', *English Historical Review*, vol. 392 (July 1984), p. 498; Howard Temperley, *British Antislavery, 1833–1870* (Columbia, SC: University of South Carolina Press, 1972), p. 40; letter from Lord Glenelg to Colonial Governors, 2 April 1838 (London, Public Record Office, CO 318/141), as quoted in M. Craton, J. Walvin and D. Wright, *Slavery, Abolition and Emancipation: Black Slaves and the British Empire* (London: Longman, 1976), p. 342.

175 Letter from Thomas Milner Gibson to George Wilson, 29 October 1841, as quoted in Alex Tyrrell, ' "Woman's Mission" and pressure group politics in Britain, 1825–60', *Bulletin of the John Rylands University Library*, vol. 63 (1980), p. 213.

4 ANTI-SLAVERY IN THE FABRIC OF WOMEN'S LIVES

1 'Memorial of Lucy Townsend', *The Twenty-Second Report of the Ladies' Negro's Friend Society for Birmingham* (Birmingham: Hudson, 1847); Lucy Townsend, 'Scrap Book on Negro Slaves', 'Album' and 'Autographs', MSS Brit. Emp. S.4, 5, 6, in RHL.

2 Sara W. Sturge, *Memoir of Mary Lloyd of Wednesbury, 1795–1865* (printed for private circulation, 1921).

3 Ann Taylor Gilbert, *Autobiography and Other Memorials of Mrs Gilbert*, 2 vols (1874).

4 Letter from Ann Gilbert to Mary Ann Rawson, 9 April 1838, Papers of H.J. Wilson and M.A. Rawson, MD 2019, Sheffield City Library.

5 Norma Taylor, 'The Life of Mary Anne Rawson' and other unpublished sources in Sheffield Central Library; Rawson Family Papers, John Rylands University Library, Manchester; N.B. Lewis, 'The abolitionist Movement in Sheffield, 1823–1833', *Bulletin of the John Rylands Library*, vol. 18, no. 2 (July 1934).

6 Coltman Family Papers, Leicestershire Records Office; *A Brief Sketch of the Life and Labours of Mrs Elizabeth Heyrick* (Leicester: Crossley and Clarke, 1862); Kenneth Corfield, 'Elizabeth Heyrick: radical Quaker' in Gail Malmgreen (ed.), *Religion in the Lives of English Women, 1750–1930* (London: Croom Helm, 1986), pp. 41–67.

7 Susanna Watts Scrapbook, Leicester Public Library; *Hymns and Poems of the late Mrs Susanna Watts, with a Few Recollections of Her Life* (Leicester: J. Waddington, 1842).

8 Josiah C. Wedgwood, *A History of the Wedgwood Family* (London: St Catherine Press, 1908), especially pp. 178–79.

9 Manuscript material in Friends House Library, London; Gail Malmgreen, 'Anne Knight and the radical subculture', *Quaker History*, vol. 71, no. 2 (Fall 1982), pp. 100–13.

10 Anna M. Stoddart, *Elizabeth Pease Nichol* (London: J.M. Dent, 1899).

11 *Life of Mary Anne Schimmelpenninck*, 2 vols (London: Longman, Brown, Green, Longmans & Roberts, 1858).

12 Isabel Grubb, 'An anti-slavery enthusiast, 1826', *Journal of the Friends Historical Society*, vol. 31 (1934), pp. 21–26.

13 Samuel Roberts, *Some Memorials of the Family of Roberts*, 3rd edn (Sheffield: Northend, 1924).

14 Typescript 'Dictionary of Quaker Biography', Friends House Library, London.

15 My thanks to the curator of Norris Museum, Huntingdon, for this information.

16 Alex Tyrrell, *Joseph Sturge and the Moral Radical Party in Early Victorian England* (London: Helm, 1987).

17 L.E. O'Rorke (ed.), *The Life and Friendships of Catherine Marsh* (London: Longmans, 1917).

18 Cecilia Lucy Brightwell, *Memorials of the Life of Amelia Opie* (Norwich: Fletcher & Alexander, 1854).

19 For Mary Dudley see *Annual Monitor*, 1849, p. 39; for Elizabeth Dudley see typescript 'Dictionary of Quaker Biography', Friends House Library, London.

20 Typescript 'Dictionary of Quaker biography', Friends House Library, London.

21 Sir George Stephen, *Anti-Slavery Recollections: In a Series of Letters Addressed to Mrs Beecher Stowe* (London: Thomas Hatchard, 1854), p. 197; see also Patricia M. Pugh, *Calendar of the Papers of Sir Thomas Fowell Buxton, 1786–1845*, introduction (London: List and Index Society Special Series, 1980).

22 Obituary in *Annual Monitor*, 1861, p. 39.

23 Letter of J. Robson to J.S. Robson, 30 October 1826, MSS Portfolio 38.65, in Friends Library, London; typescript 'Dictionary of Quaker Biography', in Friends House Library, London.

24 For Anna Gurney see Pugh, *Calendar of the Papers of Sir Thomas Fowell Buxton*, introduction.

25 For Wright's view on slavery see: An Englishwoman [Frances Wright], *Views of Society and Manners in America* (London: Longman, Hurst, Rees, Orme & Brown, 1821), pp. 62–77, 422–27, 515–23.

26 This is a very rough estimate based on the existence of a minimum of seventy-three groups with an average membership of perhaps one hundred women. There were twice as many men's societies and thus possibly twice as many male subscribers.

27 See, for example, *Third Report of the Female Society for Birmingham . . . for the Relief of British Negro Slaves* (Birmingham: B. Hudson, 1828), p. 22.

28 *Report of the Sheffield Female Anti-Slavery Society* (Sheffield, 1827), p. 3.

29 *Third Annual Report of the Ladies' Association for Salisbury . . . in Aid of the Cause of Negro Emancipation* (Calne, 1828), p. 7; 'Minute Book of the Ladies' Society for the Relief of Negro Slaves', Birmingham Central Library Archives Dept., entry for 26 November 1829.

30 'Minute Book of the Ladies' Society for the Relief of Negro Slaves', entry for 26 November 1829, p. 98.

31 Alan D. Gilbert, *Religion and Society in Industrial England: Church, Chapel and Social Change, 1740–1914* (London: Longman, 1976), Table 3.1, p. 83. (By 'artisan' Gilbert means skilled workers employed in factories and domestic industry.)

32 This does not seem a great exaggeration when there were 5,136 female signatures out of a population of some 24,000 men, women and children (see Eric J. Evans, *The Forging of the Modern State* (London: Longman, 1983), Appendix Eiii, p. 408).

33 *The Patriot*, vol. VI, no. 353 (21 August 1837), p. 532.

34 *The Philanthropist*, 20 July 1837, p. 3.

35 Letter from Maria Hope Jones to Miss Dudley, Bryn Hyfryd, 11 August 1837, MSS Brit. Emp. S18, C3/20, in RHL.
36 Dorothy Thompson, *The Chartists* (London: Temple Smith, 1984), including ch. 7 on 'The Women'.
37 Alex Tyrrell, 'The "Moral Radical Party" and the Anglo-Jamaican campaign for the abolition of the negro apprenticeship system', *English Historical Review*, vol. 392 (July 1984), pp. 481–502.
38 For Sturge's Chartist sympathies see Betty Fladeland, *Abolitionists and Working-Class Problems in the Age of Industrialization* (London: Macmillan, 1984), ch. 3.
39 Thompson, *The Chartists*, p. 140.
40 Glasgow Ladies' Auxiliary Emancipation Society, *Three Years' Female Anti-Slavery Effort, in Britain and America* (Glasgow: Aird & Russell, 1837), pp. 65–71; *Darlington Ladies' Society for the Universal Abolition of Slavery* (Rules and Report c. 1837 [n.d.], Darlington Branch Library, Durham); letter from Jane Smeal to Elizabeth Pease, Glasgow, 21 December 1836, printed in Clare Taylor (ed.), *British and American Abolitionists: an Episode in Transatlantic Understanding* (Edinburgh: Edinburgh University Press, 1974), p. 24.
41 For women leading Chartist processions see Thompson, *The Chartists*, p. 120.
42 Letter signed 'M.G.', Edinburgh, 14 April 1838, printed in *The British Emancipator*, no. 15 (9 May 1838), p. 86; no. 16 (16 May 1838), p. 94.
43 Peter Fryer, *Staying Power: the History of Black People in Britain* (London: Pluto Press, 1984), pp. 130–31.
44 Moira Ferguson (ed.), *The History of Mary Prince, a West Indian Slave, Related by Herself* (London: Pandora, 1987). This is a reprint of the 1831 original edition, with a useful new introduction.
45 Ibid., p. 78.
46 Ibid., p. 87.
47 Ibid., p. 81.
48 *Seventh Report of the Ladies' Negro's Friend Society, for Birmingham . . .* (Birmingham: B. Hudson, 1832), pp. 38–39.
49 *Journal of the House of Commons*, session 1829, vol. LXXXIV, p. 404. The petition is reproduced as Appendix I in Ferguson (ed.), *The History of Mary Prince*, p. 116.
50 Ferguson (ed.), *The History of Mary Prince*, pp. 87–88.
51 Ibid., pp. 82, 83.
52 Ibid., p. 89.
53 Ibid., p. 45.
54 Ibid., pp. 64, 84.
55 Ibid., pp. 114–15.
56 Ibid., pp. 45–46.
57 Ibid.
58 'Minute Book of the Ladies' Society for the Relief of Negro Slaves', Birmingham Central Library Archives Dept., minutes of Annual Meeting, 12 April 1831.
59 Ferguson (ed.) *The History of Mary Prince*, p. 82.
60 Ibid., p. 106.
61 Ibid., p. 105.
62 Ibid., p. 45.
63 *The Times*, 1 March 1833, pp. 6–7.
64 'Anti-Slavery correspondence, 1821–32', statement signed by Mary (John) Capper, Clapton, 9 April 1830, Temp. MSS 101/3, Friends House Library,

London; 'Minutes of a Standing Committee of the Meeting for Sufferings Appointed to Aid in Promoting the Total Abolition of the Slave Trade', Minute Book no. 2, entry for 11 May 1830, Friends House Library, London. Mary Capper's husband John was a member of the Quaker anti-slavery committee.

65 'Anti-Slavery correspondence, 1821-32', letter from Elizabeth Dudley to Peter Bedford *et al.*, Devonshire House, [n.d.], Temp. MSS 101/3, Friends House Library.

5 PERSPECTIVES, PRINCIPLES AND POLICIES

1 For male activists' views see James Walvin, 'The propaganda of anti-slavery', in James Walvin (ed.), *Slavery and British Society, 1776–1846* (London: Macmillan, 1982), pp. 63–67.

2 'Address to the Ladies of Great-Britain . . .', *The Humming Bird*, vol. I, no. 7 (June 1825), pp. 195–96.

3 *First Report of the Female Society for Birmingham . . . for the Relief of British Negro Slaves* (Birmingham: B. Hudson, 1826), p. 9.

4 *The Negro Slave. A Tale. Addressed to the Women of Great Britain* (London: Harvey & Darton, 1830), p. 70.

5 *A Vindication of Female Anti-Slavery Associations* (London: Female Anti-Slavery Society [n.d.]), p. 3.

6 [Elizabeth Heyrick], *Appeal to the Hearts and Consciences of British Women* (Leicester: Cockshaw, 1828), [p. 3].

7 Speech quoted in *Anti-Slavery Reporter*, vol. IV, no. 8 (May 1831), p. 257, and also in *Seventh Report of the Ladies' Negro's Friend Society, for Birmingham . . .* (Birmingham: B. Hudson, 1832), p. 26.

8 Ibid.

9 *Second Report of the Committee of the Society for the Mitigation and Gradual Abolition of Slavery Throughout the British Dominions* (London: Ellerton & Henderson, 1825), Appendix K, p. 168.

10 Viscountess Knutsford, *The Life and Letters of Zachary Macaulay* (London: Arnold, 1900), p. 433.

11 *A Picture of Colonial Slavery, in the Year 1828, Addressed Especially to the Ladies of Great Britain*, (London: Anti-Slavery Society, 1828), pp. 5–6.

12 'Address to the Ladies of Great-Britain . . .', *The Humming Bird*, vol. I, no. 7 (June 1825), pp. 195–203.

13 Frank Prochaska, *Women and Philanthropy in Nineteenth Century England* (Oxford: Oxford University Press, 1980), p. 30.

14 A Lady, *A Dialogue Between a Well-Wisher and a Friend to the Slaves in the British Colonies* (London: S. Bagster Jr, [n.d.]), p. 3.

15 *Second Report of the Ladies Association for Calne . . . in Aid of the Cause of Negro Emancipation* (Calne: W. Baily, 1827), pp. 3–4.

16 *A Vindication of Female Anti-Slavery Associations* (London: Female Anti-Slavery Society, [n.d.]), pp. 3–4.

17 See, for example, *Ladies Society for the Relief of Negro Slaves. Founding Meeting Held West-Bromwich, 8th April 1825*.

18 *First Report of the Female Society, for Birmingham*, p. 3.

19 See, for example, A Lady, *A Dialogue*; *A Vindication of Female Anti-Slavery Associations*; [Heyrick], *Appeal to the Hearts and Consciences of British Women*; [Elizabeth Heyrick], 'Apology for Ladies' Anti-Slavery Associations', in *The*

Genius of Universal Emancipation, 3rd series, vol. II, no. 7 (December 1831), p. 110.

20 *Twentieth Report from the Select Committee on Public Petitions* (London: House of Commons, 1833), Appendix no. 701.

21 *Berkshire Chronicle*, 25 December 1830.

22 *Nineteenth Report from the Select Committee on Public Petitions* (London: House of Commons, 1833), Appendix no. 673.

23 See Leonore Davidoff and Catherine Hall, *Family Fortunes: Men and Women of the English Middle Class, 1780–1850* (London: Hutchinson, 1987), p. 430.

24 *Genius of Universal Emancipation*, new series, vol. I, no. 16 (October 1827), p. 126.

25 These seals, listed in the *Rules and Resolutions of the Dublin Ladies' Anti-Slavery Society* (Dublin: printed for the Society, 1828), p. 16, were supplied by the Female Society for Birmingham (see account for supply of seals etc. to Dublin in *Third Report of the Female Society for Birmingham . . . for the Relief of British Negro Slaves* (Birmingham: B. Hudson, 1828), p. 54). The motto 'Am I not a Woman and a Sister' was later adopted by American women abolitionists, first appearing at the head of the 'Ladies Department' in the *Liberator* (vol. II, no. 2 (January 1832), p. 6). Walvin incorrectly describes the image and motto as an American innovation of 1838 (J.R.W. [James Walvin], 'A woman and a sister', *Slavery and Abolition*, vol. 4, no. 1 (May 1983), pp. 1–2).

26 'An appeal from British ladies to the West India planters', handwritten draft in Lucy Townsend, 'Scrap Book on Negro Slaves', MSS Brit. Emp. S.4, in RHL, pp. 127–34.

27 Poem included in 'Female Society for Birmingham, etc., for the Relief of British Negro Slaves. Album', in Birmingham Central Library, Archives Dept.

28 Printed at head of the *Third Report of the Female Society for Birmingham*.

29 *Anti-Slavery Scrap Book* (London: Harvey and Darton, 1829). The book was probably produced by the Peckham Ladies' African and Anti-Slavery Society.

30 See text of the Birmingham women's 1830 Address to the Queen in 'Minute Book of the Ladies Society for the Relief of Negro Slaves', in Birmingham Central Library Archives Dept., entry for 23 December 1830; text of 1833 petition from the ladies of Market Lavington to the House of Commons in *Nineteenth Report from the Select Committee on Public Petitions*, Appendix no. 675.

31 *Appendix to the Votes and Proceedings of the House of Commons, Session 1830–1*, p. 78. For similar points in a petition from the women of Bolton see *Bolton Chronicle*, 4 May 1833.

32 For a discussion of the Owenite debate on sex slavery see Barbara Taylor, *Eve and the New Jerusalem: Socialism and Feminism in the Nineteenth Century* (London: Virago, 1983), pp. 32–48.

33 Extract from Anna Gurney and Sarah Buxton's 'Journal', Buxton Papers, vol. XII, pp. 111–13, MSS Brit. Emp. S.444, in RHL.

34 'Minute Book of the Ladies' Society for the Relief of Negro Slaves', entry for 8 April 1828; *Second Report of the Ladies' Association for Calne*, p. 4.

35 *Ladies' Society for the Relief of Negro Slaves* [founding resolutions], resolution 10.

36 See, for example, the sheet giving 'Explanation on the contents of the Society's Album' in 'Female Society for Birmingham. . . . Album'.

37 Lucille Mathurin, *The Rebel Woman in the British West Indies During Slavery*

(Institute of Jamaica, 1975); Rhoda E. Reddock, 'Women and slavery in the Caribbean: a feminist perspective', *Latin American Perspectives*, vol. 12, issue 44, no. 1 (Winter 1985), pp. 63–80; Hilary McD. Beckles, *Natural Rebels: A social history of enslaved black women in Barbados* (London: Zed Books, 1989); Barbara Bush, *Slave Women in Caribbean Society, 1650–1838* (Bloomington, IN: Indiana University Press, 1990).

38 [Elizabeth Heyrick], *Immediate, not Gradual Abolition; or, an Inquiry into the Shortest, Safest, and Most Effectual Means of Getting Rid of West-Indian Slavery* (London: Hatchard, 1824). For discussions of this pamphlet see David Brion Davis, 'The emergence of immediatism in British and American anti-slavery thought', *Mississipi Valley Historical Review*, 49 (1962–63), pp. 209–30; and Kenneth Corfield, 'Elizabeth Heyrick: radical Quaker', in Gail Malmgreen (ed.), *Religion in the Lives of English Women* (London: Croom Helm, 1986), pp. 41–67.

39 *A Brief Sketch of the Life and Labours of Mrs Elizabeth Heyrick* (Leicester: Crossley & Clarke, 1862), p. 19.

40 Davis, 'The emergence of immediatism', pp. 209–18.

41 Andrew Thomson, *Substance of the Speech Delivered at the Meeting of the Edinburgh Society for the Abolition of Slavery, on October 19, 1830* (Edinburgh: Whyte, 1830). Another provincial abolitionist, Samuel Roberts of Sheffield, had expressed support for immediate emancipation in 1823 in 'A Letter to John Bull. With a Sketch of a Plan for the Safe, Speedy and Effectual Abolition of Slavery' (quoted in *Autobiography and Select Remains of the Late Samuel Roberts* (London: Longman, Brown, Green & Longmans, 1849), p. 102), but this seems to have recieved little attention.

42 For a useful overview of the development of support for immediate emancipation see Davis, 'The Emergence of Immediatism'.

43 [Heyrick], *Immediate, not Gradual Abolition*, p. 5.

44 Ibid., p. 15.

45 Ibid., p. 8.

46 Ibid., p. 9.

47 Ibid.

48 Ibid., p. 7.

49 Ibid.

50 Ibid., p. 18.

51 Ibid., p. 10.

52 Ibid., p. 19.

53 Ibid., p. 14.

54 Ibid., p. 22.

55 Ibid., p. 6.

56 Ibid., p. 7.

57 Ibid., p. 4.

58 [Elizabeth Heyrick], *An Enquiry Which of the Two Parties is Best Entitled to Freedom? The Slave or the Slave-Holder?* (London: Baldwin, Cradock & Joy, 1824), pp. 5–6.

59 Ibid., p. 19.

60 Ibid., p. 28.

61 [Elizabeth Heyrick], *Letters on the Necessity of a Prompt Extinction of British Colonial Slavery* (London, 1826).

62 Ibid., p. 5.

63 Ibid., p. 24.

64 [Elizabeth Heyrick], 'Apology for Ladies' Anti-Slavery Associations', p. 110.

65 Corfield, 'Elizabeth Heyrick', pp. 44–47.

66 [Heyrick], *Letters*, p. 164. Emphasis in original. Corfield ('Elizabeth Heyrick', p. 45) attributes the letter to the Quaker secretary of the Calne society, but it might alternatively have been written by co-secretary and co-founder Lucy Townsend.

67 *Report of the Sheffield Female Anti-Slavery Society* (Sheffield, 1827), especially pp. 4, 10.

68 *A Vindication of Female Anti-Slavery Associations*, pp. 5–6, 8. An identical text, in slightly different order, comprises pp. 5–14 of the *Second Report of the Female Society for Clifton . . . in Aid of the Cause of Negro Emancipation* (Bristol: T.D. Clarke, [1828]).

69 *First Report of the Committee of the Newcastle upon Tyne Society for Promoting the Gradual Abolition of Slavery Throughout the British Dominions* (Newcastle: Mitchell, 1825), pp. 4–5.

70 *First Report of the Rochester and Chatham Anti-Slavery Society* (Strood: Sweet, 1828), p. 13.

71 For Roberts' isolation on the immediatist issue, see the report of his speech at an anti-slavery meeting in the *Sheffield Iris*, 24 January 1826. His society petitioned Parliament for the amelioration of slavery between 1825 and 1828 (see N.B. Lewis, 'The Abolitionist Movement in Sheffield, 1823–1833', offprint of *Bulletin of the John Ryland Library*, vol. 18, no. 2 (July 1934), pp. 5–6).

72 *Fourth Annual Report, of the Ladies' Association for Salisbury, Calne* (Calne: T.P. Baily, 1829), pp. 6–7; 'Devizes anti-slavery meeting', *Anti-Slavery Monthly Reporter*, vol. III, no. 20 (October 1830), p. 414. While Corfield ('Elizabeth Heyrick', p. 45) argues that the Ladies' Association for Salisbury was the first women's society to become immediatist this is not borne out by the society's reports (see *Second Report of the Ladies' Association for Calne; Third Annual Report of the Ladies' Association for Salisbury . . . in Aid of the Cause of Negro Emancipation* (Calne: Baily, 1828).

73 Lucy Townsend, 'Autographs', MSS Brit. Emp. S.5, in RHL, pp. 317–18 (letters from John Philip to Lucy Townsend, London, 26 April 1829, and from Emma to Charlotte Townsend, [Manchester], 11 June 1829); 'Minute Book of the Ladies' Society for the Relief of Negro Slaves', entry for 8 April 1830.

74 'At a General Meeting of the Members of the Birmingham Anti-Slavery Society' ([printed sheet, 1830]).

75 Thomson, *Substance of the Speech*; Charles E.H.Orpen, *The Principles, Plans, and Objects of the 'Hibernian Negro's Friend Society'* (Dublin: 1831), p. 6.

76 'Committee on Slavery Minute Book', MSS Brit. Emp. S.20 E.2/3, in RHL, entry for 27 May 1830; 'Proceedings of the General Meeting of the Anti-Slavery Society', *Anti-Slavery Monthly Reporter*, vol. III, no. 13 (June 1830).

77 The Committee of the Leicester Auxiliary Anti-Slavery Society, *An Address on the State of Slavery in the West India Islands* (Leicester: T. Combe, 1824), pp. 20–21.

78 *Speeches delivered in the town-hall in Beverley, at a public meeting, convened by the right worshipful the Mayor, for the purpose of petitioning Parliament to abolish slavery in the West Indies* (Beverley, Beverley Anti-Slavery Association, 1824), p. 11.

79 *First Report of the Rochester and Chatham Anti-Slavery Society* (London: Sweet, 1828), pp. 13–15; *First Annual Report of the Edinburgh Society for Promoting the*

Mitigation and Ultimate Abolition of Negro Slavery (Edinburgh: Abernethy & Walker, 1824), pp. 5, 8–9.

80 [Sheffield Female Anti-Slavery Society], *Appeal of the Friends of the Negro to the British People; on behalf of the slaves in their colonies* (Sheffield: J. Blackwell, Iris Office, 1830), p. 7.

81 [Sheffield Female Anti-Slavery Society], *Appeal of the Friends of the Negro to the British People*, pp. 6–7.

82 [Heyrick], *Letters*, letter IV, p. 164. Emphasis in original.

83 *Report of the Sheffield Female Anti-Slavery Society* (1827), p. 10. Emphasis in original.

84 Davis, 'The emergence of immediatism', p. 228.

85 Catherine Hutton, 'Hasty sketch of the Coltman family' (1802), Coltman MSS 15D57, item 387, Leicester Museum Archives Dept.

86 Report of the Sheffield Female Anti-Slavery Society for 1829, in 'Auxiliary Society for the Relief of Negro Slaves. Instituted at Sheffield', Minute Book, Eng. MS 743, John Rylands University Library, Manchester, entry for 10 November 1829.

87 There is a valuable discussion of these pamphlets in Corfield, 'Elizabeth Heyrick', pp. 53–59, and a full list of the pamphlets in note 3, p. 61.

88 Taylor, *Eve and the New Jerusalem*.

89 Corfield, 'Elizabeth Heyrick', p. 42.

90 J. Coltman Jr, to Mrs Heyrick (1797), Coltman MSS 15D57, item 34, Leicester Museum, Archives Dept.

91 See Hutton, 'Hasty sketch of the Coltman family' (1802); Samuel Coltman, 'Memoirs of letters of the Coltman family', vols II and III, Coltman MSS 15D57, items 387 and 449–50, Leicester Museum, Archives Dept.

92 [Heyrick], *Immediate, not Gradual Abolition*, p. 18.

93 Letter [incomplete] from Sarah Wedgwood, Camp Hill, 19 September 1830, Anne Knight Correspondence, Friends House Library, London.

94 Davis, 'The emergence of immediatism', p. 220; Corfield, 'Elizabeth Heyrick', p. 48.

95 [Heyrick], *An Enquiry*, p. 22. Emphasis in original.

96 *A Brief Sketch of the Life and Labours of Mrs Elizabeth Heyrick*, p. 19.

97 *The Baptist Magazine*, vol. XVII (1825), pp. 29, 154–57.

98 *The Christian Observer*, vol. XXIV, no. 9 (September 1824), pp. 569–70.

99 'Committee on Slavery Minute Book', entries for 8 June, 8 December 1824.

100 Anthropos [Mr Mathews of Histon, Cambs.], *The Rights of Man. (Not Paines,) but the Rights of Man, in the West Indies* (London: Knight and Lacy, 1824), especially p. 34.

101 Letter from Zachary Macaulay to Henry Brougham, 25 March 1825, Macaulay Family Papers, Henry Huntington Library, as quoted in Edith Hurwitz, *Politics and the Public Conscience* (London: George Allen and Unwin, 1973), p. 32.

102 *Second Annual Report of the Edinburgh Society for Promoting the Mitigation and Ultimate Abolition of Negro Slavery* (Edinburgh: Anderson and Bryce, 1825), catalogue of books belonging to the society; *First Annual Report of the Aberdeen Anti-Slavery Society for Promoting the Mitigation and Ultimate Abolition of Negro Slavery* (Aberdeen: D. Chalmers and Co., 1826), p. 22.

103 Thomson, *Substance of the Speech*, pp. 3–4.

104 Letter from Andrew Thomson to Lucy Townsend, Edinburgh, 18 November 1830, in Townsend, 'Autographs', p. 326. This letter was printed along with extracts of Thomson's speech as Appendix no. 1 of the

'Report of the Female Society for Birmingham' in *Christian Advocate*, no. 80 (16 May 1831). Thomson's pamphlet was distributed by the Ladies' Association for Liverpool (see handwritten list at back of 'Album' among Cropper Family Papers, Merseyside Record Office, Liverpool).

105 'Committee on Slavery Minute Book', entries for 7 September, 19 October, 2 November, 23 December 1825.

106 [Heyrick], *Letters*, 'Advertisement'.

107 'Minute Book of the Ladies' Society for the Relief of Negro Slaves', entry for 8 April 1830, p. 100.

108 'Committee on Slavery Minute Book', entry for 27 May 1830.

109 *Account of the Receipts and Disbursements of the Anti-Slavery Society, for the Years 1829 and 1830; with a List of Subscribers*, ([London: S. Bagster Jr, 1830]).

110 *Report of the Agency Committee of the Anti-Slavery Society* (London: S. Bagster Jr, 1832), p. 2.

111 Letter from Margaret Crouch to John Crisp, St Ives, 18 August 1831, MSS Brit. Emp. S18 C156/148A, 149, in RHL.

112 Corfield, 'Elizabeth Heyrick', p. 51.

113 [Heyrick], *Appeal to the Hearts and Consciences of British Women*, pp. 3–4.

114 The outline of the dispute at Sheffield given here has been reconstructed from 'Anti-Slavery Letters' and 'Anti-Slavery Letters and Papers', Eng. MSS 741, 742, Rawson Family Papers, John Rylands Library, Manchester.

115 'Anti-Slavery Letters and Papers', item 63, Eng. MSS 742, Rawson Family Papers.

116 Letter from L. Palmer to M.A. Rawson, Sheffield, item 82 of 'Anti-Slavery Letters', Eng. MSS 741, Rawson Family Papers.

117 An Englishwoman, *An Address to the Females of Great Britain, on the Propriety of their Petitioning Parliament for the Abolition of Negro Slavery* (London: J.G. & F. Rivington, 1833), pp. 5–6.

118 Ibid., pp. 9–10.

119 Ibid., p. 10.

6 THE TRANSATLANTIC SISTERHOOD

1 For an account of the society see Howard Temperley, *British Antislavery, 1833–1870* (Columbia, SC: University of South Carolina Press, 1972), ch. 3.

2 *Proceedings at the First Public Meeting of the Society for the Extinction of the Slave Trade, and for the Civilization of Africa* (London: W. Clowes & Sons, 1840).

3 See letters and notes among Buxton Papers, vol. 18, pp. 55, 100 a–d, 128, 156–57; vol. 19, pp. 36–42; vol. 20A, p. 462–69, MSS Brit. Emp. S.444, in RHL. For a useful sketch of their work see Patricia M. Pugh's Introduction to the *Calendar of the Papers of Sir Thomas Fowell Buxton, 1786–1845*, List and Index Society Special Series, vol. 13 (1980), pp. i–iv.

4 Mrs Jane M. Widgins [to Anna Gurney], 1841, Buxton Papers, vol. 20, p. 153 a–d, MSS Brit. Emp. S.444, in RHL; *Darlington Ladies' Anti-Slavery and British India Society*, [report, c. 1839].

5 T.F. Buxton to Duchess of Sutherland, 26 December 1840, Buxton Papers, vol. 20, p. 92–94.

6 For a discussion of the nature of slavery in India see Mark Naidis, 'The abolitionists and Indian slavery', *Journal of Asian History*, vol. 15, no. 2 (1981), pp. 146–58.

7 For a useful overview of the activities of the society see John Hyslop Bell,

British Folks and British India Fifty Years Ago: Joseph Pease and his Contemporaries (London: Heywood, [1891]).

8 See Anna M. Stoddart, *Elizabeth Pease Nichol* (London: J.M. Dent, 1899) for a general assessment of Pease's work for the society, based on manuscript material much of which is no longer available.

9 Stoddart, *Elizabeth Pease Nichol*, pp. 86, 91–92, 99; letters from George Thompson to Elizabeth Pease, London, 27 March and 5 April 1839, as quoted in Bell, *British Folks and British India*, pp. 58–59; extract of letter from Elizabeth Pease to Sarah M. Grimke, London, 11 July 1839, printed in *Sixth Report of the Boston Female Anti-Slavery Society* (Boston: Dow & Jackson, 1839), p. 39; letters from Elizabeth Pease to Maria Weston Chapman, 11 July, 28 September and 26 October 1839, printed as items 48, 55, and 56 in Clare Taylor, *British and American Abolitionists: An Episode in Transatlantic Understanding* (Edinburgh: Edinburgh University Press, 1974), pp. 72, 84.

10 Letter from Mary Wigham to M.W. Chapman, 1 April 1839, printed as item [46] in Taylor, *British and American Abolitionists*, p. 69; 'Report of the Ladies' Auxiliary Society. Presented 1st August 1839', printed as a supplement to the *Fifth Annual Report of the Glasgow Emancipation Society* (Glasgow: John Young & Co., 1839).

11 *Report of the Sheffield Ladies' Association for the Universal Abolition of Slavery. February 19 1839* (Sheffield, 1839), pp. 12–13.

12 This act didn't remove slavery, however, since debt bondage was an economic and social problem which couldn't simply be solved by legislation (see Naidis, 'The Abolitionists and Indian Slavery', pp. 155, 158).

13 *First Annual Report of the British and Foreign Anti-Slavery Society* (London: Johnston and Barrett, 1840), pp. 4, 5. The formation of the BFASS is described in Temperley, *British Antislavery*, ch. iv.

14 *First Annual Report of the British and Foreign Anti-Slavery Society*, pp. 6, 9; Minute Book of the British and Foreign Anti-Slavery Society, vol. 1, pp. 23, 34, 54–55, 127, MSS Brit. Emp. S.20, E2/6, in RHL.

15 *Address from the Committee of the British and Foreign Anti-Slavery Society to the Women of England* (London: Johnston and Barrett, [1840]); *Anti-Slavery Reporter*, vol. I, no. 1 (January 1840), p. 3.

16 Douglas H. Maynard, 'The world's anti-slavery convention of 1840', *Mississippi Valley Historical Review*, vol. 47 (1960–61), pp. 452–71.

17 For a general account of the development of anti-slavery factions in Britain in the 1840s see Temperley, *British Antislavery*, pp. 209–20.

18 These figures are extrapolated from the cumulative contribution lists attached to the *First to Fifth Annual Reports of the British and Foreign Anti-Slavery Society* (London: Johnston & Barrett, 1840–45). For a full list of ladies' associations donating to the BFASS see the Appendix.

19 See Elizabeth Pease's correspondence, MS A.1.2. vol. 10, no. 37; vol. 11, pp. 155, 156; vol. 12, part 1, pp. 1, 19, 66, 149, 150, 151 in BPL.

20 Charles Lenox Remond to Maria Weston Chapman, Manchester, 16 November 1841, MS A.9.2. vol. 15, part 1, no. 93, in BPL.

21 John A. Collins, *Right and Wrong Among the Abolitionists of the United States* (Glasgow: George Gallie, 1841), introductory letter and p. 73.

22 Letter quoted in the *Liberator*, vol. XI, no. 31 (July 1840), p. 123. This was one of a series of her letters to Garrison published in his anti-slavery periodical the *Liberator* between 1840 and 1847. Note that the term 'new organisation' was used to refer to the anti-Garrisonian American and Foreign Anti-Slavery Society.

23 Robert LeBaron Bingham, 'The Glasgow Emancipation Society, 1833–76', unpublished M.Litt. thesis, University of Glasgow, 1973, p. 156; Duncan C. Rice, *The Scots Abolitionists, 1833–1861* (Baton Rouge: Louisiana State University Press, 1981), p. 146.

24 Contribution lists in the *Fifth to Eleventh Annual Reports of the British and Foreign Anti-Slavery Society* (London: Johnston & Barrett, 1844–50). Note that from 1850 contributions are listed for the current year only rather than cumulatively.

25 *Fifteenth to Twentieth Annual Reports of the British and Foreign Anti-Slavery Society* (London: Johnston & Barrett, 1854–59).

26 *Anti-Slavery Reporter*, vol. I, no. 16 (January 1854), pp. 126–27.

27 For the great importance of these bazaars as sources of finance see Benjamin Quarles, 'Sources of abolitionists' income', *Mississippi Valley Historical Review*, vol. 32, pp. 63–76.

28 *Address of the Female Anti-Slavery Society of Boston, United States, to the Women of Great Britain* (October 1839); *Anti-Slavery Reporter*, vol. VI, no. 14 (July 1845), p. 128; new series, vol. I, no. 4 (April 1846), p. 58; no. 9 (September 1846), p. 132; *British Friend*, vol. III, no. 7 (August 1845), pp. 107, 110–11.

29 Committee of the Glasgow Female Anti-Slavery Society, *Appeal to the Ladies of Great Britain, in Behalf of the American Slave*; 'Thirteenth National Anti-Slavery Bazaar', *Liberator*, vol. XVII, no. 5 (29 January 1847), p. 17; *Anti-Slavery Reporter*, 3rd series, vol. II, no. 8 (August 1854), p. 191.

30 Friends of Freedom, *The Liberty Bell* (Boston, MA: Anti-Slavery Fair/ National Anti-Slavery Bazaar, 1845–58).

31 *Address of the Committee of the Belfast Ladies' Anti-Slavery Society to the Ladies of Ulster* (Belfast, 23 September 1846); *North Star*, vol. I, no. 24 (9 June, 1848), [p. 2]; vol. II, no. 3 (12 January 1849), [p. 2].

32 See 'extract of a letter from Mr Wm Smeal to W. Wells Brown December 12th 1850', MS A.9.2. vol. 25, no. 50, in BPL. For more on the Glasgow splits see Rice, *The Scots Abolitionists*, p. 156; 'Scottish Anti-Slavery Bazaar', *Anti-Slavery Reporter*, new series, vol. VII, no. 84 (December 1852), p. 191; 'The Glasgow Female New Association for the Abolition of Slavery', on back page of *Letter from Mrs H.B. Stowe, to the Ladies' New Anti-Slavery Society of Glasgow* (Glasgow: John Mackay, 1854).

33 *Anti-Slavery Reporter*, 3rd series, vol. I, no. 5 (May 1853), p. 116; vol. IV, no. 5 (May 1856), p. 129; *Annual Report of the Edinburgh Ladies' Emancipation Society for the Year 1854*, p. 14; MSS Brit. Emp. S.18, C 1/12, C 34/137, in RHL.

34 *Anti-Slavery Reporter*, new series, vol. VII, no. 84 (1 December 1852), p. 183; 3rd series, vol. I, no. 5 (May 1853), p. 100; no. 10 (October 1853), p. 200; vol. II, no. 1 (January 1854), p. 7; no. 5 (May 1854), p. 101; accounts in *Fourteenth and Fifteenth Annual Reports of the British and Foreign Anti-Slavery Society* (London: Johnston & Barrett, 1853–54).

35 Betty Fladeland, *Men and Brothers: Anglo-American Antislavery Cooperation* (Urbana: University of Illinois Press, 1972) is the standard work on the transatlantic movement which, despite its title, includes a considerable amount of information on women abolitionists.

36 *Liberator*, vol. III, no. 28 (13 July 1833), p. 111; Wendell Phillips Garrison and Francis Jackson Garrison, *William Lloyd Garrison 1805–1879: the Story of his Life as Told by his Children* (New York: The Century Co., 1885), vol. I, p. 366.

37 Agency Society for the Universal Abolition of Negro Slavery, and the Slave Trade Throughout the World, *To the Anti-Slavery Associations, and the Friends of Negro Emancipation Throughout the United Kingdom* (London, 1834).

38 Anthony J. Barker, *Captain Charles Stuart, Anglo-American Abolitionist* (Baton Rouge: Louisiana State University Press, 1986), chs 4, 5; C. Duncan Rice, 'The Anti-Slavery Mission of George Thompson to the United States, 1834–1835', *Journal of American Studies*, vol. 2, no. 1 (April 1968), pp. 13–21; Glasgow Ladies' Auxiliary Emancipation Society, *Three Years' Female Anti-Slavery Effort, in Britain and America* . . . (Glasgow: Aird & Russell, 1837), pp. 9–10.

39 *Liberator*, vol. VI, no. 22 (28 May 1836), p. 85; vol. VII, no. 43 (20 October 1837), p. 172.

40 'Second Report of the Ladies' Auxiliary Society. Presented 1st August 1839', incorporated in the *Fifth Annual Report of the Glasgow Emancipation Society*, p. 41.

41 For a list of female correspondents see Glasgow Ladies' Auxiliary Emancipation Society, *Three Years' Female Anti-Slavery Effort*, p. 6; for male correspondents see *Fifth Annual Report of the Glasgow Emancipation Society*, p. 7.

42 Glasgow Ladies' Auxiliary Emancipation Society, *Three Years' Female Anti-Slavery Effort*, pp. 25–26, 58.

43 Copy of letter from A. Weld to Elizabeth Pease, 17 March 1837, New York, MS 957, 1st letter, in BPL; Maria Weston Chapman to Elizabeth Pease, 30 December 1837, printed as item 39 in Taylor, *British and American Abolitionists*, p. 63.

44 *The Durham Chronicle* of 16 December 1836, as quoted in the *Liberator*, vol. VII, no. 8 (18 February 1837), p. 30; *Liberator*, vol. VII, no. 32 (4 August 1837), p. 127.

45 Boston Female Anti-Slavery Society, *First to Fifth Annual Reports* (Boston: Isaac Knapp, 1835–39); *British Emancipator*, no. 45 (29 May 1839), p. 251; no. 50 (7 August 1839), p. 276.

46 Letter from Abby Ann Cox to George Thompson, New York, 9 December 1835, as quoted in Glasgow Ladies' Auxiliary Emancipation Society, *Three Years' Female Anti-Slavery Effort*, p. 24.

47 Boston Female Anti-Slavery Society, *Right and Wrong in Boston, in 1836. Annual Report* . . . (Boston: Isaac Knapp, 1836), p. 79.

48 Quoted in the *Liberator*, vol. VII, no. 10 (4 March 1837), p. 38.

49 [Harriet Martineau], Negro slavery', *Monthly Repository*, no. 4 (1830), pp. 4–9; Harriet Martineau, 'Demerara. A Tale', *Illustrations of Political Economy* (London: Charles Fox, 1834), vol. II, p. 141.

50 *Harriet Martineau's Autobiography with Memorials by Maria Weston Chapman*, 3 vols (London: Smith, Elder, 1877), vol. II, pp. 1–92.

51 Harriet Martineau, *Retrospect of Western Travel*, 3 vols (London: Saunders and Otley, 1838), vol. II, p. 156.

52 See letter in *Daily Advertiser* quoted in *Liberator*, vol. V, no. 51, 19 December 1835.

53 Letter from W.L. Garrison to Mary Benson, Brooklyn, 27 November 1835; and letter from W.L. Garrison to S.J. May, Brooklyn, 5 December 1835, printed as letter nos. 229, 232 in Walter M. Merrill and Louis Ruchames (eds), *The Letters of William Lloyd Garrison*, 6 vols (Cambridge, MA: Belknap Press of Harvard University Press, 1971–81), vol. II.

54 Letter from J.G. Birney to Lewis Tappan, 28 November 1835, as quoted in Dwight L. Dumond (ed.), *The Letters of James G. Birney, 1831–57* (New York: Appleton-Century, 1938), vol. I, p. 274–77.

55 Letter from Harriet Martineau to Abby Kelly, Westminster, 20 June

1838, as printed in *Harriet Martineau's Autobiography with Memorials by Maria Weston Chapman*, vol. III, pp. 223–24.

56 Martineau, *Retrospect of Western Travel*, pp. 148–65; Harriet Martineau, *Society in America*, 3 vols (London: Saunders and Otley, 1837), vol. II, pp. 162–79, 193–99, 312–52.

57 R.W. Webb, *Harriet Martineau: A Radical Victorian* (London: Heinemann, 1960), p. 161.

58 Harriet Martineau, 'Views of Slavery and Emancipation'; from 'Society in America' (New York: American Anti-Slavery Society, 1837).

59 *The Martyr Age in the United States of America, with an Appeal on Behalf of the Oberlin Institute in Aid of the Abolition of Slavery* (Newcastle: J. Blackwell, 1840).

60 Douglas Cameron Riach, 'Ireland and the campaign against American slavery, 1830–1860', unpublished Ph.D. thesis, University of Edinburgh, 1976, p. 75 (information taken from letter from R.D. Webb to A.W. Weston, Dublin, 5 July 1849, in BPL).

61 Boston Female Anti-Slavery Society, *Right and Wrong in Boston, in 1837. Annual Report . . .* (Boston: Isaac Knapp, 1837), p. 39.

62 Ibid., p. 85.

63 Boston Female Anti-Slavery Society, *Fifth Annual Report* (1838), p. 22.

64 These are in the BPL. There is a useful published selection of these in Taylor, *British and American Abolitionists*.

65 There are fifteen letters to/from six British/Irish women among the J.G. Birney Papers in William Clements Library, Ann Arbor, Michigan; and fifty-two letters to/from fifteen women among the papers of Lewis Tappan in the Library of Congress.

66 *Liberator*, vol. XVII, no. 1 (1 January 1847), pp. 1, 3; *Sixth Report of the Glasgow Female Anti-Slavery Society* (Glasgow: David Russell, 1851), p. 4; *British Friend*, vol. IV, no. 11 (November 1846), pp. 294–95.

67 *Anti-Slavery Reporter*, new series, vol. VI, no. 65 (May 1851), p. 181.

68 Letter from Fanny Tribe to John Tredgold, Bristol, 10 October 1840; letters from Fanny Tribe to John Scoble, Bristol, 24 February 1843, 1 February 1844, 5 February 1846, 6 February 1847, 18 February 1848, MSS Brit. Emp. S.18, C.10/128, C.22/86–90, in RHL; letter from Frances Armstrong to Samuel May, Clifton Vale, 16 February 1846, printed as item [195] in Taylor, *British and American Abolitionists*. p. 251; Fanny Tribe to John Scoble, Kingsdown, 13 June 1851, MSS Brit. Emp. S.18 C.22/91, 91a, in RHL; *Special Report of the Bristol and Clifton Ladies' Anti-Slavery Society . . .* (London: John Snow, 1852), pp. 21–31.

69 *Special Report of the Bristol and Clifton Ladies' Anti-Slavery Society*, pp. 16–20; Minute Book of the Bristol and Clifton Ladies' Anti-Slavery Society (henceforth BCLASS), among Estlin papers, Dr Williams's Library, London, entries for 27 March and 15 May 1851; letter from Mary Estlin to Miss Weston, Bristol, 8 May 1851, p. 70, MS A.9.2. vol. 25, no. 87, in BPL; *Anti-Slavery Reporter*, new series, vol. VI, no. 65 (1 May 1851), p. 70.

70 Minute Book of the BCLASS, entries for 6 and 13 February 1851; letter from Mary Estlin to Miss Weston, 13 February 1851, MS A.9.2. vol. 25, p. 63, in BPL; *Special Report of the Bristol and Clifton Ladies' Anti-Slavery Society*, pp. 14–15.

71 For Estlin's letters see MS A.1.2 vols 22–25, 35–36, 39; MS A.9.2. vols 20–23, 25–29; MS B.1.6. vols 4–6, 13; MS A.7.2; MS A.7.3, in BPL; selected letters printed in Taylor, *British and American Abolitionists*, items 175, 223, 323, 327, 331, 336, 341, 342, 360, 374, 403, 463, 478, 479, 483.

72 Mary Estlin to Miss Anne W. Weston, Bristol, 11 October 1851, MS A.9.2. vol. 25, p. 126, in BPL; Mary Estlin to M.W. Chapman, Bristol, 17 October 1851, MS A.9.2. vol. 29, p. 13, in BPL; Minute Book of the BCLASS, entry for 13 November 1851.

73 Minute Book of the BCLASS, entry for 13 November 1851.

74 Minute Book of the British and Foreign Anti-Slavery Society, vol. 3, entries for 5 December 1851, 2 January 1852, MSS Brit. Emp. S.20 E2/8, in RHL.

75 Mary Estlin to M.W. Chapman, Bristol, 16 February 1852, MS A.7.3., p. 43, in BPL; Mary Estlin to Miss [Caroline?] Weston, Bristol, 30 April 1852, MS A.7.3., p. 45, in BPL; Minute Book of the BCLASS, entry for 7 May 1852.

76 Mary Estlin to [Caroline?] Weston, Bristol, 26 February 1852, MS A.7.3., p. 45, in BPL; Minute Book of the BCLASS, entries for 19 February and 7 May 1852; Bristol and Clifton Ladies' Anti-Slavery Society (compilers), *Statements Respecting the American Abolitionists; by their Opponents and their Friends: Indicating the Present Struggle Between Slavery and Freedom in the U.S.A.* (Dublin: Webb & Chapman, 1852).

77 *Special Report of the Bristol and Clifton Ladies' Anti-Slavery Society;* Minute Book of the BCLASS, entry for 16 September 1852.

78 Mary Estlin to Caroline Weston, 21 March 1852, MS A.9.2. vol. 26, no. 19, in BPL; Mary Estlin to L. Chamerovzow, Bristol, 10 April 1853, MS Brit. Emp. S. 18 C30/131, in RHL.

79 Mary Estlin to Miss [Caroline?] Weston, Taunton, 6 November 1853, MS A.7.3., p. 75, in BPL; Mary Estlin to M.W. Chapman, Bristol, 9 December 1853, MS A.9.2. vol. 27, no. 85, in BPL.

80 Minute Book of the BCLASS, entries for 15 December 1853, 11 February 1854; Mary Estlin to [Caroline?] Weston, Bristol, 16 January 1854, MS A.7.3., p. 78, in BPL; F.W. Chesson to M.W. Chapman, Manchester, 17 January 1854, printed as item [348] in Taylor, *British and American Abolitionists*, p. 404.

81 Mary Estlin to [Caroline?] Weston, Bristol, 16 January 1854, MS A.7.3., p. 78, in BPL.

82 Minute Book of the BCLASS, entry for 9 June 1854.

83 Correspondence between Louis Chamerovzow and Mary Estlin, London, Paris and Clevedon, 31 July to 28 September 1854, MS A.1.2. vol. 24, pp. 87, 88, 97, 99, 102, 122; vol. 25, p. 93, in BPL.

84 Mary Estlin to M.W. Chapman, 6 August 1854, MS A.7.3., p. 84, in BPL; A.W. Weston to Mary Estlin, Versailles, 20 August 1854, MS A.1.2. vol. 25, p. 90, in BPL; *Anti-Slavery Reporter*, 3rd series, vol. II, no. 8 (August 1854), p. 191.

85 James Goodfellow, *The Print of His Shoe: Forty Years' Missionary Experience in the Southside of Edinburgh* (Edinburgh: Oliphant, Anderson & Ferrier, 1906), pp. 71–78 (including photograph); *Farewell meeting for Presentation of an Address of Sympathy and Regret to Eliza Wigham on the Occasion of Her Leaving Edinburgh, 20th April 1898* (National Library of Scotland); *Eliza Wigham. A Brief Memorial. Reprinted and Revised from the 'Annual Monitor'*, ([London: 1901]) (National Library of Scotland); Charles J. Smith, *Historic South Edinburgh* (Haddington: Charles Skilton, 1986), vol. III, pp. 26–27; E.M. Mein, 'Miss Eliza Wigham' (undated typescript in Edinburgh Central Library).

86 MSS letters in BPL; selected letters printed in Taylor, *British and American Abolitionists*, items 293, 365, 396, 411, 422, 424, 425, 444.

87 See Wigham family tree in Taylor, *British and American Abolitionists*, Appendix II.

88 For events in Edinburgh and elsewhere in Scotland following the convention see Rice, *The Scots Abolitionists*, ch. 4.

89 For details of the campaign see Bingham, 'The Glasgow Emancipation Society', ch. 5; and Rice, *The Scots Abolitionists*, ch. 5.

90 The texts of the remonstrances are given in the *Report of the Edinburgh Ladies' Emancipation Society, for the Last Year, Passed at Their Annual Meeting, Held May 27th, 1846* (Edinburgh: H. Armour, [1846]), and the *Annual Report of the Edinburgh Ladies' Emancipation Society* (Edinburgh: H. Armour, 1847). See also *Laws Adopted at the Formation of the Free Church Anti-Slavery Society, September 1846.*

91 Letter from Eliza Wigham to Mary Estlin, Edinburgh, 13 September 1850, MS A.7.3., p. 12, in BPL; 'Expression of sentiment tendered by members of the Edinburgh Ladies' Emancipation Society to the meeting of the Committee, held August 1st 1850', printed as item [291] in Taylor, *British and American Abolitionists*, p. 346.

92 Letter from A.W. Weston to Mary Estlin, 6 April 1851, MS A.7.2.10, in BPL.

93 Letter from Eliza Wigham to Rev. S. May Jr, Edinburgh, 15 March 1855, in BPL.

94 Jane Wigham to [M.W. Chapman?], Edinburgh, 9 November 1853, MS A.9.2., vol. 27, p. 66, in BPL; Eliza Wigham to Louis Chamerovzow, Edinburgh, 11 April and 19 October 1853, MS Brit. Emp. S.18, C37/61 and 62, in RHL.

95 See, for example, *Anti-Slavery Reporter*, new series, vol. VII, no. 76 (April 1852), p. 64. For reports see *Annual Reports of the Edinburgh Ladies' Emancipation Society for the Year 1854, and the Years Ending March 1857, 1859, and 1860* (Edinburgh: H. Armour, 1855, 1857, 1859, 1860).

96 Duncan Rice, ' "Humanity Sold for Sugar!" The British Abolitionist Response to Free Trade in Slave-Grown Sugar', *The Historical Journal*, vol. 13, no. 3 (1970), pp. 402–18.

97 *Anti-Slavery Reporter*, new series, vol. II, no. 13 (January 1847), p. 1.

98 For a general account of the promotion of 'free'- in preference to slave-grown cotton see Louis Billington, 'British Humanitarians and American Cotton, 1840-1860', *Journal of American Studies*, vol. 11 (1977), pp. 313–34.

99 The circular on the memorial was printed in the *Anti-Slavery Reporter*, new series, vol. IV, no. 41 (May 1849), p. 73. The text of the memorial was printed in the *Tenth Annual Report of the British and Foreign Anti-Slavery Society* (London: Johnston & Barrett, 1849), pp. 137–38.

100 *British Friend*, vol. VII (June 1849), pp. 147–48; *Anti-Slavery Reporter*, new series, vol. V, no. 52 (1 April 1850).

101 *Anti-Slavery Reporter*, new series, vol. V, no. 53 (May 1850), p. 73; no. 54 (June 1850), pp. 85–86; Louisa Bigg to the secretary of the BFASS, April 1849, MSS Brit. Emp. S.18, C13/90, in RHL.

102 Louisa Bigg, MSS Brit. Emp. S.18, C13/90, in RHL.

103 Thomas and Emma R. Pumphrey (compilers), *Henry and Anna Richardson* (Newcastle-upon-Tyne, 1892) (with portrait); 'Anna Richardson', obituary in *Annual Monitor*, 1893, pp. 104–08; J.W. Steele, *Historical Sketch of Society of Friends in Newcastle and Gateshead* (1899), pp. 189–92 (with portrait).

104 *Anti-Slavery Reporter*, new series, vol. IV, no. 41 (May 1847), p. 76.

105 *British Friend*, vol. VI, no. 4 (September 1848), pp. 103–05.

106 Letter from A.H. Richardson to John Scoble, Newcastle-upon-Tyne, 4

August 1851, MSS Brit. Emp. S.18, C21/27, in RHL. For Garnet's lecturing tour to women see *Anti-Slavery Reporter*, new series, vol. V, no. 58 (October 1850), p. 160; no. 59 (November 1850), p. 175; vol. VI, no. 61 (January 1851). For more on Garnet and the 'free'-produce movement see R.J.M. Blackett, *Building an Antislavery Wall: Black Americans in the Atlantic Abolitionist Movement, 1830–1860* (Baton Rouge: Louisiana State University Press, 1983), ch. 3.

107 *The Slave*, no. 1 (January 1851), pp. 1, 3. For list of 'free'-produce associations see Appendix.

108 Louis Chamerovzow to Miss Moore, London, 13 January 1853, MSS Brit. Emp. S.18, C37/128, in RHL.

109 Letter from Louis Chamerovzow to Anna Richardson, London, 13 January 1853, MSS Brit. Emp. S.18 C37/122, in RHL. For such a list of suppliers see *The Ladies' Free-Grown Cotton Movement*, document in John Rylands Library, Manchester (Anti-Slavery Pamphlets, R. 107337, Box 16, no. 22).

110 *Anti-Slavery Reporter*, 3rd series, vol. I, no. 8 (August 1853), p. 177; letter from A.H. Richardson to Louis Chamerovzow, MSS Brit. Emp. S.18, C35/100, in RHL.

111 See *The Slave*, no. 31 (July 1853), p. 25.

112 Letter from A.H. Richardson to L. Chamerovzow, Newcastle, 4 November 1854, MSS Brit. Emp. S.18, C35/101, in RHL.

113 See Minute Book of the British and Foreign Anti-Slavery Society, vol. 3, entries for 6 October and 29, 30 December 1854, MSS Brit. Emp. S.20, E2/8, in RHL.

114 *British Friend*, vol. XVI (August 1858), p. 211; Anna H. Richardson, *Anti-Slavery Memoranda* (Newcastle: printed for private circulation, 1860).

115 Billington, 'British humanitarians', pp. 313–34. For an account of the central place that cotton occupied in the Atlantic economy at this period, see Frank Thistlethwaite, *America and the Atlantic Community: Anglo-American Aspects, 1790–1850* (New York: Harper & Row, 1959), ch. 1.

116 Frederick Douglass, *The Life and Times of Frederick Douglass* (Hartford, CT: Park Publishing Co., 1882), p. 256; 'To the Friends of the Slave' (Newcastle, 14 February 1854) [printed circular] and letter from Henry Richardson to Louis Chamerovzow, 23 February 1854, MSS Brit. Emp. S.18, C35/109, 110, in RHL.

117 *Anti-Slavery Reporter*, new series, vol. VII, no. 84 (December 1852), p. 191.

118 See resolution of Bristol and Clifton Ladies' Anti-Slavery Society, quoted in *Anti-Slavery Advocate*, vol. I, no. 3 (December 1852), p. 21.

119 See 'The history of William and Ellen Craft . . .' (August 1852) [printed sheet soliciting contributions].

120 George F. Bosworth, *Essex Hall, Walthamstow and the Cogan Associations* (Walthamstow Antiquarian Society, Official Publication No. 5, 1918).

121 Minutes of the Ladies' Society to Aid Fugitives from Slavery, MSS Brit. Emp. S.22, G85, in RHL.

122 *Ladies Society to Aid Fugitives from Slavery. Report* (London: printed for private circulation, 1855).

123 See, for example, Lucy Browne to M.W. Chapman, Riverside, 15 October 1846, MS A.4.6A vol. 1, no. 103, in BPL.

124 Letter from J.B. Estlin to Samuel May, Bristol, 12 January 1847, MS B.1.6. vol. 2, no. 42, printed as item [248] in Taylor, *British and American Abolitionists*, p. 305.

125 *Anti-Slavery Reporter*, 3rd series, vol. I (August 1853), pp. 175–76, as quoted

in Douglas A. Lorimer, *Colour, Class and the Victorians: English Attitudes to the Negro in the Mid-Nineteenth Century* (Leicester: Leicester University Press, 1978), p. 58.

126 Julia and Eliza Griffiths, 'Address to the Anti-Slavery Ladies of Great Britain and Ireland', *North Star*, vol. II, no. 39 (21 September 1849), p. 27; *Third Annual Report of the Festival Held by the Rochester Ladies' Anti-Slavery Sewing Society*, [Rochester, 1854]; *North Star*, vol. VI, no. 7 (4 February 1853, [p. 2]).

127 A considerable amount of information on Griffiths' aid to Douglass is scattered in Philip S. Foner, *Frederick Douglass: a Biography* (New York: Citadel Press, 1966). See also Erwin Palmer, 'A partnership in the Abolition movement', *The University of Rochester Library Bulletin*, vol. 26, no. 1 (1970), pp. 1–19. Neither account contains a great deal on her activities after her return to England.

128 Douglass, *The Life and Times of Frederick Douglass*, p. 268.

129 Foner, *Frederick Douglass*, pp. 338, 342–43, 352.

130 These societies are listed in the Appendix. For information on their formation see *Anti-Slavery Reporter*, 3rd series, vol. IV, no. 11 (November 1856), p. 251; no. 12 (December 1856), p. 270; vol. V, no. 1 (January 1857), pp. 23, 24; no. 3 (March 1857), pp. 71, 72; no. 4 (April 1857), pp. 76–78; no. 5 (May 1857), pp. 116, 119; no. 6 (June 1857), p. 143; *Formation of the Irish Metropolitan Ladies' Anti-Slavery Association, with a Report for the Irish Contributors of 1856 to the Rochester Anti-Slavery Bazaar* (Dublin: R. Chapman, 1857).

131 *Anti-Slavery Advocate*, vol. II, no. 2 (February 1857), p. 11; no. 7 (July 1857), pp. 50–51; no. 16 (April 1858), p. 126.

132 William and Ellen Craft, *Running a Thousand Miles for Freedom; or, the Escape of William and Ellen Craft from Slavery* (London: William Tweedie, 1860).

133 Letter from H. Martineau to Lucy[?], Ambleside, 5 April 1851, Letters of Harriet Martineau, Ref. WDX 482/4, Cumbria Record Office.

134 C. Peter Ripley (ed.), *The Black Abolitionist Papers*, vol. I (Chapel Hill, NC: University of North Carolina Press, 1985), p. 243; R.J.M. Blackett, 'Fugitive slaves in Britain: the odyssey of William and Ellen Craft', *Journal of American Studies*, vol. 12, no. 1 (1978), pp. 41–62.

135 *Anti-Slavery Advocate*, vol. I, no. 3 (December 1852), p. 22. For further information on the Crafts see William and Ellen Craft, *Running a Thousand Miles for Freedom*; Blackett, 'Fugitive Slaves in Britain', pp. 41–62.

136 For short accounts of Remond's life see Dorothy B. Porter, 'Sarah Parker Remond, Abolitionist and Physician', *Journal of Negro History*, no. 20 (July 1935), pp. 287–93; Ruth Bogin, 'Sarah Parker Remond: Black Abolitionist from Salem', *Essex Institute Historical Collections*, no. 110 (April 1974), pp. 120–50.

137 'Sarah Parker Remond', in Matthew Davenport Hill (ed.), *Our Examplars, Poor and Rich; or, Biographical Sketches of Men and Women Who Have, by an Extraordinary Use of Their Opportunities, Benefited Their Fellow-Creatures* (London: Cassell, Petter & Galpin, 1861), pp. 276–86. This is a short autobiography by Remond.

138 Quote from ibid., p. 277.

139 Letter from Mentia Taylor to the Rev. Samuel May Jr, 14 February 1866, MS B.1.6, vol. 10, no. 39, in BPL.

140 *Anti-Slavery Advocate*, vol. II, no. 26 (February 1859), p. 201; no. 27 (March 1859), p. 211; no. 28 (April 1859), pp. 221–24; no. 29 (May 1859), p. 232; no. 31 (July 1859), pp. 249–50; no. 32 (August 1859), p. 255; no. 33 (September 1859), pp. 266–67; no. 34 (October 1859), pp. 273–75; no. 35

(November 1859), p. 283; no. 38 (February 1860), p. 306; no. 47 (November 1860), p. 377; no. 50 (February 1861), p. 399. See also reports in the *Anti-Slavery Reporter*, 3rd series, vol. VII, no. 7 (July 1859), p. 148; vol. VIII, no. 1 (January 1860), p. 13; no. 11 (November 1860), p. 271.

141 See, for example, the report of her lecture in Dublin in *Anti-Slavery Reporter*, 3rd series, vol. VII, no. 4 (April 1859), p. 73.

142 Report of Remond's lecture in the Music Hall, Store Street, London, 1 June 1859, in reply to a pro-slavery lecture by Lola Montez, in *Anti-Slavery Reporter*, 3rd series, vol. VII, no. 7 (July 1859), p. 150.

143 Speech by Sarah P. Remond delivered in the Music Hall, Warrington, 24 January 1859, as quoted in Ripley (ed.), *The Black Abolitionist Papers*, vol. I, document 73.

144 Speech by Sarah P. Remond, delivered at the Red Lion Hotel, Warrington, 2 February 1859, reported in *Warrington Times*, 5 February 1859, as quoted in Ripley (ed.), *The Black Abolitionist Papers*, vol. I, document 74.

145 Ibid.

146 Hill (ed.), *Our Exemplars*, pp. 277, 280.

147 Ripley (ed.), *The Black Abolitionist Papers*, vol. I, document 80.

148 Letter from Elizabeth Pease to Maria Weston Chapman, Darlington, 23 April 1840, MS A.9.2. vol. 13, pp. 55–56, in BPL.

149 See F.J. Klingberg, 'Harriet Beecher Stowe and social reform in England', *American Historical Review*, vol. 43 (1937–38), pp. 542–52.

150 Rebecca Whitelegge to Mary Estlin, 23 August [1853], MS A.9.2. vol. 27, no. 86, in BPL.

151 Jane P. Tompkins, 'Sentimental power: *Uncle Tom's Cabin* and the politics of literary history', in Elaine Showalter (ed.), *The New Feminist Criticism* (London: Virago, 1985), pp. 81–104 (quotations from pp. 83, 90).

152 *Anti-Slavery Reporter*, 3rd series, vol. I, no. 7 (July 1853), p. 150.

153 *The Uncle Tom's Cabin Almanack or Abolitionist Memento. 1853* (London: John Cassell, [1853]).

154 Angela Davis, *Women, Race and Class* (London: Women's Press, 1982), pp. 27–31; David W. Levy, 'Racial stereotypes in antislavery fiction', *Phylon*, vol. 31, no. 3 (Fall 1970), pp. 265–79; Jacqueline Kaye, 'Literary images of slavery and resistance: the cases of *Uncle Tom's Cabin* and *Cecilia Valdes*', *Slavery and Abolition*, vol. 5, no. 2 (September 1984), pp. 105–17.

155 Tompkins, 'Sentimental power', p. 90.

156 *Anti-Slavery Reporter*, 3rd series, vol. I, no. 6 (June 1853), pp. 123–25, 139–43. For a general account of her visit see Forrest Wilson, *Crusader in Crinoline: the Life of Harriet Beecher Stowe* (London: Hutchinson, 1942), pp. 207–32.

157 For a full list of the thirty-four women who attended the launch and the thirty additional women who signified their support see *The Times*, 29 November 1852, p. 8.

158 For the full text of the original address see *The Times*, 29 November 1852, p. 8.

159 The text of the BFASS and Shaftesbury letters was printed in the *Anti-Slavery Reporter*, 3rd series, vol. I, no. 2 (February 1853), p. 30.

160 See *Anti-Slavery Reporter*, 3rd series, vol. I, no. 1 (January 1853), pp. 10–11; file of letters relating to the amended address linked to the BFASS, MSS Brit. Emp. S.18, C114, in RHL.

161 MSS Brit. Emp. S.18, C114/78, C114/148, in RHL.

162 Letter from the Rev. George Jones of Wolston near Coventry to the Ladies' Committee for the Amended Address, 17 January 1853, MSS Brit. Emp.

NOTES

S.18, C114/96, in RHL. A similar point was made by Ann Priestman of Malton in Yorkshire, MSS Brit. Emp. S.18, C114/116, in RHL.

163 *Anti-Slavery Reporter*, 3rd series, vol. I, no. 4 (April 1853), p. 83; no. 6 (June 1853), pp. 123–25, 127, 139–43.

164 For the favourable response of Ohio women abolitionists see *Anti-Slavery Reporter*, 3rd series, vol. I, no. 9 (September 1853), pp. 198–200.

165 See text of the Duchess of Sutherland's statement at the launching of the address, *The Times*, 29 November 1852, p. 8.

166 Tyler's letter, which had originally appeared in the *Richmond Enquirer* of 28 January 1853, was reprinted in full in *The Times* of 15 February 1853.

167 Evelyn L. Pugh, 'Women and slavery: Julia Gardiner Tyler and the Duchess of Sutherland', *Virginia Magazine of History and Biography*, vol. 88, no. 2 (1980), pp. 187–202.

168 'Englishwoman', *A Letter to Those Ladies Who Met at Stafford House in Particular, and to the Women of England in General, on Slavery at Home* (London: James Ridgeway, 1853). For the image of the seamstress see Helene E. Roberts, 'Marriage, Redundancy and Sin', in Martha Vicinus (ed.), *Suffer and Be Still* (London: Methuen, 1972), pp. 58–62.

169 *Reynolds Newspaper*, 27 March 1853, p. 8.

170 'A Briton', *The Fashionable Philanthropy of the Day. Some Plain Speaking About American Slavery. A Letter Addressed to the Stoweites of England and Scotland* (London: Hope, 1853).

171 *Anti-Slavery Reporter*, 3rd series, vol. I, no. 2 (February 1853), pp. 37–38; *'Bread Upon the Waters', or, Letters, Illustrative, Moral, and Practical, Addressed Generally to the Women of Great Britain and Ireland, on the Subject of the "Stafford House Memorial", Recently Transmitted to the Women of the United States, Concluding with an Appeal to Gentlemen Connected with the Cotton Question* (London: W. & F.G. Cash, 1853), especially pp. 26–40; 'an Englishwoman' [Mrs Henry Grey], *Remarks Occasioned by Strictures in The Courier and New York Enquirer of December 1852, Upon the Stafford House Address. In a Letter to a Friend in the United States* (London: Hamilton, Adams, & Co., 1853).

172 Patricia Hollis, 'Anti-slavery and British working-class radicalism in the years of reform', in Christine Bolt and Seymour Drescher (eds), *Anti-Slavery, Religion and Reform: Essays in Memory of Roger Anstey* (Folkestone: Dawson, 1980), ch. 14.

173 Letter from Katherine Fry to Louisa Pely, 19 November 1840, Buxton Papers, vol. 20, pp. 37–43, MSS Brit. Emp. S.444, in RHL.

174 This phrase was used by Miss Ruthwell, Bradford treasurer of the Power Loom Weaver's Society, in a speech in 1845, quoted in Dorothy Thompson, *The Chartists* (London: Temple Smith, 1984), p. 136.

175 Emma Martin, *The Missionary Jubilee Panic* (1844), p. 3, as quoted in Barbara Taylor, *Eve and the New Jerusalem: Socialism and Feminism in the Nineteenth Century* (London: Virago, 1983), p. 152.

176 Betty Fladeland, ' "Our Cause Being One and the Same": Abolitionists and Chartism', in James Walvin (ed.), *Slavery and British Society, 1776–1846* (London: Macmillan, 1982), ch. iii.

177 Letter from Mary Carpenter to M.W. Chapman, Bristol, 31 October 1847, MS A.9.2. v. 23, p. 58, in BPL; letter from J.B. Estlin to the Rev. S. May Jr, Bristol, 17 October 1847, MS B.1.6. vol. 2, no. 59, in BPL.

178 Letter from M.A. Estlin to A.W. Weston, Bristol, 15 November 1850, MS A.9.2. vol. 25, no. 44, in BPL.

NOTES

179 Committee of the Glasgow Female Anti-Slavery Society, *An Appeal to the Ladies of Great Britain, in Behalf of the American Slave* (Glasgow: John McLeod, 1841), p. 15; *Annual Report of the Glasgow Female Anti-Slavery Society* (Glasgow: Temperance Press, 1842), [p. 19].
180 Letter from Abby Kimber to George Thompson, Kimberton, 26 November 1840, printed as item [88] in Taylor, *British and American Abolitionists*, p. 125. For Chartists in the Glasgow Emancipation Society see Fladeland, 'Abolitionists and Chartism', pp. 85–86.
181 Fladeland, in 'Abolitionists and Chartism', discusses Harriet Martineau's attitude to Chartism (pp. 73–75) and mentions Elizabeth Pease's support (p. 87).
182 Letter from Elizabeth Pease to Anne Warren Weston, MS A.9.2 vol. 15, part 1, no. 50, in BPL, as printed in Taylor, *British and American Abolitionists*, item 109, p. 154.
183 Harriet Gairdner to J.A. Collins, Edinburgh, 25 November 1840, MS A.1.2. vol. 10, p. 54, in BPL.
184 Letter from Elizabeth Pease to Wendell and Ann Phillips, Darlington, 16 August 1842, MS A.1.2. vol. 12 (2), no. 79, in BPL, printed as item [131] in Taylor, *British and American Abolitionists*, p. 180.
185 Ibid.
186 Ibid.
187 Letter from Elizabeth Pease to Wendell and Ann Phillips, Feethams, 29 September 1842, MS A.1.2. vol. 12 (2), no. 94, in BPL, printed as item [134] in Taylor, *British and American Abolitionists*, pp. 182–84.
188 Letter from Elizabeth Pease to Anne Warren Weston, Darlington, 30 December 1841, MS A.9.2. vol. 15, part 1, no. 122, in BPL, printed as item [114] in Taylor, *British and American Abolitionists*, p. 159.
189 Letters from Elizabeth Pease to A.W. Weston, London, 24 June 1841; Elizabeth Pease to W. and A. Phillips, Darlington, 16 August and 29 September 1842; Elizabeth Pease to J.A. Collins, Darlington, 12 May [1841?], printed as items [109], [131], [134] and [105] respectively in Taylor, *British and American Abolitionists*, pp. 151, 154, 179.

7 THE 'WOMAN QUESTION'

1 For a good general account of these developments see Blanche Glassman Hersch, *The Slavery of Sex: Feminist-Abolitionists in America* (Urbana: University of Illinois Press, 1978); for the convention see Dorothy Sterling (ed.), *Turning the World Upside Down: the Anti-Slavery Convention of American Women Held in New York City May 9–12, 1837* (New York: Feminist Press, 1987); for a valuable recent discussion of the relationship between anti-slavery and feminism see Jean Fagan Yellin, *Women and Sisters: The Antislavery Feminists in American Culture* (New Haven: Yale University Press, 1989).
2 The convention was reported in Britain in the *Christian Advocate*, vol. VIII, no. 39 (3 July 1837), p. 215, and in Ireland in the Irish Temperance and Literary Gazette, no. 55 (25 November 1837).
3 Harriet Martineau, *Society in America*, 3 vols (London: Saunders & Otley, 1837), vol. I, pp. 199–207; vol. III, pp. 16–118; Valerie Kossew Pichanick, *Harriet Martineau: The Woman and Her Work* (Ann Arbor: University of Michigan Press, 1980), p. 93 (see also pp. 92–99). For another discussion of Martineau's feminism see Gaby Weiner, 'Harriet Martineau: a reassess-

247

ment', in Dale Spender (ed.), *Feminist Theorists: Three Centuries of Women's Intellectual Traditions* (London: Women's Press, 1983), pp. 60–73.

4 Martineau, *Society in America*, vol. I, p. 201, 203, 204; vol. III, p. 106.

5 Martineau, *Society in America*, vol. III, p. 112; vol. I, p. 206.

6 See especially 'Kate', 'An appeal to woman', *The New Moral World*, vol. I, no. 42 (15 August 1835), pp. 335–36; Mrs Leman Grimstone, 'Female education', *The New Moral World*, vol. I, no. 17 (21 February 1835), pp. 132–35.

7 Barbara Taylor, *Eve and the New Jerusalem: Socialism and Feminism in the Nineteenth Century* (London: Virago, 1983); Dorothy Thompson, *The Chartists* (London: Temple Smith, 1984), p. 124; Ray Strachey, *The Cause: A Short History of the Women's Movement in Great Britain* (London: Virago, 1978), pp. 30–40; Lilian Lewis Shiman, ' "Changes are Dangerous": women and temperance in Victorian England', in Gail Malmgreen (ed.), *Religion in the Lives of English Women* (London: Croom Helm, 1986), ch. 8.

8 Gail Malmgreen, 'Anne Knight and the radical subculture', *Quaker History*, vol. 71, no. 2 (Fall 1982), pp. 100–13.

9 Ibid., p. 105.

10 Anne Knight to William Lloyd Garrison, Paris, 14 March 1838, MS A.1.2. vol. 7, no. 13, in BPL; Anne Knight to Angelina Grimké, Paris, July 1838, Weld-Grimké Papers, William Clements Library, Ann Arbor, Michigan.

11 Anne Knight to Maria Weston Chapman, London, 30 October 1839, printed as item 57 in Clare Taylor (ed.), *British and American Abolitionists: An Episode in Transatlantic Understanding* (Edinburgh: Edinburgh University Press, 1974), p. 85.

12 Sarah M. Grimké to Elizabeth Pease, Brookline, Massachusetts, 18 December 1837, Ms. A.1.2. vol. 41, p. 25, in BPL.

13 Letter from Elizabeth Pease to Angelina Grimké, Darlington, 12 February 1838, printed in Gilbert H. Barnes and Dwight L. Dumond (eds), *Letters of Theodore Dwight Weld, Angelina Grimké Weld and Sarah Grimké, 1822–1844* (New York: American Historical Association, 1934), vol. II, p. 545.

14 Ibid.

15 Ibid. For Sarah Grimké's response, arguing that discussion of women's rights was necessary to enable women to play a full part in the anti-slavery movement, see letter from Grimké to Pease, Fort Lee, 16 November 1838, MS 957, 6th letter, in BPL.

16 Glasgow Ladies' Auxiliary Emancipation Society, *Three Years' Female Anti-Slavery Effort in Britain and America . . .* (Glasgow: Aird and Russell, 1837), pp. 27–28.

17 *Proceedings of the General Anti-Slavery Convention, Called by the Committee of the British and Foreign Anti-Slavery Society, and Held in London, from Friday, June 12th, to Tuesday, June 23rd, 1840* (London: Johnston and Barrett, 1841). For the effect of the convention on the development of the British anti-slavery movement see Douglas H. Maynard, 'The World's Anti-Slavery Convention of 1840', *Mississippi Valley Historical Review*, vol. 47 (1960–61), pp. 452–71. For accounts of the convention which deal with the 'woman question' see Donald R. Kennon, ' "An Apple of Discord': the woman question at the world's anti-slavery convention of 1840', *Slavery and Abolition*, vol. 5, no. 3 (December 1984), pp. 244–66; Clare Taylor, 'Romantic reform and Anglo-American women: London, the 1840 convention and its aftermath' (unpublished typescript in British Library, 1981); and Alex Tyrrell, 'Woman's Mission' and pressure group politics in Britain, 1825–60', *Bulletin of the John Rylands University Library*, vol. 63 (1980), pp. 194–230.

NOTES

18 For a valuable beginning see Kathryn Kish Sklar, ' "Women who speak for an entire nation": American and British women compared at the World Anti-Slavery Convention, London, 1840', *Pacific Historical Review*, 1990, pp. 453–99.
19 Elizabeth Pease to [?], London, 17 July 1840, printed as item [66] in Taylor, *British and American Abolitionists*, p. 101.
20 See Frederick B. Tolles (ed.), *Slavery and 'the Woman Question': Lucretia Mott's Diary of Her Visit to Great Britain to Attend the World's Anti-Slavery Convention of 1840*, supplement no. 23 to the *Journal of the Friends' Historical Society* (Haverford, PA: Friends' Historical Association, 1952).
21 Tolles, *Slavery and 'the Woman Question'*, diary entry for 27 June 1840.
22 Sarah Pugh to Richard and Hannah Webb, 2 July 1840, MS A.1.2., vol. 9, p. 66, in BPL, as quoted in Sklar, ' "Women who speak for an entire nation" ', p. 476.
23 Letter from William Lloyd Garrison to Henry Clarke Wright, Brooklyn, August 1840, printed as item [73] in Taylor, *British and American Abolitionists*, p. 110.
24 Elizabeth Cady Stanton, *Eighty Years and More* (London: T. Fisher Unwin, 1898), p. 82. Stanton included an almost identical statement in Elizabeth Cady Stanton, Susan B. Anthony and Matilda Joslyn Gage (eds), *History of Woman Suffrage*, 3 vols, (Rochester: Charles Mann, 1887), vol. I, p. 62.
25 Letter from Anne Knight to Maria Weston Chapman, England, 4 August 1840, MS A.9.2. vol. 13, p. 49, in BPL. For Knight's attempt to convert leading Dublin Quaker abolitionists Richard and Hannah Webb to women's rights see letter from Anne Knight to Richard and Hannah Webb, Chelmsford, 12 October 1841, MS A.1.2. vol. 12, pt 1, p. 118, in BPL.
26 See Marion Ramelson, *The Petticoat Rebellion* (London: Lawrence & Wishart, 1967), pp. 72–73; Stanton *et al.*, *History of Woman Suffrage*, vol. III, pp. 837–38; Malmgreen, 'Anne Knight and the radical subculture'.
27 Account of the 1840 Convention by Maria Waring, among A. Webb, 'Copies of letters by Sarah Poole', MS A.1.2. vol. 9, no. 60, in BPL.
28 For a detailed account of Stuart's attacks on the Garrisonians see Anthony J. Barker, *Captain Charles Stuart, Anglo-American Abolitionist* (Baton Rouge: Louisiana State University Press, 1986), ch. 9. Stuart's 1841 broadsheet condemning the 'woman-intruding' society is reprinted in Barnes and Dumond, *Letters of Theodore Dwight Weld*, vol. II, pp. 858–60; for Pease's criticism of Stuart's inconsistency on 'women's rights' see letter from Elizabeth Pease to William Smeal, Darlington, 14 February 1841, MS A.1.2. vol. 11, p. 68, in BPL.
29 Elizabeth Pease to [Charles Stuart], Darlington, 28 September 1840, MS A.1.1. vol. 10, p. 3, in BPL.
30 Elizabeth Pease to John A. Collins, Darlington, 14 December 1840, MS A.1.2. vol. 10, p. 93, in BPL.
31 Letter from Elizabeth Pease to W.L. Garrison, Darlington, 1 May 1843, as printed in the *Liberator*, vol. XIII, no. 21 (26 May 1843).
32 Margaret Howitt (ed.), *Mary Howitt, An Autobiography* (London: William Isbister, 1889), 2 vols.
33 Stanton *et al.*, *History of Woman Suffrage*, vol. III, p.838.
34 Helen Blackburn, *Women's Suffrage: A Record of the Women's Suffrage Movement in the British Isles* (London: Williams & Norgate, 1902), p. 19.
35 Stanton *et al.*, *History of Woman Suffrage*, p. 838.
36 Eugene R. Rasor, 'Elizabeth A. Ashurt' entry in Joseph O. Baylen and

Norbert J. Gossman (eds), *Biographical Dictionary of Modern British Radicals*, vol. II: 1830–1870 (Brighton: Harvester, 1984).

37 Marion Reid, *A Plea for Woman* (Edinburgh: Polygon, 1988). Reprint of first edition of 1843 published by William Tait of Edinburgh.

38 Letter from Elizabeth Pease to W.L. Garrison, Darlington, 26 April 1844, printed in the *Liberator*, vol. XIV, no. 21 (24 May 1844), p. 85; Anne Knight to W.L. Garrison, Moores, 10 June 1845, MS A.1.2. vol. 15, p. 39, in BPL. Anne Knight's annotated copy of the book is preserved in Friends House Library, London.

39 A Philanthropist, *Domestic Tyranny, or Woman in Chains* (London: Whittaker & Co., 1841), p. 55.

40 Esther Sturge to Maria Weston Chapman, London, 14 April 1842, MS A.9.2. vol. 17, no. 52, in BPL.

41 Eustace R. Conder, *Josiah Conder: A Memoir* (London: John Snow, 1857), p. 318.

42 Letters from Mary Caroline Braithwaite to Joseph G. Birney, Kendal, 28 November 1840 and 3 February 1841, microfilm of J.G. Birney Papers, William Clements Library, University of Michigan.

43 Sarah Dymond to John Tredgold, Taunton, 10 August 1840, MSS Brit. Emp. S.18, C6/120a, in RHL; letter from Sarah Dymond and Charles Stuart to Angelina G. Weld, 4 November 1842, in Barnes and Dumond, *Letters of Theodore Dwight Weld*, vol. II, p. 944.

44 Josiah Gilbert (ed), *Autobiography and Other Memorials of Mrs Gilbert (Formerly Ann Taylor)*, 2 vols (London: King & Co, 1874), vol. II, pp. 185–88.

45 For a discussion of evangelicalism and anti-slavery see Louis Billington, 'Some connections between British and American reform movements 1830–1860. With special reference to the anti-slavery movement', unpublished MA dissertation, University of Bristol, 1966, pp. 88–95, 121–22. For tensions between evangelicals and Hicksite Quakers and Unitarians in the movement see David Malcolm Turley, 'Relations Between British and American Abolitionists from British Emancipation to the American Civil War', unpublished Ph.D. thesis, University of Cambridge, 1970, ch. 1.

46 For religious controversy and its effect on British women's reactions to events at the convention see Sklar, ' "Women Who Speak for an Entire Nation" ', pp. 477–81; for the intertwining of evangelical opposition to 'women's rights' and 'infidelity' in provoking splits in the Glasgow anti-slavery movement see Robert LeBaron Bingham, 'The Glasgow Emancipation Society, 1833–76', unpublished M.Litt. thesis, University of Glasgow, 1973, ch. 4.

47 *Seventh Annual Report of the Glasgow Emancipation Society* (Glasgow: Aird & Russell, 1841); Committee of the Glasgow Female Anti-Slavery Society, *An Appeal to the Ladies of Great Britain, in Behalf of the American Slave* (Glasgow, 1841).

48 Elizabeth Pease to W.L. Garrison, Ben Rhydding, 9 July 1852, MS A.1.2. vol. 21, p. 50, in BPL.

49 Frank Prochaska, *Women and Philanthropy in Nineteenth Century England* (Oxford: Oxford University Press, 1980), pp. 30–31 and Appendix I, which lists only one society with a mixed committee formed prior to 1858.

50 For Lupton's interest in women's rights see letter from Harriet Lupton to Maria Weston Chapman, Headingley, 6 June 1852, MS A.9.2. vol. 26, p. 37, in BPL. An account of the Leeds society, which ignores female initiatives and ascribes its formation to the efforts of Wilson Armistead (1819–68), its Quaker president, has been written by Irene E. Goodyear, 'Wilson Armi-

stead and the Leeds Antislavery Movement', reprinted from *The Publication of the Thoresby Society. Miscellany*, vol. XVI, part 2, pp. 113–19.

51 These developments can be traced in a series of letters which Pugh wrote to Bristol anti-slavery activist Mary Estlin, among Estlin Papers, Dr Williams's Library, London, ref. nos. 24.121.19, 20, 24, 25, 27.

52 See title page of *First Annual Report of the Leeds Antislavery Association* (Leeds: W. Walker, 1854). For a similar use of the combined slogan see the title page of *Annual Report of the Edinburgh Ladies' Emancipation Society* (Edinburgh: H. Armour, 1866).

53 *First Annual Report of the Leeds Antislavery Association*; letter from Harriet Lupton to Mary Estlin, Headingly, 27 October 1853, MS A.9.2. vol. 27, no. 72, in BPL.

54 Letter from Rebecca Moore to R.D. Webb, London, 30 November 1854, MS A.1.2. vol. 26, p. 37, in BPL; Minute Book of the Bristol and Clifton Ladies' Anti-Slavery Society [hereinafter BCLASS], among Estlin Papers, Dr Williams's Library, London, entry for 24 November 1854.

55 Minute Book of the BCLASS, entries for 16 and 24 November 1854.

56 Douglas Cameron Riach, 'Ireland and the campaign against American slavery, 1830–1860', unpublished Ph.D. thesis, University of Edinburgh, 1976, pp. 131–33, 313.

57 Rebecca Whitelegge to Mary Estlin, 10 December [1852] and 23 August [1853], MS A.9.2. vol. 27, nos. 86 and 57, in BPL; Mary Estlin to M.W. Chapman, Edinburgh, 29 September 1855, MS A.7.3., p. 89, in BPL.

58 *Annual Report of the Edinburgh Ladies' Emancipation Society* (1855). McLaren was the radical Lord Provost of Edinburgh.

59 'To the Anti-Slavery Conference to be held in London on the 29th and 30th November, 1854', letter signed on behalf of the Edinburgh Ladies' Emancipation Society by Sarah Wigham *et al.*, Edinburgh, 27 November 1854, MSS Brit. Emp. S.18, C110/222, in RHL.

60 Minute Book of the BCLASS, entries for 16 and 24 November 1854.

61 While the letters concerned do not survive, their contents may be deduced from the Rev. S.A. Steinthal's replies of 1 October and 1 and 4 November 1853, MSS Brit. Emp. S.18, C36/93, 94, S.22, G85, in RHL.

62 *London Anti-Slavery Conference. Papers Read and Statements Made, 29th and 30th of November, 1854* (London: 1854).

63 Rebecca Moore to R.D. Webb, London, 30 November 1854, MS A.1.2. vol. 24, p. 169, in BPL.

64 *Anti-Slavery Reporter*, 3rd series, vol. VII, no. 7 (July 1853), p. 150.

65 See Strachey, *The Cause*, pp. 87, 93–94. The best account of the development of feminism over this period is contained in Jane Rendall, *The Origins of Modern Feminism: Women in Britain, France and the United States, 1780–1860* (Basingstoke: Macmillan, 1985).

66 Letter [fragment] from Samuel May to R.D. Webb, [1859], printed as item [387] in Taylor, *British and American Abolitionists*, p. 437.

67 Letter from R.D. Webb to Samuel May, Dublin, 10 March 1859, printed as item [388] in Taylor, *British and American Abolitionists*, p. 438.

68 Minutes of the London Emancipation Committee, George Thompson Papers, John Rylands Library, Manchester.

69 M.W. Chapman to S.P. Remond, Weymouth Landing, 4 September 1859, Estlin Papers, 24.122.28, Dr Williams's Library, London; *Anti-Slavery Advocate*, no. 33 (September 1859), p. 262.

70 Minutes of the London Emancipation Committee, minutes for 8 October

1859. The minutes of the meeting on 22 July 1859 reveal that this last committee meeting prior to the public meeting of 1 August was attended by men only.

71 Minutes of the London Emancipation Committee, 5 August 1859 to 24 February 1860.

72 *Westminster Review*, vol. CXXVIII (1887), pp. 165–73 (quote from p. 168).

73 Judith R. Walkowitz, *Prostitution and Victorian Society: Women, Class, and the State* (Cambridge: Cambridge University Press, 1980), Table I, [pp. 126–27]; Paul McHugh, *Prostitution and Victorian Social Reform* (London: Croom Helm, 1980), pp. 170–71.

74 Quoted in Glen Petrie, *A Singular Iniquity: The Campaigns of Josephine Butler* (London: Macmillan, 1971), p. 44.

75 See McHugh, *Prostitution and Victorian Social Reform*, pp. 171, 240–41.

76 Josephine E. Butler, *Personal Reminiscences of a Great Crusade* (London: Horace Marshall, 1896), p. 81.

77 Josephine E. Butler (ed.), *Women's Work and Women's Culture* (London: Macmillan, 1869), introduction, pp. lv–lvii.

78 See especially Walkowitz, *Prostitution and Victorian Society*, pp. 110, 146, 255.

79 Stanton *et al.*, *History of Woman Suffrage*, vol. III, p. 840.

80 *First and Second Reports of the Ladies' London Emancipation Society* (London: Levey, 1864, 1865); Olive Banks, *Biographical Dictionary of British Feminists* (Brighton: Harvester, 1985), vol. I; Strachey, *The Cause*.

81 *Women's Suffrage Journal*, vol. I, no. 1 (March 1870), pp. 7, 8.

82 For members of the Birmingham suffrage committee see ibid., p. 7.

83 Mentia Taylor to Rev. Samuel May Jr, London, postmarked 10 January 1866, MS B.1.6. vol. 10, no. 30, in BPL; Sarah Pugh to Elizabeth Pease Nichol, Germantown, Philadelphia, 15 April 1867, MS A.1.2. vol. 35, p. 15B, in BPL; Eliza Wigham to William Lloyd Garrison, Dublin, 1 May 1868, MS A.1.2. vol. 36, p. 22, in BPL. See also letters from Sarah Pugh to Mary Estlin, Germantown, 31 January, 27 August, 7 December 1869; Oliver Johnson to Mary Estlin, New York, 14 February 1869; W.L. Garrison to Mary Estlin, Roxbury, 8 October 1868, items 24.121.76, 77, 78; 24.125.25; 24.124.7 of Estlin Papers, Dr Williams's Library, London.

84 M.W. Chapman to Mary Estlin, Staten Island, 17 March [n.y.], Weymouth, 25 November 1875; Frank J. Garrison to Mary Estlin, 1876–81, items 24.122.53, 54; 24.124.8–20, Estlin Papers, Dr Williams's Library, London.

85 William Lloyd Garrison to Elizabeth Pease Nichol, Roxbury, 26 September 1869, as quoted in Walter M. Merrill and Louis Ruchames (eds), *Letters of William Lloyd Garrison*, 6 vols (Cambridge: Belknap Press, 1971–81), vol. VI, no. 36.

86 Letter from Mary Burton to Elizabeth Pease Nichol, Edinburgh, 1 August 1877, MS A.1.2. vol. 39, p. 117, in BPL. Mary Burton was a prominent Scottish lecturer on women's suffrage.

87 Sklar, ' "Women who speak for an entire nation" ', p. 498.

88 Ibid., p. 499.

8 A LINGERING CONCERN

1 Betty Fladeland, *Men and Brothers: Anglo-American Antislavery Co-operation* (Urbana: University of Illinois Press, 1972), ch. 16; Douglas Charles Stange, *British Unitarians Against American Slavery, 1833–65* (Cransbury: Associated University Press, 1984), ch. 8; T.J. Vaughan, 'The British Freedmen's Aid

Movement, 1863–9', unpublished M.Litt. thesis, University of Bristol, 1971; Christine Bolt, *The Anti-Slavery Movement and Reconstruction: A Study in Anglo-American Co-operation, 1833–77* (London: Oxford University Press, 1969).

2 Howard Temperley, *British Antislavery, 1833–1870* (Columbia, SC: University of South Carolina Press, 1972), pp. 251–53, 256–57; Bolt, *The Anti-Slavery Movement and Reconstruction*, p. 31; Douglas A. Lorimer, *Colour, Class and the Victorians: English Attitudes to the Negro in the Mid-Nineteenth Century* (Leicester: Leicester University Press, 1978), ch. 8.

3 R.D. Webb to the Westons, Greenfield, Kilgobbin, Co. Dublin [n.d.] and R.D. Webb to Samuel May Jr, Dublin, 12 March 1862, MS A.9.2. vol. 16, part 2, no. 20 and MS B.1.6 vol. 15, in BPL, quoted as items [408] and [427] in Clare Taylor (ed.), *British and American Abolitionists: An Episode in Transatlantic Understanding* (Edinburgh: Edinburgh University Press, 1974), pp. 456, 479. For assessments of the great importance of Martineau's *Daily News* articles by her biographers see Valerie Kossew Pichanick, *Harriet Martineau: the Woman and her Work, 1802–76* (Ann Arbor: University of Michigan Press, 1980), p. 213; R.K. Webb, *Harriet Martineau: a Radical Victorian* (London: Heineman, 1960), pp. 329.

4 *Daily News*, 30 August 1861, leader 2, p. 4; 11 October 1861, leader 1, p. 4. The identification of these and other leaders as the work of Martineau is based on R.K. Webb's typescript compilation, 'A Handlist of contributions to the *Daily News* by Harriet Martineau 1852–1866', a copy of which is lodged in the British Library [ref: x.905/188].

5 See, for example, *Daily News*, 20 July 1861, leader 3, p. 4; 30 August 1861, leader 2, p. 4; 26 September 1861, leader 2, p. 4; 18 December 1861, leader 3, p. 4; 21 December 1861, leader 3, p. 4; 1 March 1862, leader 2, p. 4; 25 March 1862, leader 3, p. 4; 28 March 1862, leader 2, p. 4; 7 May 1862, leader 2, p. 4; 28 May 1862, leader 2, p. 4.

6 Lorimer, *Colour, Class and the Victorians*, pp. 164–68.

7 Daily News, 3 October 1861, leader 1, p. 4; 10 October 1861, leader 1, p. 4.

8 *Daily News*, 18 December 1861, leader 3, p. 4.

9 Temperley, *British Antislavery*, p. 254.

10 Harriet Beecher Stowe, *A Reply to 'the Affectionate and Christian Address of Many Thousands of Women of Great Britain and Ireland, to their Sisters, the Women of the United States of America'* (London: Sampson Low, 1863).

11 *Anti-Slavery Reporter*, 3rd series, vol. XI, no. 2 (March 1863), p. 56; Wendell Phillips and Francis Jackson Garrison, *William Lloyd Garrison 1805–1879: the Story of His Life* (New York: The Century Co., 1885), p. 73. For a hostile, pro-Southern response to the *Reply* see Civis Anglicus, *A Voice from the Motherland, Answering Mrs H. Beecher Stowe's Appeal* (London: Trubner, 1863).

12 *Anti-Slavery Reporter*, 3rd series, vol. XI, no. 3 (March 1863), p. 52.

13 [Frances Power Cobbe], *Rejoinder to Mrs Stowe's Reply to the Address of the Women of England* (London: Emily Faithfull, 1863). Cobbe is identified as the author of this pamphlet in *First Annual Report of the Ladies' London Emancipation Society* (London, 1864), footnote on p. 4.

14 *First Annual Report of the Ladies' London Emancipation Society; Second Annual Report of the Ladies' London Emancipation Society* (London: Levey, 1865); *Anti-Slavery Reporter*, 3rd series, vol. XII, no. 2 (February 1864), p. 47; no. 3 (March 1864), p. 70; no. 4 (April 1864), p. 73; no. 5 (May 1864), p. 119; vol. XIII, no. 3 (March 1865), pp. 70–71.

15 See advertisement in *Anti-Slavery Advocate*, vol. III, no. 4 (April 1863), p. 32.

16 *First Annual Report of the Ladies' London Emancipation Society*.

17 *Standard*, 3 October 1862, p. 4c, as quoted in Lorimer, *Colour, Class and the Victorians*, p. 168.

18 The tracts were: no. 1 – Frances Power Cobbe, *The Red Flag in John Bull's Eyes*; no. 2 – Isa Craig (ed.), *The Essence of Slavery*; no. 3 – J.E. Cairnes, *Who are the Canters?*; no. 4 – Edward Dicey, *Labour and Slavery*; no. 5 – Loring Moody (compiler), *The Destruction of the Republic and of all Constitutional Liberty, the Object of the Rebellion*; no. 6 – Emily Shirreff, *The Chivalry of the South*; no. 7 – Sarah Parker Remond, *The Negroes and Anglo-Africans as Freedmen and Soldiers*; no. 8 – J.M. Ludlow, *American Slavery. Reprinted from 'Good Words'*; no. 9 – M.D. Conway, *Benjamin Banneker, the Negro Astronomer*; no. 10 – Mrs P.A. Taylor (compiler), *Professor Huxley on the Negro Question*; no. 11 – Emily Shirreff, *A Few More Words on the Chivalry of the South*; no. 12 – *The Humanity of the Confederates, or, the Massacre at Fort Pillow*. All the tracts were published in London by Emily Faithfull in 1863–64.

19 For a useful discussion of the background to and impact of the book see introduction to John A. Scott (ed.), *Journal of a Residence on a Georgia Plantation in 1838–1839 by Frances Anne Kemble* (London: Jonathan Cape, 1961, original edition 1863).

20 Reviews appeared in the *Athenaeum*, 6 June 1863, and the *London Spectator*, 30 May 1863; see John A. Scott (ed.), *Journal*, introduction, p. liv. Chapter 19 of the *Journal* was entitled 'Women in Slavery'.

21 Edward Yates, *A Letter to the Women of England, on Slavery in the Southern States of America; Considered Especially in reference to the Condition of the Female Slaves* (London: John Snow, 1863).

22 Lydia Maria Child (ed.), *The Deeper Wrong; or, Incidents in the Life of a Slave Girl. Written by Herself* (London: W. Tweedie, 1862).

23 Review in *Morning Star*, 10 March 1862.

24 *First Report of the Ladies' London Emancipation Society*, p. 10; *Report of the Committee of the Edinburgh Ladies' Emancipation Society for the Year ending March 3, 1864*, [Edinburgh, 1864], p. 1.

25 *Daily News*, 14 July 1862, leader 1, p. 4, 17 July 1862, leader 3, p. 1.

26 *Anti-Slavery Reporter*, 3rd series, vol. X, no. 10 (October 1862), p. 240.

27 See John Watts, *The Facts of the Cotton Famine* (London: Simpkin, Marshall, & Co, 1866), pp. 205, 278.

28 See Mary Ellison, *Support for Secession: Lancashire and the American Civil War* (Chicago: University of Chicago Press, 1972), table of 'occupations of adults over 20 in Lancashire in 1861', p. 223.

29 George Thompson to W.L. Garrison, 24 December 1862, MS A.1.2. vol. 31, no. 167, in BPL.

30 Ellison, *Support for Secession*, pp. 80–81.

31 Watts, *The Facts of the Cotton Famine*, pp. 267, 270.

32 Bolt, *The Anti-Slavery Movement and Reconstruction*, p. 114.

33 'Minute Book of the Ladies Society for the Relief of Negro Slaves', entry for 12 April 1831; letter from Elizabeth Evans to Robert Stokes, Woodbridge, 15 March 1837, MSS Brit. Emp. S.18, C2/73, in RHL; letter from Anne Cropper to the New England Ladies' Anti-Slavery Societies, Liverpool, 4 April 1837, quoted in *Right and Wrong in Boston. Annual Report of the Boston Female Anti-Slavery Society* (Boston: Isaac Knapp, 1837), p. 104; Esther Copley, *A History of Slavery, and its Abolition*, 2nd edn (London: Houlston & Stoneman, 1839), pp. 575–6.

34 'Birmingham Antislavery Society Minute Book', entries for January 1834 and June and July 1835.

35 *The Jamaica Education Society, Under the Management of the Baptist Missioniaries. Report* (Birmingham: J.W. Stowell, 11 May 1838).

36 *Eighth Report of the Ladies' Negro's Friend Society, for Birmingham* (Birmingham: B. Hudson, 1833), p. 23.

37 *Ninth Report of the Ladies' Negro's Friend Society, for Birmingham* (Birmingham: B. Hudson, 1834), pp. 12–13.

38 Ibid., accounts on pp. 45–48; *Eleventh Report of the Ladies' Negro's Friend Society, for Birmingham* (Birmingham: Hudson, 1836), pp. 14–20; 'Minute Book of the Ladies' Society for the Relief of Negro Slaves', entries for annual meetings on 11 March 1834, 14 April 1835, 8 March 1836, 14 March 1837, 17 April 1838; *The Jamaica Education Society . . . Report.*

39 Copley, *A History of Slavery*, pp. 575–76; *Ninth Report of the Ladies' Negro's Friend Society, for Birmingham*, p. 13; 'Minute Book of the Ladies Society for the Relief of Negro Slaves', entry for 11 March 1834. This entry gives the name of the teacher as Lucy Kingdon.

40 *Irish Friend*, vol. I, no. 11 (1 September 1838), p. 87: letter to the editor on 'African Instruction' from M[ary] Dudley, South-Grove, Peckham, 6 August 1838. For response from Irish women to the appeal see *Irish Friend*, vol. II, no. 4 (1 April 1839), pp. 26–27: 'Schools in Africa. An Address to Children on Behalf of the Sable Children of Africa'; vol. II, no. 5 (1 May 1839), p. 37; no. 6 (1 June 1839), p. 48.

41 *Report of the Sheffield Ladies' Association for the Universal Abolition of Slavery. February 19, 1839* (Sheffield: Robert Leader, 1839), [p. 5]; notice of annual meeting and bazaar in *Sheffield Patriot*, 19 February 1839; poem 'the Ladies Bazaar' in *Sheffield Patriot*, 5 March 1839; appeal of Mary Anne Rawson printed in *The Edinburgh Ladies' Emancipation Society. MDCCCXL*; Mary Anne Rawson, *The Thompson Normal School, Jamaica* (Sheffield: Robert Leader, 1845).

42 *Report of the Committee of the Edinburgh Ladies' Emancipation Society for the Year ending March 3, 1864*, p. 2. In 1862 the society had given a small donation to a girls' school in Liberia (see *Annual Report of the Edinburgh Ladies' Emancipation Society . . . ending March 4, 1862* (Edinburgh: H. Armour, 1862), [p. 27].

43 *Anti-Slavery Reporter*, 3rd series, vol. VIII, no. 10 (October 1860), p. 268. See also *Thirty-Sixth, Thirty-Ninth and Fortieth Reports of the Ladies' Negro's Friend Society, for Birmingham ...* (Birmingham: B. Hudson, 1861, 1864, 1865).

44 *Freed-Man*, no. 15 (October 1866), p. 32; no. 17 (December 1866), pp. 71, 76; no. 18 (January 1867), p. 82; no. 20 (March 1867), pp. 117–21, p. 124; no. 21 (April 1867), pp. 134–37; no. 22 (May 1867), p. 152; no. 23 (June 1867), p. 161; no. 24 (July 1867), pp. 180, 184–86; no. 26 (September 1867), p. 220.

45 Lorimer, *Colour, Class and the Victorians*, p. 176.

46 *Freed-Man*, no. 18 (January 1867), pp. 84–88; no. 20 (March 1867), p. 116.

47 *Anti-Slavery Reporter*, 3rd series, vol. VIII, no. 11 (November 1860), p. 271; vol. IX, no. 1 (January 1861), p. 24; no. 4 (April 1861), p. 95; no. 6 (June 1861), p. 123; no. 7 (July 1861), p. 145; no. 12 (December 1861), p. 278; no. 8 (August 1862), p. 182.

48 'The emancipated American slaves', *British Friend*, vol. XX (1862), p. 175.

49 *To the Friends of Abolition* (Bristol: Ackland [1863]). This circular is printed in full in the *Anti-Slavery Reporter*, 3rd series, vol. XI, no. 2 (February 1863), p. 48.

50 The estimate of a total of fifty societies by the end of the Civil War is taken from Howard Temperley, 'British anti-slavery' in Patricia Hollis (ed.),

Pressure from Without in Early Victorian England (London: Edward Arnolt, 1974), p. 50. The list of women's committees is compiled from various sources, including the *Freedmen's Aid Reporter*, the *Freedman*, the *British Friend*.

51 *Report No. I. Report of the Central Committee of the Society of Friends for the Relief of the Emancipated Negroes of the United States, for the Three Months Ending 6th Month 1st, 1865. Also List of Subscriptions and Letters from America* (London: Richard Barrett, 1865); *Report No. II . . . Ending 9th Month, 1865 . . .; Report No. III . . . Ending 3rd Month, 1866;* minute books of the Central Committee of the Society of Friends for the Relief of the Emancipated Slaves of North America, Friends House Library, London; minutes of the National Committee of British Freedmen's Aid Associations and of the National Freedmen's Aid Union, MSS Brit. Emp. S.27, G88, in RHL; letters to the secretaries of the National Freedmen's Aid Union, MSS Brit. Emp. S.18 C38–40, C117–121, S.22 G87, in RHL.

52 Mary Ann Estlin to Caroline Weston, Bristol, 17 and 19 May 1865, MS A.4.2. vol. 32, no. 38, in BPL.

53 *Friend*, new series, vol. V (1865), pp. 77–78, 142, 156.

54 *Thirty-Ninth Report of the Ladies' Negro's Friend Society, for Birmingham* (Birmingham: B. Hudson, 1864), p. 21; *Fortieth Report of the Ladies' Negro's Friend Society, for Birmingham* (Birmingham: B. Hudson, 1865), pp. 55–72.

55 *Anti-Slavery Reporter*, 3rd series, vol. XII, no. 4 (April 1864), pp. 95–96; no. 5 (May 1864), p. 101; *Annual Report of the Birmingham and Midland Freedmen's-Aid Association, to May 19, 1865* (Birmingham: White & Pike, 1865), [p. 5]; *Friend*, new series, vol. V (1865), p. 141; *Thirty-Ninth Report of the Ladies' Negro's Friend Society, for Birmingham* p. 25. For Mrs Joseph Sturge's involvement see *Sixty-Eighth Report of the Ladies' Negro's Friend Society, for Birmingham . . .* (Birmingham: Hudson, 1893), p. 13–14; *Seventy-First Report of the Ladies' Negro's Friend Society, for Birmingham . . .* (Birmingham: Hudson, 1896), p. 10.

56 Obituary of Lydia Sturge in *Sixty-Eighth Report of the Ladies' Negro's Friend Society, for Birmingham . . .* (1893), pp. 12–16.

57 *Annual Report of the Birmingham and Midland Freedmen's-Aid Association*, pp. 8, 22; *Freedmen's-Aid Reporter*, vol. I, no. 10 (February 1867), p. 112; new series, no. 2 (December 1867), p. 36.

58 *Freedmen's-Aid Reporter*, vol. I, no. 4 (August 1866), pp. 38–39; no. 8 (December 1866), p. 83.

59 *Freed-Man*, no. 2 (September 1865), p. 19; no. 3 (October 1865), p. 50.

60 *Freed-Man*, no. 8 (March 1866), p. 212; no. 10 (May 1866), pp. 339–40; *Freedmen's-Aid Reporter*, vol. I, no. 5 (September 1866), p. 49; no. 8 (December 1866), p. 89; no. 9 (January 1867), p. 95; no. 10 (February 1867), pp. 101, 104, 106.

61 See, for example, the Brighton circular printed in the *Freedmen's-Aid Reporter*, vol. I, no. 7 (November 1866), pp. 65, 67. This circular was signed by Elizabeth B. Prideaux, formerly an officer of the Brighton Ladies' Anti-Slavery Association, which became inactive about 1861.

62 *Freed-Man*, no. 8 (March 1866), pp. 204–11; no. 9 (April 1866), p. 232; and various entries in *Freedmen's-Aid Reporter*.

63 *Freedmen's-Aid Reporter*, new series, no. 2 (December 1867), p. 20.

64 For details of events in Jamaica see Bernard Semmel, *The Governor Eyre Controversy* (London: MacGibbon & Kee, 1962).

65 Letters from Mary Edmundson to Louis Chamerovzow, Dublin, 15 November 1865; Isabella Waring Maxwell to Louis Chamerovzow, Killifaddy, 19 January 1866, MSS Brit. Emp. S.18 C30/122 and C 34/39, in RHL.

66 Semmel, *The Governor Eyre Controversy*; Lorimer, *Colour, Class and the Victorians*, ch. 9; Christine Bolt, *Victorian Attitudes to Race* (London: Routledge & Kegan Paul, 1971), ch. 3.

67 *Anti-Slavery Reporter*, 3rd series, vol. XV, no. 5 (May 1867), p. 101; vol. XVI, no. 1 (January 1868), p. 20.

68 *Annual Report of the Edinburgh Ladies' Emancipation Society . . . ending 15th February 1866* (Edinburgh: H. Armour, 1866), p. 25; 'Special contributions for the Jamaica matter' listed in *Anti-Slavery Reporter*, 3rd series, vol. XIV, no. 3 (March 1866), p. 85; no. 4 (April 1866), p. 113; no. 9 (September 1866), p. 234. Only one donation from a men's auxiliary is listed.

69 See accounts in the *Forty-First Report of the Ladies' Negro's Friend Society, for Birmingham . . .* (1866) and the *Annual Report of the Edinburgh Ladies' Emancipation Society . . . Ending 4th April 1867* (1867).

70 *Annual Report of the Edinburgh Ladies' Emancipation Society . . . Ending 15th February 1866* (1866), p. 25.

71 *Thirty-Sixth, Thirty-Ninth and Fortieth Reports of the Ladies' Negro's Friend Society, for Birmingham . . .* (1861, 1864, 1865); reports of the society's meetings in the *Anti-Slavery Reporter*, 3rd series, vol. VIII, no. 10 (October 1860), p. 268; vol. IX, no. 7 (July 1861), p. 145; vol. X, no. 8 (August 1862), p. 182; vol. XII, no. 4 (April 1864), p. 95.

72 *Anti-Slavery Reporter*, 3rd series, vol. VIII, no. 3 (March 1859), p. 72; no. 6 (June 1859), p. 144; no. 10 (October 1859), pp. 217–18; vol. IX, no. 1 (January 1860), pp. 12–13; no. 3 (March 1860), p. 67. Edinburgh women sent a similar petition; see *Annual Report of the Edinburgh Ladies' Emancipation Society . . . Ending March, 1859* (1859), p. 9.

73 *The Labour Question in the West Indies. Three Letters from Ernest Noel, Esq. . . . and also, Extracts from the Correspondence of the New York Times* (Birmingham: printed for the Ladies' Negro's Friend Society, by Hudson, [c. 1860]); review in *Anti-Slavery Reporter*, 3rd series, vol. VIII, no. 10 (October 1860), pp. 267–68. See also *Thirty-Sixth Report of the Ladies' Negro's Friend Society, for Birmingham . . .* (1861).

74 *Fortieth Report of the Ladies' Negro's Friend Society, for Birmingham* (1865), pp. 21–24.

75 See report of meeting in *Anti-Slavery Reporter*, 3rd series, vol. XIV, no. 3 (March 1866), pp. 86–87.

76 *Forty-First Report of the Ladies' Negro's Friend Society, for Birmingham. . .* (1866), pp. 6–10.

77 *Anti-Slavery Reporter*, 3rd series, vol. XVI, no. 1 (January 1868), p. 20.

78 *Annual Report of the Edinburgh Ladies' Emancipation Society . . . Ending 4th April 1867*, p. 3.

79 *Anti-Slavery Reporter*, 3rd series, vol. XVII, no. 1 (January 1869), p. 184.

80 *Annual Report of the Edinburgh Ladies' Emancipation Society . . . Ending 4th April 1867*, p. 3.

81 Letter from Sarah P. Remond to the editor, *Daily News*, 22 November 1868, as quoted in C. Peter Ripley, *The Black Abolitionist Papers*, vol. I (Chapel Hill, NC: University of North Carolina Press, [c. 1985]), document 102.

82 *Friend*, new series, vol. XVIII (1878), pp. 239–42.

83 *Anti-Caste*, vol. I, no. 1 (March 1888), p. 1; no. 2 (April 1888), p. 4.

84 *To the Friends of Justice and Humanity Everywhere, Especially Those who Interest Themselves in the Future of the Coloured Race; Also to the Remnant of the Anti-Slavery Workers, and the Members of the Society of Friends*, Estlin Papers, Dr Williams's Library, London [ref: 24.128 (20)].

85 Bolt, *The Anti-Slavery Movement and Reconstruction*, pp. 139–40.

86 *Life of Frances Power Cobbe as Told by Herself* (London: Swan Sonnenschein, 1904), p. 283.

9 ANTI-SLAVERY AND WOMEN: A NEW PICTURE

1 *Retrospect of the Work of Half-a-Century of the Ladies' Negro's Friend Society, for Birmingham, Leicester, West Bromwich, Wednesbury, Dudley, Stourbridge, and Other Places. Established 1825* (London: E. Newman, 1875).

SELECT BIBLIOGRAPHY

Detailed references to primary sources and to biographical works and published papers are given in the endnotes. This bibliography is intended as a selective guide to the secondary literature.

BOOKS

Anstey, Roger. *The Atlantic Slave Trade and British Abolition 1760–1810*. London: Macmillan, 1975.

Anstey, Roger and Hair, P.E.H. (eds). *Liverpool, the African Slave Trade, and Abolition*. Historical Society of Lancashire and Cheshire, Occasional Series 2, 1979.

Banks, Olive. *Faces of Feminism*. Oxford: Martin Robertson, 1981.

Barker, Anthony J. *The African Link: British Attitudes to the Negro in the Era of the Atlantic Slave Trade, 1550–1807*. London: Frank Cass, 1978.

Beckles, Hilary McD. *Natural Rebels: A Social History of Enslaved Black Women in Barbados*. London: Zed Books, 1989.

Blackburn, Robin. *The Overthrow of Colonial Slavery, 1776–1848*. London: Verso, 1988.

Blackett, R.J.M. *Building an Antislavery Wall: Black Americans in the Atlantic Abolitionist Movement, 1830–1860*. Baton Rouge: Louisiana State University Press, 1983.

Bolt, Christine. *The Anti-Slavery Movement and Reconstruction: A Study in Anglo-American Co-operation, 1833–77*. London: Oxford University Press, 1969.

——. *Victorian Attitudes to Race*. London: Routledge & Kegan Paul, 1971.

Bolt, Christine and Drescher, Seymour (eds). *Anti-Slavery, Religion and Reform: Essays in Memory of Roger Anstey*. Folkestone: Dawson, 1980.

Bush, Barbara. *Slave Women in Caribbean Society, 1650–1838*. Bloomington: Indiana University Press, 1990.

Cott, Nancy F. *The Bonds of Womanhood: 'Woman's Sphere' in New England, 1780–1835*. New Haven: Yale University Press, 1977.

Coupland, Sir Reginald. *The British Anti-Slavery Movement*. London: Frank Cass, 1964 edn.

Cowherd, Raymond G. *The Politics of English Dissent: The Religious Aspects of Liberal and Humanitarian Reform Movements from 1815 to 1848*. London: Epworth Press, 1959.

Craton, Michael. *Testing the Chains: Resistance to Slavery in the British West Indies*. Ithaca: Cornell University Press, 1982.

Curtin, Philip D. *The Atlantic Slave Trade: A Census*. Madison: University of Wisconsin Press, 1969.
——. *The Image of Africa. British Ideas and Action, 1780–1850*. London: Macmillan, 1965.
Davidoff, Leonore and Hall, Catherine. *Family Fortunes: Men and Women of the English Middle Class, 1780–1850*. London: Hutchinson, 1987.
Davis, Angela. *Women, Race and Class*. London: Women's Press, 1982.
Davis, David Brion. *The Problem of Slavery in Western Culture*. Ithaca: Cornell University Press, 1966.
——. *The Problem of Slavery in the Age of Revolution, 1770–1823*. Ithaca: Cornell University Press, 1975.
——. *Slavery and Human Progress*. New York: Oxford University Press, 1984.
Drescher, Seymour. *Econocide: British Slavery in the Era of Abolition*. Pittsburgh: University of Pittsburgh Press, 1977.
——. *Capitalism and Antislavery: British Mobilization in Comparative Perspective*. Basingstoke: Macmillan, 1986.
Dykes, Eva B. *The Negro in English Romantic Thought, or a Study in Sympathy for the Oppressed*. Washington, DC: Associated Publishers, 1942.
Edwards, Paul and Walvin, James. *Black Personalities in the Era of the Slave Trade*. London: Macmillan, 1983.
Ellison, Mary. *Support for Secession – Lancashire and the American Civil War*. Chicago: University of Chicago Press, 1972.
Eltis, David and Walvin, James (eds). *The Abolition of the Atlantic Slave Trade: Origins and Effects in Europe, Africa, and the Americas*. Madison: University of Wisconsin Press, 1981.
Fairchild, Hoxie Neale. *The Noble Savage: A Study in Romantic Naturalism*. New York: Columbia University Press, 1928.
Fladeland, Betty. *Men and Brothers: Anglo-American Antislavery Co-operation*. Urbana: University of Illinois Press, 1972.
Frost, William J. (ed.). *The Quaker Origins of Antislavery*. Norwood, PA: Norwood Editions, 1980.
Fryer, Peter. *Staying Power: The History of Black People in Britain*. London: Pluto Press, 1984.
Hempton, David. *Methodism and Politics in British Society, 1750–1850*. London: Hutchinson, 1984.
Hersch, Blanche Glassman. *The Slavery of Sex. Feminist-Abolitionists in America*. Urbana: University of Illinois Press, 1978.
Hollis, Patricia (ed.). *Pressure from Without in Early Victorian England*. London: Edward Arnolt, 1974.
Holt, Raymond V. *The Unitarian Contribution to Social Progress in England*. 2nd edn. London: Lindsey Press, 1952.
Hooks, Bell. *Ain't I a Woman: Black Women and Feminism*. London: Pluto Press, 1982.
Howse, Ernest Marshall. *Saints in Politics*. London: George Allen & Unwin, 1953.
Hurwitz, Edith F. *Politics and the Public Conscience: Slave Emancipation and the Abolitionist Movement in Britain*. London: George Allen & Unwin, 1973.
Klingberg, Frank Joseph. *The Anti-Slavery Movement in England: A Study in English Humanitarianism*. New Haven: Yale Historical Publications, 1926.
Lorimer, Douglas A. *Colour, Class and the Victorians: English Attitudes to the Negro in the Mid-Nineteenth Century*. Leicester: Leicester University Press, 1978.
McCullough, Norman Verrle. *The Negro in English Literature: A Critical Introduction*. Ilfracombe: Arthur H. Stockwell, 1962.

McHugh, Paul. *Prostitution and Victorian Social Reform*. London: Croom Helm, 1980.

McKendrick, Neil; Brewer, John; and Plumb, J.H. *The Birth of a Consumer Society: The Commercialization of Eighteenth-Century England*. London: Europa Publications, 1982.

Malmgreen, Gail. *Neither Bread nor Roses: Utopian Feminists and the English Working Class, 1800–1850*. Brighton: John L. Noyce, 1978.

—— (ed.). *Religion in the Lives of English Women 1760–1930*. London: Croom Helm, 1986.

Mathurin, Lucille. *The Rebel Woman in the British West Indies During Slavery*. Kingston: Institute of Jamaica, 1975.

Mendus, Susan and Rendall, Jane. *Sexuality and Subordination*. London: Routledge & Kegan Paul, 1989.

Miers, Suzanne. *Britain and the Ending of the Slave Trade*. London: Longman, 1975.

Newton, Judith L.; Ryan, Mary P.; and Walkowitz, Judith R. (eds). *Sex and Class in Women's History*. (History Workshop Series). London: Routledge & Kegan Paul, 1983.

Nuermberger, Ruth Ketring. *The Free Produce Movement. A Quaker Protest Against Slavery*. Durham, NC: Duke University Press, 1942.

Perry, Lewis and Fellman, Michael (eds). *Antislavery Reconsidered: New Perspectives on the Abolitionists*. Baton Rouge: Louisiana State University Press, 1979.

Poovey, Mary. *Uneven Developments: The Ideological Work of Gender in Mid-Victorian England*. London: Virago, 1989.

Porter, Dale H. *The Abolition of the Slave Trade in England, 1784–1807*. Hamden, CT.: Archon Books, 1970.

Prochaska, Frank. *Women and Philanthropy in Nineteenth Century England*. Oxford: Oxford University Press, 1980.

Rendall, Jane. *The Origins of Modern Feminism: Women in Britain, France and the United States, 1780–1860*. Basingstoke: Macmillan, 1985.

—— (ed.). *Equal or Different: Women's Politics, 1800–1914*. Oxford: Blackwell, 1987.

Rice, C. Duncan. *The Scots Abolitionists, 1833–1861*. Baton Rouge: Louisiana State University Press, 1981.

Rogers, Katherine M. *Feminism in Eighteenth-Century England*. Brighton: Harvester, 1982.

Royle, Edward and Walvin, James. *English Radicals and Reformers, 1760–1848*. Brighton: Harvester, 1982.

Scott, Joan Wallach. *Gender and the Politics of History*. New York: Columbia University Press, 1988.

Semmel, Bernard. *The Governor Eyre Controversy*. London: MacGibbon & Kee, 1962.

Sharistanian, Janet (ed.). *Gender, Ideology and Action: Historical Perspectives on Women's Public Lives*. (Contributions in *Women's Studies*, no. 67.) Westport: Greenwood Press, 1986.

Shyllon, F.O. *Black Slaves in Britain*. London: Oxford University Press, 1974.

——. *Black People in Britain, 1555–1833*. London: Oxford University Press, 1977.

Solow, Barbara L. and Engerman, Stanley L. (eds). *British Capitalism and Caribbean Slavery: The Legacy of Eric Williams*. Cambridge: Cambridge University Press, 1987.

Stange, Douglas Charles. *British Unitarians Against American Slavery, 1833–65*. Cransbury: Associated University Press, 1984.

Strachey, Ray. *The Cause. A Short History of the Women's Movement in Great Britain*. London: Virago, 1978 edn.

Sypher, Wylie. *Guinea's Captive Kings: British Anti-Slavery Literature of the Eighteenth*

Century. Chapel Hill: University of North Carolina Press, 1942; New York: Octagon, 1969.

Taylor, Barbara. *Eve and the New Jerusalem: Socialism and Feminism in the Nineteenth Century*. London: Virago, 1983.

Temperley, Howard. *British Antislavery, 1833–1870*. Columbia, SC: University of South Carolina Press, 1972.

Thistlethwaite, Frank. *America and the Atlantic Community: Anglo American Aspects, 1790–1850*. New York: Harper & Row, 1959.

Thomis, Malcolm I. and Jennifer Grimmett. *Women in Protest, 1800–1850*. London: Croom Helm, 1982.

Thompson, Dorothy. *The Chartists*. London: Temple Smith, 1984.

Tollis, Frederick B. *Quakers and the Atlantic Culture*. New York: Macmillan, 1960.

Turner, Mary. *Slaves and Missionaries: The Disintegration of Jamaican Slave Society, 1787–1834*. Urbana: University of Illinois Press, 1982.

Vicinus, Martha (ed.). *Suffer and Be Still: Women in the Victorian Age*. London: Methuen, 1980.

——. *A Widening Sphere: Changing Roles of Victorian Women*. London: Methuen, 1980.

Walkowitz, Judith R. *Prostitution and Victorian Society: Women, Class and the State*. Cambridge: Cambridge University Press, 1980.

Walvin, James. *Black and White: The Negro in English Society 1555–1945*. London: Allen Lane, 1973.

—— (ed.). *Slavery and British Society, 1776–1846*. London: Macmillan, 1982.

——. *England, Slaves and Freedom, 1776–1838*. Basingstoke: Macmillan, 1986.

Williams, Eric. *Capitalism and Slavery*. Chapel Hill: University of North Carolina Press, 1944.

Yellin, Jean Fagan. *Women and Sisters: The Antislavery Feminists in American Culture*. New Haven: Yale University Press, 1989.

ARTICLES

Amos, Valerie and Parmar, Pratibha. 'Challenging imperial feminism', *Feminist Review*, 17 (Autumn 1984), 3–19.

Anstey, Roger T. 'Capitalism and slavery: a critique', *Economic History Review*, 2nd series, 21 (1968), 307–20.

——. 'A re-interpretation of the abolition of the British slave trade, 1806–1807', *English Historical Review*, 37 (1972), 304–32.

——. 'Parliamentary reform, Methodism and anti-slavery politics, 1829–1833', *Slavery and Abolition*, 2, 3 (December 1981), 209–26.

Ashworth, John. 'The relationship between capitalism and humanitarianism', *American Historical Review*, 92, 4 (October 1987), 813–28.

Beckles, Hilary. 'The 200 years war: slave resistance in the British West Indies: an overview of the historiography', *Jamaica Historical Review*, 13 (1982), 1–10.

Billington, Louis. 'British humanitarians and American cotton, 1840–1860', *Journal of American Studies*, 11 (1977), 313–34.

Billington, Louis and Billington, Rosamund. ' "A burning zeal for righteousness": women in the British anti-slavery movement, 1820–1860', in Jane Rendall (ed.), *Equal or Different: Women's Politics, 1800–1914* (Basingstoke: Macmillan, 1985), pp. 82–111.

Blackett, R.J.M. 'Fugitive slaves in Britain: the odyssey of William and Ellen Craft', *Journal of American Studies*, 12 (1978), 41–61.

Bogin, Ruth. 'Sarah Parker Remond: black abolitionist from Salem', *Essex Institute Historical Collections*, 110 (April 1974), 120–50.

Braidwood, Stephen J. 'Initiatives and organisation of the black poor 1786–1787', *Slavery and Abolition*, 3, 3 (December 1982), 211–27.

Carby, Hazel V. 'White woman listen! black feminism and the boundaries of sisterhood', in Centre for Contemporary Cultural Studies, *The Empire Strikes Back: Race and Racism in 70s Britain* (London: Hutchinson, 1982), 212–35.

Corfield, Kenneth. 'Elizabeth Heyrick: radical Quaker', in Gail Malmgreen (ed.), *Religion in the Lives of English Women* (London: Croom Helm, 1986), 41–67.

Davis, David B. 'The emergence of immediatism in British and American anti-slavery thought', *The Mississipi Valley Historical Review*, 49 (1962–63), 209–30.

——. 'Reflections on abolitionism and ideological hegemony', *American Historical Review*, 92, 4 (October 1987), 797–812.

Davis, D.B. and Temperley, H. 'Capitalism, slavery and ideology', *Past and Present*, 75 (May 1977), 94–118.

Drescher, S. 'Cart whip and billy roller: or antislavery and reform symbolism in industrializing Britain', *Journal of Social History*, 15 (1981–82), 3–24.

Eley, Geoff. 'Re-thinking the political: social history and political culture in eighteenth and nineteenth century Britain', *Archiv Für Sozialgeschichte*, 21 (1981), 427–57.

Fladeland, Betty. 'Abolitionist pressures on the Concert of Europe, 1814–1822', *Journal of Modern History*, 38 (1966), 355–73.

Fraser, Peter. 'Public petitioning and Parliament before 1832', *History*, 46 (1961), 195–211.

Frost, J. William. 'The origins of the Quaker crusade against slavery: a review of recent literature', *Quaker History*, 67, 1 (Spring 1978), 42–58.

Goodyear, Irene E. 'Wilson Armistead and the Leeds anti-slavery movement', reprinted from *Thoresby Society Miscellany*, 16, part 2, 113–29.

Gross, Izhak. 'The abolition of negro slavery and British parliamentary politics, 1832–3', *Historical Journal*, 23, 1 (1980), 63–85.

——. 'Parliament and the abolition of negro apprenticeship, 1835–1838', *English Historical Review*, 96 (1981), 560–76.

Hall, Stuart. 'The problem of ideology – Marxism without guarantees', in Betty Matthews (ed.), *Marx: A Hundred Years On* (London: Lawrence & Wishart, 1983), 57–85.

Haskell, Thomas L. 'Capitalism and the origins of the humanitarian sensibility', *American Historical Review*, 90, 2 (April 1985), 339–61; 90, 5 (December 1985), 547–66.

——. 'Convention and hegemonic interest in the debate over antislavery: a reply to Davis and Ashworth', *American Historical Review*, 92, 4 (October 1987), 829–76.

Holt, Thomas C. ' "An empire over the mind": emancipation, race, and ideology in the British West Indies and the American South', in J. Morgan Kousser and James M. McPherson (eds), *Region, Race, and Reconstruction, Essays in Honour of C. Vann Woodward* (New York: Oxford University Press, 1982), 283–307.

Hooks, Bel. 'Sisterhood: political solidarity between women', *Feminist Review*, 23 (Summer 1986), 125–38.

Hunt, E.N. 'The anti-slave trade agitation in Manchester', *Transactions of the Lancashire and Cheshire Antiquarian Society*, 79 (1977), 46–72.

Jennings, Judith. 'The American Revolution and the testimony of British Quakers against the slave trade', *Quaker History*, 70 (Spring 1981), 99ff.

Kaye, Jacqueline. 'Literary images of slavery and resistance: the case of *Uncle Tom's Cabin* and *Cecilia Valdes*', *Slavery and Abolition*, 5, 2 (September 1984), 105–17.

Kennon, Donald R. ' "An apple of discord": the woman question at the World's Anti-Slavery Convention of 1840', *Slavery and Abolition*, 5, 3 (December 1984), 244–66.

Klingberg, F.K. 'Harriet Beecher Stowe and social reform in England', *American Historical Review*, 43 (1937–38), 542–52.

Levy, David W. 'Racial stereotypes in antislavery fiction', *Phylon*, 31, 3 (Fall 1970), 265–79.

Lewis, N.B. 'The abolitionist movement in Sheffield, 1823–1833', reprinted from *Bulletin of the John Rylands Library*, 18, 2 (July 1934).

Leys, Colin. 'Petitioning in the nineteenth and twentieth centuries', *Political Studies*, 3, 1 (February 1955), 45–64.

Lorimer, Douglas A. 'Black slaves and English liberty: a re-examination of racial slavery in England', *Immigrants and Minorities*, 3, 2 (July 1984), 121–50.

Malmgreen, Gail. 'Anne Knight and the radical subculture', *Quaker History*, 71, 2 (Fall 1982), 100–13.

McKendrick, Neil. 'Home demand and economic growth: a new view of the role of women and children in the Industrial Revolution', in Neil McKendrick (ed.), *Historical Perspectives: studies in English thought and society in honour of J.H. Plumb*, (London: Europa Publications, 1974), 152–210.

Maynard, Douglas H. 'The World's Anti-Slavery Convention of 1840', *Mississippi Valley Historical Review*, 47 (1960–61), 452–71.

Minchinton, Walker E. 'Williams and Drescher: abolition and emancipation', *Slavery and Abolition*, 4, 2 (September 1983), 81–105.

Palmer, Erwin. 'A partnership in the abolition movement', *University of Rochester Library Bulletin*, 26, 1 (1970).

Pole, J.R. 'Slavery and revolution: the conscience of the rich', *Historical Journal*, 20 (1977), 505–06.

Porter, Dorothy B. 'Sarah Parker Remond, abolitionist and physician', *Journal of Negro History*, 20, 3 (July 1935), 287–93.

Prochaska, F.K. 'Women in English philanthropy, 1790–1830', *International Review of Social History*, 19 (1974), 426–45.

Pugh, Evelyn L. 'Women and slavery: Julia Gardiner Tyler and the Duchess of Sutherland', *Virginia Magazine of History and Biography*, 188, 2 (1980), 187–202.

Reddock, Rhoda E. 'Women and slavery in the Caribbean: a feminist perspective', *Latin American Perspectives*, 12, 44, 1 (Winter 1985), 63–80.

Rees, Alan M. 'English Friends and the abolition of the slave trade', *The Bulletin of the Friends Historical Association*, 44, 2 (Autumn 1955), 74–87.

Rice, C. Duncan. 'The anti-slavery mission of George Thompson to the United States, 1834–1835', *Journal of American Studies*, 2, 1 (April 1968), 13–21.

——. ' "Humanity sold for Sugar!" The British abolitionist response to free trade in slave-grown sugar', *The Historical Journal*, 13, 3 (1970), 402–18.

Schupf, Harriet Warm. 'Single women and social reform in mid-nineteenth century England: the case of Mary Carpenter', *Victorian Studies*, 17 (March 1974), 301–17.

Sklar, Kathryn Kish. ' "Women who speak for an entire nation": American and British women compared at the World Anti-Slavery Convention, London, 1840', *Pacific Historical Review*, 1990, 453–99.

Summers, Anne. 'A home from home – women's philanthropic work in the nineteenth century', in Sandra Burman (ed.), *Fit Work for Women* (London: Croom Helm, 1979), 33–63.

Thomas, Paul. 'Changing attitudes in an expanding empire: the anti-slavery movement, 1760–1783', *Slavery and Abolition*, 5, 1 (May 1984), 50–72.

Thompson, Dorothy. 'Women and nineteenth century radical politics: a lost dimension', in Juliet Mitchell and Ann Oakley (eds), *The Rights and Wrongs of Women* (Harmondsworth: Penguin, 1976), 112–38.

Tompkins, Jane P. 'Sentimental power: *Uncle Tom's Cabin* and the politics of literary history', in Elaine Showalter (ed.), *The New Feminist Criticism* (London: Virago, 1985), 81–104.

Tyrrell, Alex. ' "Women's mission" and pressure group politics in Britain, 1825–60', *Bulletin of the John Rylands University Library*, 63 (1980), 194–230.

——. 'The "moral radical party" and the Anglo-Jamaican campaign for the abolition of the negro apprenticeship system', *English Historical Review*, 392 (July 1984), 481–502.

Walvin, James. 'The impact of slavery on British radical politics', in Vera Rubin and Arthur Tuden (eds), *Comparative Perspectives on Slavery in New World Plantation Societies* (New York: Annals of the New York Academy of Sciences, 1977), vol. 292, 347–48.

THESES AND OTHER UNPUBLISHED MATERIAL

Halbersleben, Karen Irene. ' "She hath done what she could": women's participation in the British antislavery movement, 1825–1870', unpublished Ph.D. thesis, State University of New York at Buffalo, 1987.

Midgley, Clare. 'Women Anti-Slavery Campaigners in Britain, 1787–1868', unpublished Ph.D. thesis, University of Kent, 1989.

Society of Friends. Typescript multi-volume 'Dictionary of Quaker Biography' in Friends House Library, London.

INDEX

Babbington, Lydia 18
Babbington, Thomas 18; opposes
 ladies' associations 48
Baldwin, Edward 50
Balfour, Clara Lucas 157
baptism and freedom 14
Baptist Magazine, The 64–5; on
 Immediate Not Gradual Abolition 113
Baptists: and anti-slavery campaign
 81; and female petitioning 64–5;
 missionaries 54
Barbados 10
Barbauld, Anna Laetitia 26–7; poetry
 31–2; praises Wilberforce 32
bazaars 126, 132, 152, 202; Boston
 126, 134, 142, 169; Rochester (NY)
 126, 142
Beaumont Mrs John 1
Bedford College for Ladies 143, 163
Behn, Aphra 29–30
Belle Assemblée, La 25
Bible 48
Bible Society 50, 82, 94, 13; *see also*
 British and Foreign Bible Society
Biggs, Caroline Ashurst 174
Biggs, Matilda Ashurst 164
Billington, Louis 3, 44, 46, 139
Billington, Rosamund 3, 44, 46
Birkett, Mary 34, 35, 36; on
 abstention 39; on Christianisation
 53
Birmingham: Carr's Lane Chapel 97;
 Chartism 85; door-to-door
 canvassing 61; negroes' aid 55;
 working classes 85; *see also* Female
 Society for Birmingham
Birmingham and Midland
 Freedmen's Aid Association 189,
 190
Birmingham Ladies' Negro's Friend
 Society 137, 186, 189; Eyre
 controversy 193; Impey supports
 194; Jamaica Investment Fund 191;
 see also Female Society for
 Birmingham
Birney, James G. 80, 130
Birney, Joseph 165
'Black Society' 12
Blackburn, Robin 4
blacks: abolitionists 6, 12, 89, 138,
 139, 140–5, 155, 157, 170–2, 181,
 193–4, 196, 199, 205; aid to freed

56; American citizenship 145; anti-
slavery campaign 6; children
fashionable 9–10; committees
11–12; demonstration planned 86;
educators 91–2; and Jamaica 190,
192; madonna and child
iconography 205; organisation 12;
in paintings 9–10, 12, 13, 205;
qualities 187; radicalism 14;
resettlement of 12; resistence 11,
86–92; riots 190; servants and
iconography 205; servants, unpaid
86; sexual stereotypes 174;
sexuality 14, 33; stereotypes
146–8, 174, 192; support
undermined 193; trial entitlement
193–4; as victims 6, 91, 203, 204;
welfare, concern for 196–7; *see also*
slavery; slaves
Blake, William 29, 30, 204
Bolt, Christine 185, 191, 196
Bond of Brotherhood, the 138–9
Boston Anti-Slavery Bazaar 126,
134, 142, 169
Boston Female Anti-Slavery Society
126, 129, 130; reports 131
Bowring, Dr John 160
boycott 35–40, 49–50, 57, 58, 202;
abolition, immediate 116;
abstention 35–6; cotton 137;
effects of 40; ladies' associations
125; and Royal family 137; rum
35; Sophia Sturge 80; sugar 35, 63,
70, 72, 76, 79, 137; working
classes 84, 85, 203–4; *see also*
abstention
Bradburn, Samuel 23, 35
Bright, Miss 181
Bristol and Clifton Ladies' Anti-
Slavery Society 133, 169, 172; and
BFASS 133–5; and Fugitive Slave
Act 133; *Special Report* 135
British and Foreign Anti-Slavery
Society (BFASS) 121, 133–5, 168,
171, 187; abstention 137; and
American Anti-Slavery Society
170; annual income 127; auxiliaries
133; donations 125; Estlin against
134; female conference obstructed
161; female delegates 170; female
exclusions 123, 124, 159; female
initiatives 137; feminism 176; and